OPIUM AND FOREIGN POLICY

WILLIAM O. WALKER III

The Anglo-American

Search for Order in

Asia, 1912–1954

Opium
and
Foreign
Policy

The University of North Carolina Press

Chapel Hill and London

Library of Congress Cataloging-in-Publication Data
Walker, William O., 1946–
    Opium and foreign policy : the Anglo-American search for order in
Asia, 1912–1954 / by William O. Walker III.
      p. cm.
    Includes bibliographical references and index.
    ISBN 0-8078-1970-0 (alk. paper)
    1. Opium trade—East Asia—History—20th century. 2. China—
Foreign relations. 3. Japan—Foreign relations. I. Title.
HV5816.W33   1991
363.4′5′09510904—dc20   90-26026
                                                  CIP

The paper in this book meets the guidelines for permanence and durability of the Committee on Production Guidelines for Book Longevity of
the Council on Library Resources.

Manufactured in the United States of America
95 94 93 92 91   5 4 3 2 1

For Sandy and Buzz and Jane

Life is the product of a contingent past,
not the inevitable and predictable result
of simple, timeless laws of nature.

—Stephen Jay Gould,
  The Flamingo's Smile

CONTENTS

MAPS

This book is an interpretive history of opium control in Asia in the years between the fall of the Manchu (Ch'ing) dynasty and the defeat of France in Indochina. Multiarchival research locates it in the broader context of Anglo-American foreign policy objectives across the Pacific. Great Britain and the United States were the nations not only most concerned about maintaining a Western presence in Asia in the first half of the twentieth century but also most active in the world opium control movement. For the period encompassed by this study, Asia captured the attention of the movement more than any other region.

The study of opium control possesses intrinsic interest, currently enhanced by the public's perception of drugs as a threat to society. The history of inter-American drug control is explored in an earlier book, and this one assesses the extent to which Western nations encouraged antiopium activity in non-Western societies during a time of great political turmoil and revolutionary upheaval.[1] As a means of doing so, this book views opium usage, trafficking, and control as evidence of particular cultural outlooks. In China and Southeast Asia, external pressure for control constitutes a form of cultural interaction, that is, the process of conflict and cooperation that arises out of different, competing perspectives on the place of opium in society. Gradual changes over time in the political and economic role of opium underscore the possibility of cultural transformation.[2]

The opium cultures of Asia affected Anglo-American relations after 1912. Policymakers in London and Washington did not always agree on how to deal with the presence of opium and its derivatives, morphine and heroin, in a given society. Their varying responses were related to larger policy considerations in significant ways.

Generally, the British valued their economic position and prospects more than they supported strict controls on opium—at least through the mid-1940s. Specifically, they realized how hard it would be in the short term to eliminate the habit of opium smoking. On the one hand, smoking posed no immediate threat to the security of Great Britain's economic activities. On the other, leadership in a struggle against opium smoking could have had uncontrollable consequences. With far less at stake in Asia strategically or economically until the Second World War, the United States consistently adhered to a policy opposing the cultivation of opium and advocated the cessation of opium smoking. Opium control was on occasion a contentious issue in Anglo-American relations, but that fact did not adequately explain either opium's importance in Western relations with Japan before 1945 or its place in postwar security policy in Asia in the first decade of the cold war. After mid-1945, officials in London and Washington differed considerably over the appropriate response to communism and nationalism and the appropriate role for opium control in the policymaking process.

Chapter 1 constructs an interpretive framework for Part One and surveys the seventy-five-year period before 1912. Opium in China was then a major issue in British foreign policy because of its moral and economic implications. Debate raged over the proper place of opium in the Middle Kingdom, a controversy that contributed directly to the downfall of the Manchu dynasty.

Chapters 2 through 5 describe opium as a kind of culture in itself, the zeal of Western reformers with their ethnocentric attitudes, wariness of Japan's ultimate intentions in China, and tension in the Anglo-American relationship over which nation would set the tone for a Western presence in East Asia. These chapters also show how perceptions about the social role of opium helped shape China policy, generally, and opium policy, specifically, in London, Washington, and, to an extent, Tokyo. Chapter 2 details the domestic and foreign impediments to control in China through 1924–25, when the League of Nations convened two major antiopium conferences.

Chapter 3 finds opium becoming a fundamental issue in Sino-Japanese relations in the late 1920s and shows the inability of Western nations appreciably to affect the situation. Indeed, British and U.S. representatives in China could do little but report how opium served the political and economic interests of the Nationalist regime. For nearly four years after the Mukden Incident, Chiang Kai-shek sought to tighten his hold on power by employing opium as one means for doing so; this is the subject of Chapter 4. Chiang carefully focused attention on Japanese elements in North China and Manchuria for their major role in a burgeoning narcotics traffic. At the same time, he rationalized the opium trade throughout the provinces of China under his authority and depended heavily on the revenues therefrom—while promising U.S. and British officials that a program of strict control was at hand.

Chapter 5 describes how events outran Chiang's efforts to turn the opium and narcotics scene to his own ends. Neither domestic foes, notably the Communists, nor Western proponents of control were disposed to accept indefinitely his reasons for the delay in bringing about control of opium. Only the aggressive actions of Japanese forces in the summer of 1937 prevented opium from contributing further to the political difficulties ensnaring Chiang's government.

Part Two analyzes the role of opium as an important element in the development of Anglo-American security policy throughout Asia from 1937 on. Chapter 6 shows how Japanese involvement with the narcotics trade in China impaired Tokyo's relations with the West in the two years before the Second World War began in Europe. Policymakers in the United States believed that Japan was partly trying to conquer China with narcotics. Officials in the Foreign Office were rather less certain but grew alarmed as Japanese actions posed increasing threats to important British interests in South China. When war did come from Europe, the nature of the Anglo-American relationship in Asia underwent a radical transformation.

Chapter 7 examines that change during the war through the lens provided by antiopium policy. Narcotics control officials in the United States defined opium as a strategic commodity and tried to restrict Japanese access to it. In so doing, they hoped to prepare the way for a major postwar antiopium drive throughout Asia. A renewed effort to eliminate opium smoking therefore became part of a vague anticolonial commitment on the part of President Franklin D. Roosevelt.

American hopes of reducing opium's hold on Asia turned to dust in the early postwar years, as Chapter 8 explains. Chiang Kai-shek's government, bogged down in a civil war against Mao Zedong's forces, was in no position to serve as an example to other Asian nations in the cause of drug control. Moreover, nationalists outside of China proved to be less amenable to direction from the West, even on issues such as suppression of opium cultivation and smoking, than officials had anticipated. Indeed, the British and the Americans disagreed about the pace of suppression in Burma, while the French essentially ignored pleas for opium control in Indochina.

Opium control had become something of a hostage to U.S. national security policy by 1950. Chapter 9 argues that drug control officials consciously altered their goals in deference to larger policy priorities. Government authorities apparently tolerated a thriving opium traffic in the Golden Triangle in the hope of preventing the spread of Chinese Communist influence. The British largely shared U.S. fears of Communist expansion and the security threat it would pose in Southeast Asia, but they did not agree with all the methods adopted to check communism's possible advance. The chronic tension in Anglo-American postwar relations, clearly evident by the mid-1950s, showed how unlikely then was the imposition of Western-style order in Asia.

Of course, neither Great Britain nor the United States could have defined the political agenda in Asia in the 1950s. So far as opium goes, Washington's security policy decisions meant indefinite delay in the movement toward control. In the late 1980s, while public attention and U.S. government programs rightly focused on problems generated by a booming trade in cocaine and crack from South America, opium, opiate, and marijuana abuse, efficient narcotics-trafficking syndicates, and money-laundering operations facilitated by bank secrecy laws proliferated throughout Asia.[3] The conclusion addresses some of these dilemmas currently vexing proponents of narcotics control by discussing the limits of policymaking within a historical context.

The obstacles to drug control in Asia are as great as ever. In the opinion of the House Select Committee on Narcotics Abuse and Control, failure to recognize the threat contained in the present situation "could have serious long term implications for stability in the region."[4] At the same time, U.S. funds and equipment offer some hope for the partial eradication of poppy crops in Burma and Laos. The future is least optimistic in Laos, where opium and marijuana cultivation may be bringing badly needed cash reserves into the country.[5]

Unfortunately, history teaches far fewer lessons than we sometimes believe. Nevertheless, the current drug situation in Southeast Asia may not be anywhere near as tractable as officials on the scene or policymakers in Washington expect. The social and economic conditions that long ago gave rise to the opium cultures of the region surely persist today, albeit in altered form.[6] And who can know whether future political developments, of regional or international importance, will return opium to the grim stature it enjoyed during the American years in Indochina?

Delaware, Ohio
November 1990

ACKNOWLEDGMENTS

It is a great pleasure to acknowledge the support of Lewis Bateman for this book and to thank my friend Douglas Clark Kinder, whose constant encouragement throughout the research and writing kept my spirits up whenever the going was slow. I am highly appreciative of all the dedicated archivists and staff people at the repositories mentioned in the bibliography; they helped to make research for the book that much easier.

I am also grateful to the members of the Faculty Personnel Committee at Ohio Wesleyan University, who first awarded me a Thomas E. Wenzlau Faculty Development Grant in 1987 to facilitate a final research trip. My colleagues also granted me a special faculty leave for spring semester 1988, which allowed me to write without having to worry about other obligations.

Indispensable as always for the scholar of international history are the official records of the United States, housed at the National Archives in Washington, D.C., and at the Washington National Records Center in Suitland, Maryland. I especially wish to thank the individuals who handle the military and diplomatic records. Sadly, the federal archives did not benefit from the spending frenzy of the 1980s. The deterioration of service, not the fault of an overburdened staff, will prevent future generations of scholars from knowing the joys of working in Milt Gustafson's "shop" on levels 5E and 6E of the National Archives. I know of no way adequately to repay my friends there who have assisted me over the years.

Even more than impecunious funding, unnecessary classification of records threatens to compromise the integrity of research on foreign relations. Freedom of Information Act requests are no longer dealt with expeditiously; the workload is overwhelming. Further, the great frustration of scholars with the classification system itself is entirely justified. One is tempted in this post—

cold-war era to call it Stalinist, but scholars know the system to be simply American. May a change come soon.

On a happier note, I am pleased to thank the Social Science Research Council for awarding me an SSRC–MacArthur Foundation Fellowship in International Peace and Security for the years 1988–90. The work undertaken in the course of the fellowship slowed somewhat the completion of the book but allowed me to strengthen its analytical framework. I came to rely on specialists in international relations who conduct decision-making studies. Their work is acknowledged by its presence in the notes, but special thanks are extended to Richard Ned Lebow of Cornell University; he taught me much—both in his classroom and literally on the run.

Individually, thanks go to the readers of the manuscript for the University of North Carolina Press; the participants in the Peace Studies Program's dinner seminar at Cornell; Sandra Kisner, who put the final draft on a usable disk; Stevie Champion, a superb copyeditor; William J. vanden Heuval for his generous interview; and Kathleen Weibel, former head of libraries at Ohio Wesleyan University. Others who read all or portions of the manuscript or discussed the subject with me include Jim Gillam, Gary Hess, Mike Hogan, Richard Immerman, Doug and Connie Kinder, Mel Leffler, Jane Kate Leonard, Doug Little, Bob McMahon, Kathryn Meyer, Terry Parssinen, Don Rodgers, Michael Schaller, Mark Selden, Richard Spall, and especially Waldo Heinrichs.

The dedication is to my sister Sandy, who remains an inspiration to me; and to Bob Buzzanco and Jane Kelso, who made this book possible by extending to me their floor, their couch, their food, and their love. For them and their son Kelsey, h.l.v.s.

A NOTE ON TRANSLITERATION

For Chinese names, places, words, and phrases, I have chosen to use the Wade-Giles romanization because it is used in the documentary record for the period I am concerned with. I have, however, employed the *pinyin* system for the names of Communist officials and for the capital of China, Beijing, after 1 October 1949. The rendering of names and places in Southeast Asia follows customary English-language usage. If there is no fixed convention, I have adopted the usage appearing most often in the documentary record.

PART ONE

Great Britain,

the United States,

and Opium in

East Asia to 1937

ONE

Opium and the West in China to 1912

Opium "constitutes such a grave danger not only to the welfare of humanity but to the peace of the East that it has become a problem for the world at large."[1] So declared Kaku Sagataro in 1916. Then head of the opium monopoly bureau of the government of Formosa, Kaku surely understood that since at least the early 1800s, opium had played havoc with the Chinese economy, engendered often undesirable social changes, and altered the shape of domestic politics in the Middle Kingdom. In sum, opium had contributed to both the fall of the Ch'ing dynasty and subsequent instability in East Asia.

In the same years, Western interest in opium initially ignored the societal problems it would cause. The promise of economic gain largely defined the contours of Sino-Western relations concerning opium, especially with Great Britain, prior to the early twentieth century. A movement favoring reform, or opium control in some form, began around 1900, emerging both from within and outside of China—although the domestic impetus proved to be indispensable for even modest reform. By the start of the first international antiopium conference in 1909, the United States and Britain were at odds over the pace and scope of opium control, a disagreement that reflected the British Empire's lengthy economic attachment to the trade. Even so, both powers assumed that the opium problem was one of supply. Had they focused more on the issue of demand, they might have more fully appreciated Kaku's ominous assessment. An overview of the Anglo-American experience with opium in China through the 1911 Revolution shows why the Western perspective was so limited.

Early Conflicts over Opium

Opium posed a momentous threat to the established order in Ch'ing China. The Chinese had used opium, or *ya p'ien*, brought to the Middle Kingdom from the Near East, as a medicine for more than a millennium. The British East India Company first carried Indian opium to China at the end of the Ming dynasty. Both Ming and early Manchu authorities reacted with greater alarm to the "smoke-plant," or tobacco, which Fukien traders imported from Spanish Manila, than to opium. Before long, sailors were mixing opium with tobacco and smoking the compound. An imperial edict in 1729, the first to outlaw opium smoking and associated activities, had no effect on the developing habit.[2]

The Ch'ing dynasty reached a crossroads in the early nineteenth century. Opium smoking (ya-p'ien-yen) and an increasing commerce in Indian opium were symptomatic of the troubles plaguing the dynasty. Social problems, along with economic turmoil, helped to undermine popular faith in the imperial mandate. Moreover, employment prospects for the educated elite were limited and tax officials exacted from the peasantry vital revenues for the Manchu government.[3] Assisting the decline of Confucian order was the East India Company. Granted an opium monopoly in Bengal in 1773, the company's agents probed the limits of the China market through the seasonal trading system at Canton, which had long enriched dynastic bureaucrats in Peking. If trade with foreigners was theoretically scorned as part of Manchu orthodoxy, it was nevertheless quietly welcomed for the fiscal and personal financial rewards it offered. The company's business in Patna opium grew rapidly after initially serving as a balance to the Canton tea trade.[4]

By the time company officials added privately produced Malwa opium from western India to the trade in 1830, a refined system of smuggling was well established. In a legal sense, company officials could argue that their hands were clean. Private buyers from Calcutta purchased company opium and sent it on consignment to agency houses at Canton, such as the British firm, Jardine, Matheson, and Company. Agents, dealing with what was still in theory a legitimate commodity, never actually sold opium in China. When the brown mud in the holds of their ships reached the coastal waters near Canton, it became contraband. Chinese merchants then transferred the opium to floating warehouses, clandestinely sold the precious cargo, and turned over the profits to the agency houses.[5] Some 5,000 chests of opium, each weighing 145 pounds, reached China in 1820; the annual average for the next decade was more than three times that amount. And in 1834, the final year of its monopoly of the China trade, the East India Company sent as many as 20,000 chests of opium to Canton—all quite legally.[6]

With ya-p'ien-yen existing in nearly all provinces and at all levels of society and with imports of Bengal, Malwa, and Turkish opium rising dramatically, corruption abounded in the opium trade. River police at Canton and local authorities, called "mandarins" by Westerners, controlled lucrative smuggling operations. Antiopium proclamations became mere devices to assure poorly paid officials a decent income. Nor, of course, were British sailors immune from such rewards as the illegal trade could offer. Just after the first Opium War, a British consul warned that opium was corrupting Britain's merchant marine.[7]

Commerce in opium so altered the terms of Sino-British trade that Chinese merchants surrendered a commodity far more valuable than silk or tea. The flight of silver shook the Ch'ing dynasty to its foundations. On the eve of the Opium War, China, with perhaps 10 million addicts, was spending nearly half of its total revenue on opium. John King Fairbank found that "the demand for opium [in the mid-1830s] had been built up by Chinese rather than foreign distributors."[8] Yet Western and Chinese merchants readily collaborated with minor officials to promote the opium trade to their mutual benefit. The scarcity of silver, despite prohibitions against its export, threw the economic consequences of their actions onto the peasants, whose relative tax burden grew dramatically.[9] Therein may lie the roots of popular antiopium agitation, which reformers and revolutionaries later called upon to bolster the cause of opium control.

The appeal of opium smoking to the gentry, or *shen-shih*, and peasants in the 1830s is understandable in general and specific terms. Members of societies experiencing uncontrollable and potentially destructive changes often seek solace in substances that mitigate harsh daily realities. So it was that Spanish conquerors noticed among Indians a marked use of *pulque* in the Valley of Mexico and the chewing of coca leaves in the Andes of Peru.[10] The difference in China was that the foreigners brought the anodyne with them as a business proposition. The drama unfolding around the opium trade in the 1830s could scarcely have been more compelling. Put simply, Westerners were engaged in an attempt to promote and define commercial and cultural order in Asia. As British and some American firms jockeyed for comparative economic advantages that meant nothing to the mandarins and hongs of Canton, the foreigners were prepared to use force if necessary to impose both opium and their values on the Chinese.[11]

Such was the substance of the cultural conflict then raging in China. The Canton trading system, constructed to keep foreigners at a respectful distance, threatened the growth of commercial capitalism. The imperial tribute system and Chinese reluctance to trade had to be overcome. The Canton system quickly gave way, and opium reigned as the agent of Western success.[12]

The Tao-kuang Emperor responded to this development by requesting memorials from high-ranking mandarins including Lin Tse-hsu, the often honored governor-general of Hupei and Honan. Opium addicts, Lin believed, should face severe penalties if they refused to give up their habit. In addition, the authorities should smash the opium distribution network; foreign merchants should be dealt with judiciously but must give up their supplies of the drug and agree to end the trade. In December 1838, the emperor sent Lin to Canton as *Ch'in-ch'ai ta-ch'en*, or special high commissioner, with plenipotentiary powers. Lin's charge was nothing less than to halt the prolific commerce in opium and to deter the *fan kuei*, or foreign barbarians, from continuing the trade.[13]

Lin proceeded to act in ways true to the Confucian diplomatic tradition, which assumed a Sinocentric world. On reaching Canton in March 1839, Lin pressed his tactical advantage with a show of force against the temporarily vulnerable foreigners. At the same time, he moved quickly against opium smugglers and dealers, at times exacting the harshest of penalties. Then, writing magnanimously from the position of a superior to an inferior, Lin asked Queen Victoria to put an end to poppy cultivation and the manufacture of opium in India. Since opium, he observed, "is not permitted to do harm to your own country, then even less should you let it be passed on to the harm of other countries—how much less to China!" Failure to act, he reminded Her Majesty, would result in the termination of legal commerce at Canton. The British superintendent of trade there, the ambitious Captain Charles Elliot, soon persuaded the opium merchants to turn over their stores to Commissioner Lin in exchange for an uncertain promise of reimbursement from the Crown. By the end of June, more than 21,000 chests of opium were destroyed and the foreigners in Canton fled to Macao.[14]

Lin's accomplishment could not be called a victory, though, since the British government defended the opium entrepreneurs. Elliot and the other fan kuei regrouped first at Macao and then at Hong Kong, where they refused to submit to imperial judicial authority. Independent of any single incident, Lord Palmerston determined in early November that a punitive naval expedition should sail to China to demand satisfaction for the injuries done to British subjects, shipping, and property. Petitions to the foreign minister for military action included those of the cotton industry, exporters and manufacturers alike, whose leaders were worried about the future of the India-England-Canton trade.[15] With opium serving as the pretext, military conflict was at hand between Britain and China.

In the first phase of the war, Lin's promises to the Tao-kuang Emperor that war could be avoided and opium banished from China's shores seemed as empty as prior imperial pronouncements against opium. This momentous setback cost the Ch'in-ch'ai the unalloyed support of the emperor, and the weakness of the imperial army and navy hastened his undoing. Lin was stripped of his commission.[16] A subsequent attempt to end the war, the Convention of Chuenpi, agreed on in January 1841 by Lin's successor, Ch'i-shan, and Captain Elliot, was disavowed at Whitehall and in Peking. The abortive convention ceded Hong Kong to Britain, reopened Canton to trade, established diplomatic equality between the two lands, and provided for an indemnity. While Whitehall deemed the terms insufficient, Peking found the concessions too excessive.[17]

A second phase of the war brought great bloodshed, especially on the Chinese side; Ch'ing troops could not match superior British forces. Shanghai had fallen by the early summer of 1842, and the emperor believed that Tientsin and Peking were soon to follow. Instead, the British sailed up the Yangtze, apparently intent on taking Nanking. The prospect of having the former Ming capital fall to the fan kuei brought the Opium War to an end. From this setback the dynasty would never fully recover. The Treaty of Nanking, while remaining silent on the issue of opium, opened China to more than a century of diplomatic, commercial, and missionary penetration from abroad.[18]

The Consequences of the Opium War

By definition, the opium crisis compromised the rationale underlying Manchu foreign policy: merely to fight the fan kuei risked the unity of the empire. Lin Tse-hsu recognized as much when he recommended after the war that China develop a strategy of deterrence by appropriating Western military techniques.[19] Moreover, the failure of Ch'ing prohibitions against the opium trade and opium smoking throughout the early 1800s further impugned dynastic authority. In retrospect, it is not difficult to understand why a major uprising against the Manchus, the Taiping Rebellion, loomed on the horizon, even as the first unequal treaty was being signed.[20]

British entry to the Middle Kingdom was replete with its own unfortunate legacies. A foreign policy calling for free trade, which portended a radical restructuring of international relations, could not succeed without ultimate recourse to drug addiction and war. Previewed in the notorious Napier Mission of 1834, this situation hardly enhanced the reputation of the policy's diverse advocates—free trade opponents of colonialism, Radicals, Lord Palmerston, and the Whigs.[21] To be sure, not all Englishmen found opium for silver an acceptable exchange. Yet some of those most likely to dissent on moral grounds from the Foreign Office's China policy were in no position to do so. On the same vessels with opium traveled the Word of God. And while many Chinese found much to worship in opium, few felt other than hostility at the prospect of Christian salvation. But idolatry, the early missionaries knew, contained its own ironic consequences. "Will not," Robert Morrison asked, "like sins produce like punishments?"[22] In other words, Asian heretics deserved the scourge of opium.

The United States also took advantage of the opium trade to carve out a place in China. Commercial relations were irregular during the early decades of independence until 1805, when some Americans entered the trade. None was more successful than the Boston firm of Russell and Company, whose ship, the *Lintin*, named for an island that held opium in the Gulf of Canton, carried Turkish and Persian opium to Canton. The company formally abandoned the trade in February 1839, but a few of its ships later may have handled opium on consignment for other agency houses. The steady growth of commercial involvement across the Pacific necessitated regular diplomatic contact with China. Nonetheless, even in the wake of the 1843 mission led by Caleb Cushing, domestic priorities such as continental expansion left Sino-American relations in the shadow of Anglo-Chinese interaction.[23]

The carrying of opium into Chinese waters, though legitimate under British laws, troubled consuls in the treaty ports. The ports could not adequately serve their intended purpose of encouraging Anglo-Chinese commerce if distinctions had to be made about what constituted licit trade. To remedy the situation, a system of receiving stations was established at anchorages just outside the ports. British consuls took no official notice of the stations, and the opium trade flourished unimpeded by legal difficulties. Better to serve both sellers and smugglers, the Crown Colony of Hong Kong began operating within a few years as a warehouse and distribution center.[24]

Despite treaty provisions, the Manchus were loath to deal with the fan kuei on equal terms. Yet clinging to a Sinocentric foreign policy provoked additional conflict with foreigners and further imperiled the Ch'ing dynasty.[25] Neither the Tao-kuang Emperor nor his successor, the Hsien-feng Emperor, who acceded to the throne in 1850, ever came to terms with the contraband trade in opium. Prohibiting the use of opium was rarely out of fashion in Peking, whereas serious attempts at control were out of the question. Opium production in China soon began to thrive, especially in the provinces of Yunnan, Kweichow, Shensi, and Szechwan.[26] Only with the renewal of hostilities between China and Britain in 1856, during the Taiping Rebellion, did the emperor respond by contemplating regulation or legalization of the opium trade.[27]

The British were then seeking greater diplomatic and commercial concessions than the Tao-kuang Emperor had accepted to end the first Opium War. They were joined by the French, who entered the fray after one of their missionaries, accused of working with anti-Ch'ing rebels in Kwangsi province, was executed.[28] Should not servants of God, the allies wondered, be allowed to travel freely throughout China? The allies also insisted that the Chinese open more treaty ports, allow diplomats to live in Peking, permit unlimited travel within the country, and, of course, legalize opium.

Negotiators effectively wrote these provisions into the Treaty of Tientsin in June 1858, but one year later the Chinese refused to exchange ratifications, deciding instead to renew hostilities with the fan kuei. By mid-October 1860, the war against Britain and France was nearly over. To chasten the emperor, the allies burned the Summer Palace northwest of Peking. Their cause lost, thousands of Ch'ing troops rioted in the streets of the capital. With the ratification of the Treaty of Tientsin, the opium wars had ended.[29]

No less essential than before to the economic well-being of India, opium—not mentioned by name in the peace treaty—could now legally be sold at treaty ports, where it would be taxed at 30 taels per picul. (This figure was equivalent to 39.9 ounces of standard silver per 133.33 pounds of opium.) For British consuls, worries about association with smuggled opium would finally be over; they could look forward to pressing additional commercial interests on the Chinese. In the early 1860s, a spirit of conciliation toward the fan kuei hastened an illusory Manchu restoration. Westerners, especially the British who had a clear stake in the survival of the dynasty, worked with imperial officials and helped quash the Taiping Rebellion.[30]

At war's end, however, all was not well within the Chinese Empire. Fundamental political and social changes, including local militarization, allowed the lower gentry gradually to gain considerable influence over local government as a landlord class that would later dominate rural affairs, most notably rent and tax collection. This development held great significance for the last half century of Manchu rule because it broke important ties between the central government and local powers, whether provincial elites, landlords, or militarists. Further, the creation in the 1850s of regional armies to fight the rebels set a precedent that could not easily be undone. Personal loyalty replaced deference to imperial authority; after the 1911 Revolution, similarly structured armies played a destructive political role as forces for autonomous warlords.[31]

The Taiping Rebellion was already showing signs of fatal internal weaknesses by the time the Manchus turned their full attention to its suppression. When Taiping military pressure mounted against Shanghai, an entrepôt of crucial importance for government customs revenues and the spread of Western commerce, foreign forces joined the fight against the rebels. They did so to protect the gains won after more than twenty years of conflict. Foreign merchants, missionaries, and diplomats would not have accepted with equanimity a return to the status they held prior to 1839.

Though not the most important consideration, the opium trade figured in the British decision to aid the dynasty. The possibility of losing opium revenues was unacceptable to Whitehall. Given Taiping strictures against opium and Ch'ing reluctance to countenance the drug in any formal way, such a development was reasonably feared.[32] At the least, curtailing the trade would have meant considerable disarray in colonial policy. In the background loomed the likely diminution of Great Britain's international standing, especially if trading policy was markedly circumscribed. Opium may not have set the direction of the Foreign Office's China policy, but it surely helped show the way.

China's problems afforded the United States an opportunity to advance its own interests and contributed to the myth of a special relationship between the two countries. This good fortune was not immediately apparent early in the war with Britain and France. The American minister, William B. Reed, abandoned the instructions of Secretary of State Lewis Cass and supported the British demand that the dynasty accept the opium trade. In other important diplomatic matters, though, Reed broke with his counterparts and condemned some aspects of the privilege of extraterritoriality. He doubted as well the wisdom of acquiring colonies at China's expense. Reed's cautious, if brief ministry, along with that of his successor, John E. Ward, won for the United States concessions similar to those Britain and France had gone to war to obtain.[33]

A self-strengthening movement, entailing both internal reform and, as Lin Tse-hsu had advocated, the acquisition of foreign military technology, emerged in the aftermath of war but ultimately failed to reinvigorate the dynasty. The problem was that major setbacks in foreign policy plagued the Manchus throughout the remainder of the nineteenth century. In the Treaty of St. Petersburg in 1881, Russia received a large indemnity after nearly detaching the Ili River Valley and other strategic areas from Sinkiang. War with France three years later removed traditional imperial influence from Annam and demonstrated just how powerful foreign adversaries might be whether

Ch'ing leaders adopted conciliatory or aggressive foreign policy tactics. Then, following defeat in the Sino-Japanese War of 1894–95, the beleaguered dynasty ceded Formosa to Japan and paid an indemnity to avoid losing the Liaotung Peninsula. To Korea, where Japan's influence as an agent of modernization had grown steadily after 1885, China extended formal recognition of independence. Over the next several years, foreign powers maneuvered to obtain additional concessions from the Manchus.[34]

Opium and China's Political Economy

As these critical events were played out to China's detriment, opium left no aspect of national life untouched. Legitimation and taxation of the trade neither ended smuggling nor prevented clandestine extralegal distribution networks from developing. At the same time, there ensued a scramble for the potentially lucrative revenues that encouraged not only the continued import of Indian opium but also domestic production of poppies on good land and bad.[35] In short, China was becoming dependent on opium.

In 1863, still in the early years of his long service to the Imperial Maritime Customs, the Englishman Robert Hart offered an explanation for the incidence of smuggling. "My advice," he wrote, "is to direct the authorities to lower the tax: they are levying 158 TLs [taels] on each chest: no wonder the smuggling increases. As to asking the ministers to do anything, it [would] only make them laugh at us: their orders would be useless unless supplemented by their cruisers, and to expect them to do our own revenue work would be too much."[36] Though referring to conditions in Foochow, Hart's analysis suggested opium's central role in much of the Chinese economy. The question was: Could the dynasty rely on opium taxes to meet revenue needs without, however, inadvertently consigning many more Chinese to dependence on opium?

Attempting to answer this query sheds light on the decline of Manchu authority and indicates how opium became further ingrained in Chinese culture. During the Taiping Rebellion, *li-chin*, or likin, taxes were developed to help pay regional armies; easily collected, this duty applied to commercial goods in transit between market towns. Because of its essentially local nature, likin revenue was rarely reported in full even after the government nationalized the tax. Likin, while not the sole means of funding, helped create regional power bases with the potential to act outside of Peking's authority.[37]

Opium, of course, was a perfect commodity for the likin system. Jonathan

Spence has found a close link in the 1870s and 1880s between opium likin and military self-strengthening and modernizing activities in such places as Kwangtung, Taiwan, and Szechwan.[38] Imports of opium reached a level of slightly more than 80,000 chests in the mid-1880s and stabilized around 50,000 chests in the early 1900s as more and more *mou* were given over to poppy production. (China may have been home to 15 million addicts by 1890.)[39]

Widespread demand for opium made it politically difficult to create a workable system of taxation, since control over likin revenues on domestic opium generated much controversy. The Board of Revenue tried in 1887 to fix the rate at 45 taels per picul, but Ch'ing authorities remained susceptible to the corruption and graft that were never far from the opium trade. In the 1890s, when the government considered replacing domestic likin with a more integrated collection system, the effort faltered much to the dismay of Robert Hart.[40] Vested interests ranging from criminals and peasants to merchants and officials wanted the underground opium economy to continue. From no influential corner of the empire did there emanate a persuasive voice calling for more effective controls. The profit motive, in effect, dwarfed any movement toward opium reform.

Kuo Sung-tao, China's first envoy to London, decried opium's debilitating impact on his distant homeland. "Among the injuries that Westerners do us," he wrote in 1877 to Li Hung-chang, one of the most powerful leaders of the self-strengthening movement, "there is nothing more serious than opium. . . . For several decades it has been the national humiliation, it has exhausted our financial power and poisoned and injured the lives of our people, but there is not a single person whose conscience is weighed down by it."[41]

In such a situation, foreign agitation alone could not bring about a decrease in opium production or smoking in China. Moreover, foreigners and nationals who participated in the commerce in opium were unlikely to preside over its demise. By the turn of the century, perhaps as many as one-fourth of all Chinese smoked prepared opium. Imports of Indian opium had peaked some years earlier, but domestic growth showed no sign of abating.[42] Missionaries tended to blame the Chinese for their difficulties with opium and claimed that "the evil [spread] . . . more and more every year" as Ch'ing mandarins tolerated the growth of poppies in order to enrich themselves.[43]

Reflecting this sentiment, organized foreign opposition to opium waned briefly in the mid-1880s. No nation trading opium followed the American example of 1880, at which time a supplementary treaty to the 1844 Treaty of Wanghsia absolutely forbade U.S. citizens from participating in the trade. Yet blaming British policy for the presence of opium in China begs the basic question; nor is it accurate solely to attack the opium policy of the Indian government. Ch'ing leaders, aptly concluded the controversial Royal Opium Commission in 1895, had to accept a share of the burden for the perpetuation of opium as a lucrative enterprise.[44]

The dissenting minority report of the commission condemned arguments supporting the trade based on financial considerations and urged its suppression. Speaking of India, Henry J. Wilson wrote that "it is altogether unworthy for a great dependency of the British Empire to be thus engaged in a traffic which produces such widespread misery and disaster." Although opium's place in the Indian economy was diminishing, movement to eliminate it as a source of revenue came only after the Manchu government initiated its own antiopium campaign.[45]

Antiopium efforts remained halfhearted until the crisis of the late 1890s amid foreign competition for commercial, financial, and territorial spheres of influence in China. The empire could neither assert its sovereignty nor defend itself in any meaningful way. Even the Open Door policy of the United States exposed the weakness of the Manchu dynasty more than it contributed to a closer relationship between the two countries. The failed Boxer Uprising, which arose, as Joseph W. Esherick shows, in opposition to the foreign presence in China, proved again that the self-strengthening movement could not ameliorate China's divisive internal problems.[46]

Even before the foreign powers forced the humiliating Boxer Protocol on China in September 1901, Confucian scholars and influential officials were outlining a program of reform. K'ang Yu-wei, a Cantonese scholar, proposed a radical defense of the state and Confucianism by the infusion of Western ideas concerning defense, governmental administration, and the economy. Meiji Japan and Peter the Great's Russia served as models for K'ang, but his writings portrayed Confucius as a reformer and called for the embourgeoisement of China from above.[47] Other, moderate reformers, led by Chang Chih-tung, a powerful scholar-official, found the West less worthy of emulation. It was Chang's intent to show why the Chinese people above all should protect the Ch'ing dynasty. Though an advocate of Western learning, Chang put his differences with K'ang most clearly in the famous dictum from his book, *Ch'uan-hsueh p'ien* ("Exhortation to Study"): "Chinese learning for the fundamental principles, Western learning for practical application."[48]

In September 1898, Empress Dowager Tz'u-hsi overcame through a coup d'état the influence of K'ang and his followers on imperial policy, thereby ending one hundred days of reform and giving Chang's moderate faction a chance to carry out its ideas in defense of the beleaguered dynasty. Destroying the pernicious opium business was essential to effective reform. "Therefore I say," wrote Chang, "the development of education is the medicine to use for the suppression of opium."[49] Chang also drew on means other than education to combat opium. Beginning in 1900 as viceroy of Hupei and Hunan, he imposed a consolidated tax of 115 taels per picul on native raw opium in the hope of discouraging its growth; prepared opium would pay double the rate. On 7 May 1906, an imperial edict extended the new tax to all provinces of China proper; Manchuria was to be included at a later date.[50] The first sustained attack on opium since the time of Lin Tse-hsu was at hand.

Opium Reform

Some Western missionaries later argued that their entreaties had led directly to China's antiopium campaign,[51] but such claims overlooked the indigenous reform sentiments of the day. For example, Chinese students returning from Japan agitated for opium control after seeing a government monopoly there and on the island of Formosa apparently reduce the incidence of smoking.[52] Contributing to the impetus for reform were recommendations contained in an American report on opium use in the Philippines. More thorough in its work than the Royal Opium Commission, the Philippine Commission investigated conditions in the Far East and publicly supported in 1905 a policy designed to reduce supply by placing strict prohibitions on opium importation, sale, and use over a period of three years.[53]

In the autumn of 1906, the throne bowed to the reform spirit and issued an edict mandating the cessation of poppy cultivation over a ten-year period and requiring, based on the Formosan model, licenses for smokers. Those under sixty years of age gradually had to stop smoking. The decree also prohibited other opium-related activities, especially smoking by government employees. No less an observer than H. B. Morse was moved to conclude that the "effect on the nation was electrical."[54]

It remained for Manchu officials to sign an agreement with the British to halt the importation of Indian opium. Activity by antiopium societies in both countries helped promote, but did not guarantee, the adoption of an accord. Skepticism about China's good faith and ability to implement its own edicts, along with some reluctance in India to give up a reliable source of revenue, slowed the policymaking and diplomatic process. Negotiations began in January 1907 and resulted at year's end in a Sino-British agreement to act jointly to reduce smuggling, curb the trade in prepared opium between Hong Kong and China, and, most important, reduce during a three-year trial period opium shipped from India to China by 5,100 chests annually. This figure amounted to 10 percent of the average annual trade in the years 1901 to 1905.[55] Reports from consuls and missionaries would monitor for Whitehall the effectiveness of China's opium control activity.[56]

Efforts to save Ch'ing rule through a broad reform program delayed the dynasty's fall for a few years. Yet, as one of the reforms, prohibiting the growth of opium poppies would bring much hardship to those provinces where peasants faced the loss of their primary cash crop. Only three provinces produced fewer than 2,000 piculs per year—Fukien, Kiangsi, and Kwangtung. Producing between 3,000 and 10,000 piculs among the provinces touching the coast were Chekiang, Kiangsu, Shantung, and Chihli; those in the same range along the Yangtze were Hunan, Hupei, and Anhwei. Also falling into this category were the inland provinces of Honan, Shansi, Kansu, and Kwangsi. The provinces producing more than 10,000 piculs were Manchuria with only a fifty-year history of poppy growth, Shensi, Kweichow, Yunnan, and Szechwan with an astounding harvest of not less than 250,000 piculs.[57]

However daunting the task, China achieved considerable success. Nearly four-fifths of all opium land was given over to the production of food crops by 1911. Public pressure in most provinces produced real accomplishments; Hupei, Anhwei, Kansu, Kweichow, and Szechwan were notable exceptions. Opium smoking also decreased in much of China after 1909 thanks to public condemnation of the habit. Major exceptions could be found in the provinces just listed.[58]

China's antiopium record demonstrated sufficient progress for Great Britain to agree in May 1911 to extend the provisional agreement of 1907 until 1917, at which time imports of Indian opium would cease. Appeals from the House of Commons, British antiopium associations, and the Chinese National Anti-Opium Society to end the trade sooner proved unavailing, however. The society also petitioned the Wai-wu Pu (Ministry of Foreign Affairs), urging antiopium action independent of any accord with the British.[59]

In the name of reform, the United States began to step out of the British shadow. Even before Great Britain and China reached their first accord, U.S. officials, with the encouragement of missionaries throughout Asia, began to plan for an international antiopium meeting.[60] Would China attend such a gathering? Doing so might be a way to hasten the end of the Indian trade, but would the Wai-wu Pu willingly place China's fate in the hands of foreign powers? What would be the domestic response to such a decision? Department of State officials apparently never considered these questions and assumed that the Ch'ing government would welcome the chance to discuss the opium situation in an international forum.[61] Whatever reservations they may have held, Chinese officials decided to attend.[62]

The deliberations of the International Opium Commission began at Shanghai on 1 February 1909. Named as American commissioners were Dr. Hamilton Wright, a renowned student of tropical diseases in the Far East; Charles C. Tenney, who had lived a long time in China as a missionary and was serving as Chinese secretary in the American legation at Peking; and Charles H. Brent, the Episcopal bishop of the Philippines, who headed the delegation. Tenney's preparations focused on the situation in China. Morphine imports from Japan were becoming a matter of concern because of their increasing use as a cheap substitute for prepared opium. Japan had not yet agreed to end the sale of morphine and needles for injection; thus, an imperial prohibition against their importation could not go into effect. Overtures by Washington to Tokyo were successful by the end of September 1908, and morphine prohibition went into effect in China on 1 January 1909.[63]

As a commission, the parley at Shanghai could make no binding decisions. Turning this limitation against the British, one commissioner, Tuan Fang, questioned Britain's good faith because of Whitehall's continued reliance on the outmoded unequal treaties. Yet the Chinese (and the Americans) were unable to broaden the scope of the agenda on questions of importance to China or on the issue of future multilateral action against opium and its related activities. Resolutions adopted at Shanghai merely thanked China for its campaign against opium, encouraged diplomatic contacts looking toward future opium control agreements, and stressed the need for producer nations to control opium exports.[64]

China's delegates performed notably at Shanghai, using the opportunity to make a statement about the larger costs of the opium trade. T'ang Kuo-an pointed out that the price was ultimately borne by all nations doing business with China.[65] What T'ang did not say was that China was paying the greatest price. The campaign against opium smoking and cultivation meant the loss of vital revenue. A projected increase in the salt tax would make up only part of the deficit.[66]

Anglo-American narcotics relations became strained as a result of the meeting at Shanghai. The United States could not understand British reluctance to move rapidly toward comprehensive opium controls; American authorities rejected arguments made on economic grounds for continuing opium cultivation and trade. The rationales for and against the trade, posited in the Royal

Opium Commission and Philippine Commission reports respectively, had not appreciably changed by 1909. For years to come, suspicion and doubt would mark opium relations between the two powers. Often obscuring the common objective of reducing illicit drug supplies, the animus between the United States and Britain made more difficult a realistic appraisal of the opium situation in Asia.

Having brought the trade in Indian opium to China, the British were reluctant to give it up until China controlled its domestic traffic and cultivation. Opium merchants suspected that Manchu officials were more interested in cornering a greater share of the trade's revenues than in actually eliminating it.[67] Despite reports of decreasing poppy growth in southwestern China and Manchuria, doubts persisted concerning Chinese intentions. Sir Edward Grey, British foreign secretary, and Sir John Jordan, His Majesty's minister in Peking, feared that uncertified opium—that is, opium of diverse origins shipped to China outside of the official Indian trade—would drive down the price of Indian opium.[68]

What British officials failed to realize was that they no longer dominated the opium situation in China. The Chinese were trying against the odds to eradicate opium smoking. For humanitarian reasons and in an attempt to enhance its influence in the Far East partly at the expense of Britain, the United States wanted to move discussions of narcotics problems to the international arena. The State Department thus asked interested governments to attend an antiopium meeting at The Hague, scheduled to begin in late 1911. Possibly hoping to deflect attention from his country's opium policies in China, India, and the dominions, Grey delayed accepting the invitation. The Japanese also mistrusted Chinese, if not American, intentions. As one of several manufacturers of morphine, Japan recognized its potential as a substitute for opium, wanted a share of the growing market for the drug, and accordingly refused to consent to more than strict supervision of its manufacture and trade.[69]

Less than two months before the first meeting at The Hague on 1 December, a revolt began against the Manchus. Forces set in motion in domestic politics and foreign affairs at the time of the Taiping Rebellion, together with the expectations attendant to the imperial reform programs of 1901–11, created a situation in which revolutionists successfully wrested power from the dynasty. Provincial alliances between the gentry and merchants, along with the intellectual and moral force of revolutionary propaganda and activities, broke the hold of a Manchu-controlled Confucian tradition on the educated populace. Xenophobia in the form of Han racism among the peasants played a considerable role in hastening the revolution, as did the increasing autonomy of important military leaders such as Yuan Shih-k'ai. On 12 February 1912 the Hsuan-t'ung Emperor abdicated his throne, and the next day Sun Yat-sen turned over to Yuan Shih-k'ai the presidency of the Chinese Republic.[70]

Discussions at The Hague brought the issue of Chinese stability to the fore, so far as it was related to the matter of opium. The United States tried unsuccessfully to help China by supporting the formalization of the Shanghai resolutions and by proposing that the convention under consideration be divided into two parts—one for prepared and raw opium, the other for morphine and cocaine. Despite the lack of adequate controls on the traffic in morphine and cocaine, and with no provision calling for the creation of an administrative agency, the 1912 Hague Convention remained the basis of American narcotics foreign policy until 1931. The agreement strongly urged the powers to do their best to reduce illicit traffic in prepared opium (Chapter II, Article 6) and raw opium.[71]

The British report on the meeting at The Hague detailed the opium problems facing the new Chinese government. Not coincidentally, it also condemned Hamilton Wright's leadership of the U.S. delegation (and by implication the Sino-American opium relationship), charging that he "was responsible for a number of useless and irritating proposals" and was "singularly wanting in those qualities of clear-mindedness, moderation, and respect for the ideas of others which are essential for success in an international gathering of this kind." As for the Chinese, they were treated gingerly despite "constantly endeavouring to pose as the protagonists in the matter of opium reform and to divert attention from their own shortcomings." This final remark no doubt was in reference to the opium smoking and domestic trafficking that had reappeared in the wake of revolution. The British commissioners noted, too, that the Japanese delegation played but a small role at The Hague, perhaps because its interests were upheld in Chapter III, which concerned cocaine and morphine.[72]

Japan's limited participation at The Hague surely owed much to the changing nature of its role in Asia. Neither victory over China in 1894–95 nor defeat of Russia in 1904–5 brought Japan the stature it sought. Alliance agreements with the British in 1902, 1905, and 1911 recognized Japan's unique strategic position in East Asia but assumed a comity of objectives, including defense of the status quo until Russia was no longer a regional threat, preservation of China's integrity if only to preclude military conflict destructive of commercial interests, and enhancement of economic opportunities through the protection of Japan's naval-building program. A prominent role in the lucrative morphine trade, which the antiopium reforms had not eliminated and which no manufacturing nation was then willing to renounce, linked Japan's commercial goals with its broader foreign policy objectives in China.[73]

Conclusion

The 1911 anti-Manchu revolt affected policy thinking in Japan and exposed the latent strains in the union with Britain and, implicitly, in relations with other powers, notably the United States. Japan's interests in Manchuria and China had grown steadily after the inception of the Anglo-Japanese alliance in 1902. With dynastic abdication virtually certain, Tokyo initially hoped for the creation of a constitutional monarchy over which it might exert some influence. Yet some Japanese officials and the *genro*, or "elder statesmen," such as Prince Yamagata Aritomo, saw a republic, favored by the West, as a possible threat to Japan's strategic, financial, and commercial interests.[74] The likelihood of disputes among the foreign powers arising from China's revolution ended when it became clear that Yuan would uphold the conservative order in China.

Where did opium fit as Japan redefined its China policy? Above all, the Formosan experience convinced the Japanese that the Chinese had an affinity for opium and probably morphine. Opium smokers in Formosa came primarily from Fukien and the Hakka minority in Kwangtung. (Ironically, Hakkas had formed the heart of the Taiping Rebellion, which strongly condemned opium usage.) Chances for gradual suppression of the practice of opium smoking were lessened by the realization that addicts "would rather die than leave off its use" and the conclusion of a Formosan opium monopoly official that "this practice . . . is carried on secretly in private houses and can seldom be detected."[75] To the extent, then, that authorities in Japan were disposed to see the Chinese as inveterate consumers of opium, they were likewise inclined to pursue a China policy that reflected a sense of cultural superiority.

The events related to opium in the fall of the Manchu dynasty tended to stigmatize the Chinese as an inferior people. Given its own dynamic rise to major power status in Asia and its record of opium suppression, Japan could scarcely have expressed sympathy for the vicissitudes of China's antiopium efforts. One prominent pattern in Chinese foreign relations since the Opium War clearly demonstrated that failed or partial opium control helped induce additional forms of exploitation.

How opium control in republican China fared, therefore, held profound implications. To rid the land of opium smoking and poppy cultivation would restore a mandate to rule that the Manchus had lost. Moreover, beyond East Asia, success in opium control offered a promise that China would be taken seriously as a regional power and perhaps more. Successfully combating opium would present other Asian nations facing similar problems, many of whom were then in a colonial status, with the example that Asians themselves might destroy a notorious symbol of foreign domination—something that no international conference could accomplish. Thus it was that Yuan Shih-k'ai, beginning in 1912, deemed it imperative to revive the late Ch'ing efforts against opium. Unfortunately, the revolution did not eliminate the weaknesses related to opium in Chinese society and politics, and there remained many Chinese and foreigners who were prepared to take advantage of them as opportunities inevitably arose.

TWO

Obstacles to Opium Control in China, 1912–1926

Sentiments favoring opium control faded even during Yuan Shih-k'ai's presidency. Neither his regime nor its immediate successors found a way to overcome the financial lure of the opium trade to would-be entrepreneurs. Nor could they disabuse foreigners of the belief that many Chinese had no interest in purging their land, or themselves, of opium. And yet attempts by Japanese elements to introduce opium and morphine into North China and Manchuria moved London and Washington to promote antiopium activity in China. In a sense, opium control became one way to contain Japanese ambition in East Asia at the time of the First World War and after. What the British and the Americans failed fully to realize, with their attention understandably focused on broader policy considerations, was the hold of the poppy on Chinese society. In any case, containment of Japan via opium control would founder, as revealed at the Geneva opium conferences of 1924–25, on tactical differences, which helped to open the door to further Japanese adventurism in China.

A relatively strong China, free from the menace of opium after the revolution, might have played a more constructive role in regional and international affairs in East Asia. That development would have been no small matter as Great Britain turned its attention to European events and the United States sought a more consistent Asian policy. But it was not to be. The hope that the revolution might bring order and stability to China vanished, replaced by the sadly familiar presence of foreign intrigue and intractable domestic political and economic difficulties that continued well into the 1920s.

Yuan Shih-k'ai and Opium Suppression

Not a revolutionary himself, Yuan presided over a country engulfed in revolutionary times. He was similar in that regard to his approximate contemporaries, Francisco Madero in Mexico and Alexander Kerensky in Russia. Yuan had risen to prominence as a protégé of Li Hung-chang, a powerful conservative official who had been instrumental in the development of the military self-strengthening movement. Following Li's example, Yuan built support for himself by demanding loyalty from his several armies. At the time of Empress Dowager Tz'u-hsi's reaction against the Hundred Days reform, Yuan's military prowess made him indispensable to the throne.[1] Yuan Shih-k'ai was not simply a militarist by experience or inclination; he was well prepared in November 1901 to succeed Li Hung-chang as governor-general of Chihli and run it as a model province.

Reform comprised an integral part of Yuan's program in Chihli, and the control of opium became one measure of his success.[2] H. B. Morse estimated that the province's farmers produced between 5,000 and 10,000 piculs of opium at the time. Interested foreign observers, such as Minister W. W. Rockhill of the United States, recorded Yuan Shih-k'ai's progress against opium.[3] Yuan acted in one instance with the help of the Tientsin Chamber of Commerce to establish a monopoly bureau for the production and sale of opium. Run as a business venture, the bureau tried to control opium by regulating its source. Merchants, financially strapped local officials who had to fund a variety of reforms, and the chamber of commerce shared the monopoly's profits on a 50–40–10 basis.[4] Other provinces followed Chihli's example of opium control to a greater or lesser extent.

As president, though, Yuan had to deal with opium in a broader context. Revolutionists and revolutionaries—the distinction is Frederic Wakeman, Jr.'s—briefly united with him to promote suppression nationwide. Given the loss of revenue that effective control portended, major economic difficulties were sure to follow a successful antiopium effort. Yuan nevertheless issued a presidential order in late October 1912 reaffirming his opposition to the cultivation, manufacture, and trafficking in "the all-destroying weed . . . which threatens to annihilate both our country and our race."[5] Sir John Jordan encouraged Yuan to act forcefully, and he reminded Lu Cheng-hsiang, the minister for foreign affairs, that importers of Indian opium would be more likely to carry out the agreement of May 1911 if the trade in native opium were eliminated.[6]

Failure to restrict native opium conceivably had more serious ramifications than continuance of the Indian trade. Sir Edward Grey all but made recognition of Yuan's regime in 1912 dependent on the suppression of opium. Looking for assurances that the domestic campaign would take on the vigor of the prerevolutionary effort, the foreign minister told Jordan that the "continued failure of the Central Government to impose its will throughout the country . . . must materially retard the recognition of the Chinese Republic by His Majesty's Government, unless a considerable improvement in that respect is shown before the time comes for recognition."[7] That recognition ultimately was not held hostage to opium control indicates the general credibility of Yuan Shih-k'ai's antiopium commitment. Jordan, with his incisive knowledge of China and sympathy for Yuan Shih-k'ai, told Grey in mid-1912: "[T]here seems to be no reason to doubt the sincerity of the President."[8]

Evidence amply demonstrates that recrudescence of poppy cultivation constituted a grave problem for the young republic. As usual, missionaries provided much of the information by which the British assessed the course of opium control. In the province of Yunnan, farmers north of Yunnanfu were sowing poppy fields at the insistence of their landlords and threatening to harm anyone who attempted to stop them. In Szechwan, where spreading revolutionary disorder forced missionaries briefly to withdraw from the countryside, opium control fared well only where the new republican provincial government exercised its authority. The situation was even worse in Kansu, where officials, in effect, ordered farmers to grow opium poppies in order to overcome local economic hardships.[9]

China's problems with opium raise a question relevant to more than just the Chinese situation. That is, can opium growth, consumption, and traffic be controlled in the midst of a revolution? The evidence suggests that control is possible. In Yuan's China, control depended as much on commitment as on ideology. Jordan believed that so long as Chinese leaders were "unwilling to alienate the people by enforcing drastic measures of suppression," it was reasonable to question the republic's antiopium commitment. Yet by December 1912 he reported: "Drastic measures are being adopted nearly everywhere to suppress the cultivation, trade, and consumption of opium, and there is no evidence of any discrimination in favour of the native drug."[10] With a perspective forged in Britain's own experiences with opium, Jordan deemed "practical" the proposals advocating a gradual period for total suppression.[11]

China's willingness to try to control foreign and domestic opium is essential to understanding the nexus between revolution and opium control. The fervor accompanying deeply rooted change is not sufficient in itself to effect the profound social and cultural transformation inherent in opium suppression.

Widespread popular and institutional support are necessary for suppression to succeed. Fortunately for China, in the aftermath of the 1911 Revolution, these preconditions existed among many of the Chinese people. Although Yuan Shih-k'ai's attempts to extend political centralization were resisted in many provinces, his leadership in the antiopium struggle was accepted, however briefly, because it gave useful national expression to a common objective.[12]

Elsewhere in Asia, colonial administrations kept revolutionary sentiments under control, thereby undermining the few inchoate radical nationalist pleas for opium suppression. Poppy cultivation persisted, especially at the Burma-China border, unimpeded by the strictures Yunnanese officials attempted to enforce. In French Indochina, where the legitimate trade in Indian opium continued, antiopium appeals fell on deaf ears. Authorities there sought to profit from the trade by importing either Indian or Yunnanese opium for the Saigon monopoly.[13] In 1920, during the Socialist Congress at Tours, the man later known as Ho Chi Minh condemned these "predatory [French] capitalists," asserting that "they do all they can to poison us with opium and besot us with alcohol."[14]

The myriad of problems confronting Yuan Shih-k'ai prevented a final settlement of the opium, let alone the narcotics, issue. In the first place, Yuan's prior administrative experience convinced opponents that he would attempt to consolidate his power without regard for republican scruples, which he did by increasing his military support along the Yangtze and by flouting the power of the national assembly. These maneuvers helped set off the Second Revolution in the summer of 1913, in which nine mostly southern provinces distanced themselves from Yuan and thus exposed the frailty of republican government in China.[15]

While fundamentally the product of unstable domestic conditions, China's troubles also derived from concurrent developments in foreign relations. Chinese integrity depended largely on its economic health, and the prognosis in 1913 was not good. Opium alone had a remarkably detrimental effect on the nation's economy. In U.S. equivalents on a yearly basis, the Chinese people spent over $150 million consuming foreign and native opium. If land given over to poppy cultivation had been planted with crops such as wheat or other grains, farmers would have realized some $100 million. Moreover, opium smoking reduced the productive power of smokers by perhaps $300 million annually.[16]

China's economic weakness set off another scramble for greater influence by the foreign powers. Through a proposed consortium Reorganization Loan, the British hoped to increase China's diplomatic and financial indebtedness to the Crown in order to expand the opportunities for trade and, in so doing, prevent Japanese expansion into Britain's economic sphere of interest in the Yangtze Valley.[17] Yuan Shih-k'ai surely saw his economic options diminishing; he had to accept the appointment of a foreigner as inspector of the salt gabelle, thus reducing revenue available to pay the nation's administrative expenses.[18]

Willing to do virtually anything to solidify his hold on power, Yuan attempted to re-create the monarchy in 1915 with the help of Frank J. Goodnow, an expert on public administration and constitutional law from Columbia University, who drafted a provisional constitution.[19] Adding to Yuan's troubles, the Twenty-One Demands of May showed that Japanese ambition was growing even as domestic support for his regime steadily eroded.[20] British and American responses to the demands focused in the short term more on the possibility of Japanese expansion in Manchuria and Shantung than on the critical weaknesses of Yuan's government.[21] In effect, they were minimizing the profound importance of opium for China's political and economic stability. President Woodrow Wilson merely informed both China and Japan that the negotiations regarding the Twenty-One Demands should not impair American rights under the Open Door policy.[22] Most disturbing to Grey was the realization that his Far Eastern policy was in some disarray; strains in the alliance with Japan rendered all the more important the presence of a stable regime in Peking.[23]

In short, neither Western power wanted to see Japan virtually dismantle China; nor were they prepared to accept Japan as an equal power. On the contrary, a relatively weakened, but stable China would receive Anglo-American diplomatic solicitude in exchange for political and economic influence in domestic affairs. At the same time, a strong Japan would be admonished to act responsibly in pursuit of its interests; ultimately, this advice would extend to the issue of manufactured narcotics in China.

The Opium Combine

Even had Yuan Shih-k'ai's attempt to restore the monarchy been warmly received, China's financial situation would not have substantially improved. The salt gabelle did not have the same potential for fiscal manipulation as taxes on opium. It is hardly surprising, then, that Yuan and his immediate successors tried to squeeze additional revenue from the opium business.[24]

By March 1915, merchants in Shanghai moved to create a central combine under which existing stocks of imported opium would be transferred to Pe-king's control. In theory, the combine was intended to reduce smuggling and provide aged smokers with a reliable source of opium. Authorities believed that suppression campaigns would continue and that the combine was not a retrograde step. Merchants in Shanghai even promised a rebate of sorts to the government for every chest of opium sold in Kiangsu, Kiangsi, and Kwang-tung. The arrangement would end on the date that imports of Indian opium were officially to cease, 31 March 1917. Sir John Jordan found the entire affair objectionable and predicted the resumption of native poppy cultivation along with an upsurge in smuggling from Shanghai.[25]

Following Yuan's death in mid-1916, suppression became even more prob-lematic. Price-fixing was keeping the cost of imported opium artificially high while guaranteeing the combine a regular supply. The provisions of an agree-ment with the merchants gave control of the estimated 2,100 chests to the government. Payment to participants in the Shanghai Opium Combine would be made in the form of 6 percent, ten-year bonds. In theory, the opium was intended for medicinal needs only; yet, if it were sold for other purposes such as smoking, it would greatly improve the financial condition of whoever con-trolled the proceeds.[26] Despite the enticement of desperately needed revenue, the government delayed taking possession of the combine's opium. Wanting to minimize its losses, the combine in April 1917 addressed a memorandum to Feng Kuo-chang, then vice-president, calling upon the government to take delivery. Peking, however, had temporarily defaulted on its agreement with the combine.[27] Not until 1918 would there be a final disposition of the opium in question.

American Views of Opium Suppression

Free from Britain's colonial entanglement with opium, the United States ad-vocated a rapid road to suppression. Such a development would have meant a radical change in Chinese culture, which Western missionaries had long espoused. Missionaries, of course, often set the tone for official American per-ceptions about China and opium; they knew well that the dramatic changes suppression would bring were impossible if the Chinese people cared more for some pleasing soporific than they did for the cross. Learning fairly super-ficial lessons despite numerous inquiries into the reasons for opium smoking, they tended to blame opium's victims for their plight. James W. Bashford, the principal Methodist Episcopal bishop in China, found the government in Peking "ignorant, corrupt, and impotent" and deemed the masses "unskilled in modern industries." Also disparaging was Charles Denby, U.S. minister to China for thirteen years after 1885. His musings on opium betrayed his lack of knowledge about a society vastly different from his own. "The only thing that can be said for it," he wrote in 1905, "is that China-grown opium will eventually cut off the Indian trade, and at least enable the people to spend in their country the money which they devote to their own perdition."[28]

The missionaries under Bashford's charge closely watched the opium situation in their districts. As more than passive observers, the ministers of the Methodist Board of Foreign Missions tried to show the way toward opium suppression in the regions where they labored. Arthur Schlesinger, Jr., describes the missionaries as agents of a kind of cultural imperialism whose presence accentuated the contradictions in Chinese society. By 1918, the apparent futility of their efforts led them to depict "a great moral calamity [in] China."[29]

While generally sharing this pessimistic assessment about the deleterious effects of opium on the Chinese people, U.S. officials nevertheless sought to fashion an East Asian policy that dealt with opium as part of broader Anglo-American concerns. Sometime between the issuance of the Twenty-One Demands in 1915 and the signing of the Lansing-Ishii Agreement in November 1917, they succeeded in doing so. Bishop Bashford may have contributed indirectly to this effort when he wrote to President Wilson and Secretary of State William Jennings Bryan in the spring of 1915 detailing the Japanese threat to important American religious and economic interests in China. Bashford assured Bryan that "the United States is acting in the best interests of China in quietly but firmly protesting against her absorption by Japan."[30] The Wilson administration believed that the 1917 agreement reiterated its avowed commitment to China's integrity. The British, despite preferring an overt recognition of their interests, welcomed this cautious statement of U.S. policy.[31]

The politics of opium in China were forcing the two powers to reappraise how they had previously dealt with the opium issue. Merely ending the import trade was no panacea. This is not to argue that policymakers in London or Washington had acted precipitously at Shanghai and The Hague. Rather, it suggests that moral and diplomatic suasion also had to be based on a realistic analysis of the domestic situation. The British, led by the unflagging efforts of Sir John Jordan, had already begun to act in such a fashion, but the corresponding breakthrough in U.S. understanding of the enormity of the opium situation came more slowly.

The change was apparent in America's reaction to the opium combine proposal. What the United States had worked to eliminate in the Philippines, an opium monopoly, was virtually certain to begin operating in China, especially since, diplomat John Van Antwerp MacMurray believed, "prominent members of the present government are interested [in it]." With the monopoly would come a breakdown of social and economic order as a result of opium smuggling from Persia and elsewhere; increased poppy cultivation and opium smoking were sure to follow. Ambassador Walter Hines Page of the United States reported from London that Britain also opposed the prospective monopoly as being contrary to the spirit of the 1912 Hague Opium Convention and the Anglo-Chinese agreement of 1911. When the Chinese government reached an agreement with the Shanghai Opium Combine in mid-1918 and actually took control of at least 1,200 chests, the Foreign Office and the State Department protested the arrangement.[32]

By the end of November, pressure against the government moved President Hsu Shih-ch'ang, once a military protégé of Yuan Shih-k'ai, to decide to destroy the nearly eighty tons of opium in a costly public burning at Shanghai. The actual incineration took place in specially constructed furnaces over an eight-day period ending on 25 January 1919.[33] Supportive memorials were sent to Hsu Shih-ch'ang from several antiopium societies in China that were then in the process of consolidating their activities into the International Anti-Opium Association (Peking). Among those influential in the formation of the association were Elizabeth Washburn Wright (Mrs. Hamilton Wright); a number of foreigners living in Peking, including Protestant ministers; and A. E. Blanco, of the Chinese Maritime Customs, who later headed the Anti-Opium Information Bureau in Geneva and became an ardent supporter of Chiang Kai-shek's opium suppression measures.[34]

Backing for Hsu also came from H. G. W. Woodhead, editor of the *Peking & Tientsin Times*; Dr. Wu Lien-teh, physician and Chinese delegate to two of the Hague opium conferences; and, at Shanghai, the Reverend A. L. Warn-shuis of the International Missions Council. President Hsu, who was about to order some 17 million taels worth of opium burned, agreed to serve as patron of the antiopium association. When V. K. Wellington Koo (Ku Wei-chiun), China's minister in Washington, conveyed the decision to Elizabeth Wright, he praised her efforts and those of her late husband in the crusade against opium.[35]

Sir John Jordan congratulated the Peking government on the wisdom of its action, calling Hsu Shih-ch'ang "an enlightened ruler." Jordan, who had served as British minister since 1906, rejoiced that "we have removed finally the stigma attaching in the popular mind to our connection with this traffic" but added the caveat that "by keeping our own hands clean in the future we can continue to exercise pressure to prevent the exploitation of China by other countries."[36] Not all those celebrating the burning of the combine's opium stocks shared Jordan's evaluation of the British role. Thomas Sammons, the U.S. consul, intimated that the British had only a shallow faith in Hsu's anti-opium professions. And journalist Ellen N. LaMotte charged that the merchants in the Shanghai combine were "unofficial agents" for the British government. In the appendix of a book written while in China, she commented on the impending burning of opium: "America to the rescue! It must have been a close squeak for poor old China."[37]

Sammons and LaMotte, as did many other Americans before 1931, assumed that only strict suppression was acceptable opium policy. Their attitude derived from the experiences of the United States with opium smoking in the Philippines nearly two decades before and from long-standing opposition to Great Britain's participation in the Indian trade. Although the trade with China had ended, it continued to serve government monopolies in British possessions elsewhere in Asia. Yet, in rejecting a monopoly even as a catalyst for suppression, U.S. officials found it difficult to distinguish between friends and enemies in the fight against opium. Given the existing situation in China around 1920, this hard-line stance made for questionable policy and impaired relations with Great Britain.

The Failure of Opium Control

The First World War and the domestic political chaos of the time gravely damaged the cause of opium control in China. Not realizing that this was happening, Minister Paul Reinsch of the United States welcomed Hsu's decision requesting that foreign missionaries supply the government with information about opium cultivation. Reinsch hoped to find in Hsu the requisite moral strength to bring dissident factions in China together.[38] The American minister, a progressive, former professor from Wisconsin, also took as a favorable sign a decision by the government and the International Anti-Opium Association at Peking to send a telegram to the Paris Peace Conference imploring the conferees to put on the agenda opium and morphine suppression.[39] The State Department initially opposed placing the issue of opium before the conference but soon reversed itself. British officials took the lead at Paris in getting a drafting committee to consider several proposals and prepare what became Article 295 of the Treaty of Versailles, whereby ratification of the Versailles pact meant accepting the 1912 Hague Opium Convention.[40]

Nonetheless, other developments at the time indicated just how unlikely opium control actually was. A burgeoning illicit trade in morphine was over-running part of the country; Japanese nationals were increasingly active in the morphine business and were peddling opium in Manchuria and North China; and the failure in 1919 to repair the break in relations between northern and southern factions guaranteed that provincial and regional warlords would dominate Chinese politics. Basic to their hold on power were the tax revenues warlords received as a result of revitalized opium poppy cultivation. In sum, neither officials in Peking nor the military government in Canton were capable of preventing opium and narcotics from again menacing China.

Concerning morphine, or morphia, it is uncertain who first brought it to China or when; only in 1892 did Chinese customs begin recording its impor-tation. Raising the tax on morphine in 1903 drove the drug underground and literally into the arms of Chinese users. The trade was outlawed in 1907 by agreement of China and the foreign powers except under a physician's signa-ture. Yet by 1915, Japan was importing nearly 360,000 ounces of morphine from Great Britain. Because of the stringency of Japanese laws controlling mor-phine, much of it was shipped to China where extraterritorial privileges kept it hidden from local customs officials.[41]

During the war large-scale illicit production and trafficking by Japanese, Koreans, Formosans, and Chinese occurred in Manchuria and in the Tsingtao region. Missionaries and the *North-China Daily News* blamed the Japanese for the trade in morphine. Jordan concurred but thought that Chinese enforce-ment of existing restrictions might induce Japanese officials to clamp down on the trade. Bowing to pressure from antiopium societies, including one in Ed-inburgh where two-thirds of Britain's morphine for export was manufactured, His Majesty's Government tied exports to legitimate needs in Japan and the Kwantung Leased Territory. Foreign Secretary Arthur Balfour in July 1917 instructed Sir Conyngham Greene, the ambassador in Tokyo, to inform the Japanese government of the decision. Taken as an emergency wartime mea-sure, the restrictions, which Tokyo accepted, were to be lifted at the end of the war.[42]

American observers, including Elizabeth Wright, reacted strongly against reports of Japanese participation in the morphine traffic. Another American, E. Carleton Baker, U.S. consul general at Mukden, on learning that the Japa-nese had prohibited their nationals from trading in drugs, commented that "their desire is simply to hoodwink the world and to go through the motions of suppressing the evil." Although, as Baker noted, the Chinese were "disposed to buy" opium and morphine, U.S. representatives agreed with the *North-*

China Daily News that Japanese officials, manufacturers, and financiers were responsible for the vast majority of the eighteen tons of morphine imported into Manchuria in 1918.[43]

Although there is reliable evidence showing that the Japanese military administration in Tientsin was intimately involved in the morphine trade, it is not clear that this activity was condoned in Tokyo. The press there expressed concern over the damage opiates were doing to Japanese honor and prestige abroad; after being urged to do so by the Anglophile Count Soejima Michimasa, the cautious premier, Hara Kei (Takashi), promised in February 1919 to act against the trade.[44] Hara's decision was probably linked to other foreign policy goals. Japan hoped to place a statement on racial or national equality in the covenant of the League of Nations. Yet because of strong opposition by Australia and New Zealand, the attempt got nowhere—leaving Tokyo to register its regret about the failure of the conference to support the proposal. Hara nevertheless pressed on with his campaign against the narcotics traffic. From his vantage point in Peking, Jordan accepted declarations by Japanese military officials that they had decided to abolish the opium administration in Tsingtao and the Kwantung leasehold and would crack down on the morphine trade.[45]

Meanwhile, the cultivation of native opium was undoing more than a decade of suppression activity. Officials in Peking, known as the Chihli Clique, were no more able to do anything about it than foreign missionaries and diplomats who charted its revival. By mid-1920, extensive cultivation could be found in part of Fukien, western regions of Honan, and Shensi, provinces under the nominal control of Peking. Similar conditions were evident where the Canton government presumably held sway: in Hunan, southwestern Hupei, part of Fukien, Kweichow, Yunnan, and Szechwan. Chihli, Kwantung, Kiangsu, Shansi, and Kansu were relatively free of cultivation, as were Anhwei and Kiangsi. The same could be said for Chekiang, Kwangtung, and most of Kwangsi. Small amounts of opium were then being grown in Manchuria.[46]

In Shensi, the *tuchun*, or military governor, was openly defying orders from Peking and insisting that peasants sow their fields with poppy seeds. Decrying the threat to "China's national interests," Jordan protested to the Ministry of Foreign Affairs, the Wai-chiao Pu (formerly, the Wai-wu Pu), encouraging it to make an example of the tuchun, and Reinsch made his similar position clear in "pointed terms." In truth, there was little more either man could do in the face of a virtual breakdown of national authority.[47]

With provincial officials opposing the Chihli clique, the Western objective of a stable China became increasingly elusive. The warlord period, which

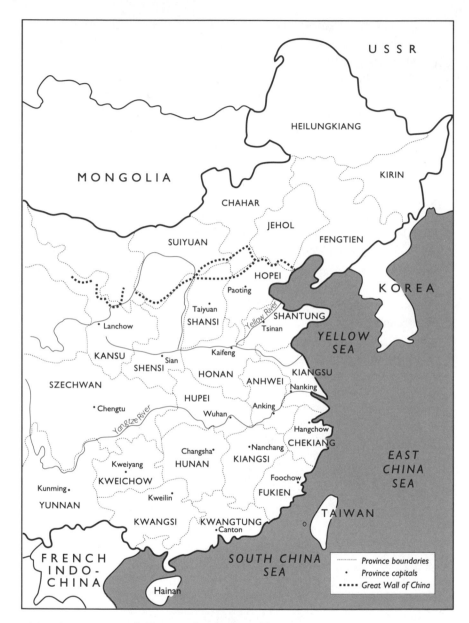

Map 1. Provinces of China under the Republic

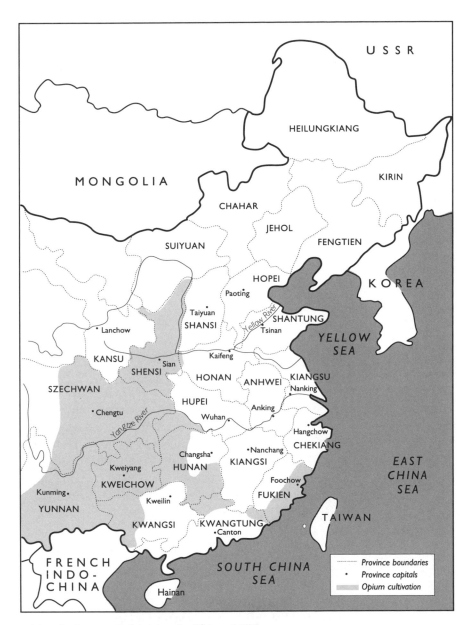

Map 2. Opium Cultivation in China, 1920

lasted until 1928, effectively compromised the cause of opium control. Whether enlightened or reactionary, warlords contended for personal or provincial power with all the means at their disposal. Even Feng Yü-hsiang, the "Christian General," failed to end completely the opium business in Shensi after helping in mid-1921 to oust the notorious Ch'en Shu-fan. The number of warlords reached the hundreds; retention of autonomy and convenience, if not sheer opportunism, dictated deference to Peking's authority. Early in the 1920s allegiances shifted as easily, it seemed, as new heads of state, cabinets, or legislatures took a turn at running the government.[48]

To enjoy the amenities of power, which meant funding their personal armies, warlords enforced—often with the help of landlords—a remarkably varied system of fees and taxes. In those provinces where opium grew abundantly or where opium traffic was heavy, suppression bureaus taxed opium in the guise of fines because there existed no real alternative money crop to finance the warlords. Ironically, foreign concern about customs and salt revenues helped turn the tuchuns and local warlords to opium, a source of income they could better control.[49]

Within the chaos that permeated China arose a rough nationalism, especially as seen in the lofty ideals of the May Fourth Movement.[50] First to take advantage of this renascent spirit were Dr. Sun Yat-sen and his followers, whose political fortunes had waned after Yuan Shih-k'ai declared the Kuomintang (Nationalist party, or KMT) illegal in November 1913. To enhance his authority, Sun reorganized the party in October 1919, two months after prolonged negotiations with northern officials failed to resolve their differences.[51] Sun Yat-sen gave the military government at Canton its legitimacy. Then, as provisional president of China in May 1921, he proclaimed his support for federalism, peaceful reunification, the open door, and industrialization. Sun soon established an alliance with some northern militarists, including the Fengtien general, Chang Tso-lin, but an attempt to unify China failed and Sun fled to Shanghai in August 1922.

To be sure, warlord rule brought crippling economic and social distress to China: opium poppies were planted in times of extreme famine, government administration became meaningless in many provinces, and the dislocation of legitimate trade impeded industrial growth and the modernization of agriculture. Furthermore, banditry flourished and Chinese politics became even more militarized, thereby completing a process begun during the Taiping Rebellion. Whether or not out of genuine conviction, warlords often held their forces together with appeals to national patriotism. (Feng Yü-hsiang particularly impressed his troops in this way.)

No one could have known immediately after 1920 whether opium suppression would find a place in China, no matter who dominated national politics. Hsu Shih-ch'ang's ouster did not augur well for suppression in the short term, yet the antiopium movement did not entirely disappear. Peking's International Anti-Opium Association and foreign missionaries continued to inveigh against poppy growth. Despite increasing personal risks, Christians condemned slogans such as those distributed in Fukien exclaiming: "Salvation from Poverty through Opium-growing." At the same time, though, their reports indicated that they were having little impact on the situation.[52]

Antiopium agitation made little headway, leading the general secretary of the International Anti-Opium Association, the Reverend Arthur Sowerby, to write the Opium Advisory Committee (OAC) of the League of Nations demanding the cessation of the Indian trade. Even if India were willing to reduce production, argued L. J. Kershaw of the India Office, Turkish and Persian opium would soon replace Indian supplies. The association strongly disagreed, termed Britain "blameworthy in the common judgment of the world," and deemed India beyond redemption since it "persistently and obstinately continued to produce opium in ever increasing amounts."[53]

With a marked degree of noblesse oblige, officials in London rarely sought to disabuse the International Anti-Opium Association of its ideas concerning British or Indian culpability for conditions in China.[54] What concerned the British government more than anything else was the dismal situation in China. In a dispatch to Sir Beilby Austin, Jordan's successor in Peking, Foreign Secretary Lord Curzon chided the association for not paying adequate attention to the recrudescence of opium cultivation in much of the nation. Curzon felt that if China's "culpable negligence" in curbing the appetite for opium were reversed, then Britain's policy of gradual restriction in its colonies would be more effective. At that time, contributing as it were to Britain's sense of superiority, smuggling from Hong Kong had diminished despite the increasing importance of opium in China.[55]

The Issue of Legalization

By the end of 1923, conditions were worse than they had been at any time since 1911. Opium was grown widely and sold openly throughout southern and southwestern China. Vast quantities of Yunnanese opium were traded with interior cities and French Indochina. Conservative reports had production increasing by 50 percent in Yunnan in 1922. Tax revenues, three times those of 1921, were collected on production, transport, and export, while protection costs were based on a journey's length.[56] Conditions were scarcely better elsewhere. In the Yangtze Valley from Chungking in Szechwan to Ichang in Hupei, the river was a ribbon of opium. Poppies were grown in Kansu to offset the unfavorable trade balance; in Shensi, wages were often paid in opium. Opium saturated the district of Amoy in Fukien. And though cultivation was still limited in Chihli and Manchuria, smuggling and related clandestine activities there could not easily be controlled.[57]

Threatening to compound the situation was a movement to legalize the opium business. The promise of great revenues for Peking would have been motivation enough to create a monopoly. Moreover, as proponents realized, legalization might break the power of the warlords. Over 4 million acres throughout the country were producing opium instead of cotton, cereals, rice, wheat, potatoes, or beans on behalf of tuchuns who protected poppy plants and established local opium suppression bureaus to supply themselves with needed revenue.[58]

As early as mid-1922, the *Peking & Tientsin Times* reported that a demand for legalization based on fiscal needs would likely arise. Authorities in Peking increasingly linked the regime's financial stability with the issues of militarism and Chinese security, and the paper disclosed that 40 percent of the nation's revenue went for military expenses of $200 million (Mex.) per year. Disbanding the armed forces in the hope of undercutting the power of the tuchuns would cost an additional $100–$200 million (Mex.). To some, including Sir Francis Aglen, inspector general of the Chinese Maritime Customs, an opium monopoly seemed a logical, if temporary, solution. Opium revenues would fund a real suppression campaign and pay for the disbandment of some 1 million men; the nearly 370,000 remaining soldiers would provide necessary security for China.[59]

Opposition to Aglen's point of view came from Sir John Jordan, then an assessor with the OAC in Geneva, the U.S. government, and the International Anti-Opium Association.[60] By April 1924, the new Chinese Government Opium Suppression Board was working directly with the association to promote control in the areas under Peking's rule. These efforts accomplished little since ostensibly loyal province leaders were encouraging poppy cultivation, which the Bank of China assisted, at least in the case of Kansu, by transferring large amounts of silver to local branches.[61] Despite protests, Christians were being forced to plant opium poppies in Fukien, for example, at the same time as their mission houses were being looted.[62] Even so, at an OAC meeting in August 1924, China's delegate claimed that cultivation was being controlled effectively. Given this disingenuous position, it is not surprising that negotiations earlier in the year with Japan over opium and morphine traffic failed to produce an agreement.[63] Tokyo had no incentive to do more than play a diplomatic waiting game. As always, the Japanese view of the Chinese and their affinity for opium was hardly complimentary.

The projected government opium monopoly further undermined Chinese credibility with the Western powers.[64] By early 1925, local monopolies were operating under the control of militarists throughout the country. British doubts about the propriety of a monopoly differed somewhat from those of the United States, however. It could scarcely be otherwise for London, given the existence of opium-smoking monopolies in Britain's Far Eastern territories. Reservations derived from the absence of a stable political environment under which a monopoly might operate.[65]

The Foreign Office hoped to minimize Anglo-American differences by proposing that a commission of inquiry into the opium-smoking situation be sent to the Far East following two antiopium conferences that were scheduled to begin at Geneva in November 1924.[66] The First Geneva Opium Conference, at which the United States was not a formal participant, dealt with opium smoking in Asia; the second considered the issues of production and manufacturing. The major question facing delegates to the first conference was how to curtail the trade in prepared opium. The conferees supported government monopolies on the importation, sale, and distribution of opium; prohibition on the use of opium by minors; control on commerce in raw and prepared opium through import certificates; and the exchange of information on smuggling.[67]

What the first conference failed to do was set a date by which opium smoking would cease, thus incurring the wrath of the U.S. delegation. Horrified at what he saw as the prospect of opium legalization in Asia, Bishop Charles H. Brent drew on the moral authority of American opposition to opium smoking and urged the powers not to sign the agreement. Nor was the United States placated by the promise of some future inquiry so long as opium monopolies still operated.[68] Compromise therefore proved impossible. On 7 February 1925, the president of the second conference, Herluf Zahle of Denmark, announced the withdrawal of the Chinese and American delegations. The pretext for China's exit was that the Geneva conferences had not adequately dealt with the subject of prepared opium.[69]

The British blamed what happened at Geneva squarely on conditions in China. Only when the government curtailed poppy cultivation would the elimination of opium smoking—to take place over a fifteen-year period—be possible, concluded Lord Robert Cecil in an interdepartmental conference held at the Foreign Office. As for the United States, Lord Cecil deeply regretted the American departure from Geneva, believing that the second conference had fashioned a convention aimed at controlling the manufacture and traffic in opium and other drugs through the creation of an import and export certificate system and the establishment of the Permanent Central Opium Board (PCOB) to handle information on production, consumption, and traffic in drugs.[70] Many years later, Herbert L. May, an American drug expert who subsequently worked for the PCOB, claimed that it "was a mistake for the Americans to walk out" of the second Geneva conference.[71]

Geneva's Legacy for China

The outcome of the Geneva meetings meant that opium-smoking monopolies would continue to operate in the Far East. That China was too weak to put a viable monopoly into effect paradoxically worked to Peking's benefit in the immediate aftermath of Geneva. Solicitude for China in the United States increased noticeably. The Opium Committee (later the Opium Research Committee) of the Foreign Policy Association (FPA) sent representatives to OAC meetings and regularly encouraged U.S. officials to do more to help China.[72]

Representative Stephen G. Porter, the powerful chairman of the House Foreign Affairs Committee who led the American exit from Geneva, asked the State Department to determine if a portion of the Boxer indemnity could be remitted to China for opium control by the government and selected anti-opium groups, including the International Anti-Opium Association. The State Department rejected the proposal as untimely but, in response to other pressures, began to reconsider its position on extraterritorial rights. Substantive change on that issue by foreign powers might have altered the status of their concessions as havens for the drug trade.[73]

In a surprising development, the meetings at Geneva briefly brought the United States and Japan closer together over the issue of the illicit narcotics trade. Missionaries and diplomats alike had long expressed skepticism about Japanese actions and intentions regarding the flow of morphine into China. Rowland McLean Cross of the American Board of Commissioners of Foreign Missions could recall that missionaries in Japan "were saddened and concerned by what was happening in China." To Cross and those serving in North China, the Japanese army was the source of narcotics problems.[74] Six weeks before the first Geneva conference, information reaching the State Department indicated that the morphine traffic in Kwantung genuinely concerned Tokyo. Consequently, Porter, as chairman of the American delegation, sought to work closely with the Japanese. In turn, Japan's representative largely supported Washington's proposals despite contrary British advice. Relations between the former allies, it seems, had become cordial at best.[75]

For the first time, Britain found itself outside the mainstream of antiopium activity in Asia. Yet officials at the Foreign Office and diplomats in China could take comfort in their intimate knowledge of the Asian situation. The Geneva agreements gave them a useful tool for monitoring Japanese intentions in China; this was significant since the Washington Conference of 1921–22 had accorded Japan status as a major power in East Asia. In addition, their experience convinced them that multilateral deliberations were useless unless followed by meaningful action on the scene. In the mid-1920s, this meant China's adoption of a realistic program to curb the production of opium. Thus, China would have to establish a monopoly-style program as Britain had proposed at the first Geneva conference. Until that happened, or without the intervention of unrelated events, British influence in China would be somewhat diminished in comparison to the special relationship with the United States and the suddenly improved relations with Japan.[76]

Conclusion

The foreign powers knew that China had to solve its domestic political problems in order to break opium's hold over its future well-being. The United States was not then prepared to take China's part in disputes with other nations.[77] Ominously, it was unlikely that Japan's ambitions in China had been entirely fulfilled, Shidehara Kijūrō's conciliatory foreign policy notwithstanding.[78] Although Sun Yat-sen had relied on revenues from the opium business while alive, despite knowing the hazards of such an expedient action, his death in March 1925 raised the prospect of renewed antiopium activity— especially in light of his Final Testament urging China to strive for real independence and equality. H. H. Kung (K'ung Hsiang-hsi) later characterized the will as an effort "to give guidance to the people."[79] Opium reform, let alone a defense of Chinese integrity, could not occur, however, so long as political and economic discord threatened the country.

A divided and weakened China was finding, as it had before, a kind of friendship with the United States and, to a lesser extent, with Great Britain. Yet their individual and mutual interests rendered them scarcely more than uncertain allies, if that is not too strong a term. The monopoly question had strained Anglo-American relations in the Far East and would continue to do so. Ironically, whereas a stronger China would not have received similar solicitude from the West, it might have been better able to meet the external challenges to its authority that soon appeared. Political reintegration in China was not a foregone conclusion in 1926, but a renewed campaign to unify the country would capture the attention of all interested parties, including the advocates of opium suppression. The outcome of that effort would further clarify the interrelationship of opium, international politics, and security in Asia in subsequent years.

THREE

Opium's Threat to Security
in Asia, 1926–1931

The prospects for opium control in China immediately after the Geneva conferences could scarcely have been more remote. Proponents of control felt stymied at every turn and fashioning a workable program seemed like a Sisyphean task. As they had for some years, the tuchuns effectively stood in the way of reform. Opposition to opium by several organizations within China, continued exhortation by foreign missionaries against opium smoking and poppy cultivation, and the well-intentioned efforts of the Opium Advisory Committee to curb the opium traffic had no discernible impact on most warlords. Although foreigners participated in the opium and narcotics trade, the Chinese themselves were largely responsible for the cultural devastation that opium wrought. However painful for antiopium advocates to admit, this conclusion was as true in the late 1920s as it had been following the Opium War in 1842. Sadly, far too many Chinese looked upon their compatriots with the same disdain displayed by non-Chinese purveyors of opium and narcotics.

Despite the odds, foreigners were counting on the return of stability to China. The Japanese, for example, ensconced in the Shantung Peninsula and in Manchuria from Mukden to the port of Dairen, were trying peacefully to expand their economic presence beyond the Great Wall into North China. Civilian and military leaders in Tokyo believed that strategic security was impossible without such influence.[1] Shidehara Kijūrō's accommodating China policy appealed to the other two foreign powers directly concerned with the opium situation in Asia. Put another way, if Tokyo were vigilant against the morphine trade, its efforts might redound to Japan's credit in other issues involving the major powers in China.

In London, protecting imperial economic interests remained the centerpiece of Far Eastern policy. Domestic chaos in China or a Sino-Japanese conflict would threaten London's economic policies.[2] Knowing that opium could foster instability, the Foreign Office began moving after 1925 toward opium reform in its own Asian possessions and urged China to do the same. In this way Great Britain emphasized, as it had since the Washington Conference, the importance of Chinese integrity to its own objectives in Asia.

After leaving Geneva, the United States far more than Britain believed that its interests were protected in part by cordial relations between Tokyo and Peking. But the renewal of antiforeign sentiment in China, highlighted by the incident on 30 May 1925 at Shanghai, confirmed for Secretary of State Frank B. Kellogg the need to promote a progressive foreign presence in China on major issues like tariffs and extraterritoriality. Ironically, London's tentative move in the same direction induced Washington to alter its China policy and act more forcefully in support of Chinese nationalism.[3] In so doing, the United States was prepared to place Sino-American relations on a more solid footing should China's domestic situation improve.

Until the Kuomintang's Northern Expedition (1926–28) succeeded in unifying China, the goal of stability, so dear to foreigners, was all but precluded by the tuchuns, who secured their power by the collection of land and opium taxes. In the case of opium, the choice of market routes could determine which warlords prospered and which fell from power, just as the absence of railroad lines had destroyed some towns in the nineteenth-century American West. Centralized rule in China became a virtual fiction around 1925 as prominent warlords, allied in cliques with others in the pursuit of temporarily similar objectives, gave little thought to the security or future of the nation. Until the demise of the warlord era became more of a certainty in 1928, Chinese opium control remained on hold.[4]

British Opium Policy after Geneva

The relative lack of attention to the Chinese opium situation in British and American diplomatic records between early 1925 and late 1927 indicates, first of all, the chaos of the contemporary political scene. Reporting on opium-related developments became less important than detailing broader events. Second, it shows the persistence of antiforeign sentiment since even missionary reports were sparse at the time.[5] John V. A. MacMurray, the U.S. minister to China, surely spoke for much of the foreign community when he told Joseph C. Grew in February 1927: "We are living in a China that is absolutely incomprehensible to those who have not known it since May, 1925."[6]

What the Foreign Office endeavored to do then, in order to further its antiopium activities, was to address conditions elsewhere in the Far East, particularly as they affected colonial economic matters. Nearly a century of involvement with opium had convinced the British that opium could not be isolated from general security concerns. Exports from India declined after 1919 but were still eliciting interest in Parliament. Saigon imported the most Indian opium, followed by Singapore and Bangkok.[7] Of immediate concern was the Portuguese colony of Macao, which was seeking increased opium supplies. Foreign Secretary Austen Chamberlain ruled that control at Macao was too lax to permit additional exports; the India Office agreed, noting that Macao was a major center of the illicit traffic where authorities "admittedly countenance a considerable export trade which has no legitimate explanation."[8]

Making Chamberlain's decision relatively easy was India's opium situation. The time for export restriction was at hand, since India was relying less and less on the opium trade for revenue. The inability of officials there to control opium exports to French Indochina, which surely exceeded legitimate requirements, persuaded the Foreign Office to make a change. In that regard, Malcolm Delevingne of the Home Office urged Chamberlain to approach the French to arrange for the progressive reduction of imports at Saigon. Delevingne knew, however, that the Indochina government also had to do more to restrict opium imports, whether from India, Persia, or Yunnan.[9] The decision gradually to reduce exports from India to French Indochina was made at an interdepartmental meeting in January 1926.[10]

Changing export policy brought with it additional dilemmas for British policymakers. Chief among these was the question of how the opium-smoking monopolies in British colonies, which were entitled to continue operations under both the 1912 Hague and 1925 Geneva conventions, would procure opium as India ceased to be a source. The Colonial Office responded that the monopolies would draw from other, unspecified sources.[11] Production records pointed to Persia as the likely source at the time.

The situation in the Straits Settlements and Malaya also merited Whitehall's attention. Nearly half of all revenue for the Straits came from opium in 1925, and the Malayan economy could hardly function without income from opium. The Foreign Office judged that it might take as long as twenty years for a replacement fund to be fully effective.[12] Before a decision was made about what to do, an interdepartmental meeting of representatives from the Home Office, the Colonial Office, and the Foreign Office convened in late November 1926 to discuss an alarming rise in Persian opium consumption in Malaya. A boom in the rubber market had led to an unexpected increase in demand for opium among the resident Chinese, who were earning more than before.[13]

The assumption underlying the policy deliberations was that, until China took responsible action against cultivation, opium smoking would continue to threaten the security of all colonies housing a substantial minority Chinese population. Talks with Malay officials showed conditions to be far worse than imagined. Smuggling was on the rise, opium law offenders crowded Malay jails, and the taint of corruption was attaching itself to public servants. Given this situation, only a partial improvement of conditions was possible. The interdepartmental committee urged the Malay government to continue registering smokers and to plan for the eventual rationing of opium. The pattern of decision making in the case of Malaya reveals an incremental response to the opium problem there. While satisfying the needs of policymakers in the short term, the chosen strategy appears to have been used in this case in order to avoid dealing directly with the issue.[14]

Smuggling and corruption also attended the opium trade in Asian nations outside the European colonial system. Conditions were so troublesome in Siam by late 1927 that officials in Bangkok wanted to discuss with their counterparts in Malaya and the Dutch East Indies ways of combating smuggling. Nearly 20 percent of the national revenue in Siam came from opium sales. Wanting to adhere to the 1925 Geneva agreement, the government hoped to reduce that figure to less than 15 percent by implementing a system of registration and rationing. Yet, as was the case wherever Chinese minorities lived in Asia, lowering limits on official imports of prepared opium was likely to result in renewed smuggling.[15] Officials in Bangkok were not alone in not knowing how to handle such a nettlesome situation.

Authorities in London nevertheless put considerable faith in the registration-cum-rationing scheme. Before the profusion of poppy planting in China, opium production in India had held the key to effective control. The less India depended on income from opium sales, the easier it would be to phase out smoking monopolies in the colonies. In that way British policy would serve as a practical model for Asian countries searching for a way to restrict over time the consumption of prepared opium.

Other than the extensive growth of opium in China, after 1925 two problems stood in the way of what Whitehall could term a foreign policy success. The first was the growth of Persia's opium trade with the Far East, particularly Japan. A League of Nations commission studied the situation and recommended the planting of substitute crops as a way to gradually reduce dependence on opium revenues; it also encouraged the development of various light industries.[16] Promises by the Persian government to try to put the proposals into effect and the recent history of antinarcotics activity by Japan partly encouraged officials in London to believe that the issue could be resolved satisfactorily.

The other problem had to do with continuing American opposition to British opium policy. Because Whitehall's policy was a part of its overall Far Eastern strategy, an attempt had to be made to repair the bad feelings. London needed the support of the United States in Asia and was disturbed by the inconsistency and, in the case of opium, what it saw as myopia in American policy.[17]

The crucial difference between the two nations concerned the 1925 Geneva opium agreement, which seemed to tolerate opium-smoking monopolies as sources of revenue. The United States, though, espoused control at the source and restricting drug production solely to medical and scientific needs. Policymakers in the Home Office did not discount the wisdom of placing limits on manufacturing but hoped that U.S. officials might implement the 1925 accord as an essential step in that direction.[18] For Delevingne, the problem was also one of distribution, since narcotics manufactured in Germany and Japan were falling into illicit channels.[19]

The United States refused, however, to reexamine its position on the 1925 agreement. In fact, for a few years after the Geneva meetings, Representative Stephen G. Porter and other Americans encouraged some governments to ignore the accord in favor of the 1912 Hague Opium Convention. Why, then, did the Foreign Office persist in efforts to bring the State Department around to its way of thinking?[20] Since policymakers in London and Washington did not believe that a manufacturing limitation agreement was possible in the late 1920s, the answer must lie elsewhere. After the Washington Conference, British strategists pursued improved relations with the United States as a brake on Japanese ambitions in China. Anglo-American amity in the matter of opium control would help realize that objective. Whatever else it may have been, the British antiopium program in the Far East became a fundamental part of an anti-Japanese strategy.[21] Events in China would have much to do with the success or failure of that strategy.

Nationalist China and Opium Suppression

Years after the Northern Expedition, Li Tsung-jen, son of a Confucian scholar and one of the leaders of the Kwangsi Clique, recalled that the National Revolutionary Army received its pay from the Ministry of Finance, which drew on the "Opium Prohibition Special Tax" for funds. Nationalist leaders rationalized this action as a step toward prohibition, yet such a justification was a far cry from Sun Yat-sen's 1924 declaration that "the problem of Opium Suppression in China is synonymous with the problem of good government. For . . . opium cannot co-exist with a National Government deriving its power and authority from the people."[22]

To the extent possible, the leaders of the Nationalist forces doing much of the fighting during the Northern Expedition enjoyed widespread support without relying on opium revenues. Li Tsung-jen was known as a progressive militarist; Yen Hsi-shan, who refrained from joining the National Revolutionary Army until June 1927, held power as "model governor" of Shansi; Li Chi-shen, prominent in the Kwangtung Army and loyal to the Kwangsi Clique, became the chief of staff, then commander, of the Fourth Corps of the National Revolutionary Army; and Feng Yü-hsiang, the Christian General, was a man of historically shifting loyalties in scrambles for power and prestige in warlord politics in North China. Compared to their forces, the Whampoa Military Academy–trained First Army Corps, which served as Chiang Kai-shek's base of power, did relatively little fighting.[23]

Success in the campaign for Chinese reunification improved the chances for a reform movement within China.[24] As Chiang Kai-shek and his supporters tried to exploit the widespread demand for reform, one question they naturally asked was what to do about the opium situation. Following the warlord precedent of using opium income for their personal use, they turned to a monopoly system. (China's early exit from Geneva in 1925 had not resulted from any real opposition to Britain's monopoly proposal.)[25] The reality facing the Kuomintang was that Chinese opium smokers would not easily give up their habit even in favorable circumstances.

What transpired in the first years of Nationalist rule was an ingenious response to the opium problem. After a brief experiment with a monopoly, the Nationalists adopted a policy of total suppression, at least publicly. Yet the structure of authority in the Nationalist government made it difficult to know what was really going on concerning opium.[26] In fact, the government kept open the suppression or prohibition bureaus that best served its revenue needs. The Ministry of Finance under T. V. Soong had nominal control of the Nationalist Opium Suppression Bureau, but it is doubtful that Soong personally decided how revenues from Chekiang or Kiangsu, for example, would be expended.[27] In some provinces such as Szechwan, Yunnan, Kweichow, and perhaps Kwangsi, where effective Nationalist authority did not extend, suppression meant working through the existing opium businesses. The French in Indochina were particularly reluctant to see Yunnan dry up as a source, and the carrying trade through Tonkin assured Canton a regular opium supply.[28]

With its hold on power fairly secure after mid-1928, the KMT promulgated an Opium Suppression Act and Regulations that were scheduled to take effect on 1 March 1929; thereafter, addicts would be treated as criminals. Then, from 1 to 10 November in Nanking, the government held an Opium Suppression Conference. Garfield Huang, general secretary of the National Anti-Opium Association, pronounced the sincerity of the Nationalist leadership "beyond dispute."[29] Prior to the conference, the association believed that the people of China viewed the opium situation with "most serious alarm." Chiang Kai-shek, by then in control of the party, government, and military, promised that control would start at the top; the government would no longer depend on opium for revenue. Military and political officials profiting from the trade were ordered to stop the taxing of opium. Other leaders of the reunification campaign and prominent figures in the new government, including the respected Hu Han-min and Feng Yü-hsiang, also spoke out against the evils of opium at the conference.[30]

Foreign diplomats apparently did not take the antiopium pledges as seriously as did the National Anti-Opium Association. For example, J. F. Brenan in Shanghai doubted the good faith of the KMT concerning suppression,[31] but all such expressions of disbelief hardly mattered. Through their professed opium suppression program, the Nationalists were trying to play foreign powers off against one another as if doing so would validate their antiopium strategy.

British officials knew that their own gradualist approach to control would fail in the near term unless the Chinese were serious about suppression. Other than the reports in the journal of the National Anti-Opium Association, *Opium: A World Problem*, available evidence for the late 1920s shows the practical limits of Whitehall's policy. Minister Sir Miles Lampson was advocating limits on poppy growth, the adoption of a feasible monopoly scheme, and a regional study of opium smoking. Rather frustrated, he lamented that "the plain truth is that in practice the [opium] trade still flourishes like a young bay tree. . . . The opium question in China is an open scandal, but, conditions in this country being what they are, there is little that any outside influence can do to effect an improvement."[32]

In contrast, the Nationalists had every reason to be pleased with themselves. Proclaiming a policy of thorough suppression allowed China to buy time for its opium program with Washington, while developments on other fronts were strengthening relations between the two nations. A strong indication of this improvement came in a letter from Garfield Huang to Alfred Sao-ke Sze in May 1929. "Your favorable association with people of the United States," Huang wrote, "has to a great extent helped to bring about the perfect understanding that now exists between America and China in regard to the opium issue."[33]

American and British officials tried to confirm whether the Nanking government actually was working to suppress opium. However, for every report of effective antiopium activity, contrary evidence left foreign observers increasingly skeptical. This was especially true in Fukien, Kwangtung, and Kwangsi—where the authority of the Nanking government faced a brief and abortive challenge in early 1929. (There was no pretense about suppression in Yunnan; Nationalist directives carried little weight there, and opium shipments often received military protection.)[34] In sum, Nanking permitted the opium business, as needed, solely for the purpose of producing revenue.[35] Even with the Nationalists firmly entrenched in power, opium suppression still had far to go in China to meet Anglo-American expectations. Yet selective antiopium activity permitted Kuomintang leaders to cope with a nationwide problem perhaps as well as any regime had managed to do since the days of Yuan Shih-k'ai.

Shanghai, the Kuomintang, and Opium Suppression

The struggle for Shanghai in the early months of 1927 marked a contest for the soul of the Nationalist revolution. At its end, the Kuomintang Left and the Communists were effectively isolated from the revolutionary coalition, and the crucial foreign commercial and financial presence in Shanghai's International Settlement and French Concession remained intact. More than any other power, Britain was relieved since Shanghai, as Wm. Roger Louis has written, was its "financial, commercial, and industrial base on the Asian mainland." Despite the concurrent antiforeignism, exemplified by the Nanking Incident on 24 March, better times were at hand in China's relations with the Western powers. The taking of Shanghai on 21 March by troops of the National Revolutionary Army presaged an end to the threat to Nationalist and foreign interests there.[36] It also allowed KMT officials to reap additional political profits from their antiopium policy.

Victory in Shanghai underlined the importance of Chiang Kai-shek and his military and business associates to stability in China. Yet it would be erroneous to see Chiang's supremacy in Kuomintang politics as inevitable in the uncertain months of 1927–28. On the road to power, the party necessarily had to rely on a kind of praetorian nationalism, which, in turn, significantly influenced the Chinese political scene once power was achieved. That is, militarism suffused nationalism.[37] H. H. Kung warned Chiang not to rely too heavily on the military prowess of warlords to unify China but to form a relation with them on the basis of broad, mutual interests. Yet in order to seize power, the man whom Hearst journalist George E. Sokolsky called the "Ningpo Napoleon" could no more follow that prescription than the Yangtze River could fail to flow into the South China Sea.[38]

Not all the military men active in the Nanking government saw in that relationship an alliance of long duration. Li Tsung-jen, a member of the State Council on its inauguration on 10 October 1928, termed Chiang Kai-shek, its chairman, unqualified for top leadership. Li observed in his reminiscences that Chiang "had a personality that could hardly be admired. He had, in his earlier years, learned all the mean tricks possible, while he was a member of the Green Gang in Shanghai."[39] While Li's remarks can be construed as disgruntled caviling by one who later fell out of favor, they should not be summarily dismissed. Chiang's ties to Shanghai's underworld via the Green Gang, or Ch'ing-pang, facilitate a better understanding of opium suppression in the early years of Nationalist rule.

Its location and cosmopolitan environment had long made Shanghai an important entrepôt for the illicit opium business. Before the Ch'ing dynasty's campaign against opium, the International Settlement offered the trade a safe home. With the formal end of the Indian trade in 1917, powerful Chinese interests set out to capture the market in smuggled domestic and foreign opium for Shanghai. Throughout the early 1920s traffickers and the Shanghai Municipal Police battled over the trade. At length, the opium lords could not be denied. In April 1925, at a meeting with the police chief of the French Concession, they had reached an agreement providing that the police there would be paid monthly *pour fermer les yeux*. With the connivance of naval and military personnel, opium—some from Persia or Turkey, usually from Szechwan and Yunnan—flowed freely into the Shanghai area. Favored merchants in the French Concession, selected by Tu Yueh-sheng, Chang Hsiao-lin, and Huang Chin-jung of the Green Gang, took charge of the opium business by the late 1920s.[40]

Tu, while deferential to the elder Huang, was the real leader of this "trinity of scoundrels." His acquaintance with Chiang Kai-shek predated the reunification campaign, and he performed a vital service for Chiang as members of the Green Gang attacked leftist labor groups in mid-April, thus eliminating Shanghai as an important Communist stronghold. The Green Gang also helped sever the brief alliance between Chiang Kai-shek and the Shanghai capitalists, who thought that Chiang was one of their own. Chiang evidently had cultivated their support merely to obtain money for military campaigns in the north. In compensation for Tu's efforts on his behalf, Chiang replaced T. V. Soong, whose ties to Shanghai capitalists were real, as minister of finance and stood aside as Tu and his associates tightened their grip on criminal activities in Shanghai.[41] Tu's control over illegal opium was a mainstay of his operations. To protect himself from occasionally overly zealous municipal authorities, he evidently took out Portuguese citizenship and worked out of the friendly confines of the French Concession, where he served as a member of the French Municipal Council.[42]

The cartelization of Shanghai's opium business by friends of Chiang Kai-shek assisted the government in its relations with foreign powers. Few observers took the opium suppression bureaus seriously at Shanghai or elsewhere, but, in a larger sense, that did not matter. Their very failure allowed the government to charge foreigners in the International Settlement with hindering the enforcement of the Opium Suppression Act. In a sense, Nanking officials were subtly attacking extraterritorial rights, which they wanted the powers to relinquish at once. Given the desire in Washington and London to see opium control succeed in China and in light of the dearth of reliable information about conditions in Shanghai, Malcolm Delevingne only stated the obvious when he observed that "Chinese representatives at Geneva can get away with almost any absurd statement they choose to make."[43] Miles Lampson counseled patience, arguing that an appeal to the OAC about conditions in Shanghai must come from the city's municipal council for extraterritoriality to cease being a smoke screen for Nanking.[44]

While the resurgence of nationalism under the Kuomintang held out the promise of stability to the West, it possessed even more profound implications for relations with Japan. Officials in Tokyo had never been as sanguine about the revival of nationalism as their British and American counterparts. An anti-Japanese boycott, which began in June 1927, added to their uneasiness and evoked fears about their nation's interests in Shantung. On the surface, the KMT sponsored the boycott to extract further donations from merchants in Shanghai, but, in light of simultaneous developments concerning Japan and opium and the Tsinan Incident in May 1928, the boycott underlined the potentially explosive nature of relations between Nanking and Tokyo. The problem was that trouble with China might undermine Japan's largely favorable reception in Britain and the United States, an attitude Shidehara had carefully cultivated.[45] Retired army general Tanaka Giichi, who advocated a far less conciliatory policy toward China, became prime minister and also replaced Shidehara as foreign minister just as Chiang moved against the Communists in Shanghai. The concatenation of events in 1927–28 from Shanghai to Shantung to Manchuria previewed the coming breakdown of the fragile state of security in East Asia.

Japan's Battle with Narcotics in China

Japan's spotty record on opium control in the decade after the downfall of the Ch'ing dynasty had damaged its international standing. Greater vigilance by Tokyo in the mid-1920s partially rectified the situation. Nevertheless, in reflecting on his fact-finding mission to Japan in 1926 for the Foreign Policy Association, Herbert L. May recalled that, despite a laudable performance in controlling opium smoking at home, the "Japanese were manufacturing drugs on a large scale and the government was just closing its eyes to what was going on."[46]

The National Anti-Opium Association also thought that great numbers of Chinese were put at risk by Japan's opium policies. The association's journal, *Opium: A World Problem*, published an article denouncing Tokyo for failing to devise plans for dealing with opium and morphine addicts in Formosa and Korea. Writing in the shadow of the Tsinan Incident and alleging that perhaps four-fifths of the Japanese casualties in that clash were drug traffickers, the author declared that "the friendship between China and Japan is on the point of bankruptcy."[47]

Like most Chinese provincial leaders in the warlord era, Japanese officials in North China endeavored to profit from the opium and morphine trade. What focused international scrutiny on their efforts was their dealing in morphine as well as prepared opium. Tokyo's relations with Chang Tso-lin greatly compounded the situation. The ambitious Fengtien warlord had a lust for power and a love of the opium pipe. Throughout the 1920s, Chang did Tokyo's bidding in Manchuria, looking after Japanese economic interests in ways that complemented his own broader political objectives. Like others of his generation, he indulged heavily in opium both for its intoxicating and revenue-producing qualities. Thus, proponents of opium control could not easily determine who dominated the extensive morphine trade and pervasive opium smoking in areas under Chang's control. Never a puppet, the independent Chang finally angered extremist Kwantung Army officers, who had him assassinated in June 1928. Rather than plunging Manchuria into chaos and providing a pretext for the introduction of additional Japanese forces, the killing brought to power Chang's son, Chang Hsueh-liang. The Young Marshal quickly made common cause with the Kuomintang, thereby temporarily frustrating Japanese goals in Manchuria. Just as important for present purposes, Chang Hsueh-liang did not altogether share his father's attachment to opium.[48]

Satō Naotake, who represented Japan on the Opium Advisory Committee, knew that a change of leadership in Manchuria meant trouble for his government on the issue of drug control. A career diplomat with long service in Europe, Satō advocated close ties with the United States and Great Britain. In July 1928, he admitted to Delevingne that Japan's opium record in Kwantung was a poor one but claimed that jurisdictional uncertainties in the leasehold prevented responsible officials from exercising adequate control over narcotics. The State Department's John Kenneth Caldwell found Satō's argument unpersuasive but seemed willing to seek a solution to the problem.[49]

The proposed strategy called for consuls in China and Manchuria to exchange information on the illicit drug traffic. British ambassador Sir John Tilley reported from Tokyo in November 1929 that Shidehara, again foreign minister after the fall of Tanaka's Cabinet, favored the conclusion of a consular arrangement with London and Washington. Within a year, Japan agreed to cooperate at most major ports and cities. The port of Dairen, however, was not included in the agreement due to the need to consult further with military authorities in Kwantung.[50]

Neither the Tanaka government nor Baron Shidehara ever found a way to overcome the disparity between Japan's declared antinarcotics policy and the reality of the situation in Dairen. Their response to Western overtures for action approximated the kind of overly vigilant reaction to stressful situations that decision makers experience when they find a possible response to a serious policy problem but have insufficient time for its implementation. This insight into the decision-making process helps us understand why the establishment of a Kwantung Government Monopoly Bureau in July 1928 alarmed Tokyo's critics.[51] Conditions in Kwantung probably deteriorated somewhat after Shidehara's return as foreign minister. Accordingly, charges by the National Anti-Opium Association that the government of Japan was violating the 1912 Hague Opium Convention there were technically accurate.[52] At the same time, Japanese militarism, in the form of the Kwantung Army, came to symbolize a bold, coercive means of defending putative national economic interests in Manchuria, irrespective of the decisions made by civilian officials in

Tokyo. Before long, involvement by elements of the Kwantung Army in narcotics trafficking posed a grave threat to North China as well as Manchuria.

Opium and Security in East Asia

Around 1930, opium, whether prepared for smoking or in some manufactured form, affected the security of East Asia. In the case of China, the Nationalist government could not easily turn its back on a source of revenue that helped to secure its hold on power. Yet the price paid in Chinese stability for dependence on opium was a heavy one. So long as Shanghai remained the major center of the opium trade, provincial leaders—who retained a residual warlord mentality—would farm opium as before. By November 1928, a severe famine plagued at least nine provinces north of the Yangtze. Spared were the Manchurian provinces and those closest to Shanghai; Shantung, Shensi, and Honan suffered most. Opium worsened conditions in Hupei, Honan, and Shensi where forced poppy cultivation and the illicit trade continued. Farmers in Kansu reportedly had to sell excess grain and their children in order to pay a compulsory opium tax.[53]

How opium imperiled China is no mystery. With T. V. Soong serving again as finance minister after Chiang Kai-shek returned to power in January 1928, Nanking's financial standing improved considerably. By year's end, the government was able to obtain a special loan for famine relief secured by Maritime Customs revenues. Yet this indebtedness likely resulted in greater reliance in the short term on income from opium. Tariff autonomy would not take effect until 1929; salt revenues partially serviced loans secured earlier by regimes in Peking; kerosene and tobacco taxes were not yet adequate to meet obligations incurred by emergency loans; and likin, to be abolished within two years, had never been a dependable source of government revenue.[54]

Thus, opium maintained its great economic importance, as became apparent in the earliest reports of the Commission of Financial Experts, headed by Edwin W. Kemmerer of Princeton University, which went to China in 1929. Nanking then only had full financial authority over Kiangsu, Chekiang, Anhwei, and Kiangsi. Proposed taxes were based more on how much revenue was needed than on the ability of people to pay. With a currency linked to silver, a decline in the metal's price would increase the cost of foreign debt repayment, which had to be made in gold. The commission concluded that government revenues would not cover expenditures other than annual service charges on externally secured obligations. Military expenses and the lack of authority in the provinces were two major impediments to a stable financial structure. Unsecured indebtedness to domestic banks put added pressure on officials to find a reliable source of revenue.[55] The complexity of the situation made it fairly easy, the commission realized, for Nanking to adopt the subterfuge of opium suppression in its quest for financial credibility.

Just as opium-related issues left the people of China in a precarious state, so, too, did opium endanger regional economic stability. At length, the success or failure of opium control held important implications for international politics in Asia around 1930. At the First Geneva Opium Conference, Great Britain had tried to allay American fears about the limited agenda by promising to take a close look at opium smoking within its possessions and other areas of the Far East. The British proposed in August 1928 that a Commission of Enquiry be sent to examine the situation. The League of Nations Council and Assembly endorsed the idea and appointed a commission by March 1929.[56] Tokyo and Nanking initially responded favorably to the inquiry, but China soon put forth a debilitating proviso, asking that the probe be extended, as a League report noted, "to all countries without exception which produce or manufacture opium, its derivatives and other drugs, and that China [be] represented on the Commission."[57]

Nanking's reservation, which apparently originated during the Opium Suppression Conference, made it all but impossible for the commission to visit China. Both the government and the National Anti-Opium Association feared the attention that the commission would focus on China. The association denounced reliance on opium revenues in Far Eastern territories while proclaiming that "the Chinese as a people are inborn haters of opium."[58]

Between September 1929 and May 1930, the Commission of Enquiry visited French Indochina, Siam, Burma, the Straits Settlements, the Malay States, Hong Kong, the Philippine Islands, Formosa, Macao, the South Manchuria Railway Zone, Chosen (Korea), and the Kwantung Leased Territory. Commissioners, under the leadership of Sweden's Eric Einar Ekstrand, could have gone to Shanghai's International Settlement but refrained from doing so because of China's objections to the mission. Local officials in all places visited by the commission related the difficulties presented by opium smuggled out of China, often marked for smoking by overseas Chinese. In contrast to the view of the National Anti-Opium Association, the commissioners believed that "more than any other people the Chinese are from early life familiar with opium smoking."[59]

The commissioners uncovered little opposition to opium smoking anywhere they went. What Ekstrand and the others saw as a social problem had the potential of becoming a pronounced threat to economic security since the illicit commerce in opium created an underground, alternative economy wherever it existed. Changing the situation would not be easy: "In the face of unlimited supplies of opium and the extensive illicit traffic, which is inevitable in these circumstances, the final suppression of opium-smoking is not yet within sight."[60]

The brief visit of the commissioners to the Kwantung Leased Territory underscored the difficulty of suppression. Both British and American officials there believed that the whole affair was orchestrated to leave a positive impression. William R. Langdon, the U.S. consul, scoffed at the antiopium campaign conducted during the visit "after all these years of indifference." Yet whatever the actual intentions of local civil authorities, the demand for narcotics by Chinese in the Kwantung region played into the hands of those willing to exploit that weakness.[61]

The Commission of Enquiry could only recommend the gradual suppression of opium smoking by curtailing the amount of prepared opium available. Unless nations, especially China, limited cultivation and genuinely sought to cure opium addiction, programs for control would fail. Dependence on opium for revenue was merely one dimension of the problem. Ultimately, opium posed a threat that went beyond Asia. Its cultivation led to the extensive production of, and illicit traffic in, morphine and heroin, which constituted "a more serious menace to the whole world than the smoking or eating of opium in the Far-East."[62]

Despite the ethnocentricity in the commission's observation, the real fear it conveyed should not be overlooked. The comment prefigured the next international attempt to control opium and thereby promote Asian security. In mid-November 1931, the Conference for the Suppression of Opium Smoking met at Bangkok. Washington sent an observer, but the Chinese refused to attend. The Foreign Office did not mind Nanking's absence, since China would have raised the contentious issue of extraterritoriality. Delevingne was prepared to counter such a diversion by discussing Kuomintang opium profits.[63] Equally significant, the Foreign Office worried that an attack on the rights of foreign powers in China might harm Nanking's relations with other countries.[64] By the time the conference began, however, that concern had been rendered moot by Japanese actions in Manchuria.

The presence of the United States at Bangkok was encouraged by the Foreign Office for several reasons. The Commission of Enquiry had visited the Philippines, and the United States could contribute significantly to a discussion about opium smoking; indeed, even unofficial participation might mute undue American criticism of the conference. At the prodding of the Foreign Policy Association and with the help of Caldwell in the State Department, the United States had reevaluated its attitude toward the OAC and worked closely with Delevingne and others to produce an accord reached earlier that year at the Conference for the Limitation of the Manufacture of Narcotic Drugs.[65] Because of the pessimistic tone in the Commission of Enquiry's report and Whitehall's negative assessment of conditions in China, British officials welcomed whatever Anglo-American harmony they could find.

The Department of State sent Caldwell to Bangkok with some misgivings. The conference was essentially a follow-up to the First Geneva Opium Conference, a gathering Washington had found of little value. Also, the Hearst press had criticized Caldwell for his performance at the manufacturing limitation conference, claiming that he had given in on matters of substance to the British. Secretary of State Henry L. Stimson instructed Caldwell to make it clear that the United States still adhered to a policy of "complete statutory prohibition of the importation, manufacture, sale, possession or use of prepared opium, coupled with active enforcement of such prohibition." He further urged Caldwell to speak out against smuggling from the Far East, which was becoming an increasing problem for the United States.[66]

The Bangkok conference generally disappointed the British, for it accomplished little regarding opium smoking. Failing even to endorse the work of the Commission of Enquiry made it difficult to condemn China's cultivation of poppies or the smuggling of Chinese opium. And yet, in light of the deepening crisis in Manchuria, reports by Caldwell and Delevingne of cordial discussions about U.S. opium policy surely provided some comfort to Whitehall at the time.[67] Although a complete meeting of the minds in Washington and London was unlikely, the Foreign Office sought a close working relationship with the Americans as part of its overall strategy of protecting British interests in the Far East. For U.S. officials, improved relations with Britain naturally followed from the reconsideration of its role in the international antinarcotics movement. Convergence on other policy matters such as extraterritoriality remained less desirable but was not summarily dismissed.

The United States moved in other ways to revise its opium policy. Caldwell informed Nelson Trusler Johnson, who began serving as minister to China in early 1930, that Stuart J. Fuller would rejoin the State Department as an expert on narcotics. Fuller's experience as a consular official in Tientsin some years before prepared him well for his new post.[68] A major change in the administration of domestic control also contributed to the renovation of narcotics foreign policy. Congress created in 1930 the Federal Bureau of Narcotics

(FBN) as an independent agency within the Treasury Department to coordinate U.S. drug control policies. Like Fuller, its activist commissioner, Harry J. Anslinger of Pennsylvania, had begun his government career in the consular service. His work on narcotics for Treasury in the late 1920s led him to see domestic and foreign drug policy as closely linked. The underpinnings of Anslinger's perspective, formed in his youth and during Prohibition as a consular official, predisposed him to believe that threats to the nation's well-being, whether by alcohol or narcotics, emanated largely from foreign sources.[69]

Anslinger and Fuller wasted no time in projecting an American presence abroad. Anslinger sent Elizabeth Washburn Wright to the Philippines after the visit of the Ekstrand Commission to bolster the U.S. policy of absolute prohibition regarding opium smoking. Her mission was also meant to convey interest in the broader objectives of the commission rather than blind opposition to its efforts.[70] Fuller avidly took up his work in the State Department and at Geneva, where he replaced Caldwell at OAC meetings. In the spring of 1932 he and Anslinger attended the fifteenth session of the OAC, where Fuller reported that "we kept in constant touch with each other and worked in complete accord." The two Americans also met away from the OAC with officials of other countries, including M. D. Perrins of the Home Office, to gather and exchange information on the world narcotics situation. Fuller judged the secret talks "the most directly effective and useful work in conjunction with the suppression of the illicit traffic performed during the fifteenth session."[71] A review of conditions in China does not indicate how these activities helped reduce opium as a threat to security.

The Opium Crisis in China, 1930–1931

While the Western powers were finding common ground in their struggles against opium, the Nanking government saw its hold on power begin to slip. "The Chinese revolution has failed," Lloyd E. Eastman quotes Chiang Kai-shek as lamenting in 1932. J. Heng Liu (Liu Jui-heng), who would serve as chairman of the National Opium Suppression Commission from 1930 to 1935, saw a nation in chaos: "I feel very much discouraged and wonder if the revolution is worthwhile." Dr. K. C. Wu (Wu Kuo-cheng) recalled: "Unfortunately, after Dr. Sun's death, Chiang Kai-shek came into power. He paid lip service to Dr. Sun's ideals, but he never tried wholeheartedly to put them into practice."[72]

As always, troubles with opium compounded the situation. Few provinces escaped some connection with the opium business. H. G. W. Woodhead, editor of the *China Yearbook*, estimated that production in 1930 could not be less than 200,000 piculs, or about 12,000 tons. The *Ta-kung-pao* (a Tientsin paper known as "L'Impartial") claimed that officials mandated poppy farming wherever possible and then punished the poorest offenders of the suppression laws in order to show their fidelity to the government's antiopium campaign.[73]

The grip of opium on China was remarkable. Growers and dealers in Yunnan, for instance, sought better ways to get opium to market, including several attempts to fly it to the coast. Missionaries estimated that perhaps 20 percent of all shipments carried by coolies through Kweichow was disappearing. The unreliable nature of the opium supply generated a crisis in Yunnan, causing Lung Yun, the provincial chairman, temporarily to resign in 1931.[74] Soldiers often guarded opium shipments through Szechwan and Kweichow. Sporadic banditry arose among heavily taxed peasants as a protest against the whole opium phenomenon but was overwhelmed by the pervasiveness of the trade.[75] A movement to restrict morphine production in Szechwan proved to be moderately successful, but local authorities, in particular Liu Hsiang, acted to protect their vested interest in prepared opium. Put simply, the demand for morphine had grown so great that complete suppression was impossible. The Hsing Chi Company, a Shanghai morphine operation, was buying over $250,000 (U.S.) worth of morphine monthly from its branch in Chungking.[76]

Opium reappeared in great quantities in 1931 along the Fukien coast. As elsewhere, growing was compulsory and local military officials taxed the crop in the name of suppression.[77] In Shanghai, illicit Persian and Indian opium arrived by sea, Yunnanese opium often came through French Indochina, and opium from Szechwan traveled the Yangtze River by way of Ichang, Hankow, and Nanking. Whenever a new shipment arrived, military authorities kept municipal police away until distribution was completed. Tu Yueh-sheng apparently arranged with T. V. Soong in May 1930 for seven hundred cases of Persian opium to land at Shanghai in return for a handsome payment to the Ministry of Finance.[78]

What was happening below the Yangtze had its counterpart in Manchuria. A smuggling ring in Jehol distributed opium throughout Manchuria and North China, bringing a substantial income to the provincial chairman, T'ang Yu-lin. O. Edmund Clubb described the activities of the old warlord as "patently not the stuff of which heroes are made." T'ang had created a distribution network around Mukden in Fengtien that was composed of Chinese postal authorities, rail employees in the South Manchuria Railway Zone, and Japanese police.[79] One new police chief in Mukden foolishly raided the home and warehouses of T'ang Yu-lin, but the misunderstanding was quickly cleared up and T'ang's operations continued.[80] Adding to the misery his illicit opium business caused, morphine and heroin traffic spread from Dairen to northern Manchuria. The *China Weekly Review* blamed much of the opium and narcotics trade on Japanese soldiers and foreign civilians who were still protected by archaic extraterritorial rights.[81]

The Anglo-American response to the opium crisis tended to blame the situation on the Chinese government. Both London and Washington found Nanking's attitude hypocritical. On the issue of suppression, Miles Lampson declared: "I instinctively mistrust Chinese sincerity in all such matters." John MacMurray, whose hostility toward Nanking for once found acceptance among his colleagues, proclaimed: "What the Chinese really need is a modicum of political honesty."[82] Hoping to soften criticism of China's record, the chief of the publicity section of the National Opium Suppression Committee wrote Anslinger in July 1930 to claim modest improvements in recent months "in spite of political disorder prevailing in the country." The greatest obstacle to control, he told the FBN commissioner, was still extraterritoriality. As the preceding indicates, Western diplomats in China did not take such arguments seriously. Woo Kai-seng, China's representative at the OAC, encountered considerable skepticism when he tried to explain his government's inability to deal effectively with opium. In contrast, Japan's representatives left the OAC meetings in 1930 and 1931 relatively unscathed.[83]

Criticism of China became even sharper after December 1930, when Nanking again considered the formal creation of an opium monopoly. Although the British theoretically favored monopolies as a practical means of moving toward prohibition, a monopoly in China seemed to promise further governmental reliance on opium for revenue. This dependency meant continued subjugation of thousands of Chinese to the ravages of addiction almost as a matter of official policy. It seems clear that during its early years, Chiang Kai-shek's government had not tried to implement a policy of genuine suppression but followed instead a course of action destined to make the situation worse. As the *Shanghai Evening Post and Mercury* concluded, the opium suppression campaign was a fiasco.[84]

Nelson Johnson protested the possibility of a monopoly to C. T. Wang, minister of foreign affairs. When he spoke with T. V. Soong, he was told that a monopoly would help curb the power of the militarists, bring dependence on opium revenues under control, and gradually eliminate the use of opium in China. Soong's own position on the monopoly remains unclear. His arguments to Johnson resembled those of Dr. Wu Lien-teh, a monopoly advocate who served as a delegate in 1911–12 to the antiopium conference at The Hague.[85] Most likely, Soong supported a monopoly because it might help him undercut the power of Chiang Kai-shek and his friends in the Shanghai underworld. So argued American consuls, and recent scholarship essentially confirms their analysis. Yet, like others before and after him, Soong nearly lost his life when he attempted to challenge the existing order in Shanghai.[86]

Conclusion

China's opium crisis ostensibly threatened to increase drug smuggling to the United States, as Stanley K. Hornbeck of the Division of Far Eastern Affairs reminded Johnson. Equally as significant, the failure to control the opium and narcotics traffic coincided with disabling political crises in Tokyo and Nanking. Strong leadership was absent in both cases. The Kwantung Army brought to a head in Manchuria the issues of Japan's economic and treaty rights as Shidehara's policies were increasingly subjected to attacks at home. Even a temporary retreat in Manchuria probably would have brought the Cabinet down.

In China, the Kuomintang nominally presided over a nation thoroughly rent by factional divisions. In economic terms, as financial adviser Arthur N. Young contended, this meant more problems with the deficit and compounded "the great difficulty of cutting military expenditures." Chang Hsueh-liang and Yen Hsi-shan struggled for control in the north; and Kwangtung and Kwangsi militarists supported a rebel regime in Canton. The Communists remained a major force in central China. As we have seen, opium was a significant element in any explanation of the social and political turmoil plaguing China at the time. With its authority effectively circumscribed, the Nanking government banked its future and the security of China on the likelihood of a mutually beneficial relationship with Chang Hsueh-liang.[87]

The Mukden Incident of 18 September 1931 and the subsequent confrontation between China and Japan destroyed the international order that had existed for a decade in East Asia. The actions of the Kwantung Army, in which opium and narcotics operations had a key role, now threatened Tokyo's formerly cooperative relations with the West. Unless some accommodation could be found, Great Britain and the United States would find more common ground than ever in their strategic objectives in the Far East. Inevitably, that meant formulating a revised China policy that, because of more important considerations, would play down the contradictions in Nanking's opium sup-pression policy in defense of Chinese integrity.

The advent of conflict with Japan did not resolve China's opium crisis. Rather, it provided Chiang Kai-shek's government with additional time to profit politically and economically from the trade. The breakdown in Japan's relations with China also turned the focus of attention on Tokyo as the prin-cipal agent of the apparently irremediable opium and narcotics business. Given his later view that the Japanese used narcotics "to debauch the Chinese and make conquest easier," Herbert L. May might have been thinking just that as he and his wife stood on a railway platform in Mukden on 17 September.[88] A new era in international politics in Asia was at hand. The role that opium would play is not well known but was no less important for that.

FOUR

China's Winning of
the West, 1931–1935

Opium and narcotics complicated the general political and military situation in Manchuria and North China after Mukden. Before long, Chiang Kai-shek's skillful manipulation of the drug issue contributed to a partial regeneration of his political stock in the West. Chiang was able to turn Japanese involvement with narcotics to his advantage because he, rather than the Kwantung Army, had the authority to devise and implement, however gradually, an antiopium strategy for much of China. In holding this trump card, as it were, he placed officials in Tokyo on the defensive. In turn, Western policymakers, while dubious about the authenticity of his antiopium commitment, could not deny Chiang's importance to their drug control objectives. Moreover, their attention to the opium issue in the early 1930s anticipated the later limits of Western tolerance for Japanese adventurism throughout Asia.

The Mukden Incident evoked cautious response from foreign observers. Sir John Simon, who became British foreign secretary in late October 1931, tried to steer a course that avoided antagonizing either Tokyo or Nanking while at the same time working closely with the United States and the League of Nations.[1] It proved to be an impossible task. American businessmen had long recognized the special interests of Japan in Manchuria, an easy concession by them since less than 10 percent of their investments were located there. In addition, some within the Department of State wanted to end the apparent fiction that arrangements devised at the Washington Conference would help China become a guardian of stability in Asia. As Mahlon F. Perkins mused from Peiping, there had been "no limit to [foreign] toleration of her misbehavior."[2]

Though viewing the actions of the Kwantung Army as purposeful, Nelson Johnson did not initially believe that the government in Tokyo planned to occupy Manchuria. He refused to condemn Japan out of hand even as its intentions became clearer. An exchange of letters with Joseph Grew showed that the two Americans recognized Japan's legitimate strategic and economic interests in China.[3] Other Americans who were closely associated with China felt a certain frustration with its problems. Arthur Young hoped that the clash at Mukden might curb the factional strife that the KMT could not halt. And Roger S. Greene of the Peiping Union Medical College doubted that the Nationalists could have prevented the attack in Manchuria. Yet, Greene noted, "the Young Marshal, Chang Hsueh-liang, could have done certain things which would have had the effect of greatly relieving the tension."[4]

A boycott of Japanese goods in the summer and autumn of 1931, described by financial adviser Oliver C. Lockhart as a form of warfare, exacerbated the crisis atmosphere in Manchuria and North China. T. V. Soong feared that the boycott would cost the government as much as $7.5 million (U.S.) per month in revenue; it would surely lead to further reliance on opium revenues. However wise or foolish, the boycott persisted and gave birth to an oath sworn to school children in Nanking:

> By the blue sky that watches over me, by the bright sun that shines on me, by the mountains and rivers of my country, by the sacred tombs of my ancestors, I swear with my warm blood and with utter sincerity that for the rest of my life I shall never use Japanese goods. May Heaven punish me should I retract my decision or change my mind.[5]

Chinese propaganda after Mukden urged retaliation against Japanese aggression in Manchuria, and bandit activity spread throughout the countryside. If these actions were meant to induce the Western powers to alter their policy and force a Japanese retreat, they failed completely. State Department officials agreed on a policy of nonrecognition. And without American assistance, appeasement was all that could be expected from Britain. Both powers adopted a policy of appeasement but for different reasons: the Foreign Office feared for the future of Britain's position in the Far East, while the State Department and President Herbert C. Hoover, showing greater concern about the world economic crisis, found comfort in a posture of moral censure. Despite showing the practical limits of British and American harmony in East Asia, their courses of action reflected a mutual, negative assessment of the Kuomintang's ability to rule China effectively or to play a major role in international relations in the region.[6] The Nationalists were intent on changing that perspective and, in part, used antiopium policy with marked success over the next few years as a means of doing so.

Opium and the Sino-Japanese Conflict, 1931–1933

Friends of China avidly took up its cause. A. E. Blanco, a Spanish national who had left a position with the Opium Section of the League of Nations Secretariat to found the Anti-Opium Information Bureau, charged in January 1932 that the Japanese had started a new opium war with their actions in Manchuria. Blanco, once employed in China's customs service, declared that three-fourths of the Japanese in South Manchuria were involved in the narcotics traffic and were protected by Tokyo's consular office.[7] In fact, the reality of the situation in Manchuria and North China did not match Blanco's allegations. To be sure, Japanese drugstores throughout the region were selling illicit narcotics. In the puppet state of Manchukuo, the Japanese army was trying to wrest control of the trade in Jehol opium from T'ang Yu-lin. Yet, in the process, innumerable Chinese, Japanese, and Koreans, with uncertain allegiances, were contending for a stake in the business. The situation worried Johnson, who rightly feared the possible movement of Japanese forces in Jehol.[8]

The contest for Jehol intensified as Chang Hsueh-liang's defending forces lost ground. T'ang's style of rule had alienated many Chinese in a region that was of considerable strategic and economic importance to the Japanese, who moved quickly to entrench themselves by rationalizing the existing opium trade through the creation of a monopoly based in Manchukuo.[9] There could have been few tears shed when T'ang finally gave way to Japanese and Manchukuo troops in February 1933 in the area one journalist termed a "Chinese Alsace-Lorraine."[10]

From his vantage point in Peiping, Johnson feared that U.S. prestige was at stake in the contest between China and Japan. Accordingly, he worried about the fate of the Washington system and surmised that Japan might "turn away from us altogether." He warned that Japan was attempting to create "a new motif in international relations," one that "we had wished to consider a buried past." Stanley K. Hornbeck viewed the situation with even greater pessimism: "The ultimate arbiter must be force. . . . Neither rules nor regulations nor resolutions nor laws nor treaties are decisive where a country is embarked upon a course such as Japan has followed."[11]

Just after the expulsion of T'ang Yu-lin, and in the wake of the report by the Lytton Commission, officials in Tokyo announced Japan's withdrawal from the League of Nations. As we will see, Tokyo's decision did not help its representatives answer questions about Manchurian opium then being asked at Geneva.[12] The Japanese military in Manchuria cared little about what effect their actions had at Geneva or in the United States; yet Johnson felt that the same could be said of those Chinese rulers who were "maintaining [their] own satrapy and extorting the maximum from the people."[13] In short, he did not believe so strongly as Hornbeck that a larger Sino-Japanese conflict was in the offing.

About two weeks before the Tangku truce of 31 May 1933, the *Peking & Tientsin Times* published a Japanese report claiming that financial recovery had begun in Jehol. The opium tax for farmers had been cut in half to five Yuan per mou, and a new purchasing system channeled opium to the provincial monopoly. The enthusiasm contained in the report should not obscure the reality of Jehol's lengthy reliance on opium for the vast majority of its revenue. It is possible that funds expended by the Tientsin Special Service Agency in a vain effort to unite anti-Nanking militarists came from Jehol's opium revenues.[14] In this regard, the International Military Tribunal for the Far East (IMTFE) singled out General Itagaki Seishirō's provocative role in Hopei in 1933. Itagaki had received a transfer from the Mukden Special Service Agency to the General Staff and was assigned to Tientsin in February. The IMTFE charged that drug trafficking financed anti-Chinese activities, with local special service agencies often controlling the traffic.[15] Itagaki was therefore well situated to take advantage of the opportunities provided to contest the KMT for dominance in North China.

Whether he did so in this particular case does not matter. Chinese officials and their foreign supporters charged then and later that narcotics and opium were powerful weapons of war employed by the Japanese government. Just before the Opium Advisory Committee met in mid-May 1933, Blanco issued a polemic warning that Manchukuo, "not bound by any international Opium Convention, threatens to become a vast center of opium production and manufacture of opium derivatives, destined for the illicit traffic." Given this state of affairs, he suggested, Nanking would be forced to create a monopoly in order to bring a measure of control to the traffic.[16] In other words, Western displeasure over the opium situation in China should be directed at Tokyo rather than the Kuomintang. Blanco was trying hard to deflect outside criticism of his Chinese friends for their renewed interest in a monopoly. Even the National Anti-Opium Association, following the lead of J. Heng Liu and Dr. K. C. Wu, now believed that a monopoly for medical purposes and limited sales for smoking was acceptable.[17]

Despite Blanco's efforts, foreign diplomats found Nanking's professed anti-opium zeal largely illusory. The situation had gotten further out of hand: Feng Yü-hsiang was reportedly making "heavy exactions from the common people";

and at Foochow and Amoy, taxes on opium funded antirebel and anti-Communist activities.[18] In North China, the Japanese and the Chinese were in effect operating competing monopolies. Even where Nanking's authority held sway without the need for allies such as Chang Hsueh-liang, opium policy—Johnson concluded—was "an open acknowledgement of the failure of the Government to eradicate [the evil] in spite of the issuance of numerous decrees, manifestos, and mandates."[19]

At the least, opium was playing a significant role by mid-1933 in defining the contours of the conflict between Japan and China. Both sides clearly were prepared to utilize the drug in various ways in order to acquire a military, political, or propaganda advantage over their foe. The victims of this quasi-opium war were the people of China, who still suffered from the scourge of the poppy. If anyone profited from their continuing misery, it was Chiang Kai-shek. How he did so shows that he was able to play on fears of Japanese sponsorship of the Manchurian drug traffic in order to help secure his place as China's principal leader, despite the challenges to his authority.

China's Opium Policy and the West, 1933–1934

Chiang clearly needed to call upon his considerable political skill. Information reaching Washington after mid-1931 indicated that an opium monopoly was a certainty in China. Would Great Britain help Nanking set it up, as one report indicated? Secretary of State Stimson even briefly considered supporting the monopoly as a partial solution for China's economic woes, and Johnson discussed the idea more than once with T. V. Soong.[20] Other Chinese authorities suggested that a monopoly would be of short duration and assured U.S. officials that suppression was ultimately more important than the opium-related revenues collected by the government.[21]

Just the same, with an official, if informal, monopoly operating by November 1933, the United States decided not to reconsider its traditional opposition for two reasons. First, the KMT did not have complete control over some provinces where poppies were grown. Second, it could not exercise meaningful jurisdiction over the distribution of raw or prepared opium—as was evident, for example, from the growing incidence of smoking in Shanghai and the opiate business in Manchuria. To the Department of State and the Bureau of Narcotics, this meant an inevitable increase in illicit drug traffic from Asia to the United States.[22]

Concern about the opium situation in China was not exactly mirrored in broader Western concerns in East Asia at the time. What, for instance, were American interests beyond the maintenance of peace? Had the world economic crisis significantly altered Britain's policies toward its colonies or China? Did the outcome of the Sino-Japanese rift really matter to either Western power? With few clear answers, the Foreign Office and the State Department sought to appease Japan and to maintain, for the time being, the fiction that the Washington system was still useful as a guide for Asian policy. As Chinese and Japanese officials knew, the gradual convergence of Anglo-American interests came about from a position of weakness that left Western policymakers little more than rhetoric to defend their interests.[23]

This virtual paralysis on questions of grave importance did not pervade Western relations with China and Japan over opium; U.S. opium policy began to tilt slightly in China's direction after officials briefly tried again to work with the Japanese. Japan's departure from the League of Nations, scheduled to take effect in March 1935, did not include leaving the OAC, so at the May 1933 meeting, Stuart J. Fuller and Harry J. Anslinger encouraged an active Japanese role. Fuller, described by Hornbeck as "a man of unusual ability, thoroughly sound judgment and inexhaustible energy," asked the Japanese to improve prior agreements for exchanging information on narcotics.[24]

The issue that led the United States away from a policy of evenhandedness was that of import certificates for Manchukuo. Fuller's opposition to Manchukuo's inclusion in the system—the singular achievement of the 1925 opium convention, as Washington saw it—came out in talks with M. D. Perrins of the Home Office after the OAC session. The United States feared that a flood of illicit narcotics would inundate China if Manchukuo legally imported drugs. Moreover, anything other than a firm policy would impute a kind of legitimacy to the government of Manchukuo, if not to its opium monopoly, which reportedly was importing Persian opium.[25]

Fuller and Anslinger had begun to doubt Tokyo's good faith on narcotics even before the May OAC session. They found Japanese cooperation suspect, particularly regarding the heroin trade around Tientsin.[26] When the OAC next convened at its autumn session, Fuller initiated a general discussion of conditions in Manchuria and in so doing indirectly challenged Japan's drug control record. He charged that even licit opium trade to Manchuria would play into the hands of traffickers. In view of the expansion of poppy cultivation in Manchuria and Jehol, the inevitable result of imports to Manchukuo would be increased smuggling of manufactured narcotics to the United States. The only solution was for Tokyo to refuse to transship opium to Manchukuo, which it recognized, and for other countries such as Switzerland and Great Britain to put aside their financial interest in the import trade.[27]

Not having mentioned Japan by name, Fuller insisted that he had not attacked its Manchurian policy despite press reports to the contrary. (His internal report to superiors on the OAC meeting chided the British for their unwillingness to adopt the U.S. position on the issue.)[28] The Chinese took heart from the disagreements among the powers. Victor Hoo Chi-tsai and Wellington Koo, also in Geneva, tried to focus even greater attention on the situation in Manchuria but failed because the OAC, it was determined, would have been considering a political question, Manchukuo, not within its competence.[29]

Fuller misunderstood the intricacies of Britain's position on opium. Whitehall was tired of supporting a weak Chinese nationalism even indirectly, as it had for years. Stability in Nanking no longer possessed a clear connection with Britain's substantial economic stake in China. Without that link and with no guarantee of active U.S. support for Western interests in the face of even greater Japanese expansion, the Foreign Office saw no reason to pursue a policy that might alienate the powerful Japanese military.[30] Accordingly, the primary consideration in Britain's opium policy became how it affected larger strategic goals.

Thus, Great Britain was chary of following the U.S. lead and drawing closer to Nanking on opium matters in 1933 and 1934. Sir Miles Lampson and others continued to chart an illicit traffic along the Yangtze to Tu Yueh-sheng in which the connivance of the Chinese navy, T. V. Soong, and Chiang himself was manifest. The lack of real control helped explain to Whitehall both support for communism in Kiangsi and persistent problems with an anti-Nanking axis in South China. Suppression campaigns against bandits, rebels, or the Communists served largely as justifications for deriving revenue from opium. At the same time, strict control of commerce in opium from Kwangsi to the Kwangtung monopoly meant serious economic troubles for Kweichow and Yunnan. The Kwangsi government and the monopoly had reached an accord in mid-1932 to regulate the trade from the southwest. With the collapse of a Fukien-based rebellion against the Kuomintang in January 1934, the pact fell apart. Ironically, Nanking's victory temporarily undercut its authority in provinces not firmly under its control. In sum, it is safe to say that policymakers in London did not believe that the Chinese road to stability, unlike the banks of the Yangtze, was lined with opium poppies.[31]

As usual, Fuller had prepared himself well before speaking at Geneva in November 1933. Remembered by Herbert L. May as a man with a "dynamic personality," he sought information about opium cultivation and morphine and heroin manufacture in Jehol and traffic from there to North China.[32] American records suggest that State Department authorities must have knowingly overlooked certain information when dealing with narcotics matters in KMT-ruled areas, however. As early as September 1931, Fuller learned about the activities of Tu Yueh-sheng. He and Anslinger knew of the bonds between Chiang and Tu and were aware of the Chinese navy's role in the Yangtze opium trade.[33] Anslinger's papers at the Harry S. Truman Library contain an undated typescript, "The Chinese Story," with an assessment of the Tu-Chiang relationship: "[Tu] trafficked in more opium and narcotics than any man then known, and conducted the most fabulous opium racket in China. He was one of the most powerful men in China, a leading pillar in the financial and political life of Shanghai. . . . Tu once save the life of Chiang and thereby gained favors for both legitimate and illicit traffics in many forms."[34]

Examples abound, but a few will suffice to show what the State Department knew about opium control in Nationalist China. Records indicate the tenuous nature of Nanking's authority and the steps taken to maintain the facade of antiopium activity. By mid-1932, for instance, Shansi ceased to be a "model" province; Yen Hsi-shan, perhaps again seeking provincial and personal autonomy, was encouraging a robust opium business. He dealt severely only with the unofficial trade.[35] An even worse situation existed in Fukien, where rebellions against Nanking seemed common. Warlords forcibly collected opium taxes from farmers who sometimes considered selling their wives and children in order to meet their obligations. Those who resisted often saw their homes burned or were shot.[36] In Yunnan in mid-1933, an antiopium association bravely proclaimed that "the black (opium) calamity is much worse than the red (communist) calamity" and asked Lung Yun to move more rapidly toward suppression.[37]

In dealing with these conditions, Chiang Kai-shek supported opium control when it enhanced his power and the authority of the KMT. By early 1934, he had exploited the inability of his adversaries to make common cause and had extended Nanking's rule to Fukien, Chekiang, Kiangsu, Anhwei, part of Kiangsi, Hunan, Hupei, Honan, Shensi, and Kansu. Elsewhere, greater or lesser challenges to the KMT still had to be met.[38] Chiang prevailed, Lloyd E. Eastman concludes, because of his military background and role in the development of the Whampoa Military Academy, because of his financial ties to Shanghai's business community and underworld, and because of his ability to manipulate contentious political and military factions.[39] Opium also proved to be a staunch ally.

In June 1931, Chiang was talking about a six-year period for implementing a centralized system of opium suppression. During that time, he would employ opium revenues to pay for antibandit campaigns. Chiang's stratagem fooled few knowing observers. An editorial in the *New Hankow Daily News* called J. Heng Liu and Dr. Wu puppets of the KMT and declared: "The whole of China depends on opium for its revenues, and whole communities depend upon opium for life."[40] One foreigner, H. G. W. Woodhead of the influential *Shanghai Evening Post and Mercury*, found Chiang's proposal praiseworthy; opium revenues would be sufficient to underwrite the government's drive to maintain order in the provinces. The politically peripatetic Wang Ching-wei, chairman of the Executive Yuan, agreed that the stability of a monopoly would improve Nanking's relations with the provinces.[41]

Meanwhile, the government, with Chiang as head of the Military Affairs Commission, issued antiopium mandates calling for the complete suppression of poppy cultivation and illicit opium traffic. Nelson Johnson found the mandates "pathetically naive and not a little ridiculous."[42] Chiang nonetheless proceeded regularly to announce prohibitions on opium-related activities and to gather a portion of the profits therefrom. Perhaps as much as $60 million (U.S.) was involved annually in the officially encouraged and protected trade; much of the income paid for independent military forces with nominal allegiance to the KMT. So-called special tax and opium suppression bureaus were created to regulate the traffic. All the while, opium consumption spread among the people of China and the crisis in agriculture worsened, thus preventing control of a famine that had riddled Kansu and Shensi.[43]

By the end of 1933, T. V. Soong's special tax bureau controlled opium from Hupei, Shensi and Kansu opium had found a stable market in Anhwei, and opium from Yunnan and Szechwan was readily available in Hankow. Chiang's Agricultural Bank of the Four Provinces (Honan, Hupei, Anhwei, and Kiangsu) distributed opium receipts to various claimants. The death penalty presumably awaited those who grew poppies in Hupei, but a dispatch about cultivation from Hankow noted: "There nevertheless exist certain facts which do not fit the picture painted by Nanking." The *Ta-kung-pao* admonished the government to "pay attention to its position and prestige, [and then] the authorities [will] find themselves able to look the people in the face."[44]

Given the extensive reports on opium seen by officials in Washington and the more neutral perspective of British authorities, and in light of the controversy over the Kuomintang's actions in China, what explains the course of U.S. policy? First, Johnson, Fuller, and probably Anslinger believed that Chiang Kai-shek ultimately would bring about some degree of opium control. That he had not done so by early 1934 was insufficient reason for losing hope. Besides, no one other than Chiang had the requisite power to implement a policy of suppression. This is not to argue that some Americans were not frustrated by developments in China. Its leaders, Johnson lamented to Owen Lattimore of the Institute of Pacific Relations, could scarcely "lift themselves above the personalities which constantly engage their attention."[45]

Fuller, however, continued to emphasize the role of Japan's army in the narcotics traffic. His growing concern over Japanese intentions was the second reason for the change in policy. Most worrisome for Fuller and his colleagues was the possibility of increased traffic in Persian opium from Manchuria to the United States. Regarding the situation in North China, he learned from Blanco that Japan might withdraw its troops from inside the Great Wall in exchange for an agreement protecting the narcotics business. At a conference held in Kuling on Chiang's initiative, Wang Ching-wei and Soong accepted the Kwantung Army's demands that friendly civil and police commissioners be allowed to take office in Peiping and Tientsin.[46]

Although the Kuling accord alarmed Fuller, his focus on the Kwantung Army's responsibility for the narcotics situation in North China dovetailed nicely with Chiang's interests. The United States would insist on an accounting from Tokyo—both on a bilateral basis and at the OAC in Geneva—regarding opium and narcotics traffic. Having one of the major Western powers support him in such a fashion would serve Chiang well unless the Japanese were prepared to resort to force. That is, Nanking's opium suppression activity needed to be only as realistic as the immediate situation demanded. The domestic drug trade would still provide substantial unofficial revenue to those who had long depended on it. At the same time, officials could crack down on opium and narcotics law violators whenever it was politically advantageous to do so.

Johnson understood as well as any policymaker the realities of opium in China. He informed Helen Howell Moorehead of the Foreign Policy Association that the "problem is one of reducing or taking away the need or craving for the drug and that until this has been done there can be no adequate control over the supply." Japanese forces, of course, were as resourceful in meeting demand as the suppliers of Tu's Green Gang. By March 1934, Johnson was putting an additional onus on the Japanese, who "have no moral scruples when it comes to opium or the use of the gun or the sword."[47] Yet it was a long way from taking Japan to task for its presumed complicity in narcotics trafficking to a serious rupture in relations. Even so, the decision of American officials to emphasize the Japanese more than the Chinese connection with the drug traffic had important consequences. First, it was a contentious issue on its own. And second, if narcotics became a part of larger disputes between Washington and Tokyo, differences would be even more difficult to resolve. In that case, the OAC might be virtually useless as a forum for discussion, just as the Mukden Incident had cost the League of Nations its credibility on major international issues.

The focus on Japan ultimately opened the door to closer U.S. relations with Chiang's Kuomintang. At least in part because of its evaluation of the narcotics situation, the United States rather than Great Britain led the move in that direction. As Johnson, in a further refinement—if not reversal—of his former position, explained to Hornbeck, "One may put any construction one wishes upon all of this, but certainly one must conclude that Chiang is taking a very realistic view of the opium situation and has reached the conclusion that he must accept it as he finds it, taking the revenue which it offers lest he leave this revenue as a weapon in the hands of his enemies."[48] Now that he had found some favor with the United States, the task remained for Chiang to accomplish approximately the same with Britain. He did not have to wait long for his opportunity.

Chiang's Opium Policy Ascendant

As Washington came to accept Chiang as China's supreme ruler, his domestic critics saw the situation in a less favorable light. Nanking's rulers, critics argued, rarely tried to get close to the people and thus failed to win their support against communism. To a former leader in the Fourth Corps, Chang Fa-k'uei, Chiang had seriously erred by not offering greater resistance to Japanese forces during fighting at Shanghai in 1932. Against the Communists, Chang charged, he "relied on military rather than political means, without which a solution of the Communist problem was impossible." Chiang further compounded his errors by accepting military leaders as provincial chairmen.[49]

An equally harsh assessment came from Yi-yun Shen Huang, whose husband Huang Fu—an expert on Japan with ties to Feng Yü-hsiang—headed Peiping's Political Reconstruction Council for two years after the Tangku truce. Though never a member of the KMT, Huang acted as its intermediary in relations with Hopei, Shantung, Shansi, Chahar, Suiyuan, and the municipalities of Peiping and Tientsin. To perform his duties as charged, Huang had to turn a blind eye to rampant governmental corruption. "Worst of all was the traffic in narcotics," his wife remembered. "In Peiping narcotic dealers even had influential support from within the city government." Party leaders offered negligible assistance, and their taxing the trade while outlawing smoking "had a built-in contradiction because it made traders lawful and users unlawful." Huang proposed an end to this practice through a scheduled prohibition program, but his suggestions went unheeded.[50]

Foreign assessments of Chiang and the KMT were not so harsh. The course of events in East Asia gradually was moving Britain's China policy closer to that of the United States. "It is a major British interest not to antagonize Japan," Sir Victor Wellesley of the Foreign Office declared in January 1934. But were Japan to "become the leader of the yellow races, . . . British influence, though not necessarily completely eliminated would be greatly reduced."[51] Aware of civilian-military tension in Tokyo over China policy, the Foreign Office carefully maintained a good working relationship with Washington despite uncertainties about American policy. Miles Lampson observed that U.S. policy in China, unlike Britain's, was still "free from the least taint of aggressive or imperialist intention." In that regard, America had to be judged a rival power, yet its policy "is [largely] identical with ours and we can and do cooperate wholeheartedly with America on all major Chinese questions."[52]

Most high British officials might not have accepted Lampson's assessment in all its particulars, but Anglo-American harmony was of signal importance. On the specific issue of opium control, his successor, Sir Alexander Cadogan, strongly concurred with Lampson's judgment. Cadogan, whose sympathies had been with China during the Manchurian crisis, supported Fuller's statements at Geneva on the narcotics situation in Manchukuo. Blame for the continuing deterioration of conditions there accordingly rested with Manchukuo and Japanese authorities.[53]

On the other hand, Foreign Secretary Sir John Simon's differences with the United States over Manchuria had not left him an unalloyed supporter of American policy. "I would untie ourselves from U.S.A. policy at the earliest possible moment," he argued. "We shall only be used as a catspaw and be deserted if the situation became difficult." Just the same, rough similarities of interest in Asian policy seemed inevitable: "While maintaining and if possible increasing our friendship with Japan I would ride with China rather than with Japan."[54]

Contemporary developments gave added weight to this position. The Amau Declaration or Doctrine of 17 April 1934 starkly reemphasized the precarious nature of British economic and financial interests should Japanese policy become equally assertive in practice. At the least, this call by Amau Fiji of the Foreign Ministry for Japan to dominate the economic future of China ostensibly contradicted Foreign Minister Hirota Kōki's determination to create a new spirit of international cooperation in Asia. Hirota's discussions with Sir Francis Lindley, the British ambassador, and Joseph C. Grew prevented the emergence of a full-blown crisis.[55] If policymakers in Britain were once disposed, as Akira Iriye holds, to seek closer ties with Japan to preserve traditional interests, officials such as Charles Orde and Sir Robert Vansittart of the Foreign Office reassessed that position in response to Amau's rhetorical boldness.[56] From his perspective, Grew concluded that the statement "expresses the policy which Japan would like to pursue," notwithstanding Hirota's conciliatory attitude toward China and other nations.[57]

On another current issue, the British worried about how communism might affect their economic interests and Chiang's ability to rule. Lampson felt that communism was alien to the Chinese; yet the unsettled domestic scene had left the door "wide open to new ideas and heresies of every kind."[58] By 1931 the KMT had largely restricted the Communist presence to Kiangsi and then tried to eliminate it through a series of bandit-suppression campaigns. The Nationalists seemingly gained political advantage over the Communists with the advent of the Long March in October 1934.[59]

Kuomintang mythology holds that opium suppression contributed to Nanking's antibandit activity. While there are stories of Red Army units tolerating opium smoking in some areas, assertions that they encouraged the practice are wrong. Chang Kuo-t'ao, who later broke with the Communist party, recalled the reaction of his troops in 1932 to the suffering of Szechwan's opium addicts. The army fed them and gave them wine to drink and opium to smoke. This gesture no doubt violated the prohibition the Red Army had placed on opium, which Edgar Snow related in his book *Red Star over China*. But, as Chang explained about his response to the dismal conditions he had witnessed, the issue was political, and, as a leader, he devised a realistic rather than a doctrinaire response. Other cadres spent the summer in northern Anhwei and Kiangsu mobilizing peasants to revolt against the imposition of opium taxes. Chang Fa-k'uei's observation that the Communists did a good job of getting close to the people takes on a tangible meaning in this context.[60]

In his dispatch on communism from Hankow in 1932, O. Edmund Clubb cited reports showing that the KMT partly financed early bandit-suppression campaigns by exacting opium taxes in Hunan. In a report on the opium traffic written two years later, he remarked: "It is not without significance that, according to the best information available, the production and consumption alike of opium are effectively suppressed in areas under the control of the Chinese Soviets."[61] None of this is to suggest that Western reactions to communism in China were unwarranted; that is not the issue. Rather, concerns over the security of traditional economic and political interests worked to Chiang's advantage by inducing the United States and Great Britain to support him as the leader most likely to bring stability to China. As part of that process, the two powers distinguished between opium and narcotics problems existing in Kuomintang China and those created in areas dominated by Japanese forces.

Chinese leaders including Wellington Koo knew, therefore, how critically important it was to keep Manchuria and North China in the public eye. Serving as ambassador to France at the time of the Amau affair, Koo told the League of Nations that Japanese designs on China emanated from "a deeper purpose of weakening the spirit and morale of the Chinese people." In this case, the agent of aggression was the Manchukuo opium monopoly.[62] Despite Koo's efforts to focus attention elsewhere, the OAC did not ignore developments in China proper. The OAC had earlier contemplated conducting an inquiry into Nanking's cooperation with foreign powers on opium and the clandestine manufacture of narcotics in China and Manchuria. Fuller and Hornbeck termed the idea impractical when it came up again in the spring of 1934, since the inquiry would founder on the issue of manufacturing. As a police matter, it raised questions of extraterritorial rights and corruption, and the likelihood of noncompliance with recommendations was great. Victor Hoo gave what amounted to provisional acceptance by his government, but the committee did not initiate the inquiry.

Reflecting later on the proposal, Fuller observed that Nanking evidently tried "getting foreigners to drag Chinese chestnuts out of the Japanese fire." True, he faulted Japan for the lamentable conditions in North China, Manchuria, and Jehol—a region with "*no laws or regulations whatever to control manufactured drugs*." But because of Washington's generally cautious Asian policy, Fuller could not offer the Chinese anything other than promises of consultation about problems posed by illicit drugs in areas under Japanese influence.[63]

Chinese officials may have been seeking just such reassurances. Their antiopium policies were being scrutinized, notably in June 1934 at the OAC, where discussions focused on China as well as Manchuria. There Fuller, joined by Sir Malcolm Delevingne, mildly rebuked the Chinese for failing to curb poppy growth and opiate manufacturing, noting a rise in imports of acid acetic anhydride, which was used for heroin production. Hoo moved to deflect criticism of Nanking by promising to discuss the OAC meeting with his superiors. He also told the delegates that the opium problem could not be solved without a general settlement of political problems in the Far East. He pointed out, too, that Nanking was including opium control in the process of national reconstruction then under way, the New Life Movement.[64] Hoo subsequently met with Nelson Johnson, pledging results if Johnson "could intimate to the Chinese Government directly the concern of the American Government . . . that [the opium question] had concrete bearing upon relations between China and the United States."[65]

Hoo's efforts demonstrated the KMT's strategy of obscuring the realities of its ties to opium in order to strengthen foreign support for Nanking against Japan. Its tactics consisted of a two-track approach. First, the New Life Movement—undertaken with great notoriety—was intended to secure Chiang Kaishek's position as leader and to regenerate China's political, social, and economic life by emphasizing the virtues of a disciplined, militarized society. Chiang modeled the movement on European fascism and Japanese militarism and infused it with a simplified Confucianism for mass appeal.[66]

Leftist opponents of his regime, including Communists, found the movement anachronistic and a bar to national integration, while foreign reformers initially responded to it with cautious enthusiasm. Under the leadership of Chiang and later Madame Chiang, the movement became a clarion call for indigenous reforms, including opium suppression, at a time when domestic criticism of the KMT was intensifying.[67] The *Peiping Chronicle* declared: "The question of opium lies at the root of almost every problem, and blocks every attempt at reconstruction." Members of a disbanded antiopium organization in Fukien termed Nanking's leaders "hypocritical and selfish." Hankow's *Central China Post* bluntly condemned China as "the world's greatest menace in the drug traffic."[68]

By late spring 1935, the New Life Movement had provided the Nanking regime with some breathing space from its critics. Woodhead wrote in his column, "One Man's Comment for Today," that "no one doubts General Chiang's sincerity in his attempt to uproot what he considers a pernicious habit." Building on their initial work in Kiangsi and Fukien, the New Life Voluntary Service Groups addressed conditions in Szechwan and Hopei by closing opium dens and visiting hospitals for addicts.[69] In its biennial report issued in May 1935, the National Christian Council of China praised the KMT's "sincere and earnest" desire to wipe out the opium menace.[70]

The second track enabled the KMT further to obscure its involvement with opium through the activities of the Blue Shirts. Created in early 1932 when Nationalist China seemed in peril, its military and ultranationalistic orientation took on a fascist cast. Blue Shirts dominated secret police activities under the direction of Tai Li, who had intimate connections with Shanghai's underworld, and suffused the membership rolls of the New Life Movement. In this

way, the Blue Shirts complemented neatly the intricate opium-related enter-
prises of the Green Gang, which Tu Yueh-sheng carefully directed from his
headquarters within Shanghai's French Concession.[71]

Having fostered a kind of cultural revolution that was nationalist in com-
plexion, Chiang exploited it for his personal advantage. From Nanchang,
he directed opium control operations in ten provinces—Honan, Chekiang,
Hunan, Kiangsu, Kiangsi, Hupei, Anhwei, Fukien, Shensi, and Kansu—
which, not coincidentally, he had also designated as bandit-suppression
zones.[72] Chiang and his subordinates then decided what was official opium
traffic, entitled to military protection, and which shipments, particularly from
the southwest on the Yangtze near Ichang, were subject to seizure. The pattern
of suppression approximated contemporary political realities; in Tientsin,
where the Japanese presence and involvement with drugs loomed large, the
government ordered numerous patients to be tattooed before they were permitted to leave a narcotics hospital.[73]

How did Great Britain and the United States react to the Kuomintang's
suppression activities? Neither nation overly praised Nanking for its efforts,
yet policymakers in London and Washington admitted that Chiang was responsible for limited progress in his nation's battle against opium. A U.S. military intelligence report explained that he was seeking "to weaken the officials
in those provinces where the power of the Central Government is shadowy or
nonexistent by destroying their revenue."[74]

The assessments of Fuller, Johnson, and Cadogan about Chinese policy reflected their awareness of the formidable obstacles to effective control. Fuller
saw in Chiang's endeavors "a plan to give to the military an additional source
of revenue." Johnson knew revenue to be the first priority of Chinese leaders;
their second was to present "a reformer's face to the now somewhat skeptical
outside world." Actually ridding the nation of the opium curse came third,
"and then weakly." In like manner, Cadogan noted the high priority given to
opium control as a device to produce revenue. Yet he concluded: "Control of
the opium traffic and the revenues attaching thereto is moreover clearly essential to the establishment of an effective Central Government, and it is to this
end that General Chiang Kai-shek appears to be working."[75]

Western authorities did not accord similar understanding to Japan when
discussing antiopium activity. Fuller found "unconvincing" Yokoyama Masayuki's explanations to the OAC about conditions near the Great Wall, particularly in view of the relatively light penalties imposed for illicit narcotics manufacturing. Indications of a potential anti-Japanese bias in the Department of
State on the eve of the November 1934 meeting came from the desk of Under

Secretary of State William Phillips. In the draft of a dispatch, Phillips wrote that Fuller should "guard against creating any impression that the American Government is assuming the position of a special critic of Japan." His final instruction replaced "Japan" with "any one government."[76] British uncertainty about Japanese intentions surely increased after talks with the president of the South Manchuria Railway, Matsuoka Yōsuke, in September 1935. Matsuoka, who would become foreign minister in July 1940, had nothing to say when asked about the traffic in narcotics.[77]

No single event had convinced Whitehall that Japan could not be trusted regarding drug trafficking. Rather, concern in the Foreign Office about North China inexorably moved British policy closer to the American position. Tokyo's difficulties with the West sprang from two sources, one cultural, one perceptual. In the first place, the KMT had effectively portrayed itself as a potential agent of opium and narcotics reform. Ultimately, this meant that Chiang would eschew profits from the drug traffic in order to protect his nation from opium. Few Japanese in Manchuria or North China could claim the same motivation. Matters of perception compounded Japan's problems greatly. Westerners fully expected Tokyo to share their antiopium sentiments, whereas Japanese perceptions, as a guide for their involvement with opium, seem to have followed the Kuomintang's practice of apparent disdain for the Chinese masses.[78]

The two Western powers were not so naive as to believe that Nanking was avidly trying to suppress opium. Yet their skepticism about Tokyo's intentions gave the Kuomintang a degree of credibility that the Kwantung Army could not match. In that sense, Chiang had won his gamble. He was in a position to gather desperately needed revenue and improve provincial political allegiance as a result of rationalizing China's domestic opium trade, while alienating neither Great Britain nor the United States.

Chiang Kai-shek's Alliance with Opium

Chiang's success was especially important since the Bureau of Narcotics charted an alarming flow of narcotics from China to the United States in the early 1930s. While some newspaper accounts blamed the traffic on smuggling from Manchukuo and Jehol, Anslinger's bureau knew the situation to be far more complex.[79] M. R. Nicholson, the Treasury Department attaché at Shanghai and his government's major source of information on Chinese opium and narcotics, submitted reports implicating Chiang Kai-shek and possibly T. V.

Soong in the heroin trade to North America.[80] The allegations were impossible to prove, but ample drugs were available for diversion into illicit channels. J. Heng Liu, whose Opium Suppression Commission Chiang would later absorb, proposed in early autumn 1934 that the Kuomintang operate a central drug laboratory to meet medical needs. The resulting illegal traffic, he explained to worried U.S. officials, "would not be used by any appreciable number of American citizens, but by Chinese in the United States."[81]

Not all Chinese agreed with the practice of profiting from the addiction of their countrymen, women, and children, but Chiang's opium apparatus enabled the generalissimo to do just that. From 1934 to 1936, the government received perhaps Y100 million per year from the opium and narcotics traffic.[82] In the provinces under Nanking's control where antibandit or anti-Communist campaigns were being waged, the government had restricted poppy cultivation by June 1935 but continued to rely on legal sales for funds.[83] In the Hankow area, branches of the Agricultural Bank of the Four Provinces collected taxes on opium traffic and remitted them to inspectorate headquarters at Nanchang. Southwestern China remained a less reliable source of income, however. John Stewart Service would reminisce about his days in Yunnan: "The whole lifestyle, the daily schedule of a city like Kunming was tied to opium smoking."[84] Lung Yun, an inveterate opium smoker and no great friend of the KMT, could not depend on Yunnan's abundant poppy fields for a good return when markets were depressed in French Indochina or on the China coast. Subsidies from Nanking partially made up income shortfalls, and government troops protected Yunnanese shipments in exchange for a percentage of the revenue.[85]

Chiang Kai-shek needed opium revenues from Yunnan to supplement funds from the salt gabelle, customs, and other sources of income for the national treasury. He therefore had to find a way to gain influence with the provincial opium trust, the Nan-seng Company. Pursuing Communist troops in Yunnan in May 1935 provided him with an opportunity since the Red Army had been interfering with opium caravans crossing Kweichow.[86] By the end of the summer, the positioning of KMT forces in Yunnan had brought the province into temporary alignment with the Nationalists.[87]

The generalissimo followed similar tactics elsewhere to entrench Kuomintang authority and gain greater control over the opium business in the southwest and the Yangtze basin. He succeeded in Kweichow when Nationalist forces proved to be more effective against the Communists than local armies from Kwangsi and Kwangtung. Chiang taught the militarists in Kwangsi a lesson about power by eliminating the province as a route for opium to the

South China coast, thereby depriving them of tax revenues to pay their troops. By mid-July, Chiang had turned much of the Yunnan-Kweichow opium enterprise over to his ally, Tu Yueh-sheng.[88] Anti-Communist activity and financial reorganization also brought Szechwan under Nanking's jurisdiction in fairly short order in 1935. Reforms there did not lead to opium suppression but brought instead stricter regulation of cultivation and sale, which ended some rogue operations. In Chengtu, a city of 500,000, the government monopoly continued to provide revenue for Chiang, catering, as Nicholson related, to city workers and poor farmers who "would rather go without food than without opium."[89]

The Kuomintang's opium particularly found its way to Shanghai. There Tu supervised a distribution network, controlled all aspects of life from underworld operations to local government and municipal finances, and "enjoyed honours reserved for Confucian scholar-officials of a bygone era." Ilona Ralf Sues, who worked for Blanco's Anti-Opium Information Bureau before visiting China in the mid-1930s, wrote: "He was by far the most powerful man in China, and the Government itself had to count with his power. . . . Tu was a combination of Al Capone and Rockefeller. . . . Tu Yueh-sen [sic] was the boss of it all."[90] Beyond just handling opium for smoking, Tu oversaw the narcotics business. As head of the Chung Wai Bank and chairman of the board of directors of the Commercial Bank of China, he easily financed his illicit dealings.[91] And in July 1935, Tu became a key member of the new opium suppression commission in the municipality of Shanghai.[92]

With Tu's dominance of Shanghai, the government had in effect cemented its alliance with opium. The Ministry of Finance could count on a reliable source of unofficial revenue, while at the same time the announcement of a six-year suppression campaign put independent operators on notice that their activities would be punished. In some instances, this meant that addicts faced the possibility of death if they did not abandon the opium habit after the end of 1936.[93]

The government did not enjoy the luxury of dealing with the opium and narcotics traffic in North China in similar fashion. Japanese, Korean, and Formosan gangsters ran the morphine and heroin trade with the protection, Nicholson thought, of Japanese authorities in the Peiping-Tientsin area. "The opium policy of Japan is calculated to ruin the Chinese race," he told his superiors.[94] The Kuomintang called upon the New Life Movement to undertake what turned out to be largely rhetorical narcotics control programs in North China. What occurred seemed more like a contest for the market between Manchukuo opium on the one hand and opium from Kansu and Shensi on the other. No matter which side won the right to ply the opium trade in the north, the local citizenry lost.[95]

Elements in the Kwantung Army undeniably sought to profit from the opium business at the expense of North China. Yet not all Japanese authorities there and in Manchuria, let alone in Tokyo, wanted to poison the Chinese populace as a matter of policy. Reports by Frank Lockhart and other consular officials cast doubts on such a sweeping conclusion. Efforts to regulate the drug trade and provide medical treatment to addicts, which cannot easily be distinguished in authenticity from similar actions in Chiang's China, did occur in Manchukuo under Japanese auspices. The *North-China Daily News* believed that Japan had little to gain from debauching the Chinese with narcotics. As it was for the Kuomintang, the whole matter was "simply a question of finance."[96]

Nonetheless, Fuller and other U.S. policymakers did not alter their view of Japanese responsibility for conditions in North China. Their virtual denial of the complexity of the situation underscored the effectiveness of Chiang Kai-shek's opium strategy and would in time allow them to interpret Japanese actions as a threat to overall Western interests in East Asia. An assessment of the KMT's opium control program by the *Ta-kung-pao* implied how successful the generalissimo had been in influencing U.S. policy: "The Government in spreading the opium poison among our children and grandchildren in its greedy search for revenue is showing itself more ferocious than tigers and wolves."[97]

The United States could not reach a similar conclusion because of the way its policy toward opium control in China had evolved. Chang Fa-k'uei understood well the political ability of Chiang Kai-shek, who "was accomplished in the art of intrigue. He knew how to cheat, intimidate, and differentiate. . . . [and] weathered each crisis by utilizing the selfish motives of his enemies."[98] Merely a slight modification in language would have made Chang's evaluation applicable to what Chiang had accomplished vis-à-vis the United States by late 1935. Not only were policymakers in Washington in his corner despite his association with opium, but Fuller apparently encouraged A. E. Blanco to assume a role in 1935 as a paid propagandist in Europe for Chinese opium policy.[99]

Conclusion

The evolution in the West of an anti-Japanese perspective on the narcotics situation in East Asia and the refusal to confront Hirota's Foreign Ministry on the issue played into the hands of Chiang Kai-shek. While holding Japan to a stricter standard of accountability than China made sense to Fuller and Anslinger, it emboldened the Kuomintang. In the near term, Chiang was able to mold an alliance with opium that rationalized poppy cultivation and the illicit trade and promised to improve China's financial picture. He extended as well the authority of the central government to provinces where it had previously been virtually ignored. The appearance of political stability and the resurgent nationalism accompanying his antiopium strategy generated a modicum of approval in Washington and London.

Chiang's success held longer-term negative consequences for relations with Japan. Even as he was putting the final touches on his opium policy in mid-1935, the Japanese army was encouraging the development of an independence movement in Hopei and Chahar.[100] The prospect of armed conflict between China and Japan, however remote, would threaten the gains Chiang's strategy had achieved. In the event a clash actually occurred, Western military assistance was no more likely than it had been after the Mukden Incident. Furthermore, the lack of a strong reaction by the Foreign Ministry in Tokyo to Fuller's statements at Geneva could only have angered Kwantung Army officers and Japanese officials in Manchukuo and North China. They would scarcely bypass an opportunity to retaliate against what they perceived both as a diplomatic slight from the West and the hypocritical nationalism in China's opium suppression campaign.

FIVE

The Deepening Crisis
in China, 1935–1937

By mid-1937, the actions of the Kwantung Army, affecting virtually all aspects of domestic and international politics in China and Japan,
would force the Western powers to take sides in the Far Eastern crisis. In the
two previous years, the drive to economic autarky, an essential part of Japan's
strategic calculations, continued even as the Army General Staff, the Imperial
Navy, and the Foreign Ministry struggled over how to draw North China further inside the Japanese orbit. Whatever their differences, decision makers
continued to perceive China as inferior and, hence, malleable to Tokyo's will.
Nanking's response, a policy of accommodation and nonresistance rather than
confrontation, lasted well into 1936. It seemed to confirm the Japanese position as well as to indicate that the Chinese were unlikely to protect traditional
British and American interests from Japanese aggression.[1]

As a result, Great Britain and the United States had to come to terms with
the realities of Japanese ambition by recognizing the need for regular consultation on major issues of mutual concern. In the case of opium control, they
worked together, usually in advance of OAC meetings. Joining forces, in a
sense, they subjected the antiopium activities of Chiang Kai-shek's government to greater critical scrutiny. While seeing more clearly that Chiang tolerated the opium traffic in order to raise revenue and extend the Kuomintang's
authority, Western policymakers gained a better appreciation of the effect of
opium and narcotics on larger developments in China, notably the spread of
Japanese influence.

The United States was seeking in the mid-1930s to follow a policy favoring
neither China nor Japan. That the national interest did not reside in Nanking
or Tokyo remained central in Stanley Hornbeck's mind. The chief of the Division of Far Eastern Affairs believed, as he had told Roosevelt in May 1933
while Stuart Fuller was addressing the Opium Advisory Committee about

opium and narcotics trafficking in Manchuria, that acting on China's behalf would "re-invigorate Japanese animus against this country" and might hasten the realization of Tokyo's goals.[2] The cautious Hornbeck, whose didactic tone and attention to detail made him difficult to work with, exerted a profound influence on Far Eastern policy. He defended the predictable world of the open door and the Washington Conference. To surrender either in response to Japan's quest for a new order in Asia "would mean that either we change our whole foreign policy . . . or make a definite and specific exception as regards the Far East."[3] Yet his evenhandedness was not doctrinaire; the United States, if need be, could work with the Chinese, who "have been and are easy-going and complacent, whereas the Japanese have been and are active, aggressive and inclined to be bellicose."[4]

The logic of Hornbeck's position led him to support the building of a strong navy in order to deter Japan from possible attack.[5] Nonetheless, President Roosevelt, an advocate of a larger navy while serving as assistant secretary in the Navy Department during the Wilson administration, refused—despite calls from the General Board, some members of Congress, and the State Department—to move quickly to increase the number of lighter craft to treaty limits. In this way, he essentially chose to maintain the passive Asian policy that had marked his administration from its inception.[6]

When the Japanese announced on 30 December 1934 that they were going to abrogate the Washington naval treaty, British and American policymakers could no longer ignore the possibility of a threat to their interests. Alarmed British officials concluded that the Japanese military ambition in the north knew few bounds and that Hirota Kōki's Foreign Ministry was in no position to impose any. Officials on both sides of the Atlantic showed some deference to each other's sensibilities. Hornbeck wanted to cultivate "an impression on their part that they lead and we follow." On major issues, however, Washington should be less flexible.[7]

Norman H. Davis, who chaired the U.S. delegation to the Second London Naval Conference in 1935, counseled patience and the development of a common strategy "as the best means of avoiding trouble with Japan or of minimizing it if it could not be avoided."[8] Just after replacing John Simon as foreign secretary, Sir Samuel Hoare told the House of Commons that His Majesty's Government and the United States were "in close touch on this matter" of North China. Even so, the Far Eastern Department feared that the United States "will not act in the Far East" and "has lost interest in the traditional American policies of the open door and the integrity of China."[9]

By late 1935, what this posturing meant to Nanking was that resources available for the defense of China's interests were limited. The campaign against communism was a calculated gamble to curry favor abroad, perhaps even in Tokyo.[10] Making things more tenuous, Chinese leadership appeared terribly inept. In one of his gloomier moments, Alexander Cadogan lamented that the KMT "are a rather inchoate body of possibly well-meaning and quite intelligent individuals without any authority or directive force." The United States essentially shared this appraisal; as a dispatch from Nelson Johnson made clear, the announced antiopium campaign did nothing to change opinion in Washington. His military attaché, Colonel Joseph W. Stilwell, dismissed opium suppression as a device to distract the Chinese people "from worrying about the National Government's failures in dealing with Japan and the communists." "The New Life Movement," Stilwell bluntly declared, "is another such smoke screen."[11]

Chiang's travails and the troubles of Nationalist China mounted steadily after mid-1935. Never distant from the heart of any issue was the question of opium and narcotics. The hopes that Chiang had raised in the West regarding opium control quickly faded. British and American narcotics policies did not revert to what they had been before Fuller's foray against conditions in Manchukuo, but neither did the KMT receive the same dispensations it had for some two years. As faith in Chiang's government gave way to concern about Japanese imperialism, visions of order and stability in East Asia ebbed as well. Only the growing specter and, finally, the reality of Japanese aggression shielded Nanking from Western obloquy.

Opium and the Economy of China

Chinese economic experts had to oversee an essentially premodern economy even in the early years of the Nanking decade. Warlords and provincial governors had maintained the traditional autonomy of the rural sector and used the land as their personal satrapy. Farmers rarely sold grains and cash crops beyond local markets, and a large proportion of tax revenues regularly stayed at home. Somewhat more modern in makeup and outlook was the urban, or nonagricultural, environment, especially in the cities of Shanghai, Peiping, Tientsin, Canton, Nanking, and Hankow where foreign commerce and manufacturing had become familiar sights.[12]

Without sufficient revenues the Kuomintang could not hope to maintain its power and authority. Fully 75 percent of its expenditures covered military costs. Arthur Young told Finance Minister H. H. Kung in September 1935 that sound fiscal management mandated the cutting of expenditures by Y5 million per month, which meant reducing military costs and grants to provincial and local officials.[13] Meanwhile, the perilous state of China's currency made fiscal reform seem less than an ideal solution. The silver purchase program of the United States in the early New Deal had resulted in the sale and smuggling of vast quantities of the metal; often-acrimonious discussions between the Department of State and the Treasury Department had not improved the situation by mid-1935. Runs on the silver holdings of major banks in Shanghai, Nanking, and Hankow threatened the national government with financial collapse.[14]

Informed observers advocated a combined program of currency reform, rural reconstruction, and banking modernization to ameliorate the crisis and modernize China's economy. Each of these steps, if honestly and successfully undertaken, would have dramatically altered the KMT's dependence on opium. Yet economic and financial experts faced the imposing task of restructuring the mainstream economy without threatening the alternative one based on opium. From mid-1935 through the outbreak of war with Japan two years later, opium exacerbated the serious problems confronting Nationalist China because of the KMT's reliance on it to mitigate domestic and foreign difficulties.

Sir Alexander Cadogan, like others before him, concluded that the opium suppression campaign "is to a large extent affected by the desire for easy revenue." Foreign and domestic foes of opium took no solace from Nanking's announcement that on 29 May 1935 Chiang would assume the duties of inspector general of opium suppression in the place of J. Heng Liu.[15] This administrative change would enable the generalissimo to protect his precious income even as the Ministry of Finance carried out a decision of October 1934 to create a managed economy, starting with the imposition of export restrictions on silver.[16]

The flight of silver need not have destabilized Chinese currency, but unregulated private sales and smuggling made destabilization a certainty. The drain on reserves also brought about credit contraction outside of Shanghai, unemployment, and numerous business failures.[17] H. H. Kung proposed greater financial centralization while allowing for the return of some revenues to loyal provinces. This would not overturn, he knew, the secret budget of the Military Affairs Commission. The KMT adopted a plan for currency reform on 3 November 1935 that ended the use of silver as a monetary standard; the *fa-pi* became China's legal tender. With silver nationalized and currency movements closely managed, four banks were entitled to issue notes: the Bank of China, the Bank of Communications, the Central Bank, and the Farmers Bank—originally the Agricultural Bank of the Four Provinces.[18]

Foreign acceptance of the plan was essential to its success. Great Britain's economic interests in the Far East led the Cabinet to send Sir Frederick Leith-Ross, its chief economic adviser, to investigate the situation and perhaps obtain Japanese acceptance of the monetary reforms.[19] British trade experts saw revamping the banking structure as conducive to the growth of free enterprise in China's cities. The influence of Leith-Ross on the adoption of a financial reconstruction program may have been indirect but, as K. P. Chen, a managing director of the Central Bank, clearly recognized, "Leith-Ross was not just a currency expert; he represented British power in the Far East."[20]

The choice of banks permitted to issue notes bore a close relationship to the KMT's involvement with opium. When the financial crisis worsened in Shanghai in the spring of 1935, the government asked Tu Yueh-sheng to help reorganize the Bank of China and the Bank of Communications in exchange for which Tu was invited to join the board of directors of the Bank of China.[21] While this action may have constituted a legitimate attempt to control the operations of major banks, that was not true regarding the Farmers Bank. Capitalized at Y7.5 million for the declared purpose of funding Communist-suppression campaigns, it probably financed opium cultivation and trade. In January 1936, the bank received the authority to issue Y100 million; this increase surely reflected the confidence of Chiang and his associates in the stable future of the opium business.[22]

Reports on capital movements and regular audits of banking practices normally accompany currency reforms and bank reorganization, but Nanking refused to allow extensive scrutiny of a bank that, in Arthur Young's words, "was generally regarded as especially close to Generalissimo Chiang." Chiang apparently blocked an audit requested by Kung at the time of the Leith-Ross mission in order to protect a reported Y200 million annual income from opium.[23]

More than renovations in the money and banking structure showed the importance of opium to the Chinese economy. Clarence E. Gauss, praised for his honesty and a hardheaded, informed view of Chinese politics (for which he was rewarded with the post of ambassador in 1941), concluded in mid-1936 that declining customs receipts "strongly influence the National Government's peculiar handling of the drug traffic." He was referring in this instance to the KMT's willingness to provide monopoly opium to registered addicts in

Shanghai.[24] From Nanking, Willys Peck wondered "whether the Chinese Government will be willing and able, after it has organized an air-tight monopoly of the importation and distribution of opium in the area directly under its control, gradually to give up such a remunerative business." Even M. R. Nicholson, whose pro-Nationalist sympathies were deeply held, reported on the extensive involvement of military officers in the opium traffic in the heart of Nanking.[25]

Neither lingering famine nor floods in rural China disrupted more than briefly the operation of the official opium trade. Although Wang Ching-wei called for rural reconstruction and an end to corruption at the final session of the National Financial Conference of May 1934, his words went unheeded—at least where opium cultivation was customarily found. The *North China Herald* reported that farmers in the frontier province of Suiyuan were growing poppies instead of food crops. The government encouraged opium production and local bankers financed the crop "because of its rapid growth and because of its ready market." The ultimate destination of the crop determined whether government troops or the Japanese army protected it in transit and governed who received the revenue from retail sales.[26]

Tales of poverty, famine, terrible death by starvation, and the remission of opium taxes to government coffers could be found from Kansu to Shensi to Szechwan. Where Chiang as opium inspector mandated the eradication of the local opium crop, it was understood that suppression should occur gradually, if at all, so as not to deprive his inspectorate of its anticipated income.[27] In the remarkable documentary record, *One Day in China: May 21, 1936*, citizens from some towns and villages used the opportunity afforded them on that special Thursday to speak out against the pervasiveness of the opium scourge in their homeland. In one vignette, a seven-year-old blind child in Kiangsu mocked Chiang's professed suppression campaign.[28]

Nowhere was the association between the government and opium any more important economically than in Shanghai. Fears of severe penalties for morphine usage turned addicts there to opium smoking, which, with the reliable assistance of Tu and the Green Gang, increased government income. By early 1937, merchants were importing Persian opium in order to cater better to the tastes of their clients.[29] Meanwhile, Chiang tried to boost revenues by requesting suppression officials in the International Settlement and the French Concession to cooperate in registering addicts and licensing opium hongs in the settlement, where Tu did not yet operate. Information available to Gauss left no doubt that Chiang "was largely inspired by a desire to obtain revenue from opium and narcotics addicts," which would end up in the vaults of the Farmers Bank in Hankow, and that Tu Yueh-sheng was supervising the entire operation.[30]

British and American diplomats tried to prevent the registration of addicts in the International Settlement, but discussions with the Shanghai Municipal Council got nowhere. Quite simply, Tu had more resources than the opponents of registration; he offered to pay off a $100,000 (U.S.) debt of the chairman of the council.[31] Tu did get the council to agree to a plan to register addicts in the settlement, yet it refused to permit the creation of opium hongs. In early July, a desperate Gauss told Stirling Fessenden, American secretary-general of the Shanghai Municipal Council, that the Consular Body might possess the authority to veto actions of the council affecting the International Settlement; thus, the council appointed a committee to study the matter further.[32] There it rested because events in North China were drawing attention away from the opium issue in Shanghai.

Chiang's suborning of the commerce in opium showed how unprepared or unwilling he and the Ministry of Finance were to put their authority to the test; popular memory of the warlord years and the role of the Kuomintang in the chaos of the times was still vivid. Moreover, rural reconstruction had been a farce; landlords, money lenders, provincial officials, merchants, and military leaders—in the words of the *North-China Daily News*—continued to "extract whatever a helpless farmer can be forced to pay."[33]

To an extent, funding the anti-Communist campaigns had provided the original justification for adopting a policy of gradual suppression. Thus, it surprised few foreign observers when the government returned to this device after mid-1935. The Chinese Communist party (CCP) constituted a fundamental threat to the ideology and authority of the Kuomintang. And, at least in West China, its propaganda against smoking found favor among local women who supported programs for education and rehabilitation. KMT charges that their Red adversaries forced peasants into the opium business had no basis in fact. While missionaries along the route of the fabled Long March bore witness to the appeal among the masses of promises of land reform, they could not similarly testify to opium-related abuses by Communist forces.[34] American authorities were aware of the CCP's antipathy to opium. They gave credence to reports that the yield of the poppy crop in eastern Kweichow fell by more than 60 percent when Communists poured into the area after leaving Kiangsi. And no less a person than Stuart Fuller admitted that the decline was "due to the ravages of Communist bandits."[35]

If nothing else, during the Long March and after, the Red Army and its supporters threatened the government's opium enterprise. KMT forces persuaded officials in provinces such as Shansi, not included in the Communist hegira, to compensate for losses elsewhere. In March 1936, a correspondent for the *Peiping Chronicle* found district magistrates conspicuously selling opium; its pungent odor was "palpable in Sian, the center of Nanking's scheme to develop the Northwest." Some opium reaching Sian may have come from Communist-held areas in northern Shensi, as government reports alleged, but Ninghsia and Kansu were doubtless the major providers. In matters concerning opium and narcotics, cause-and-effect relationships are hard to establish, but Shansi assumed an enhanced role in the opium trade shortly after Yen Hsi-shan became a member of the Central Executive Committee of the Kuomintang and vice-chairman of the Military Affairs Commission.[36]

Separating the political and economic aspects of the opium trade for other than brief analytical purposes obscures the strength of their interrelationship. While opium played an essential role in the economic planning of the Kuomintang at the highest level (as seen in the banking reorganization scheme), its economic importance simultaneously had an influence on political developments, of which the anti-Communist campaign was a prime example. In the two years just prior to the Sino-Japanese clash of July 1937, knowledgeable Western observers had seen firsthand how the political economy of the opium business made resolution of China's many difficulties far more problematic.

The North China Imbroglio

Shortly before giving way to Anthony Eden in November 1935, Samuel Hoare told the House of Commons that His Majesty's Government was watching with concern the events in North China. Specifically, he meant the Japanese-inspired autonomy movement in Hopei and Chahar, which had taken on added significance with Nanking's adoption of financial reforms. If the reforms proved effective, Nationalist control would spread throughout North China and British influence would be enhanced.[37] Both the Kwantung Army and Nanking sought to use opium and narcotics to advance their political interests in the north. Authorities in Manchukuo may have tried to aid addicts by providing hospital care free of charge. According to the *North China Herald*, though, the provincial monopoly continued to operate largely without restriction by the authorities. At Harbin and Mukden, the drug trade was in the hands of Koreans who seemed to local officials to have no other way of making a living.[38]

A lack of reliable information at the time precluded an accurate assessment of conditions in territory under the control of Japan. Should, for example, Fuller and others have seen as genuine decrees purportedly restricting the amount of acreage under cultivation? Were the decrees disingenuous or was the opium situation beyond the control of even well-meaning local authorities? Evidence suggests that the latter may have been the case. Poppy production for the monopoly centered in Jehol, long a fertile region and supplier of opium for the illicit trade, where the loan policies of local banks encouraged farmers to plan for abundant crops.[39] It would be misleading, however, to leave the implication that narcotics production and trafficking was settled policy in Japanese-dominated areas.

Extensive opium growing in Jehol and the existence of narcotics factories in the city of Mukden does not prove conclusively that Japan deliberately sought to use drugs as a weapon of war against China.[40] Hence, Namba Tsunekazu's testimony to the International Military Tribunal for the Far East in 1947 should not be dismissed out of hand. Once the vice-director of the Manchukuo Opium Monopoly Bureau, Namba testified for the defense about opium in Manchukuo; he was not a defendant. He admitted that some unscrupulous officials had made money by "taxing" commerce in opium and narcotics. Yet he described an opium control program that was hardly at variance with Nanking's. Registered addicts would purchase opium from the government monopoly; elimination would occur over a period of ten years. Those who wished to continue smoking opium after 1937 had to have a physician's certificate attesting to their need. Regarding the extensive cultivation in Jehol, Namba indicated that clandestine growth declined after 1935 and that his office had selected Jehol as a center for the production of monopoly opium because grain did not grow well there. To be sure, the narcotics situation in North China was grave, but that resulted in large part from the presence of illegal manufacturers who fled there to avoid prosecution in Manchukuo.[41]

In mid-1937, English-language newspapers in North China were reporting antinarcotics activities by Japanese consular police that generally supported Namba's later testimony. The action came in response to an order issued by the Foreign Ministry on 1 July 1936 and, in the short term, to statements about the situation in the Peiping-Tientsin area made at the OAC. From his post in Tientsin John Kenneth Caldwell put the matter in sharp focus: "[For] the first time in the history of North China, the Japanese authorities are now apparently taking action with the ostensible purpose of controlling or suppressing to a certain extent the activities of their nationals in the illegal narcotic trade." It was unknown, of course, how salutary the crackdown on drug traffickers in North China would be, but the State Department and the Federal Bureau of Narcotics doubted that positive results would be forthcoming.[42]

Had not more serious events intervened, Manchukuo's fledgling antinarcotics endeavors might have been welcomed by the West, especially in the United States where the fear of illicit traffic from Asia remained strong. The narcotics situation in North China, Japan's apparent complicity in it, and its possible ramifications for America's own drug problem concerned officials in Washington in the last year before fighting broke out in China. Foreign missionaries and the *China Weekly Review* agreed about Japanese and Korean responsibility for the trade. And from Shanghai, calling on his vast network of informants, Nicholson regularly asserted that Japan was intent on narcotizing the Chinese people—a policy put into effect, as he saw it, after the conclusion of the Tangku truce.[43]

The U.S. consul at Tientsin, David C. Berger, went even further when he described that city as perhaps "the world's premier manufacturing and distributing center for habit-forming opium derivatives" thanks to the willing participation of Japanese authorities, "particularly the more forward-looking, Kwantung Army militarists and their satellites."[44] In other words, drug traffickers—encouraged by corrupt officials—had the means to put the American people at risk. The cumulative effect of these reports from China simplified how Fuller and other U.S. drug control officials perceived Japanese objectives, thereby constraining their policymaking options.

Just the same, what was taking place on the Asian scene was far more complex than merely a crude attempt to subvert the Chinese will to resist Japanese aggression. Were that the case, then the government at Nanking would have been just as guilty as Japan was judged to be in the aftermath of the Pacific war. If Nicholson remained blind to that reality, Nelson Johnson did not. When the KMT accepted the creation of the Peiping-Tientsin Opium Suppression Inspectorate in February 1936, he knew that the objective was to reap profits from the opium trade from Shensi, Kansu, Suiyuan, and even Jehol, if possible.[45] Speaking specifically about the flood of narcotics into North China, Johnson observed:[46]

> The responsibility for the traffic does not lie entirely with the Japanese. There are those, in fact, who credit Japanese officialdom with a certain amount of desire to cooperate with Chinese authorities in the matter but lack of energy on the part of the latter in the work of suppression combined with administrative difficulties faced by the Japanese civil authori-

ties in combatting the activities of their gain-seeking subjects together result in failure at attempts at control.

Regarding the part played by the Chinese, he continued:

> It is believed that ineffectiveness of control of the strong-drugs traffic results . . . from several circumstances: 1) the Chinese people generally lack faith in the intentions and actions of the National Government and local administrative authorities as regards the general administration of the "anti-drug campaign"; 2) political debility, deriving from various causes, renders weak proposed measures of control; and 3) economic and political distress drives large numbers of people to seek any temporary relief from their suffering and despair that may be possible, no matter what may be the final consequences.

The Peiping-Tientsin inspectorate soon became the Hopei-Chahar General Purification Inspectorate, a change that underlined the centrality of the autonomy movement to Japan's quest for hegemony in North China.[47] Western observers discounted the likelihood of a clash between the two Asian nations over North China; even in mid-March 1937, the War Office in London concluded that "no responsible Chinese seriously considers taking the initiative in opposing Japan." Sir Hughe Knatchbull-Hugessen, who replaced Cadogan as ambassador to China in the autumn of 1936, believed that party politics in Japan would prevent any precipitate move on Japan's part.[48]

The United States essentially concurred with Whitehall's evaluation of the China scene. Hopes by Hirota for an amicable resolution of differences, officials lamented, had faded almost as soon as foreign legations were raised to embassy status in mid-1935. Johnson told Hornbeck in October that Japan "has reduced North China to a status similar to that of Manchuria before 1931."[49] He still believed, however, that Chiang would placate Japan short of signing a treaty or surrendering to Japanese demands. In other words, a patient Japan would realize its goals in North China.[50]

With no prospect of Anglo-American assistance against the Kwantung Army, Chiang's government used all means short of war to retard the advance of Japan too far south of the Great Wall. Opium and narcotics played an important role in that endeavor, which, along with the antinarcotics actions of some civilian officials in Manchukuo, belies the simplistic charge that Japan followed a policy of narcotization of China. In reality, opium proved to be a useful weapon for both sides in the economic and political battle for North China before the clash of armed forces.[51] Johnson, in fact, explicitly equated the opium suppression program of Manchukuo with that of Nanking; he knew that China and Japan were engaged in a heated rivalry for control of the opium and narcotics trade in North China and elsewhere.[52]

The importance of the Sino-Japanese contest over opium arguably transcends its historical time and place. By the middle of 1936, authorities in Manchukuo and Tokyo were aware of the danger in *their* growing dependence on opium. Not only was there a need for control because of the intractability of the illicit commerce, but also Japanese nationals themselves were increasingly falling victim to the lure of narcotics, something that was unacceptable to the self-proclaimed leaders of a Pan-Asian movement.[53] That state of affairs carries with it two related, fundamental lessons. First, it is not easy for a major power to maintain hegemony over a people whose culture includes an intimate relation with drugs without becoming enmeshed in that aspect of the culture. Spanish conquerors experienced firsthand the miasma of drugs and empire in the coca-growing mountain valleys of Peru. And British sailors carrying opium from India to China in the 1830s were willing to sample their precious cargo, which, to someone like Commissioner Lin, made the foreign presence in the Middle Kingdom even more objectionable. In a slightly different way, the United States underwent a roughly comparable experience in the early 1950s when it provided assistance to Kuomintang forces opposed to Mao Zedong's Communist regime.

There is another lesson, perhaps less encompassing than the first, about political legitimacy and drugs for nations that are the object of control by stronger powers, whether as client states or as adversaries. If a status-quo regime in power faces a revolutionary threat from the Left, its association with drugs hastens the loss of its authority. This seems to have been the case in China after the mid-1930s, in Vietnam in the 1940s and 1950s, and perhaps in Cuba in the late 1950s. As we have seen, even had the leaders of Nationalist China wanted to do so, they would have had difficulty breaking their great reliance on opium revenues. This situation surely resulted both from the dynamics of internal Chinese politics and from the structure of power under the Kuomintang, but it is just as certain that the contentious nature of relations with Japan impaired the prospects for opium control. Accordingly, a status-quo, lesser power that cannot overcome its dependence on drugs is doubly burdened, and its claims to legitimacy become all the more spurious in the face of determined domestic opposition.

Rural China, where such opposition flowered, had endured great suffering because of the cupidity of Kuomintang leadership. The five bandit-suppression campaigns and the extension of Nanking's power into the provinces in the early 1930s had failed to eliminate the basis for resistance to the Kuomintang. When the Sian Incident of December 1936 exposed to many in Shensi and Kansu both the personal frailties and lack of authority of the generalissimo, the Communists in Yenan pushed for a united front if only better to assume the dual mantle of national leadership and political legitimacy in the event of conflict with Japan.[54]

Years of hard struggle had prepared Mao and his comrades to command a peasant-based revolution against all enemies. "The Long March is a manifesto," he declared in "On Tactics against Japanese Imperialism." "It has proclaimed to the world that the Red Army is an army of heroes, while the imperialists and their running dogs, Chiang Kai-shek and his like, are impotent."[55] This apparent readiness to break China away from the political and diplomatic shackles of the Nanking regime must have seemed a daunting prospect even to those whose vision allowed them to see a Red star rising over China. Immediately after the Sian Incident, Mao understood that Chiang himself might necessarily play a part in the momentous changes the Communists envisioned.[56]

At most, opium control played a minor role in what took place at Sian. The Young Marshal rebelled after refusing to fight the Communists, ordered the arrest of Chiang, and advocated forming an alliance with the Soviet Union against Japan. He also demanded the release of political prisoners and implementation of Sun Yat-sen's will—both of which could be interpreted as a sign of dissatisfaction with Nanking's opium suppression policies. It is perhaps significant that a widely advertised drive against drug users and traffickers, which had been accompanied by threats of execution of offenders, did not occur. Foreigners in Tsingtao attributed the change in plans to the Sian affair.[57]

Whether or not that was the case, the narcotics situation throughout North China held grave implications for all interested parties. Neither the Nationalists nor the Japanese could escape unscathed in a contest to dominate the north. The longer the former plied the opium trade, the greater the opprobrium they would encounter at home and abroad; the latter, it appears in retrospect, wrongly and foolishly presumed that they could pursue imperial goals unfettered by narcotics. Opium-related events in the north further alarmed the United States and Great Britain. While both continued to see a Sino-Japanese War as unlikely right up to the Marco Polo Bridge Incident on 7 July 1937, they had already begun by then to reassess the severity of the threats to their interests in China. Developments in South China and on the Fukien coast, along with the pretense of opium control put forward by the

Kuomintang, contributed to perceptions in Whitehall and at the State Department that their respective interests might well be in jeopardy.

The Opium Contest outside of North China

The government in Tokyo, under great pressure from the army, deliberated about a more assertive posture in the north by 1936. In the process, the autonomy movement had effectively undermined efforts to promote harmony with China based on Hirota Kōki's three principles of October 1935.[58] Johnson more and more saw in these developments an effort by the military to eliminate Western influence in Asia.[59] While he was no more prescient than other foreigners regarding the future in China, his concerns merited more attention than they received.

The British, in particular, failed to appreciate what might happen if they responded enthusiastically to an invitation from Nanking to establish an economic presence south of the Yangtze. If anything, Tokyo's largely negative reaction to the Leith-Ross Mission and China's economic reforms should have been a warning of likely trouble. But Knatchbull-Hugessen, like others before him, tended to ignore the implications of the Amau Declaration, at least until February 1937, when he declared: "Any suggestion that we are aiming at Anglo-Japanese cooperation in China would be disastrous to the prospects of British business here."[60] The ambassador may have better appreciated the tension in Sino-Japanese affairs than his colleagues at home; they were dealing with Ambassador Yoshida Shigeru, who wanted to rebuild Anglo-Japanese friendship. The naming of Satō Naotake as minister for foreign affairs in February also raised the misleading possibility of a rapprochement with the West.[61]

In testimony to the IMTFE, witnesses contended that Japan's diplomatic maneuverings were a smoke screen designed to hide clandestine plans for further expansion. Such was the analysis after Cabinet approval on 11 August 1936 of revised "Fundamentals of National Policy," which recommended an economic offensive throughout South China. With less conclusive evidence, based largely on Nicholson's dispatches and monthly State Department political reports, the IMTFE prosecution alleged that Japanese narcotics operations in Manchuria and the north served as an agent of expansion into the next area, in this case South China—to follow the logic of the argument.[62]

The actual situation in the south during 1936 and 1937 does not readily lend itself to such a clear-cut conclusion. One year after Communist raids in

1934–35 had cut opium production in Kweichow, the official trade was again flourishing but toward Hankow instead of Kwangsi.[63] Deprived of perhaps one-half of all provincial revenues, the Kwangsi Clique, led again by Li Tsung-jen among others, sought for a final time in May 1936 to break free of Nanking by forming the Anti-Japanese National Salvation Army. The effort failed and Kwangtung and Kwangsi soon came under Nanking's control. An agreement ending the dispute provided for the remission of opium revenues to provincial treasuries, a percentage of which ended up in Nanking's special accounts.[64] Significantly, there is no indication of Japanese association with the Kwangsi-Kwangtung opium trade.

The same cannot be said for the opium and narcotics business on the Fukien coast, where the picture was less clear. Nicholson reported on Japanese clandestine activities in Amoy and Foochow but could not establish an indisputable link with the drug traffic. At most, he laid the blame for the illicit commerce at the feet of the Formosans who, he claimed, were hiding behind extraterritorial privileges proffered by Japan's consular officials while they trafficked in domestic and Persian opium as well as morphine and heroin.[65] Haldore Hanson, an American journalist known for his objectivity and later employed by the State Department, wrote an article for the *North China Herald* claiming that Japanese did not run the province's drug rackets. Depicting an upsurge in heroin and morphine usage, he blamed the Formosans, "the willing scapegoats of the Government's inability to wipe out the opium traffic."[66]

Nor, it seems, was Nanking able or willing to do much about the activities of Yeh Ching-ho, also known as Paul A. Yip and Paul Yap. Convicted of opium trafficking perhaps as early as 1925, Yeh controlled the Lu Tung Company of Amoy (later named Yu Ming) and took over the Fukien opium monopoly in July 1934. Yeh dealt with all suppliers of opium and narcotics, whether Chinese, Formosan, Persian, Manchurian, or Japanese. A naturalized citizen of Japan in order to protect himself legally if need be, he nevertheless struck a deal under which he provided funds to the KMT for its opium suppression campaign.[67] Despite Yeh's notoriety, he was too independent an operator to be branded an agent of Japanese aggression. The extreme catholicity of his interests ultimately drove him from the good graces of Nanking's opium inspectorate on the eve of the war with Japan.[68]

Tokyo does not appear before July 1937 to have embarked on a course of aggression using opium as a weapon, even though Japanese interests were not distant from the inner workings of the coastal monopoly system. The competition for revenue was keen, and no one player dominated the game. More than any other, the KMT had a hand in all facets of the trade—perhaps somewhat less so where narcotics were concerned. Nanking, of course, used opium suppression activities to political advantage: dictating the nature of control indicated greater dominance over formerly rebellious provinces such as Kwangsi and Kwangtung.

In the early months of 1937, the Foreign Office closely followed reports accusing Japan of smuggling narcotics, since an influx of drugs in the south could signal an indirect attempt to circumscribe the Western presence.[69] Yet as Chiang tried to curry favor with the West, claiming Japanese perfidy, he did not succeed as he had two years earlier. His government's antiopium campaign was largely a chimera, which Britain and America had no compelling reason to play down until July.

Criticism of China's Opium Suppression Program

Nanking's elaborately constructed scheme to give the impression of opium suppression fell apart with the reality of smuggling from China to the West. From September 1935 on, H. O. Tong used his position as superintendent of maritime customs to import opium from Persia, some of which apparently entered the illicit traffic to the United States. From the safety of Shanghai, which Sir Alexander Cadogan once called "one of the most repellant towns on earth," Tu Yueh-sheng continued to oversee the drug trade. As chairman of the Special Goods Association (Opium Merchants Union) and a member of the local opium suppression committee, Tu ruled the Shanghai underworld with a fierce, uncompromising hand. By late May 1937, Nicholson could only deplore Tu's brazenness and lament: "Under the circumstances, it is no wonder that we have so much smuggling into the U.S.A. lately."[70]

Elsewhere, the evil seemed worst in the Peiping-Tientsin area, where it touched every class of the people. In early 1937, not long after the Sian Incident, the Kuomintang reiterated its pledge to enforce the death penalty against narcotics abusers, but this stricture did not deter millions of smokers from enjoying the pleasure of a daily pipe. The China Weekly Review warned addicts that they deserved no leniency because "opium and heroin are instruments of Japanese policy." To be sure, bankers and merchants would receive another opportunity to change their ways, but common addicts could not escape what must be seen as a kind of societal triage.[71]

Chiang Kai-shek alarmed Westerners by continuing to blame foreigners in the settlements of Shanghai and elsewhere for China's persistent opium troubles. The China Weekly Review parroted the Kuomintang's line, charging a lack of cooperation by the powers. Declaring the situation all but hopeless, Chiang personally assumed responsibility in March 1936 for antiopium activities in the municipalities of Shanghai, Nanking, and Hankow.[72] Kan Nai-kuang, once a member of the Kuomintang's left wing, a former vice-minister of the interior, and director of the National Opium Suppression Commission in 1937, admitted in the spring of that year that Nanking's antiopium policy had failed. The pattern of delay, obfuscation, and competition with non-Chinese participants in the drug trade further entrenched Tu Yueh-sheng, described by Ilona Ralf Sues as a man with "a long egg-shaped head, short-cropped hair, receding forehead, no chin, [and] huge, batlike ears," as master of the Chinese opium scene.[73]

Washington's quiet support for opium control in China failed to produce a satisfactory record of accomplishment. So prior to the twenty-first OAC meeting, scheduled for May 1936, Stuart Fuller took the American case against China to London, where he spoke with Malcolm Delevingne, who was about to begin another three-year term as a member of the League of Nations' Drug Supervisory Body (which Fuller deemed "a wise choice"), Major William H. Coles of the Home Office, and Charles Orde of the Far Eastern Division of the Foreign Office. On this occasion, Canada's C. H. L. Sharman and India's G. S. Hardy were also present. No one objected to what Fuller proposed to say at Geneva about the Far Eastern situation.[74]

Fuller subsequently described to the OAC a problem of immense proportions. Total opium poppy production in China amounted to 12,000–18,000 metric tons, only 1,325 tons of which were grown in Manchuria and Jehol. Yunnan, where suppression officials ordered farmers to grow poppies, produced more than 4,600 tons; Szechwan totaled nearly as much. Shensi and Kansu also showed signs of unusually large increases in opium growth from earlier years. Opium, both domestic and that imported from Bushire in Iran, was saturating an already sodden market. Moreover, the government apparently was subsidizing the trade through the operations of the Farmers Bank.

"China will continue to be," Fuller emphasized, "a narcotic menace to the rest of the world." In 1934 alone, for which year the Chinese report to the OAC was virtually useless, some 24,000 kilograms of acid acetic anhydride were imported into Shanghai, enough to produce 4.4 million average doses of heroin. China, he claimed, had the capacity to produce thirty to sixty times the world's legitimate annual heroin requirements. All this opium and narcotics activity "cannot fail to make money for the government." As he privately acknowledged, "It is not going to be easy in 1940 to give up the rich revenues to be derived by the Government from peddling opium to its citizens."[75]

The *Shanghai Evening Post and Mercury* and the *North-China Daily News* demanded that China reply to Fuller's charges. The latter newspaper denounced Nanking's practice of blaming the drug traffic on the foreign settlements beyond its jurisdiction.[76] At the OAC meeting, Coles gave added weight to Fuller's critique by detailing the movement of opium from the Persian Gulf to China. Nearly inexplicable to the British and Americans, however, was the committee's adoption of a resolution expressing "great satisfaction" with the Chinese actions against narcotics, a move taken after China's Chen Ting condemned the situation in North China.[77]

In taking the line of least resistance by reiterating the KMT's determination to control opium and narcotics, Nanking's delegates shortened the time China spent in the uncomfortable international spotlight. Japan's Inagaki Morikatsu, consul general at Geneva, and the minister to Switzerland, Hotta Massaki, who had no experience with narcotics matters, did not enjoy the same luxury. They attended the OAC session because Japan's regular representative, Yokoyama Masayuki, was home on leave. Japan's earlier decision to withdraw from the League of Nations surely did not serve Tokyo well in this instance.

Fuller also condemned the illicit traffic to Canada and the United States from North China, claiming that the narcotics in question had been "manufactured with the permission of the Japanese Ministry of the Interior." The traffic was "carried on in part by foreigners, principally Japanese and Koreans, living under extra-territorial jurisdiction." His voice filling with emotion, Fuller concluded: "Let us face facts. Where Japanese influence advances in the Far East, what goes with it? Drug traffic." In turn, Coles urged the Japanese to take more effective action and thereby assist British officials in East Asia.[78] Despite continued irritation with conditions in China, the United States, if not Great Britain, was showing a willingness, as Hornbeck had envisioned more that two years earlier, to lean toward China in its dispute with Japan.

What transpired soon after the twenty-first session of the OAC indicated the role opium control played at that time in strategic policy planning in Tokyo and Nanking. The Ministry of Home Affairs, as if to admit Tokyo's inability to influence the actions of Japanese military personnel and civilians in China, mandated stricter control of the drug trafficking at home. However weak this step appeared to others, Joseph Grew found promising the obvious link between Japan's embarrassment at Geneva and the ministry's announcement.[79]

Meanwhile, something had to be done to improve China's image. A year earlier, when State Department officials held Chiang in higher regard, Fuller had told Johnson that the United States would not object if A. E. Blanco advised Nanking about opium suppression.[80] Blanco, as we have seen, undertook the assignment and was hard at work in the early months of 1937. He told Wellington Koo that the lack of opium-related prosecutions in Szechwan, a province with nearly 54 million inhabitants, did the government no good. "This is an absurdly low rate," he warned, "for a province well-known to be a seat of many clandestine factories for the manufacture of opium derivatives." Next, Blanco informed the generalissimo himself that China had to improve its reporting to the Opium Advisory Committee in order "to convince the world of China's success in the suppression of opium and narcotic evils." He enumerated for Chiang what ought to be included in the annual reports. Chiang immediately ordered the complicated statistics to be ready by the end of April for the twenty-second OAC session in May![81]

Chiang's action would have been even more ludicrous but for the fact that he evidently thought he could again obscure the reality of the opium situation and return China to the good graces of authorities in London and Washington. Evidence suggests that he considered falsifying information to be released to the League of Nations: "[There] may be cases when our actual work in suppression does not come up to the standards originally provided by the Suppression Program, which will quite likely arouse misunderstanding from foreign nations. In order to avoid misunderstanding all material on statistics in relation to opium and drug suppression should be scrutinized by the Military Affairs Commission before they are published."[82]

The generalissimo's statement, delineating Nanking's strategic thinking on the narcotics question, was just the kind of thing Hornbeck had in mind in his advice to Fuller before the twenty-first session of the OAC: "Continual vigilance is necessary . . . to keep most governments up to the mark and to forestall the subversive efforts of others."[83]

Fuller carried the message of preparedness to the twenty-second OAC meeting in late spring 1937, but propagandists of the fourth estate and government polemicists would distort his meaning. He asserted again that illegal drugs from Asia were reaching North America, Egypt, and even Europe in alarming proportions; he welcomed the appeal made by the OAC to both China and Japan; and he called special attention to the clandestine manufacturing of narcotics in areas of China under Japan's control, namely, Peiping, Tientsin, and Hopei, where conditions were "appalling and beyond description." He acknowledged, too, that China's record seemed to show signs of improvement although, as we have seen, the evidence was far from conclusive.[84]

The pundits had a field day following Fuller's address. The *South China Morning Post* of Hong Kong termed it "one of the strongest indictments of Japanese opium policy ever heard in the Opium Advisory Committee" and solemnly concluded: "Humanity has come to rely heavily upon American aid in the war on drugs." The paper speculated that Tokyo's opium activities in North China were not so much intended to poison the Chinese people as they were meant to provide leverage in any political discussions about the fate of the area.[85] Two other newspapers, the *Peiping News* and the *Peiping Chronicle*, also applauded what they considered to be the import of Fuller's address. The *News* welcomed his praise of Nanking "on its sincere and successful efforts to stamp out the opium habit." The *Chronicle* hoped that perhaps Tokyo would now realize "the grave injury done by the [drug] traffic to the Japanese national reputation."[86]

Subsequent remarks by Harry Anslinger and T. W. Russell (Russell Pasha) of Egypt's narcotics bureau contributed to the general misunderstanding of Fuller's remarks. Privately, Anslinger found the conditions in Japanese-occupied China "disgraceful, intolerable, and terrifying," but protests by the United States and others "should galvanize Japan to clean [things] up." Although the commissioner's words contained nothing inherently at odds with U.S. policy, had the Chinese learned of them, they clearly had the potential to give unwitting support to Chiang's dilatory tactics.[87]

It is not certain what Anslinger actually thought in mid-1937 about Sino-Japanese competition for the control of the narcotics trade. Like Fuller, he tended to oversimplify the sometimes contradictory information that reached his desk. That he found Japan more culpable became evident in a public controversy at Geneva. T. W. Russell, quoting a Chinese source that he and Anslinger deemed reliable, charged that 90 percent of all illegal narcotics marketed internationally was of Japanese origin. Moreover, some 500 kilograms of heroin reached America weekly after presumably being shipped from Tientsin by Japanese traffickers. The *Peiping Chronicle* played up the story; Fuller, who was usually careful about such allegations, accepted the general tenor of Russell's remarks.[88]

Department of State and Treasury Department officials in Washington reacted with alarm. They were concerned that the allegations, if exaggerated, would take away from Fuller's earlier, more evenhanded address, which was already suffering from undue distortion. Russell's figures were quite exaggerated: at 500 kilograms per week, nearly 28 tons of illicit heroin would reach the United States annually. Based on estimated production figures for opium in Jehol, it was possible to manufacture no more than 17 tons of heroin yearly using all of the poppies grown in the province. Nicholson, in direct contradiction of what he had reported two weeks earlier, claimed that the flow of drugs to the West was declining and disparaged Russell's "loose public statements [that] hurt rather than help the cause of narcotic suppression."[89]

It should be noted that the OAC at its spring 1937 session raised the possibility of convening a conference to consider limiting opium cultivation. First proposed several years earlier, the idea held scant appeal for U.S. policymakers. China's dubious record of opium control and Japan's continued involvement with narcotics in North China rendered the conference, as Hornbeck said of the initial proposal, "untimely, inexpedient, and impractical." The United States would not support such a gathering unless the agenda included strict limitations on raw opium for all purposes and on poppies grown for morphine extraction. Given the inability of the OAC to do more than discuss at length the Far Eastern situation, which no doubt reflected the very separate agendas in Tokyo and Nanking, the committee refrained from making a decision about the proposed meeting.[90]

Relief for China from criticism about its antiopium record did not come from the Foreign Office or the State Department in the late spring of 1937. Neither British nor U.S. policymakers objected any less, to be sure, to the situation in North China. Grew reminded his longtime friend Hugh R. Wilson, the minister in Switzerland, that "the Kwantung Army is a unit by itself" and one not easily controlled.[91] The Foreign Office shared Grew's perspective while finding uncertain, but possibly hopeful, the direction of Japanese foreign policy under General Hayashi Senjūrō, a moderate who served as premier until a dispute with the Diet over economic programs induced him to leave office in mid-June.[92] British interests at any rate did not seem to be in immediate jeopardy. By late June, Knatchbull-Hugessen may have reversed his earlier skepticism about Japanese intentions, writing Cadogan that they "have learnt a lesson and whatever their bark, I think the latrations are for public consumption and that the bite will prove much less exciting."[93]

Nor did Nanking find comfort in the English-language press. On 7 July, just hours before the Marco Polo Bridge, or Lukouchiao, Incident, the *Shanghai Evening Post and Mercury* estimated that as many as 700,000 people were making their living from the opium trade, China's only billion-dollar retail trade. Nearly 80 percent of that number lived in Kweichow, Szechwan, and Yunnan. Two days later, with armed conflict with Japan no longer as remote a possibility as before, the paper—with well-chosen words—admonished critics of the government to exercise caution: "Nanking's alliance with the former opium racketeers, now perfumed into respectability as partners of the Government, has not changed its essential nature of gangsterdom and the opium lords still know how to strike swift and hard—not infrequently with some measure of official support, though this is not to imply violence or illegality by the Government itself." The *North-China Daily News* likewise wondered whether the current state of affairs, the need for revenue, and reliance on the Shanghai underworld would postpone indefinitely the enforcement of opium suppression.[94]

Conclusion

It is idle to speculate whether opium would have become an even more contentious issue in Sino-Western relations in the summer of 1937 if China's dispute with Japan had not heated up. Nicholson's contradictory dispatches, at least one of which averred that the flow of narcotics to the West was as low as it had been in some time, suggest that a modus vivendi was possible; at a minimum, from this perspective, relations would not have worsened. There remained, of course, the Japanese presence on the opium scene to leaven any criticism of Nanking's suppression program. In any event, policymakers in Washington were predisposed by then to hold Japan to a stricter accountability where narcotics trafficking was concerned.

Nanking's ostensible suppression campaign had not stilled the many voices decrying the role of opium in the Chinese political economy. These included native and foreign Christian missionaries; Garfield Huang, who, although he had fallen out of favor in some antiopium circles, was still contributing time and his own money to the National Anti-Opium Association;[95] the most prominent English-language press; and the Communists, with whom the government was negotiating for the purpose of creating a united front against Japan. Outspoken opposition by any of these individuals or groups, except possibly the Chinese Communist party, to Nanking's opium control program could have affected Sino-Western relations for a time. Such a development would have been all the more likely had London or Washington determined that Chiang's alliance with opium constituted a threat to their larger interests.

Thanks to the incident at the Marco Polo Bridge, ties with the West did not deteriorate further. All the same, the government at Nanking needed to redeem its standing at home and abroad. Redemption would ultimately come not in the form of forgiveness for its past association with opium and narcotics but as a practical political choice. Domestically, this meant united action against Japan, with the Kuomintang playing a fundamental role as Mao Zedong had foreseen at the time of the Sian Incident. The CCP would not put aside its objective of communism, a major aspect of which had long been actual opium suppression; instead, the anti-Japanese campaign would assist its realization. The party's opposition to opium was evident not only in the lives of its leaders, such as Zhu De of Szechwan, but also in the way it responded to the masses of people whose own lives had long been ravaged by opium.[96]

Great Britain and the United States had their own reasons for putting aside past differences with the Nationalists over opium and narcotics. They had to come to terms with the issue when it became clear that the clash at the bridge could not be contained short of war. Indeed, the early successes of Japanese forces against Chinese cities considerably reduced the KMT's opium dependency. While hoping for a peaceful resolution of the conflict, the two Western powers did not ignore Japan's designs on China. As Knatchbull-Hugessen succinctly put it, "The Japanese soldier in China regards himself as a demi-god."[97]

Accordingly, it became a matter of intense debate how best to protect their individual interests. Inexorably, this process drew them closer to Chiang Kai-shek's government and to each other. The association with China at war, never a comfortable one, put the opium question in a different, less urgent light. The Anglo-American partnership, which developed in the late 1930s as the international situation worsened, became a closer union—yet one always defined by competition as well as cooperation. Within that framework, as the two powers sought to devise foreign and strategic policies to fashion an acceptable semblance of security in Asia, opium would become by the early 1950s nearly as important to an understanding of world politics across the Pacific as it had been a century before.

PART TWO

Opium and the

Anglo-American Search

for Security in Asia,

1937–1954

SIX

Japan, Narcotics, and
the West, 1937–1939

Nearly three decades of international attention to the opium and
narcotics situation had paid few dividends in Asia. The greatest impediment
to suppression remained the political and economic importance of drug production and trafficking. In China, regime stability and solvency partly depended on a close association with the poppy.

The growth of Japanese power after September 1931 affected the urgency
of suppression. It moved British and American officials toward closer collaboration on opium policy and by 1937 inclined them to view control as an
aspect of security policy, especially as Japan tried to promote a new order in
East Asia. At the same time, Western powers were proclaiming the invio-
lability of their interests without actually being in a position to defend them.
They saw in China's conflict with Japan a chance to reassert the principles of
internationalism as exemplified by the Washington treaties. Anthony Eden
defended his ministry's support for a cautious policy as being consistent with
the spirit of Washington. And Prime Minister Neville Chamberlain favored a
response to the conflict that would move matters "into channels of political
and economic cooperation."[1]

Mise-en-Scène: The Security Context in East Asia

Decision makers at the State Department and the Foreign Office had clearly
not abandoned their belief in internationalism during the trying times of the
1930s. Indeed, Japan's quest for economic autarky and China's chronic political instability made the pursuit of internationalism, Washington-style, seem
the only sensible course to follow.[2] But the British and the Americans could
not afford to look on the Asian scene in mid-1937 with the same detachment

that the Washington accords had provided them fifteen years earlier. In the inevitable recognition of a changing order, frustration was sure to arise, as it did when Sir Robert Craigie, London's new ambassador at Tokyo, reacted to the tragic shooting of Sir Hughe Knatchbull-Hugessen by wondering why the Japanese could not act "like any self-respecting European Government."[3]

Such wistfulness—at best, Eurocentric; at worst, replete with racism— could not alter the fact that internationalism was on the defensive, making security an elusive commodity.[4] Isolationism, couched in the form of neutrality legislation, further reinforced the American reluctance to see the situation in Asia for what it was. Chamberlain, hopeful for a positive change in U.S. policy, felt that the earlier legislation unfortunately constituted "an indirect but potent encouragement to aggression."[5]

The slide toward war over hostilities in China led the Foreign Office to consider conciliating Japan. Except for Craigie, few officials put any stock in that course of action. As deputy under secretary of state for foreign affairs, Sir Alexander Cadogan found Japan engaged in "the furtherance of a policy of blatant aggression."[6] Britain, therefore, was going to have to rely on the strength of Chinese opposition to Japanese imperialism for the immediate safety of its financial and commercial interests in China and beyond. In short, the time for appeasement was beginning to run out in Asia.

Whitehall's gamble led policymakers to conclude that whoever controlled China would require the kind of economic assistance that only entrepreneurial London could readily provide. That is, Britain was betting against Japan's ability not only to achieve self-sufficiency—the very goal of Ishiwara Kanji and his supporters—but also to conquer China. The realization that Great Britain's future in Asia would likely be an economic one gradually emerged from foreign and strategic policy deliberations in the late 1930s.[7] As such, Britain would come to rely on the United States as an ally of sorts, both when making policy regarding the situation in China and in deciding how best to protect British economic interests. Eden summarized neatly the conclusions of Chamberlain's Cabinet: "We must . . . lose no opportunity of cooperating with U.S. Govt."[8] It would be hard to overstate the importance of America's slow rise to globalism to the fate of Western security interests while Britain was faced with the unhappy prospect of its imperial decline.

How a power shift from London to Washington would ultimately transform the international arena could hardly have been imagined in July and August 1937. And yet, Washington's political passivity did not extend to the realm of economic foreign policy. After early 1937, financial caution by private banking interests was giving way to greater involvement in the Chinese loan market, and the prospects for trade expansion were good. Warren Pierson, president of the Export-Import Bank, called Kuomintang China "a valuable market . . . that we should [not] abandon . . . to the Japanese or anyone else." He saw the bank as a means by which the private sector would get more deeply involved in the Chinese economy. Nelson Johnson earlier warned that "the extension of Japan's political control in China would constitute an immediate threat to various established commercial interests." In the summer of 1937, with an improved Chinese economy showing signs of receptivity to the influx of foreign goods and capital, private and public officials in Washington and London were beginning to understand all too well the magnitude of the threat from Japan.[9]

Menacing then to Japan's leaders was the prospect of improved economic and political ties between China and the West or the Soviet Union. Brief hopes for a new era in Sino-Japanese relations under Satō Naotake's Foreign Ministry quickly evaporated over the issue of Japanese influence in North China; Tokyo's decision to end the autonomy movement in April did not really amount to the requisite political disengagement that might have calmed troubled waters in East Asia. Increasingly hostile rhetoric by Chiang Kai-shek suggested the alarming possibility of a rapprochement with Moscow, a development that the Anti-Comintern Pact of November 1936 had only encouraged. Not only from the vantage point of London, but on the scene in northern China as well, appeasement had no useful role to play as tension mounted between Nanking and Tokyo.[10]

The clash at the Marco Polo Bridge was not premeditated: indeed, the nascent Cabinet of Prince Konoe Fumimaro had determined to avoid a confrontation with China. Yet, after the outbreak of fighting, settling long-standing differences proved to be an impossible task. Nanking sought to retain the status quo in North China, while Tokyo tried further to diminish Kuomintang influence there. Hostilities resumed by the end of July; the possibility that negotiations might somehow contain the conflict virtually disappeared as fighting spread to Shanghai in mid-August.[11] In its wake, the Soviet Union and China signed a nonaggression pact that strengthened Chiang's determination "to lead the masses of the nation, under a single national plan, to struggle to the last." He observed in a statement issued on 30 July that "the Government's policy vis-à-vis Japanese aggression remains the same and has not changed. It is to preserve China's territorial integrity and political independence."[12]

Opium, Narcotics, and the Early War in China

The Western powers had employed similar terminology for many years in trying to protect and extend their interests. The generalissimo's call to arms, at it were, continued through the disappointing Brussels Conference of November and constituted a shrewd, but unsuccessful effort to place his nation and the West on common grounds. To do so effectively, Chiang had to mitigate the most objectionable aspects of his rule. By the spring of 1937, as we have seen, the traffic in opium and narcotics was on the verge of impairing relations with Great Britain and the United States.

Contributing to the seriousness of the situation was an article appearing in March in *Foreign Policy Reports*, the influential publication of the Foreign Policy Association. The FPA was interested in opium and narcotics matters as they pertained to the enforcement of American laws and control of the illicit traffic.[13] Helen Howell Moorehead and Professor Joseph Chamberlain gave freely of their time and their sometimes unsolicited advice to American drug control officials. In his article, "The Opium Menace in the Far East," Frederick T. Merrill examined opium's role in the Sino-Japanese relationship. He summarized conditions depressingly familiar to experts in China and the West: between 15 and 50 million Chinese used opium in some form, KMT leaders spoke the language of suppression while relying on income from the trade, and Japanese civilians and military personnel were largely responsible for uncontrollable commerce in narcotics in northern China.

Merrill found that drug peddlers of both nationalities posed grave threats to the security of China's people: "Aside from the Chinese trafficker, there is overwhelming evidence that the Japanese national is the most sinister character in the illicit drug trade north and south of the Great Wall." Like Nicholson, Merrill evidently felt that the Kuomintang was moving in the right direction. "Only a partial advance has been made," he admitted, "but apparently the Central Government is increasingly sincere in its efforts to eradicate opium."[14]

Merrill's evenhanded assessment angered authorities in Nanking. Yet A. E. Blanco had told V. K. Wellington Koo on at least two occasions that China's opium suppression activities needed to be presented in a more favorable light: "Of course the finest propaganda concerning suppression is suppression itself but meanwhile it does seem necessary to show the world that China is doing more than shooting addicts and peddlers. Naturally the efficacy of the publicity will depend not only in the presentation but in the regularity and thoroughness with which the best side of opium and drug suppression work in China is presented to the public."[15]

Nanking's response to Merrill came in the form of a request to amend the essay in a subsequent issue of *Foreign Policy Reports*. But, as Merrill informed Koo, available evidence did not deny the earnestness in Nanking's six-year plan, despite undeniable problems with its implementation: "[I] decided not to stress further those defects, which would, incidentally, distract attention from the general weight of evidence favorable to China."[16] Blanco wrote at least three letters to Merrill claiming errors in the article. Victor Hoo Chi-tsai admitted, however, that it would be difficult for the Chinese fully to counter Merrill's facts. Hoo thus saw no point in prolonging the controversy, which the FPA termed "distinctly acrimonious."[17] F. S. Chien of Nanking's Opium Suppression Commission at first wanted categorically to deny Merrill's evidence but changed his mind and warned Blanco to act cautiously: "I regret to say that there are several points which most people think are incredible but are nevertheless true."[18]

"The Opium Menace in the Far East" ultimately helped to bring about the kind of reception Blanco was seeking for the opium suppression program of his friends in China. The FPA distributed it widely within the United States and abroad; it reached many concerned public agencies and private organizations ranging from Harry Anslinger's Federal Bureau of Narcotics to the National Christian Council of China. The changes in content in the annual reports of the FBN from 1936 to 1937, as well as his actions at the twenty-second OAC session, indicate that Anslinger generally accepted Merrill's argument. About five years later, Merrill published an expanded version of the article as a book with a distinctly altered emphasis. Issued under the auspices of the Foreign Policy Association and the Institute of Pacific Relations, it was entitled *Japan and the Opium Menace*.[19]

Kuomintang authorities desperately sought to improve Nanking's international standing as war with Japan became more certain. They requested economic and material assistance from many quarters but knew, as financial expert K. P. Chen later put it, that the United States "was the only country capable of helping China." M. R. Nicholson seemed to Chen to be one American on whom the Chinese could rely to convey the urgency of their situation. China's leaders also partially wanted to use foreign assistance to enhance their credibility at home. Recollections of prominent officials and intellectuals suggest, however, that the KMT's advocacy of nationalism in the face of the threat from Japan did not really overcome its prior lack of attention to democracy.[20]

Soviet aid in the form of military advisers, money, and matériel not only helped prepare China to defend itself against Japan—however unsuccessfully—but also protected for a time Moscow's traditional strategic interests at the China border against Japanese incursions. Yet the Soviets refused to be drawn into China's war with Japan despite Chiang Kai-shek's many efforts to encourage them to take a more active role in 1937 and 1938. When Wuhan fell to Japanese forces in October, Chiang must have realized that his hopes for Soviet intervention were in vain. Even a clash in Mongolia at Nomonhan in the late spring and summer of 1939 between Soviet-Mongol forces on the one hand and Japanese-Manchukuo troops on the other did not bring Moscow into the war.[21]

Obtaining assistance from Great Britain and especially the United States proved to be no easier. Even limited diplomatic support from either power for a negotiated settlement might have been more forthcoming if contentious issues such as opium had been less troublesome. This is not to claim that policymakers responded to China's needs based on the Kuomintang's ability to suppress the illicit trade in opium. Rather, as argued in the first part of this study, the presence of opium often loomed large as Britain and America pondered the security of their interests in East Asia. Indeed, officials in the Foreign Office and the Department of State made policy with a greater appreciation for the role opium played in affecting those interests than has generally been acknowledged. It is hardly surprising therefore that, as Japanese aggression threatened to displace Western influence in China, Washington and London would take particular notice of how opium and narcotics contributed to the realization of Tokyo's goals.

Merely getting information from Japan about drug trafficking was difficult. State and Treasury officials hoped to improve the existing informal exchange of information with Japanese authorities. If such a system was going to work like the one Nicholson oversaw in Shanghai, U.S. representatives would be paying funds to anonymous informants, and to that the Japanese strongly objected. Joseph Grew saw nothing inherently wrong with routing inquiries through the embassy, perhaps because Japan's drug problems were primarily located on the Chinese mainland, but Stanley Hornbeck opposed that option.[22]

More disconcerting still were the reports that came out of an autumn meeting of the Fifth Committee of the Assembly of the League of Nations. There the delegates, led by Great Britain, questioned the worth of Japanese actions against opium, including the promulgation in July of an ordinance in Manchukuo limiting the manufacture of common opium derivatives to the production capabilities of the local monopoly. Victor Hoo, after reviewing the record, termed Tokyo's efforts "bad faith," charging that Japan was engaging in "long term chemical warfare against a whole people."[23] A State Department memorandum, initialed by Stuart Fuller in February 1938, also deplored "the serious conditions obtaining in respect of the opium and manufactured drug traffic in China north of the Yellow River, including Manchuria and Jehol," where it was difficult to determine whether effective measures were being taken to improve the situation.[24]

The course of the war made impossible the gathering of reliable information for a similar evaluation of conditions south of the Yellow River. Yet Fuller and his colleagues relied on Nicholson's informants to depict for them the extent of Japanese operations in North China. In Peiping alone, more than ten kinds of heroin were available at some eight hundred shops and opium dens.[25] Meanwhile, the *North-China Daily News* reported that, at least in the province of Shensi, suppression orders of the KMT were finally having some effect; special inspectors were enforcing regulations ordering farmers to plant all available land with wheat and other grains.[26]

However lamentable the narcotics situation in North China, some evidence suggests an awareness by high Japanese officials of the need to address conditions there. Shortly before the Marco Polo Bridge, or Lukouchiao, Incident, H. H. Kung apparently offered to reduce tariffs on Japanese goods with China if smuggling in North China were curtailed. Kung had information linking the staff of Imai Takeo, military attaché at Peiping, with the illicit traffic. Yet before Imai, who later stood out as a proponent of peace with China, could take any action, 7 July arrived. The issue became temporarily moot until 11 August, when both the Chinese prime minister, Wang Ching-hui, and the Kwantung Army commander, General Ueda Kenkichi, who was not a defendant at the Tokyo trials, issued statements to the effect that determined efforts were being made to curb the narcotics traffic in North China.[27]

Both sides probably intended the statements to serve as policy guidelines should a protracted war ensue. The KMT had already spurned negotiations and needed to mobilize China's people and resources for the coming struggle. Nor would it have served Ueda well to have to deal with ubiquitous narcotics problems while conducting battlefield campaigns and trying to establish a puppet government in the north.[28] Throughout the autumn, however, much disarray plagued the narcotics business at Tientsin and Peiping. In response, the Tientsin Peace Preservation Committee abolished existing antidrug regulations.[29] While this development alarmed foreign observers, it did not necessarily indicate that Japan was embarking on a policy of narcotization in North China—even though the International Military Tribunal for the Far

East later lent its authority to that allegation.[30] During the same period, U.S. consular officials in Harbin and Mukden regularly filed dispatches chronicling a systematic crackdown on illegal drug operations in Manchukuo.[31]

In unoccupied China, the war greatly altered the government's relationship with opium. Right after the Lukouchiao Incident, though, the KMT did not abandon the idea of expanding its opium operations into the International Settlement and the French Concession at Shanghai. Clarence Gauss feared "the spread of underworld activities," while Fuller predicted that "the smuggling of prepared opium to North America would be greatly facilitated." The issue disappeared, of course, with the spread of fighting to Shanghai.[32] China's army needed food, not an opium-laden diet—so authorities encouraged grain production. The Communists had already learned that former smokers were not necessarily good soldiers; hence, plans for the rehabilitation of some 1.3 million registered addicts, however costly to the government, could not be set aside. In Szechwan, where the Kuomintang leadership would ultimately retreat, the provincial government acted to curb the trade in smuggled opium around Chungking. Opium restriction also seemed to be the order of the day in Canton.[33]

Foreigners reacted positively to these developments. Journalist Haldore Hanson and other former skeptics agreed that Chiang was approaching the goal of complete suppression. Blanco, perhaps revealing more than he realized, told the readers of the *Manchester Guardian*: "In times of war China will realise that she cannot afford to weaken her people with opium and deprive her population of foodstuffs which could be grown on land now producing opium."[34] Other than in Fukien, where contraband opium remained a problem despite the absence of Yeh Ching-ho, suppression was becoming the patriotically expedient course to follow in a besieged nation. The Executive Yuan assumed oversight authority for opium control, but as its president Chiang remained in charge of suppression.[35]

Chinese authorities surely believed they were regaining ground lost in relations with the United States over opium from 1935 to 1937. Reporting on the spring session of the OAC, Victor Hoo discussed a proposed conference, probably to be held in 1940, to limit opium cultivation to medical and scientific needs—which did not include opium smoking. "This is the American and Chinese point of view," he declared. "However the countries having opium monopolies are very reluctant to admit that opium smoking should be prohibited within a specific time limit." With Iran, Manchuria, Jehol, and Britain's Asian possessions in mind, Hoo predicted failure for such a conference. Yet in direct contrast to China's position on the 1931 opium inquiry, he opined: "I don't think we should object to an impartial enquiry, which on the contrary would be helpful in pointing out the illicit traffic carried on by the Japanese." The Foreign Policy Association agreed with Hoo and lobbied France, the Netherlands, and Great Britain to support the proposed conference. In August 1937, Helen Moorehead discussed the opium situation with Lord Halifax, who led her to believe that Great Britain might revise its position on opium smoking.[36] The issue became moot, though, as Japanese forces expanded the war to Shanghai.

Making the Case against Japan

In the short term, the changes in China's opium situation failed to generate more than moral support from the two major Western powers. At the Brussels Conference, the Roosevelt administration reemphasized its determination to avoid placing sanctions on Japan. The president had not yet won over the public to the idea of quarantining or imposing sanctions on aggressor nations; hence, nothing was done specifically to address the needs of China.

This turn of events angered Wellington Koo, who rightly placed the blame on the United States while viewing the British in a rather more favorable light. He must have thought that the United States was following a policy of appeasement in Asia. Just the same, the conference further strained Japan's relations with the West. It also showed how meaningless the Washington treaty system had become and revealed important limits in the Anglo-American relationship. As Roosevelt put it, the United States must not appear as "a tail to the British kite."[37] Yet within these confines, the administration would move slowly in the coming months and years toward closer cooperation with Britain in Asia, albeit on its own terms.[38]

Despite not wanting to antagonize moderates in Tokyo, the State Department even before Brussels considered advising resident Americans to leave China since their safety could not be assured. Nevertheless, the Foreign Missions Conference urged all of its members to carry on with their work if at all possible; one American missionary who stayed recalled observing the sale of heroin by Japanese in North China, where authorities declined "to . . . take official notice of it."[39] British missionaries also found themselves under great duress. G. S. Moss, who had just returned from service as His Majesty's consul general at Hankow, told a meeting of the Conference of British Missionary Societies in July 1938 that missionaries were having a difficult time because of the general militarization of the countryside.[40] The threat to missionaries portended the elimination of an important source of information for Great Britain and America concerning conditions in China. Missionaries around Hankow, for example, learned that the morale of troops and the Chinese people in central China remained high even as the Kuomintang fled to Chungking.[41]

Actions taken by Japan's military, coming as a result of political decisions in Tokyo, gradually undermined the hopes of Robert Craigie and Joseph Grew that moderate elements might soon control Japan's foreign policy. Regardless of the original intentions of Premier Konoe Fumimaro and Foreign Minister Hirota Kōki, the government, one scholar aptly concludes, "had committed itself, in effect, to a policy of chastisement" by early September—however lengthy that course of action. It would become even more punitive with the brutal assault on Nanking in December.[42]

In London meanwhile, the Sino-Japanese War helped provoke a crisis between Neville Chamberlain and his foreign secretary. For some time, Anthony Eden had been advocating closer cooperation with the United States in order to check the advance of the dictator powers. Chamberlain, even after the *Panay* crisis, found untimely the idea of a reciprocal relationship with Washington that included military or economic sanctions against Japan and refused to support President Roosevelt's proposal to make a major statement on the international situation. To Oliver Harvey, Eden's private secretary, the "P.M. [was] temperamentally anti-American." In this situation, Eden felt his authority was being undermined, so he resigned on 20 February.[43]

For its part, the United States vacillated in late 1937 between trying to reinforce an outmoded internationalism through a kind of limited appeasement, as Under Secretary of State Sumner Welles desired, and moving toward a parallel or collective response to aggression, which Cordell Hull believed was a more sensible course of action. Yet by accepting Welles's position, Roosevelt may have gained greater freedom of action at home to renew a modest program of naval rearmament. Such tactics helped pave the way for the passage in May 1938 of the Vinson Act, which updated the 1934 Vinson-Trammel shipbuilding program.[44]

In the near term, this gambit did Britain little good. Sir John Pratt, a Far Eastern specialist in the Foreign Office, feared that a Japanese victory would lead to "the progressive and fairly rapid elimination of all British interests in China." Similarly, G. Warren Swire of the China Association, a trading group, lamented: "At present England has only potential cards, such as her rearmament, the pacification of Europe and economic pressure, which would have no effect on the Japanese in their present state of mind."[45] With China as the primary defender of British interests in Asia, taking other than an indirect approach in addressing disputes with Japan seemed an imprudent course to follow.

Within this policy context, Great Britain and the United States set out individually and at times in concert to bring pressure to bear against Japanese opium and narcotics activities in China. For London, the trick was somehow to keep Tokyo from responding to the concern about narcotics with threats to vital commercial interests.[46] In contrast, the United States could afford somewhat to antagonize the Japanese since America had fewer tangible interests at stake in East Asia. The Roosevelt administration, however, could do little unless the public accepted a foreign policy at variance with that permitted under restrictive neutrality. Promoting a new internationalism entailed major domestic risks in the contentious political atmosphere of 1938. Ultimately, the government needed to educate Americans in a new way of thinking about world politics. Judging by their prior actions at Geneva, officials such as Fuller and Anslinger were prepared to do just that in the field of opium control.

Precisely what constituted Japan's opium policy in China in 1938 and 1939? Relying largely on Nicholson's hyperbolic reports meant accepting the premise that Tokyo intended to use narcotics as a weapon of war against a defenseless people. More dispassionate assessments supported this view. In April 1938, for example, Colonel George V. Strong of the War Department's Intelligence Branch told Fuller that the Japanese intended to establish an opium monopoly in North China under the North China Army and in Central China under the army based at Shanghai. The government had undertaken this activity as secretly as possible so that the Foreign Ministry could deny knowledge of it.[47]

Strong implied, and Gauss and Nicholson confirmed from Shanghai, that the creation of narcotics monopolies in China led to intense wrangling over the control of profits. The army wanted the navy to have no role in the opium business, and Japanese in the municipality of Shanghai battled constantly with the Reformed Government in Nanking for a greater share of opium revenues. By October 1939, Japanese authorities were facing the daunting prospect of integrating all operating monopolies in China as the only way to overcome the parochial squabbling.[48] All of this indicated, of course, that income from the sale of opium and narcotics was insufficient to meet Japan's growing need for revenue, whether for its armies in the field or in support of its puppet governments.

Nelson Johnson understood well the economic consequences of the occupation. Income from salt, tobacco, opium, and the like could not make up for the flight of labor from China's cities and the destruction of urban industries.[49]

Sir Archibald Clark Kerr, immediate successor to the unfortunate Knatchbull-Hugessen, nevertheless noted a marked increase in drug trafficking in northern and central China. Narcotics, he informed Halifax—who followed Eden as foreign secretary without becoming so thoroughly involved with policy as his mercurial predecessor—remained a useful source of revenue.[50]

In North China and Manchuria, Westerners feared the worst when the Peiping Provisional Government abolished all antinarcotics and antiopium laws on 24 February; what next took place seemed to confirm their fears.[51] The Tientsin Bureau of Finance ordered each opium den to pay an impost of 1 percent on its gross intake. After 1 October, only 150 licensed dens could operate in the Japanese Concession, leaving John Kenneth Caldwell to wonder whether more than 300 others would move to Chinese territory and be operated by collaborators with the "special consideration" of Japanese military authorities. Nicholson likewise denounced the Japanese for permitting Tientsin to serve as "the supplying center of heroin for Europe."[52]

The Foreign Office did not fully concur in these assessments. To be sure, narcotics were manufactured in Tientsin, but the Japanese "take steps which at least seem to be aimed at remedying the situation when it gets really bad." The rest of the time, their Kuomintang-like dependence on narcotics revenues dictated their actions.[53] Most important, R. A. Butler, the under secretary of state for foreign affairs, told the House of Commons that His Majesty's Government possessed "no evidence that the increased drug traffic . . . is the outcome of any deliberate plan on the part of the Japanese Government, or that it is aimed at the systematic demoralization of the Chinese people."[54]

Butler's statement must have caused some consternation in the Department of State. The department had previously requested embassy personnel in London to report on debates in the House of Commons about narcotics, deeming such information "particularly valuable . . . at the present time."[55] As we shall presently see, Hornbeck, Fuller, and George A. Morlock, who had also begun to work on drug issues in the Division of Far Eastern Affairs, were in the process of preparing the American case against what they believed to be Japanese opium policy.

Butler held a different view of the drug situation than Sir Malcolm Delevingne, whom one scholar describes as "the prime mover of British drug legislation" and who, Fuller believed, accepted the American position favoring a complete prohibition on opium smoking.[56] Butler came to the Foreign Office from the India Office and ostensibly was predisposed to consider opium questions from a colonial perspective. The same held true for Lord Halifax, Eden's more compliant successor, whom Helen Moorehead had warned that delay in curbing smoking monopolies would have a negative effect on the American view of the proposed opium conference and might even influence how U.S. officials evaluated British policy in the Far East.[57] While Moorehead did not officially speak for the government, she was close enough to the State Department to know its thinking on the matter.

Throughout 1938 and 1939, opium in Manchukuo continued to concern officials in Washington and London. John Paton Davies, Jr., U.S. vice-consul at Mukden, noted a flurry of activity by the new Central Commission for Opium Suppression in early 1938 but concluded that antiopium laws continued "to be administered for the protection of [official] revenue" and to curb competing, illicit traffic in drugs. While posted at Mukden, Davies lived next to a small heroin factory and on occasion came upon "corpses on the mounds of rubbish," drug addicts "dumped naked into the slime." "It was difficult not to conclude," he recalled, "that the Kwantung Army was satisfied that the Chinese of Manchuria should be debauched. Dope addicts do not overthrow governments."[58]

It was just as true that addicts were poorly equipped to contribute to the well-being of a new imperial order. They were not productive subjects. Or so Nelson Johnson believed; he also felt that so long as Chiang did not respond effectively to Japanese excesses, the appeal of the Communists, "the only group of people in China [with] any real gift for leadership among the people," would grow.[59] Authorities in Tokyo had long feared the growth of communism among the Chinese peasantry, as Hirota's three principles attested. With a war on their hands, some officials both in Tokyo and Manchukuo were having second thoughts about tolerating the opium business, since it had the potential of worsening Japan's China debacle perhaps as much as anything else.

The U.S. consul at Mukden, William R. Langdon, reached a similar conclusion. Although not as well known as other Foreign Service officers of his time, Langdon's reporting was highly regarded in the Far Eastern Division.[60] Opium control for Manchukuo officials seemed like a race against time and custom. With well over 500,000 and maybe as many as 1 million smokers, they tried to educate the public and turned to medical treatment to fight the spread of addiction, and they sought to limit poppy cultivation by local Chinese.[61] When it became apparent that drug smuggling from Chosen (Korea) was threatening planned suppression programs, officials called for a meeting with their Chosen counterparts in order to consider appropriate action. One such meeting took place in December 1938, but results were meager.[62] As had others before them, authorities found it difficult to give up the lure of opium revenues.

Langdon believed that the efforts of the Central Commission for Opium Suppression went beyond mere propaganda. He reviewed steps in the government's new program to eliminate opium dependence over a ten-year period, calling attention to the restrictions in place regarding cultivation and the role of the monopoly bureau in purchasing and marketing official opium. New laws made it mandatory for smokers to register; by August 1938, more than 585,000 people had done so. Some fifty national and local infirmaries were set up to treat approximately 20,000 addicts at a time. In contrast, the older system gave rise to abuses and "consisted of measures to monopolize the opium business for revenue purposes."[63]

The fundamental question remains: How accurately did Langdon portray opium conditions in Manchukuo? The IMTFE condemned Manchukuo for exacerbating China's opium problems, and one leading scholar of Japan's war against China, Robert J. C. Butow, evidently accepts the allegations by Nicholson and others of intentional narcotization.[64] Langdon, however, argued that the authorities "must be given full credit for adopting more positive measures to eradicate opium smoking than any other Japanese colonial administration. . . . There is no reason to doubt the sincerity of the educational campaign against opium." The Foreign Office received information that essentially confirmed Langdon's point of view.[65]

Accepting reports about the rigorous nature of antiopium activity in Manchukuo is just as difficult as putting faith in the Kuomintang's early opium suppression movement. Yet, with the center of the narcotics trade well established in North China at Peiping and Tientsin, assertions of vigilance against opium become rather more credible. Moreover, supplies of opium and narcotics from Manchuria were not easily obtainable in Nanking and Shanghai; those cities obtained opium from Chosen and from Iran by way of Dairen. The utter chaos that followed the taking of Nanking disrupted any plans the Japanese may have had to use income from the sale of drugs to provide revenue for their puppet regime, the Reformed Government of the Republic of China, set up in March 1938. In fact, the Nanking puppet regime paled as an administrative agency when compared with the North China Provisional Government.[66]

Too few able-bodied Chinese remained near Hangchow, Shanghai, and Nanking to provide a reliable revenue base for the Reformed Government. Perhaps as many as 16 million people had fled the region, and few returned—thanks in large measure to the existence of guerrilla warfare. The regime could not both afford to pay troops to keep the area under control and meet its own expenses. Neither customs receipts, salt taxes, nor opium revenues were adequate for the task.[67] Great Britain's refusal to allow the use of the Maritime Customs for other than the service of foreign loans compounded the financial difficulties of the puppet regimes and prompted abusive treatment for British subjects, notably in Tientsin. Even an agreement in April 1938 to place receipts in the Yokohama Specie Bank, an act of appeasement that angered the Chinese, did not lighten the financial burden of the Reformed Government.[68]

In the meantime, opium peddlers around Nanking sold their wares in relief camps, supplied by Japanese *rōnin*, or gangsters. Some foreigners believed that this activity was part of a policy of drugging the Chinese people.[69] M. S. Bates of the United Christian Missionary Society and a professor at the University of Nanking so charged the Opium Suppression Bureau of the Reformed Government. Bates wondered: "Do either Chinese or Japanese interests require for the future a drugged people, short-lived and infecund, physically indolent and morally irresponsible?" Opium and heroin, he asserted, were supplied by the government, the Japanese army's Special Service Agency, or those under their protection.[70]

While Bates did not specifically claim that the Japanese were engaging in systematic demoralization of the Chinese, some U.S. policymakers were inclined to accept that interpretation. Morlock, for example, penned a memo similar to the Nicholson thesis and criticized Britain's R. A. Butler for being poorly informed. Refusing to consider that analyses of events other than his own were possible and noting that Japanese firms had funded the importation of considerable quantities of Iranian opium, Morlock denied that Japanese officials could be ignorant of the deal: "Nor is it believed that the Japs expected or intended to sell this opium in China for the purpose of smoking."[71]

Along with the putative opium policy of the Reformed Government at Nanking, U.S. officials pointed to the situation at Shanghai as an indication of the lengths to which the Japanese would go to further their objectives through the use of opium and narcotics. Six groups vied for control of the drug business: the Japanese army and navy, puppet regimes in Nanking and Shanghai, the independent operators of opium hongs, and representatives of Tu Yueh-sheng, who had fled when war came to his once impregnable base of operations.

Tu's flight may have helped earn him the lasting gratitude of his countrymen and women and a reputation as a great patriot, but apparently he still tried to rule the Shanghai opium and narcotics trade from his sanctuary in Hong Kong. Tu may even have struck a deal with the elusive Yeh Ching-ho, who also surfaced in Hong Kong after his run-in with the Kuomintang just before the Marco Polo Bridge Incident.[72] At length, Tu spurned a Japanese offer to coordinate the opium business in Shanghai in exchange for helping to quash resistance to Japan. His decision left the field to unskilled newcomers and former associates who found it impossible to wield similar power and authority over the trade.[73]

Throughout 1938 in the Shanghai region, Korean, Japanese, and Chinese interests failed to make much headway in organizing the opium trade. Only in 1939 did the puppet government begin to realize income from the operations.[74] The change came when the Shanghai liaison officer of the Asian Development Board, the Koain, stepped in to administer the monopoly. This action preserved for the Japanese military a share of the monopoly's profits. Gauss believed that the military held considerable responsibility "for the deplorable conditions" in Shanghai, but Clark Kerr found "no proof of the connivance of the higher Japanese military authorities" in the drug trade.[75] Both of these assessments may have been true. Given their growing exasperation with conditions in occupied China, the Americans did not always carefully differentiate between the involvement of higher- and lower-ranking officers in the opium and narcotics business.

Although the case against Japan was not as conclusive as some policymakers in Washington believed, U.S. officials still intended to use the information possessed by the State Department to obtain an accounting from Tokyo. Fuller especially wanted to put Japanese officials on the spot at the Opium Advisory Committee for the opium-related activities of the puppet governments. The British, however, could not take such direct action for several reasons. Chamberlain would not have been so inclined in 1938. After Konoe reorganized his Cabinet in May, the new foreign minister, Ugaki Kazushige, indicated that he wanted to improve relations with Great Britain. As before, Craigie saw positive signs in this development, although his hopes did not last out Ugaki's brief tenure in office.[76]

Britain was preoccupied, too, with events in Europe and was not prepared to take any steps that suggested active support for Chiang Kai-shek. Finally, most officials in the Foreign Office realized that the security of Britain's position in Asia depended on American action should trouble with Japan arise. Lacking a commitment from Washington to defend its interests, London refused to risk further alienating Tokyo on a matter such as opium. These considerations help make more explicable a Foreign Office minute of 31 May 1938 that the opium-induced devastation of the Chinese would not necessarily be fatal to British interests.[77]

America, Britain, and Japanese Accountability

The twenty-third session of the Opium Advisory Committee was scheduled to begin on 7 June 1938. Fuller intended to make a strong statement about the responsibility of officials in Tokyo for involvement in drug trafficking by the provisional governments in China. Maxwell M. Hamilton, chief of the Far Eastern Division, told Hornbeck and Welles that although the OAC "is normally not an appropriate forum . . . to make any major pronouncements in regard to policy, . . . in view of the notorious character of the illicit traffic in narcotics, we should not object to Mr. Fuller making a statement along the lines suggested by him."[78] Morlock concurred fully after he learned that 428 cases of Iranian opium had reached Tientsin in mid-April, 300 of which were in Japanese hands at Shanghai. Another 1,000 cases were being held in Macao, where the Special Service Agency of the Japanese army was trying to set up a heroin factory.[79]

Morlock feared that any heroin produced would be used to demoralize the Chinese; he worried, too, that "efforts will be made to export [it] to the United States." Anslinger, who, as requested by the State Department, would also be going to the OAC meeting, expressed similar concern. "The Japanese," he recalled in his customary style, "had coldly calculated its devastating value as forerunner to an advancing army; long before the steel missiles began to fly, opium pellets were sent as a vanguard of the military attack. . . . A systematic attempt was undertaken to undermine the Chinese population."[80]

Secretary Hull was aware of the presence of Iranian opium in China. Yet he instructed Fuller to temper his statement, observing that "it would be inadvisable for you to take a position in public meeting 'that the Japanese Government is responsible for acts of provisional governments created with its aid.'" Instead, he suggested that Fuller confine his remarks to reminding the Japanese that they had a treaty obligation to punish their subjects who imported opium into China.[81]

The secretary's memoirs do not reveal why he ignored the advice of the top officials in the Far Eastern Division; nor do the department's archives provide conclusive information. One possibility is that Langdon could not submit as soon as requested statistics on the importation of Iranian opium into Manchuria, Jehol, and North China.[82] A more speculative, but arguably more plausible explanation comes from the convergence of Grew's perspective on Japanese-American relations and the appointment of Ugaki to replace Hirota as foreign minister. By early April, Grew felt that Japan's problems with Britain—

probably the ongoing talks about customs rates—provided "a certain degree of leverage in our diplomatic negotiations, arising out of the desire of the Japanese Government to keep Japanese-American relations on an even keel."[83] Hull may have judged the time to be inopportune for what would have been an acrimonious approach to Tokyo regarding opium and narcotics. The naming of the liberal Ugaki as foreign minister on the eve of the OAC meeting surely convinced him that forbearance offered a more prudent course.

As was his wont, Fuller stopped in London before proceeding to Geneva. There he spoke with Alexander Cadogan and William Coles, who promised to consider cutting supplies for opium monopolies, thus holding out the prospect of future action against opium smoking in British colonies.[84] At Geneva, China received less criticism than before. Nigel B. Ronald, of the Far Eastern Department, who called the Japanese "accomplished liars," told U.S. officials that "Chinese authorities . . . are anxious to stamp out the illicit drug traffic."[85] In fact, Yunnan remained the one place where the Kuomintang was facing serious trouble with its suppression program. Some local opium was reaching Shanghai after traversing various circuitous routes. Since Lung Yun, a Sinicized Lolo tribesman, had never acted deferentially toward the KMT, the Japanese mistakenly thought he might be induced to support Wang Ching-wei's puppet regime, but Lung Yun's relationship with Chungking remained an important alliance of convenience for both parties during the war.[86]

Earlier hopes that the OAC might make progress on the proposed conference to control opium went unrealized because of the more pressing matter of the Far Eastern situation. Japan's representative, Amau Eiji, then minister to Switzerland, told the meeting that "my Government desires to reaffirm that its policy of suppression of the evils of the abuse of opium and other dangerous drugs remains unaltered." Amau excoriated the KMT for conditions in China, particularly in Yunnan; he blamed much of the situation in North China on the activities of Yen Hsi-shan in Shansi and also on the presence of Koreans who had fled Manchukuo.[87] In reply, Hoo condemned Japan for poisoning the Chinese population wherever its influence permeated.[88]

Fuller then spoke, blaming the laxness of the Portuguese at Macao and the war with Japan for China's recurring problems with opium and narcotics. He praised the Kuomintang's annual report to the OAC for 1936 while reviewing conditions throughout China. In marked contrast to the dispatches Langdon would soon be sending, Fuller, like Davies, found little cause for optimism in the Manchurian situation. Concerning the lamentable state of affairs in North China, he declared:

The Japanese Government has an inescapable responsibility for the importation of opium into that territory in contravention of the laws of China. I put it to you that there is no legality or legitimacy in the assumption of authority by the provisional regime at Peping, and that it is to be profoundly regretted that the Japanese Government has not exercised that restraining influence which it is in a position to exercise upon the authorities of the provisional regime.

Finally, Fuller drew attention to Shanghai, noting that no market existed for the huge quantities of Iranian opium being held there. Business conditions were bleak, and the purchasing power of the people had all but disappeared as a result of the war. As such, the opium in question must be "disposed of in the form of heroin and that mostly for export to Europe and America." According to information reaching the State Department, Mitsui Bussan Kaisha, a company that had drawn on American expertise to improve its technical capability, may have been underwriting the narcotics operations.[89]

In the strictest sense, Fuller had not violated Hull's instruction not to discuss the complicity of the Japanese government in the opium and narcotics dealings of its provisional regimes. Just the same, his remarks soon caused something of an international sensation. Amau categorically denied that the Japanese army had anything to do with the drug traffic,[90] and Japan's Foreign Ministry orally expressed its regrets to Grew regarding Fuller's statement about Japan's association with narcotics in North China. Grew personally believed that Japan was showing "a genuine desire to cooperate with us on the question of suppressing illicit international narcotics traffic." Anslinger, however, found Japan's protests "inconsistent with facts" and deemed them "confessions by avoidance."[91]

The OAC could take no effective action since Amau threatened to withdraw from the committee when the discussions became highly critical of Japan. The committee merely passed, as Fuller put it, a "comparatively weak" resolution expressing its disapproval of the narcotics situation in occupied China. In Shanghai, the *North-China Daily News* responded by ridiculing the "pious" effort of the OAC, while the *Shanghai Evening Post and Mercury* was more understanding, noting that the League of Nations could do little so long as Japan was advancing militarily.[92]

Fuller, who had uncorked his pent-up anger at what he saw as official irresponsibility in Tokyo, also expressed much dismay about the halfway resolutions of the Opium Advisory Committee. If political considerations continued to render the OAC impotent, then the United States should refuse to provide the committee with information that "is used merely to whitewash nations which unblushingly encourage the abuse of narcotic drugs and [which] have for years been feeding the illicit traffic in North America."[93] In Tokyo, Grew discussed the OAC meeting with Japanese authorities, who told him that they would have appreciated a chance for consultation before Fuller spoke. Grew, in turn, informed Washington that he valued the cooperation he was receiving about the flow of illicit drugs from Japan to North America. Admitting that diplomatic advantages, which he was "not, of course, in a position to determine," might result from actions such as Fuller's, he warned that unfavorable publicity would likely undermine existing cooperation.[94]

The point is not that Grew favored appeasement of Tokyo. As his biographer writes, "He used every means of warning the Japanese government of the rising American temper." Yet Grew did not believe that conflict between the two nations was inevitable, despite increasing U.S. concern over Japanese treatment of American citizens, their property, and general American economic interests in China. He appealed to Ugaki to keep the army and navy in check and thereby reduce the risk of engendering more serious problems.[95]

Events in both Washington and Tokyo outran any chance the foreign minister might have had to improve bilateral relations with the United States. The imminent creation of the Koain forced his resignation, since it meant further delay in settling the war with China. Also, State Department officials were busy preparing a note to Japan protesting Tokyo's refusal to uphold the principles of the open door.[96] Seen in the context of these events, it is not surprising that Hull did not respond well to Grew's efforts to reach an understanding over narcotics. The secretary, it seems, did not then want to disavow in any way Fuller's disputatious statement at Geneva.

On 12 September, the department sent Grew an eleven-page dispatch, although remonstrance might be a more appropriate word, indicating its belief in the culpability of authorities in Tokyo for the actions of the "reformed" governments in China. Prior assurances about antinarcotics activity were seen as empty promises, while recent pledges of cooperation were dismissed as perfunctory—the result of intense negative publicity.[97] The United States and China soon increased the pressure on Tokyo. Fuller, who evidently did not view his talks with British officials in a comparable light, told Sakamoto Tamao of the Japanese embassy that prior consultation about statements to the OAC would needlessly politicize the work of the committee. And Koo, drawing heavily from Fuller's speech in June, told the Council of the League that Japan was refusing to cooperate with Chinese narcotics officials. Koo spoke at

Blanco's urging after the latter suggested that the time had come to politicize the issue by placing it before the Council.[98]

The Japanese disputed Koo's assertion and likened the criticism to China's earlier condemnation of British involvement in the Canton opium trade. The blame, in other words, should fall primarily on the Chinese people's appetite for opium and narcotics. Whatever truth that charge contained had no chance for an open hearing in the autumn of 1938, since relations with the West had deteriorated. As Ugaki was resigning on 30 September, the League's Council voted to apply economic sanctions against Japan. In response, on 2 November Tokyo announced its withdrawal from further participation in all work of the League, including opium control.[99] According to the Foreign Ministry, a new order for East Asia was at hand.

At first, the British appeared to go along with the U.S. move to pressure Tokyo for the actions of the puppet governments. William Coles had spoken in support of Fuller at Geneva, and Sumner Welles and Ambassador Sir Ronald Lindsay discussed making joint or concurrent formal representations to Tokyo about the sale of opium in China.[100] That the two governments would act in concert seemed likely by mid-autumn; as Germany and Japan drew closer to forming a military alliance, Tokyo set up the China Affairs Board, and Hankow and Canton fell to Japanese forces. Moreover, the prime minister seemed prepared to concede that Japan might defeat China in the long run, thus imperiling British prestige and economic interests and perhaps the security of the Dominions.[101]

Thus, Whitehall approached the United States in January 1939 about making a protest based on the issue of self-defense against narcotics imported from China by Japanese traffickers. In due course, the State Department authorized Grew to proceed alone or together with Craigie after discussing the matter with him.[102] By March, Craigie had not received instructions from the Foreign Office to go ahead with the protest, so Grew acted alone and presented an American aide-mémoire on 13 April. The formal protest again outlined the case Fuller had made at Geneva and called upon the government in Tokyo to meet its obligations, particularly in occupied China.[103]

It is not altogether clear why Great Britain decided not to protest Japan's role in the opium traffic, which, Butler told the House of Commons, the government at the highest level viewed "with grave concern." As late as the end of July 1939, Butler reported that the government had "under immediate consideration possible representations to the Japanese Government on the drug situation in the occupied areas of China."[104] Officials in the Foreign Office may have seen some flexibility on the part of Japanese authorities that eluded

U.S. policymakers.[105] Or perhaps larger foreign and strategic policy considerations intervened, such as the Admiralty's assessment that commitments in the Mediterranean made it impossible to send a fleet to defend British interests in the Far East. Strategists agreed that if war came, only help by the United States could prevent the eclipse of Britain's position in the Pacific. In the summer of 1939, Washington made no promise to that effect.[106]

By mid-August, events like the Tientsin crisis nearly forced the British to act precipitously. Conciliation, Bradford A. Lee has written, would have threatened "to alienate America and undermine China's resistance, without moderating Japan's behavior and safeguarding British economic interests." But as Whitehall struggled to find an appropriate course of action, the German-Soviet Nonaggression Pact of 23 August threw Japanese foreign policy into a state of confusion.[107]

Conclusion

Holding Japan accountable for complicity in the opium and narcotics trade in Asia turned out to be a meaningless gesture. Tokyo denied the charges and withdrew from participation in the work of the OAC. Whitehall, however, refrained from doing anything to jeopardize its larger strategic interests in China and beyond by antagonizing Japan over narcotics unless the United States was prepared to defend those more vital interests in the event of war. Only China, therefore, was in a position to lend support to the American protest. Although preoccupied with the advance of Japanese forces, the KMT joined with the United States in firing verbal salvos until the target, Japan, tired of the exercise and walked out of the OAC. Both the KMT and the State Department were convinced that drug trafficking had become part of the fundamental makeup of the Japanese state. In that sense, the inability of Tokyo to control narcotics in occupied China proved Japan's nefarious intent.[108]

This joint endeavor supported the illusion in both countries about the harmonious nature of Sino-American relations, which would barely survive the war.[109] An extremely ill Stuart Fuller unconsciously helped to perpetuate this myth in 1939 when he told the twenty-fourth session of the OAC that "the Chinese Government deserves great credit" for its antiopium campaign. His remarks followed those of Victor Hoo, who described how the war promoted the cause of opium suppression in territory controlled by his government. For his part, Fuller claimed that conditions in Japanese-held territory had deteriorated further since June 1938 and that both China and the United States were feeling the effects.[110]

This rhetorical shadowboxing showed how far the United States had come in expecting trouble with Japan over narcotics, and it minimized chances for a dispassionate assessment of the situation in China. Even so, missionaries and diplomats moving about the countryside discovered ongoing problems with opium in areas still held by, or loyal to, the Kuomintang. "Opium-sodden" soldiers from Szechwan were seen roaming about Ichang without their weapons, while one American Foreign Service officer on a journey through Yunnan marveled at the growing and ritual smoking of opium.[111] Meanwhile, William Langdon in Mukden and George Merrell in Harbin found no reason to change their minds about the antiopium efforts of Manchukuo authorities. Problems did remain, but heroin, for one, plagued North China far more than it did Manchukuo.[112]

The coming of war in Europe had immediate consequences for British policy in Asia. Great Britain could not afford to become involved in a two-front war, so differences with Japan became less important by default but remained unresolved. Policymakers in London knew, though, that they could not stray too far from U.S. policy in charting their own course. Fortunately, the Roosevelt administration had recognized the threat to Western interests posed by a deeper advance of Japanese forces into China and possibly the rest of the region. Washington's abrogation in July 1939 of its 1911 commercial treaty with Japan demonstrated that awareness. But to what extent was the United States willing to defend those interests, defined at Whitehall primarily with reference to the fate of the empire?[113]

Obtaining a commitment from Washington would entail a cost to British prestige. In effect, U.S. authorities would want a role in defining the future of the empire as an element in Britain's strategic thinking. Hence, just as the focus of British policy in Asia turned increasingly to the issue of the integrity of its imperial interests beyond China, assuring the safety of those interests might ultimately involve a major reconsideration of Whitehall's relationship with His Majesty's colonies. The continued presence of opium-smoking monopolies constituted one aspect of that relationship that was certain to come under close scrutiny.

SEVEN

Opium and the Second World War in Asia

Officials in the Division of Far Eastern Affairs in the State Department used the outbreak of war in Europe to link drug control and broader policy considerations. Having long assumed that drugs affected the nation's security, they acted consciously to further that association. Doing so ultimately involved them in the question of the future of colonial rule in Asia and assured them a prominent place in discussions about the safety of Western interests there.

Whether they liked it or not, the British were in no position to resist these developments. London's ambassador, Lord Lothian (Philip Kerr), a Liberal peer and an unabashed believer in the need for Anglo-American cooperation, told Acting Secretary of State Sumner Welles in November 1939 that the preservation of Western interests in Asia would thereafter depend largely on U.S. policy and actions. Neither Britain nor France, Lothian acknowledged, could prevent Japan's advance anywhere in the Far East. Thus, he implied, the British were prepared to defer to American perceptions and priorities.[1] The foreign secretary, Lord Halifax, reflected this key shift in Anglo-American relations when he told the reformer and antiopium crusader, Muriel Lester, that His Majesty's Government would not seek to improve relations with Japan at the expense of China. The Japanese opium record in North China clearly stood in the way of an accommodation. "I am," he proclaimed, "as distressed as you are about the drug traffic." Given the differences between London and Tokyo over this and other issues, little improvement in relations seemed possible.[2]

The State Department did not see how relations would change without a substantial revision of Japan's China policy. Armed aggression had made a modus vivendi far more difficult, and U.S. diplomats in China felt the Japanese military believed that it was on a divine mission to bring glory to the emperor and to free the Chinese people from the oppressiveness of their own government—even if they had to rape and kill them to do so.[3] Regarding the occupied areas of eastern China, they assumed the existence of highly centralized planning: "The provision and sale of narcotics is a prominent function of the New Order in this part of China. . . . [Nearly] all reports agree that the drug problem is incomparably worse than before the war."[4] This situation, along with other political and economic developments, convinced Joseph Grew that the New Order "has come to stay." At the least, such a state of affairs would mean permanent Japanese control over Manchuria, Inner Mongolia, and North China. Writing from Peiping, Nelson Johnson concurred and predicted the exclusion from North China of virtually all American trade.[5] Whatever else it may have accomplished, Tokyo's New Order had put the West on the defensive.

Some informed opinion, with a strong sense of noblesse oblige, thought it prudent to let the Japanese discover the error of their ways. If they failed to do so, and the unchecked traffic in opium and narcotics indicated such failure, then subsequent actions by Japan in the Far East, in the words of the *Christian Science Monitor*, "can only discredit its modernism and hinder its progress toward real civilization."[6] To be sure, the creation of the Koain and the announcement of a New Order for Asia rendered this condescending perspective, shared by many in the West, utterly useless for policy purposes.

In fact, Japanese expansionism and the drive for autarky forced on the Foreign Office and the State Department a reactive policy. For the three years after Tokyo's withdrawal from the opium work of the League of Nations until the attack on Pearl Harbor, neither Washington nor London, aside from the U.S. aide-mémoire of April 1939, approached Japanese officials directly about the status of narcotics in occupied China. Both governments believed that strong representations were warranted, but raising the issue on humanitarian grounds, one possibility, seemed absurd given the brutal nature of the war. At length, overtures about narcotics proved impractical. Any appeal would have to be made on specific grounds, since representations of a general character would fail because the Japanese were turning "a blind eye" to the drug traffic.[7]

The Foreign Policy Association, through Helen Howell Moorehead, unsuccessfully petitioned Cordell Hull to raise the issue of narcotics in formal discussions about China with Japanese diplomats.[8] Although further direct representations were not forthcoming, the United States proved not to be entirely hamstrung in the late 1930s. Japanese ships arriving at American ports were subject to special attention from U.S. Customs after being trailed into port by the Coast Guard.[9]

Along with Japan's dominant position in Asia, the internal Chinese struggle for power and authority limited the ability of the West to respond to events. Wang Ching-wei had broken with the Kuomintang and was seeking some way to accommodate Japanese objectives and still retain a degree of autonomy. Drawing on lessons he had learned from Sun Yat-sen, Wang believed that the destinies of China and Japan were inextricably linked. For its part, Chiang Kai-shek's government could not spurn all thoughts of a settlement with Tokyo; the KMT's ability to sustain the united front was no sure thing—a fact that did not escape Japanese officials. Thus, the Koain, in effect, supported Wang's new "National" government after its establishment on 30 March 1940, while simultaneously prosecuting the war and looking to Chungking for an ultimate settlement.[10]

Meanwhile, Chungking pleaded with the United States for assistance to bolster confidence in its rule. Although the Roosevelt administration put together a substantial aid package for Chiang's government, a task completed in November just as Tokyo signed the "Basic Treaty" with Wang Ching-wei, Johnson doubted that U.S. help would improve the situation confronting the generalissimo. Public confidence in him had evaporated among the Communists and segments of the educated citizenry thanks to a combination of the ravages of war, increasing bureaucratic corruption, and strict thought control programs espoused by the minister of education, Ch'en Li-fu. Ho Lien described 1940 as a time when "fewer and fewer people could be found who still supported the regime."[11] Indeed, it was not clear whether Chiang would use financial and material assistance from America more against the Communists or the Japanese.[12]

In this confused situation, ample opportunities existed for opium and narcotics to play a considerable role in political and military developments. Facing mortal danger, the Chinese government could only fight so many enemies. We might ask how Chungking, given its reliance on the opium trade, could presume to protect China's people against an assault that, whether or not as a matter of settled policy, evidently included opium as a potential weapon. A. E. Blanco warned: "War will create ideal conditions for the increased illicit use of narcotics, and whether at the front or at the rear matters little to the trafficker. . . . We are on the eve of a period when everything justifies the belief that narcotics, whether cocaine, morphine and more especially heroin will make new and more victims than they have ever made . . . in the past."[13] The slight hyperbole aside, Blanco's vision of a grim future had a clear foundation.

Opium and Western Security Interests, 1939–1941

Policymakers in Washington generally shared Blanco's bleak assessment of China's narcotics scene. Seeing the situation in this way led them to treat the opium issue as part of larger security-related concerns over the fate of Western interests during the two years that Japan and the West drifted toward war. Commissioner Harry J. Anslinger appropriated on more than one occasion Madame Chiang Kai-shek's terse statement that "opium pellets long preceded lead bullets" in Japan's invasion of China.[14] The FBN chief saw in the international environment after 1 September 1939 an opportunity for his agency to play a crucial role in China's effort to resist Japan. Among other things, he approved the export of 5,000 ampoules of morphine for the Chinese Red Cross.[15] His action in December 1940 came just after the administration's decision to expand the aid package for Chungking and indicated his faith in the efficacy of the KMT's opium control program.

Anslinger's actions alone did not account for the greater importance of drugs to foreign policy. Participation by Japanese military and civilian officials in the narcotics trade proved to be even more influential. Soon after Wang's regime was set up in Nanking, the Koain instructed the Executive Yuan of the Reformed Government to organize an opium monopoly to work with or oversee the operations of local monopolies. In short order, opium suppression offices appeared at Shanghai and Soochow and in the provinces of Kiangsu, Chekiang, and Anhwei. They operated with greater or lesser success depending on the availability of opium and the honesty of the officials in charge.[16]

Opium for the monopoly came from Shensi (possibly supplied in part by forces otherwise loyal to the KMT), from Dairen, from Yunnan and Szechwan via traditional routes for smuggling, and from Iran. Looming in the shadows of the puppet government's opium activities were Yeh Ching-ho and friends of Tu Yueh-sheng, if not Tu himself, who retained close ties to key figures in the Reformed Government.[17] Starting in mid-1940, as Wang's regime looked to the narcotics trade to defray some of its operating costs, the proprietors of opium hongs in central China and along the coast complained about the scarcity of supplies of preferred opium, especially from Iran. Ironically, smuggled opium from North China so undercut the official trade that seven major hongs petitioned an office of the Koain for relief. As a solution, they called for the cultivation of poppies in local provinces, improved cooperation with suppression officials throughout China, and greater military force against smuggling.[18]

Predictability never became a hallmark of the opium trade in occupied

China. Profits decreased, for example, in the Wuhan and Shantung regions, where local authorities encouraged the smoking of opium in order to raise revenue.[19] In North China proper, opium production may have fallen off in early 1940 as business conditions greatly deteriorated. Never, though, did foreigners abandon the conviction that Japanese authorities actively, if secretly, promoted the opium trade throughout the north.[20]

Consequently, positive reports reaching Washington from Harbin and Mukden about Japanese officials did not bring about a reconsideration of the American (or British) perspective on Japan's association with illicit opium activities. In February 1940, William Langdon credited "the *de facto* authorities in Manchuria for their measures in the past two years to suppress opium and narcotic drug addiction." As he saw it, the need for "sturdy human labor to produce food and industrial materials for [the] Japanese economy" had led to the effort to control drugs.[21]

The same argument might have applied to the needs of Japan's military and civilian authorities throughout much of China, but Westerners were not prepared to test such a proposition. The official position in the State Department and the Foreign Office better resembled that expressed in a letter by a British missionary, Dr. H. S. D. Garvan, to the Foreign Mission Committee of the Church of Scotland in Edinburgh. Through its propagation of the opium trade, the Japanese had weakened the moral fiber of the people of Manchuria; official graft, bribery, and corruption littered the moral landscape of occupied China; and any attempt to improve the situation occurred only because Japanese subjects were becoming addicts. One American Congregational missionary, Alfred Dixon Heininger, later recalled that the Japanese were "raising funds and undermining the character of the Chinese people by getting them to indulge in opium."[22]

The prosecution's case at the International Military Tribunal for the Far East after the war reflected the assessment of British and American missionaries, based as it was in many respects on the observations and reports of two like-minded men, Dr. M. S. Bates and M. R. Nicholson. It did not matter that Bates admitted to a defense counsel that he had not closely investigated and compared the situation in China before and after July 1937.[23] Moreover, one prosecution witness, Oikawa Genshichi, a high-ranking official of the Koain in Shanghai and later in Tokyo, amplified what Western authorities knew about involvement in the opium trade by the Special Service Section of the Japanese army and the Koain. When Oikawa suggested that the puppet governments sought to promote a gradual decrease in the use of opium and explained that rapid suppression would have guaranteed social and economic disorder, the prosecution offered as countervailing evidence a number of Nicholson's reports for 1940.[24]

Another former Koain official, Morioka Susumu—also a witness for the prosecution—who had served at Peiping, claimed even more strongly than Oikawa that the puppet governments had honestly pursued opium suppression. Their efforts failed because the lengthy presence of the army prevented civilian officials from working in an environment conducive to effective control. Activities of the Communists also made it difficult to enforce antiopium regulations. Regarding North China, Morioka blamed the lack of control on powerful organizations that operated with great secrecy. As for the monopoly system and its policy of providing opium for addicts, he declared: "I believe that this system was an effective measure in carrying out the policy of suppressing opium as a whole."[25]

The present discussion is not meant as a rebuttal to Stuart Fuller's dictum that where the Japanese went, opium followed. He was right, although the same could have been said about Chiang's forces before the war broke out. Rather, the argument is that policy made on the basis of Fuller's perception was closely related to general developments in the international situation in China. Nicholson and Bates did not always have entirely reliable sources of information; nor were missionaries or consular personnel immune from seeing the situation in ways that served their particular, often compatible interests. The strain in Western relations with Japan generated by the opium issue owed its enhanced significance to the broader context, that is, to the general deterioration in relations. Nothing better demonstrated this state of affairs than the signing of the Tripartite Pact in September 1940, about which Herbert Feis concluded: "War with Japan came plainly into sight."[26]

Accordingly, Oikawa and Morioka may have told the truth about opium suppression in occupied China, just as it was not wholly unreasonable to expect that developments in Mukden and Harbin might be replicated elsewhere. The reality of the situation scarcely mattered, though, after the European war started and when a settlement of Sino-Japanese differences proved impossible near the end of 1940.[27] Another American loan for China, the destroyers-for-bases deal, and Britain's decision to reopen the Burma Road in October, after it had been closed for three months despite American objections, became part of a firmer Western policy toward Japan. In the context of these important developments in Anglo-American relations in the late summer and early autumn of 1940, the designation by the U.S. Army of opium as a strategic or critical commodity takes on added significance in understanding the link between opium and the search for security in Asia. Opium had to be kept out of the hands of the Axis powers.[28] Western officials equated security with limiting Japanese power so as to prevent its threatening economic interests or colonial possessions.

The course of war in China in 1941 actually may have improved the prospects for opium control. Wang Ching-wei reportedly began an antiopium propaganda campaign in May, about the same time as the existing shortage of rice in the south worsened. Smoking, of course, continued, being far too ingrained for Wang's regime to extirpate. Nonetheless, quality opium remained a scarce and precious commodity in central and southern China. Travelers between unoccupied and occupied territory even used opium as a means of exchange. So desperate were the hong operators of Shanghai to obtain opium that they sent a representative to Hong Kong to negotiate with Tu Yueh-sheng in hopes of finding additional supplies.[29]

On 13 August, the government in Tokyo promulgated new regulations for the control of narcotics. No longer could Japanese subjects or corporations manufacture crude opium or narcotics in China; outlawed, too, was poppy cultivation for manufacturing. Moreover, the trade in narcotics into and within China was greatly circumscribed. George Morlock predictably played down the impact of the regulations: "It is not likely that these laws will interfere with the activities of those Japanese who organize the distribution of drugs to Chinese addicts."[30] A ban on press coverage of the decree prevented foreign correspondents from getting information about it from the Foreign Ministry. Noteworthy, however, was the lack of public endorsement by the army and navy ministries.[31] Unfortunately, it cannot be determined whether an antiopium effort similar to that at Harbin and Mukden was getting under way elsewhere or whether military and civilian officials were intent on perpetuating the opium trade in the familiar name of suppression.

Comparable uncertainty did not obscure what was known about opium control activities in unoccupied China as the Kuomintang's six-year suppression campaign came to an end. Hoarding of opium in Szechwan and Yunnan permitted coolies and the elderly to smoke highly adulterated opium, an act one British diplomat called "a great if involuntary sacrifice in a national cause." Chinese officials even took their campaign into the disputed borderland of the Wa States of Burma.[32] Some illegal operations no doubt persisted, and Lung Yun still managed to derive a handsome income from the poppy.[33] In other parts of unoccupied China where the opium trade continued, defections from the Kuomintang to the Communist camp may have led to the introduction of controls or, at the very least, to a loss of revenue for Chungking.[34] Six months before Tokyo announced its revised antiopium regulations, the KMT took a similar step. As comprehensive as any prior mandate, the new one set down severe penalties for the possession, manufacture, transportation, sale, and consumption of opium and narcotics. Prohibited as well were poppy cultivation and the possession of smoking paraphernalia.[35]

These developments led the State Department to request a full report on drug conditions in unoccupied China in the spring of 1941. Morlock was especially interested in knowing about the situation in Yunnan.[36] He learned that poppy growth was occurring primarily in the remote western and southern sections of the province; the trade in smoking opium relied, in part, on opium from Kweichow and Burma, with smuggling along the Burma Road in the latter instance; and official connivance was protecting the trade with the province of Sikang.[37]

It took several months for Clarence E. Gauss, Johnson's successor as ambassador, to report on conditions elsewhere in unoccupied China. He described the Kuomintang's six-year suppression program as a considerable success even though the attempt to register addicts was failing and the detection of poppy cultivation remained limited. On the other hand, private opium stocks were surely depleted, opium hongs and retail shops outside of occupied areas were likely to stay closed, and cultivation had declined except in those places already mentioned. Gauss did not minimize the persistence of opium as a mainstay in the political economy of Yunnan, Sikang, and parts of Szechwan; yet, on the whole, he judged China's recent record to be encouraging (even in Yunnan), a testimony to the antiopium commitment of Chiang Kai-shek—particularly after July 1937 when suppression took on the mantle of patriotism.

Absolute suppression would await the withdrawal of the Japanese from China, greater control over the western warlords, and public recognition that suppression must endure. More than anything else, Gauss warned, the "paramount prerequisite" to long-lasting control "is the complete political and military unification of the country."[38] It was clear in Washington that Gauss intended his words to serve as a warning. The ambassador had cast a critical eye on the Kuomintang's association with opium during his earlier tenure at the Shanghai consulate. Incessant friction between the Nationalists and the Communists culminated in the New Fourth Army Incident of January 1941 and cast an ominous shadow over China, tearing at the fabric of unification even as Gauss was writing his report.[39]

Unlike his British and Soviet counterparts, who thought that the foreign powers ought to try to prevent a greater schism, Nelson Johnson resisted such an effort.[40] Yet it was difficult to adhere to that position as pressure mounted from foreigners as well as Chinese across the political spectrum for the United States to use its influence with the two sides to get them to settle their differences. Concern arose over the negative effect the rift was having on the war against Japan, but Johnson, who was on his way to Australia after his many years in China, argued that intervention by the United States would have accomplished little.[41] Gauss agreed, observing that "there can be little hope of a real united front, that is, a united front grounded upon sincere political and military cooperation." Disaffection between Nationalist and Communist forces caused great consternation in the Foreign Office. As Sir Llewellyn Woodward pointed out in his official history of British policy in the Second World War, the "continuance of Chinese resistance was of vital interest to us." As a result, getting the United States to pay closer attention to the controversy and, at the same time, extending additional Anglo-American aid to Chungking were ways of protecting British interests.[42]

No less a figure in the dispute than Mao Zedong more or less confirmed the American perspective. In a speech at Yenan on 1 February 1940, Mao denounced the regime of Wang Ching-wei and the anti-Communist hard-liners in the KMT. "They howl for unification," he said about the latter, "but what they really want is to liquidate the Communist Party, the Eighth Route and New Fourth Armies and the Shensi-Kansu-Ninghsia Border Region, on the pretext that China cannot be unified so long as these exist."[43] After the New Fourth Army Incident, only "a slight temporary easing" of the KMT-Communist tension could be expected. The united front had provided an opportunity for the Communists to engage in the work of political mobilization, that is, in the land reform and social transformation necessary to bring about a successful revolution. As we have seen, this included taking action against opium as soon as practicable but with a commitment the Kuomintang had not always possessed.[44]

The attack on Pearl Harbor did not so much change the calculations of American policymakers as it hastened the realization of British objectives. Great Britain's partnership with the United States became what some in the Foreign Office had long hoped for. The two nations would act more in agreement to advance the principles of international order than at any time since the halcyon days of the Washington system. Yet on some important issues, accommodation of differing prewar interests proved difficult, including the fate of the imperial preference system and the composition of a world monetary system. In addition, as we shall see in the context of drug control, the sensitive issue of decolonization emerged as a matter of great dispute.

Insofar as opium and narcotics pertained to the waging of war in Asia,

Anslinger seized the occasion to assert American leadership. Narcotics truly became a weapon of war, and he began to plan as well for a new order of his own design for the postwar years. In a press release in late January 1942, the commissioner declared: "We in the Treasury Department have been in a war against Japanese narcotics policy for more than ten years. . . . We have experienced Pearl Harbors many times in the past in the nature of dangerous drugs from Japan which were meant to poison the blood of the American people."[45] Determined to avoid a similar catastrophe in the future, he set out to link opium control and Allied security policy.

The Narcotics Problem outside of China

Anslinger and his colleagues knew that others than the Japanese army, its followers, and the Nationalist Chinese were directly involved in the Asian opium traffic. Years later he would charge that the Communists orchestrated an illicit trade out of their headquarters in Shensi in order to finance their military administration and thereby cause additional problems for the Kuomintang.[46] Though we will deal with these allegations in due course, they were far in the future before America entered the Pacific war. Of more immediate concern were conditions in Siam (Thailand) and, to a greater extent, Burma, French Indochina, Macao, and Hong Kong.

A report to the U.S. Congress in 1906 had detailed the use of and traffic in opium in each of these colonial areas except Macao and Thailand, an independent kingdom. While in several instances overseas Chinese were blamed for problems with opium smoking, a large share of the censure was placed on the existence of official opium monopolies and the desire for the revenues they generated.[47] By the late 1920s, the British were complaining bitterly about the failure of France to implement the 1925 Geneva Convention in Indochina, where the government was seeking exclusion from the operation of the convention but, as a French colony, could not do so.[48]

Acting independently, State Department officers reached a similar conclusion about the lax operations of the monopoly in Indochina. And like the British, they tried to persuade French officials to do something about the situation; in particular, Fuller wanted the French to curtail smuggling through Tonkin from "the opium province," as he referred to Yunnan.[49] Armed with details about sophisticated smuggling operations, he brought the matter to the attention of the Opium Advisory Committee in 1936, but his pleas for action had no discernible effect on Indochinese authorities. On the contrary, monopoly officials shortly thereafter may have purchased supplies of opium offered to them by Meo (also called Miao or Hmong) tribesmen.[50] If anything, conditions had worsened by 1940. To no avail the Saigon press demanded that the government eliminate the monopoly, yet monopoly revenues for 1941 were higher than those for 1940, which, in turn, may have exceeded the 1939 total by at least 50 percent.[51]

Of scarcely less concern to Western authorities were conditions in the Portuguese colony of Macao, located adjacent to Hong Kong with easy access to Canton. From 1911 on, Macao made its presence felt in the Chinese smuggling trade with the active participation of colonial administrators. Herbert L. May denounced Macao as "a prominent sink of iniquity" where an industrious official "could make a fortune and retire."[52] At Nicholson's urging, Fuller proclaimed to the OAC that "the Portuguese Government . . . does not cooperate in the international effort to combat the drug evil." When officials in Lisbon tried to blame the Japanese for the situation at Macao, Anslinger termed their protest and a simultaneous one by Japan "confessions by avoidance."[53] By early 1939, the Department of State was convinced that Japanese interests at Macao were operating the drug and vice rackets in South China, especially around Canton, but the Lisbon government denied the allegations as "baseless."[54]

Just as Macao was coming under intensive scrutiny, so, too, was Hong Kong. Though the British supported the U.S. position on Macao and illicit opium, they were not prepared to concede that similar conditions prevailed in Hong Kong. In fact, Hong Kong did not suffer from comparable levels of official corruption, although it probably served as a base for smuggling opium and narcotics into both China and the United States.[55]

So concerned were U.S. officials about the Crown Colony's place in what they saw as Japan's assault with narcotics on its adversaries, real and potential, that in February 1939 they sent an aide-mémoire to the Foreign Office regarding the presumed breakdown in drug control in the colony. As evidence, the State Department pointed to the presence of some three thousand opium dens in the city, and Anslinger personally wrote William H. Coles at the Home Office to convey his fears that conditions were likely to worsen since Tu Yueh-sheng had fled to Hong Kong.[56] The Foreign Office admitted that the United States had a strong case and saw the aide-mémoire as a virtual ultimatum to improve the situation. Yet if the British were prepared to acknowledge that something had to be done, they nevertheless refused to act hastily.[57]

It is worth recalling that at this time the United States wanted to make a joint appeal with the British against Japanese complicity in the drug traffic in

China. However, for larger reasons of policy and because the evidence against Japan was less conclusive than authorities would have liked, the Foreign Office decided against joining with the United States.[58] Soon after the signing of the Molotov-Ribbentrop Pact, London and Washington overcame whatever irritation the aide-mémoire may have caused. Nicholson emphasized the cooperative attitude of officials in Hong Kong on the issue of narcotics. The British informed Stanley K. Hornbeck that they were "taking active steps to suppress the traffic" and that the colony would fulfill its international obligations.[59] With the onset of the European war, the United States could hardly have asked for anything more.

In the abstract, Burmese opium did not threaten Western interests as much as the drug traffic passing through Indochina or Hong Kong and Macao. Yet policymakers in Washington deemed Burma important because of its status as a British colony. If London seriously considered the elimination of opium smoking in its Far Eastern possessions, Burma could not be excluded. Since at least the turn of the century, the eating and smoking of opium had expanded among the non-Burmese hill people and minorities of Upper Burma. In the Shan States east of the Salween River, poppy production flourished and fueled the trade in nonmonopoly opium with Thailand. Violence often accompanied smuggling operations, making control far less likely.[60] Northern Burma, as the son of Baptist missionaries later related, "was a drug culture." Its border with Yunnan, the area comprising the Wa States, remained in dispute until 1941, when it came under Burma's jurisdiction. For the most part, Chinese nationals in northern Burma smoked opium, whereas native Burmese, Indians, and hill people consumed it by eating. Among the minorities of the Kachin Hills, opium retained its traditional place in tribal ceremonies.[61]

The significance of Burmese opium for the West suddenly became greater in the summer of 1940 with the closing of the Burma Road as a result of Tokyo's demands. The road had served as a vital conduit across northern Burma for military supplies destined for Kuomintang forces in China. Even though the British portion of the aid was small compared to that of the Soviet Union or the United States, an open road symbolized both hope for the KMT and the prestige of Great Britain in Burma and India. About one month earlier, the surrender of France to Germany had resulted in the closure of another prominent supply route to China through northern French Indochina. When the time was right, the gates of Southeast Asia would lie open, in effect, to the advance of Japanese troops and influence.[62]

In marked contrast to the earlier policy of restricting opium smoking for its own sake, the wartime interest in opium in Southeast Asia fit into this larger picture in two important respects. First, authorities in the United States and Great Britain could not discount the possibility that a further breakdown in Japanese-Western relations, followed by a sweep of Japanese troops into Indochina, Burma, or elsewhere, would bring with it additional narcotics addiction as it had in China—if only as a revenue-producing device. Second, and equally ominous, was the prospect of Japan controlling virtually the entire Southeast Asian opium trade as well as a considerable proportion of the illicit commerce out of Yunnan, while simultaneously retaining access to high-quality Iranian opium shipped from Bushire.

Such developments could not have seemed farfetched by the late spring of 1941. To the alarm of Britain, Japan further entrenched itself in Southeast Asia by mediating a border dispute between Thailand and French Indochina regarding previously lost territory in Laos and Cambodia. Next, in July, Vice Admiral Jean Decoux, the governor-general of Indochina, signed an agreement permitting Japan to establish bases and station troops there, an accord that Britain and America construed as a serious threat to their security. Roosevelt tried to buy time by proposing a neutralization scheme for Indochina, while Japan's Indochina gambit raised in London the specter of imminent peril for British possessions (and for those of the Netherlands). Christopher Thorne aptly concludes: "Everything thus depended upon Washington." But the United States was not then ready to take military action.[63]

During the same period, Decoux sought from Whitehall a statement of policy on opium shipped from Iran. Would the British navy interfere with the shipments? A recent one—which temporarily had been detained—totaled eight hundred cases (each case weighed 160 pounds). The Ministry of Economic Warfare concluded that Britain could not confiscate the opium on grounds of economic warfare, despite its being carried on ships of British registry, because Whitehall had not yet declared Indochina to be enemy-controlled territory and because reasonable grounds did not exist to believe that the opium would be reexported for illicit purposes. Britain could take legal action, and then merely to refuse access to facilities for reshipment, only if the cargo passed through Singapore—in which case a reexport license would be needed.

The detained opium was released by the end of August. Even though the United States considered opium a strategic commodity, Britain did not insist that Iran cease trading it with Indochina. J. M. Troutbeck of the Ministry of Economic Warfare explained that the release was intended to serve as a friendly gesture, undertaken in the hope of improving relations with Vice

Admiral Decoux, but that detention might prove useful in the future as "a weapon of pressure." Decoux, who was pro-Vichy and who was performing a remarkable balancing act in an ultimately unsuccessful attempt to keep his regime afloat, could hardly have seen the opium issue as other than an additional problem in his relations with various powers.[64]

As the war came, U.S. officials shared his perspective but for rather different reasons. In an early attempt to analyze what the Allies would encounter if they faced the enemy in Southeast Asia, the Office of Strategic Services (OSS) described Laotians, Cambodians, and Annamese as "calm, docile races" of peasant farmers. The Cochin-Chinese, however, were "indolent and physically lazy" but somewhat intellectually superior to the people of Tonkin. Analysis of the opium situation in Indochina condemned the French administration for selling opium, declaring: "It is just another method of subjugating the natives, morally and physically, to obtain huge profits." The end result of the business, the OSS held, made the people of Indochina among the weakest in Asia.[65]

It is unknown whether this report found its way to Anslinger or Morlock, who nevertheless acted in its spirit as they set U.S. drug policy throughout the war. Bluntly put, the United States would have to save the people of Southeast Asia from their own weakness. Keeping opium out of the hands of the Japanese to the extent possible constituted the top priority in Asia. Less than two months after Pearl Harbor, the war was disrupting Japan's ability to provide the lucrative Thai market with Iranian opium, the Indian Ocean was no longer a safe place for Japanese ships, and Turkish opium was virtually unobtainable. Making the best of a similar situation in Vietnam, the official opium monopoly ordered Meo tribesmen in Laos and northern Tonkin to increase poppy production.[66]

Anslinger simultaneously maneuvered to corner the market on available opium. He pressed John D. Goodloe, vice-president of the Defense Supplies Corporation, to purchase all available stocks of opium. Anslinger first had recommended that the government buy only 500 cases of Iranian opium at $900 per case, but he and Morlock soon realized that it would be best to obtain whatever was available. William L. Clayton, then serving as deputy federal loan administrator, questioned the need for a preemptive buy such as Anslinger and Morlock had in mind. Goodloe told Clayton that the proposal "originated with the State Department and [is] considered important and urgent for political reasons." The War Production Board (WPB) finally authorized the purchase of 4,000 cases (or chests) of opium: 2,200 from Turkey, 1,300 from Iran, and 500 from India. As administrator of the wartime narcotics supply, Anslinger could act, according to WPB Directive No. 10 of 6 October 1942, as "necessary or appropriate in the public interest and to promote the National Defense."[67]

Although Japanese forces found it hard to draw on customary sources for opium, the actions of the United States did not affect the poppy-growing areas of occupied China or Southeast Asia. Hence, the Japanese military met its narcotics needs by persuasion, purchase, or force as it advanced across East Asia. If, as seems to be the case, understanding the role of opium adds substantially to our knowledge of what the Japanese Cabinet called the "China Incident," so might it also help us more fully understand American and British involvement in the Asian theater of the war. Equally as important, it is essential to see how opium policy meshed with early considerations of postwar security matters in Washington and London. It is to those matters we now turn.

Opium and the Greater East Asian War

War with Japan prevented the British and the Americans from getting reliable information about narcotics and opium in occupied China. Especially through the efforts of the vice-minister of information, Hollington K. Tong, whom John Paton Davies, Jr., described as "a general purpose contact-man for dealing with Americans," Chungking consistently asserted that Japan had enslaved at least 13 million people to opium in Manchuria alone and continued to follow a policy of narcotization throughout the country.[68] The OSS seemed to confirm this accusation when it learned that Japanese authorities were taxing the Chinese to such an extent that the latter had no choice but to grow opium in order to meet their obligations.[69]

A subsequent OSS analysis prepared in April 1945 painted a different picture, one indicating movement in the direction of opium control by the Japanese. After 1937, but especially after 1942, officials in North China were compelled to meet medical requirements for drugs for civilian and military purposes from local production. Chinese and Japanese merchants in November 1942 set up an association to regulate legitimate trade. Also, by mid-1944, officials throughout North China, Inner Mongolia, and Manchuria were trying to phase out opium smoking.[70] While this activity does not prove conclusively that the Japanese were in the process of transforming their prior association with opium and narcotics in the war with China, it does suggest that officials were finding it difficult to govern a population besotted with opium.

In areas destined for incorporation into the Greater East Asia Co-Prosperity Sphere, opium may have played its familiar role as a producer of revenue when the war expanded beyond China's borders. Prime Minister Tōjō Hideki acted in November 1942 to create a new body with jurisdiction over the economic, commercial, and cultural affairs of countries under Tokyo's influence. The Greater East Asia Ministry effectively reduced the power of the Foreign Ministry while giving more extensive authority to the military. Its importance for present purposes stems from the judgment of the International Military Tribunal for the Far East that the new ministry abetted narcotics trafficking and used the revenues to finance an aggressive war outside of China. The tribunal reasoned that the ministry must have participated in the narcotics trade because two of its agencies, the Manchurian Affairs Board and the China Affairs Board, had extensive prior involvement with the opium business.[71]

What can be pieced together from available documentation, which is understandably sparse, suggests a more complex picture. We know that officials in Indochina promoted opium cultivation by the Meo when other sources of supply dried up and that they sold opium throughout the war. Also, opium from Yunnan easily found its way into Tonkin, but not all of it reached Hong Kong or the South China coast. (Japanese forces probably did sell some opium to Chinese troops stationed near the Indochina border.) As in earlier Chinese and Japanese experiences, French subjects took so well to the opium habit that there existed a studied indifference to its persistence by Decoux's government. It is therefore worth noting that Colonel Archimedes L. K. Patti, head of the OSS-Indochina mission, recorded Ho Chi Minh as asking the French in July 1945 to initiate reforms that included a prohibition on the sale of opium. Ho, as we know, first took this position some twenty-five years earlier but received little help in this effort in 1945 since Chinese in Hanoi and Cholon had smuggled opium from Yunnan to Tonkin and Cochin-China during the war.[72]

Elsewhere, the course of the war in the Pacific portended great damage to British authority and prestige. Prime Minister Winston S. Churchill clearly recognized the importance of Burma, declaring in February 1942 that "it must be held at all costs." But Rangoon soon fell and British power seemed far less imposing than it had previously. Yet if the limits of British power were exposed, the same held true for the Japanese, who subsequently failed to hold the gains of the early months of the war. Meanwhile, the loss of Burma increased the ability of the United States to determine Allied strategy in the Asian and Pacific theaters. Anthony Eden, once again at the Foreign Office, admitted as much in the wake of the "succession of disasters" of 1942. He acknowledged that "the United States must in time become the dominant partner in Anglo-American councils."[73]

It was not altogether clear what Eden's perspective on Allied relations meant for the conduct of the war in Burma immediately after the retreat of British and Chinese forces to India. Chaos dominated the Burmese scene and the Allied response remained uncertain for a time.[74] That inability to discern an appropriate course of action presaged trouble for Japan as well, despite Tokyo's backing for the Burma Independence Army (later the Burma Defense Army) and declaration of support for Burmese independence at the time of the Great East Asia Conference in November 1943.[75]

Thanks to Allied military tactics as the war dragged on, Tokyo's forces could not guarantee the maintenance of order in Upper Burma. Local conditions played a role as well when opium smuggling did not abate among an element of the population that was long disposed to autonomy. It surely must have seemed ironic to Western authorities that specially trained narcotics police could do nothing to alter this situation. Instead, they reportedly accepted bribes to protect the illicit traffic and other criminal activity but came down hard on the Chinese who were caught in the opium network in order not to reveal how greatly they had been compromised.[76]

Japan's association with the opium trade therefore did not pay the same political and economic dividends that it had in Formosa, China, and, perhaps, French Indochina. The trade contributed to the undoing of Japan's New Order in part by undermining the morale of Japanese troops in Burma through the spread of addiction. As the OSS learned from the exploits of Detachment 101, opium's place in Upper Burma remained unassailed despite the ferocity of the war there. Tokyo's forces failed to turn the trade to their economic advantage and were left trying to induce the Shans, somewhat successfully, and the Kachins, whose antipathy to the Japanese the Allies would call upon, to collaborate in return for additional supplies of opium to help them best their Chinese competitors in the commerce.[77]

The lessons in Japan's brief, unrewarding experience with opium suggest three related conclusions about opium in China and Southeast Asia. First, opium tended to take on a life of its own, irrespective, within limits, of time or place, in those societies that grew or traded it. On closer inspection, this enigmatic, if not ahistorical phenomenon indicated the persistence over time of a culture of opium. Put differently, involvement with opium nurtured and sustained within various groups a particular way of seeing the world beyond their own frame of reference. Second, people involved with opium usually ignored great personal risks in order to continue their involvement. Breaking away from a prior reliance on opium for consumption, revenue, or both seemed more a temporary than an enduring situation, whether brought about by choice or force.

Finally, outside authorities—in this case, both Chinese and Japanese—proved less able to control a local opium situation in the name of reform or empire than they had reason to expect. The Kuomintang had been forced to come to terms with the opium lords of China prior to July 1937, and the Japanese never really succeeded in controlling smuggling problems in North China and Manchuria. While Japan's experience with opium in Formosa, for example, indicates there may be exceptions to this proposition, such a conclusion would be misleading. In Formosa, Japanese officials did not have to face the problem of opium cultivation as well as consumption by smoking, which, in any event, occurred among relatively small numbers of resident Chinese (less than 7 percent according to estimates of the Philippine Commission's Opium Investigation Committee). In a corollary to this proposition about outsiders and opium control, the Japanese had little chance of radically altering opium's traditional role in Upper Burma even with the imposing presence of more than 150,000 troops. Ironically, the very situation they endeavored to dominate instead helped to compromise their own military and security policies.

As for the KMT, its six-year campaign against opium surpassed Yuan Shih-k'ai's accomplishments and led to a revised perspective on Chiang's government. Thus, when the early months of war in Hong Kong, the Philippines, Singapore, Malaya, the Dutch East Indies, and Burma reduced the Western position in Asia to one of chaos, the British, despite serious misgivings, had to swallow the appointment of Chiang Kai-shek as commander of the Chinese theater. Particularly after the debacle in Burma, the United States saw considerable justice in a larger wartime role for the generalissimo. Even Churchill had to admit the great importance of "maintaining contact with Chiang," who was existing "on a very thin diet."[78]

By the Cairo Conference in late 1943, however, the two Western powers viewed China in a different light. U.S. officials at the highest levels were beginning to tire of Chiang's reluctance to prosecute the war while incessantly demanding Lend-Lease aid and billion-dollar loans. The British, who felt that the Americans did not appreciate Chiang's shortcomings, viewed with suspicion the Cairo Declaration—as that document pertained to the future of occupied areas, particularly prewar colonies. In other words, Whitehall doubted that Chungking could be depended on when it came to planning for the revitalization of Western interests in Asia after the war.[79]

Had major British officials considered China's wartime experience with opium in their deliberations, their uncertainty would have been even greater. Yunnan, though hardly a typical province, played a signal role in the war because of its store of strategic resources. With some difficulty, provincial officials reached an accommodation with Chungking over economic policy that markedly diminished Yunnan's previous autonomy. Politically, Lung Yun endeavored to retain a measure of autonomy, going so far as to welcome into Yunnan all manner of liberal dissidents from centralized rule. In this contentious environment, the wartime traffic in opium might well be seen as an indication of the limits of Chungking's power. While Lung Yun had ceased to rely on opium as the sine qua non of provincial revenue, he never tried to halt smoking or the opium traffic as vigorously as the six-year campaign required.[80] Nor were the Nationalists in a position to force him to do so.

The KMT attempted on occasion to extend its pre-1940 antiopium commitment, but old habits were not easily changed. We have seen how the nation's narcotics regulations were revised in early 1941. Some two years later Lieutenant Commander (later Admiral) Milton E. Miles, U.S. Navy, proposed to General Tai Li, chief of Chiang's secret police, that China establish a modern police training school. Miles was then heading a mission to gather intelligence information under Naval Group China, later known as the Sino-American Cooperative Organization (SACO). He got along well with Tai Li, who had been closely involved in the activities of the Blue Shirts, and suggested that SACO help Tai revamp his organization. Among other things, this would mean sending Federal Bureau of Narcotics instructors to China in the summer and autumn of 1943 to train Chinese personnel for their role in the overall program of crime detection and intelligence work.[81]

Tai Li's experiences left him no stranger to China's opium scene either as policeman or participant. His efforts in mid-1942 to curb the illicit traffic from Sikang to Yunnan caused much tension between Kunming and Chungking. Within the year, just before the arrival of the FBN training mission, Tai Li's secret police had apparently done an about-face. They were then seen guarding opium shipments from Sikang destined for Kwangtung and possibly Yunnan. U.S. diplomats in Chungking learned that Tu Yueh-sheng probably had a role in the traffic.[82] If that was true, it is hard not to conclude that the Kuomintang was encouraging the trade, albeit unofficially.

Support for this contention comes from several contemporary developments. In August 1943, the KMT reinvigorated its drive to curtail opium smoking, a move that indicated a recrudescence of earlier conditions— notably in the western provinces. Moreover, Chiang was dealing gingerly with

Sikang's Liu Wen-hui, whom Lloyd E. Eastman describes as "not notably en-lightened," a throwback to the warlord era. Perhaps the generalissimo was trying to accept the situation as he found it, but in so doing he reopened the Pandora's box of dependence on opium revenues and toleration of the trade for larger political objectives. To be fair, Chiang did not want to undercut his influence in Sikang in the event of trouble after the war with either the Com-munists or the nearly autonomous Szechwan-Yunnan militarists.[83]

In addition, smuggling operations were conducted between free and occu-pied China. KMT officers and provincial authorities, who refused to accept the emplacement of customs stations on the southern Yunnan border, regu-larly exchanged opium, rice, cotton, and tin for heroin pills and other opiates. Similarly illegal deals took place at the border with Burma and may partly explain the trouble that General Joseph W. Stilwell had in getting Chinese forces to mount an offensive into that country. And, of course, opium from Yunnan still served its customary markets in French Indochina. H. H. Kung as well as Tai Li and Tu Yueh-sheng were reportedly the primary beneficiaries of these various schemes.[84]

More than mere participation in the illicit opium trade impaired the Allied war effort in the China-Burma-India theater. First, Liu Wen-hui possessed virtual autonomy in newly formed Sikang. While Chiang was preparing to meet with Roosevelt and Churchill at Cairo, KMT forces fought with Liu's troops and bandits in Sikang. According to a British missionary serving with the China Inland Mission, the KMT had promoted the cultivation of opium in western Szechwan since 1938.[85] As was the case in Yunnan, this meant that troops could not fulfill their war-related assignments—assuming those obli-gations were other than protecting the opium business. One dispatch received in the Foreign Office wryly observed: "The present theoretical position is that all forms of the drug traffic are entirely prohibited in Free China."[86]

Any discussion of the place of opium in wartime China must consider Com-munist participation in the trade. Accounts by journalists, recollections of missionaries, U.S. intelligence records, and the archives of the Foreign Office indicate minimal Communist involvement with opium. One seeming excep-tion to this apparent consensus came to light when Everett F. Drumright was detailed to Sian in mid-1943. Drumright, who would survive the postwar purge of China experts in the Foreign Service, found that the Communists were selling opium but did so almost exclusively in enemy-controlled areas. They then used the proceeds to meet their own supply needs, cut off as they were from war matériel by the Kuomintang.[87]

In March 1944, the KMT permitted a group of journalists to travel to the

Border Region of Shensi. They first had to visit non-Communist areas in the northwest before spending a required minimum of three months with the Communists. Gunther Stein and Harrison Forman were among those who accepted these conditions and joined the group. Although under the control of the Communists, the Border Region seemed devoid of opium and its related problems even though pro-Kuomintang elements in Sian had led Stein and Forman to believe otherwise before they entered Communist lands.[88]

While persons close to the Chungking government had trouble accepting their positive portrayal of the situation at Yenan, Stein's and Forman's reports about communism and opium were sound. Allegations to the contrary were intended to discredit the Communists and possibly prepare the way for future anti-Communist military operations. It did appear that, where possible, Chiang was saving his best troops to do battle with the Communists. He only reluctantly decided in April 1944 to send the Y-Force, a detachment of nearly 72,000 American-equipped troops from Yunnan, into Burma to support Stilwell's drive to retake Myitkyina. (The strength of the Y-Force later dwindled to about 15,000 men.) Also in April, the Japanese launched their first major offensive in some time, Operation Ichigō, in an attempt to destroy Chinese-American air bases in South and East China. The offensive threatened the war effort when Nationalist forces adopted a largely passive role. The Communists employed guerrilla tactics and profited from Ichigō by seizing additional territory and in the process establishing relations with America's so-called Dixie Mission, which arrived at Yenan in July 1944.[89]

Eastman concludes that "Operation Ichigō caused even the people to lose confidence in Chiang." They thereby increasingly supported Yenan's reform programs, which, in the words of a U.S. Army intelligence report, did not live off the people and the country. Merrill Steele Ady, a minister of the Church of Christ in China who worked for the OSS, similarly found the KMT out of touch with the Chinese people. Raymond P. Ludden, one of the Foreign Service officers on assignment with the Dixie Mission, summed up the popular appeal of the Communists: "The simple Communist program of decent treatment, fundamental civil rights, sufficient food, and sufficient clothing for the peasants has brought about genuine unity between the Eighth Route Army and the people." Cementing the relationship was the willingness of Communist forces to engage the enemy.[90]

The decline in Chiang's stature contributed to the revival of opium problems by the end of the war. Opium-related corruption reappeared among KMT politicians, troops, and independent militarists. Even after the pro-Chiang Patrick J. Hurley had replaced Gauss as ambassador, the U.S. embassy termed "factual" a story—which but for KMT censorship would have appeared in the *Hsin Hua Jih Pao* (New China Daily), the major Communist party paper in Chungking—telling of the reemergence of opium operations from cultivation to sale without visible opposition by Kuomintang authorities.[91]

This state of affairs made compromise even less likely in China's deteriorating internal situation. In time, the lack of unity would mean trouble for the Western powers as they sought to design a postwar world in which China was projected to play a significant role. How could a nation largely at war with itself help shape the new global order promised by an Allied victory? And how could the West devise a security policy to safeguard its vital interests in a region where its influence was arguably on the decline? That is, if the Chinese were not able or willing to defend an American-cum-British update of the Washington system, what relevance did it have for other Asians? What Christopher Thorne has described as a problem in Japanese-Western relations before Pearl Harbor became an equally serious matter in relations with China and the rest of Asia: "the problem of finding a basis for coexistence among interdependent states in a multicultural world."[92]

Opium and American Anticolonialism

Roosevelt's anticolonial stance acknowledged that international relations in Asia after the war would have to take on a multicultural dimension. The West's subsequent loss of stature could scarcely have been foreseen earlier in the war when Roosevelt determined that colonial rule had no future. While strongly disagreeing with the president, no European power was in any position to object strenuously to his assessment. Churchill implored Roosevelt in August 1942, referring to the upcoming first anniversary of the Atlantic Charter, not "to give it a wider interpretation than was agreed between us at the time. Its proposed application to Asia and Africa requires much thought."[93]

As an able bureaucrat and administrator, Harry Anslinger was giving considerable thought to what the demise of colonial rule meant for the future of international opium control. For more than a decade, he had turned problematic situations to his personal or organizational advantage. In the 1930s, for example, he overcame efforts to reduce the authority of his bureau, and by the time America entered the war against the Axis, Anslinger was indispensable to the conduct of U.S. narcotics foreign policy. The course of the war, with the need to maintain a reliable source of narcotics, further enhanced his power. Anslinger also arranged for the records and key personnel of the Per-

manent Central Opium Board and the Drug Supervisory Body to be transferred to the United States for the duration of the conflict.[94] The next logical
move would entail an effort to reduce opium consumption.

In late 1942 and early 1943, Anslinger presided over meetings about the
postwar fate of opium-smoking monopolies in the Far Eastern territories of
European powers. He showed no sympathy for smokers who might suddenly
be deprived of their usual pipe of opium, noting that "monopolies had never
succeeded in keeping the smuggler out." Those in attendance on 4 December,
including Helen Moorehead, Herbert May, George Morlock, and Victor Hoo,
agreed that Great Britain held the key to the success of the projected endeavor,
since curtailing opium smoking in Burma might induce other imperial powers
to adopt a similar course of action. Moorehead presciently warned that the
British would surely see the issue as a domestic matter not susceptible to
outside influence.[95]

At a subsequent meeting in January, Anslinger declared that the poor performance in 1942 of the armed forces in the Far Eastern territories "was the
result of the opium-smoking habit" and averred that the Four Freedoms were
inconsistent with the sale of opium. His strong feelings aside, Anslinger realized that the European powers had to be persuaded that eliminating the monopolies constituted sound policy despite its potential economic and political
costs.[96] How would the British, for example, handle the likely outbreak of civil
disorder once a policy of complete suppression was decided on? And how
would anticipated losses in revenue be overcome?

Since these questions did not admit of easy answers, the Foreign Policy
Association called for a further meeting with Dutch and British officials present. The Foreign Office, aware of the prior deliberations, judged it prudent to
discuss opium smoking with other interested governments in order to influence the content of an agenda for any formal talks.[97] Malcolm Delevingne was
skeptical about what a multilateral meeting could accomplish and succeeded
in getting the British embassy to send only as an observer its second secretary,
Cecil E. King.[98]

What transpired at the meeting, held in March, convinced the embassy that
it had erred in not sending someone of greater standing. Anslinger dominated
the talks by discussing the short-term problem of what to do about opium
smoking in territories recaptured from the Japanese and the longer-range issues of monopolies and the general opium question. He held up the KMT's
antiopium program as a model for others to follow and argued that the Chinese felt stronger about controlling opium than about extraterritoriality
(which had recently been formally ended by treaty). Colonel C. H. L. Shar-

man, chief of Canada's narcotics bureau and long one of Anslinger's strongest supporters, observed that if the powers could count on production controls in China, then the monopolies could be put out of business. Otherwise, it was useless to ask the British or the Dutch to act against their interests.[99]

N. A. J. de Voogd of the Commission for the Netherlands East Indies in the United States concurred, noting that until smuggling ceased to be a major problem, only gradual restrictions on smoking would be possible. When Anslinger asked King if he had anything to say, the secretary admitted his ignorance of the subject but promised to convey the substance of the talks to higher embassy personnel. Determined not to be so ill-prepared for any future meetings, Lord Halifax, who had replaced Lord Lothian as ambassador to the United States, informed Anthony Eden that such gatherings were "attended and conducted by responsible persons . . . who may acquire unfavourable impressions of British policy in the absence of a defence or at least an exposition of the British case."[100]

Lord Halifax saw the meeting "as a reflection of the great and growing importance of the United States in international affairs." Officials in London believed that the Americans, and possibly the Chinese, had seized on the opium-smoking issue as part of an effort to promote the decline of British prestige in Asia. The events at Cairo later that year in no way disabused the British of their fears, as we have seen. F. K. Roberts of the Colonial Office argued that Americans "attach disproportionate importance to the prohibition of opium smoking while the Chinese Government, for all their failure hitherto to suppress smoking effectively in their own territories, are likely to make political capital out of any failure by His Majesty's Government to consider suppressing opium smoking in British Far Eastern possessions."[101]

The Americans failed to produce a common understanding at the March meeting. Undaunted, Morlock suggested that the State, War, Navy, and Treasury departments announce that on liberation of occupied areas, the United States would seize existing opium stocks and close all operating opium shops. The departments soon reached a basic agreement on policy although Secretary of the Navy Frank Knox observed that, rather than force a confrontation with the laws of liberated territories, which was a distinct possibility, Allied forces might adopt an interim policy of suppression on the basis of military necessity.[102]

Secretary Henry Morgenthau, Jr., of the Treasury Department minimized Knox's added warning about the literal costs of suppression, believing that the Japanese "have taken over the monopoly system in its entirety and have probably encouraged consumption." In support of the United States, the Chinese announced that their forces would "carry out vigorously the policy of suppression of opium smoking and close any agencies having monopolies of the sale of opium in the areas to be occupied by Chinese forces, without regard to whom the territory belonged." As in the cases of Burma and French Indochina, such action was certain to provide clandestine income for Chinese occupation forces—troops that in any event were not altogether welcome in either place.[103]

Finally, on 21 September 1943, the State Department sent an aide-mémoire concerning opium-smoking monopolies to the British and Dutch governments. It announced a common policy of opposition to opium smoking and the operation of monopolies in recaptured Far Eastern areas and possessions. Eden had hoped for a rather less clear-cut statement, one that accepted suppression as a long-term goal. Instead, participants at an interdepartmental meeting at the Home Office agreed to eliminate monopoly activities in Malaya, Hong Kong, and Sarawak and, after appropriate consultation, in Ceylon and Burma. In fact, Burmese authorities appeared to favor a policy of prohibition, but nothing would be done in India for some time. Already, the British knew, the Dutch were prepared to announce a policy of total prohibition on opium smoking in the Netherlands East Indies. Only the French position remained a mystery.[104]

U.S. policy had triumphed. Great Britain and the Netherlands made a joint announcement of their new positions on 10 November. In addition to statements on opium smoking and monopolies, both governments announced that the only acceptable trade in narcotics included drugs for medical and scientific purposes.[105] While Washington's success, or more accurately Morlock's and Anslinger's, achieved one of the longtime goals of U.S. narcotics foreign policy, the victory would not quickly be translated into a tangible accomplishment. U.S. policy had been made with little regard for local conditions in Upper Burma, for example, where cultivation and consumption coexisted easily. Underlying assumptions about the need to prohibit opium smoking reflected a mentality of paternalism and a presumption of cultural superiority, both of which were then under attack in Asia. Even as Japan's imperial intentions became increasingly clear to their fellow Asians, the anti-Western sentiments embodied in Tokyo's New Order remained something of a rallying cry for colonial peoples.

Public opposition to opium gave further impetus to Burmese agitation for complete independence, although Burma had no doubt profited from the operation of the opium monopoly. Authorities dismissed it with relative ease as a vestige of the colonial period. Declarations against opium must have emboldened officials in Rangoon when they contemplated the difficulty of dealing with minority peoples in Upper Burma. The authorities now had an additional weapon to employ as they endeavored to bring the hill tribes under control.[106]

Malcolm Delevingne believed that the decision on opium would serve well future Anglo-American interests in Asia. Other policymakers, perhaps more in tune with the wartime tensions between the two allies, were less sanguine about its impact. W. T. Annam of the Burma Office complained that the opium question "is, strictly speaking, a matter of internal administration in a British possession." One Foreign Office minute minimized the U.S. role in what was to some officials an unwanted change in policy: "The only legitimate American interest . . . will be their desire to protect their troops from contracting dope habits and it is presumably on that point of view alone that we shall ask Americans for their comments on the instructions which the Burma Office and the Colonial Office will draw up [regarding prohibition]."[107]

Behind this rhetorical bravado, the British hoped that the opium situation in China and Southeast Asia would not take a turn for the worse while they and other colonial powers were coming to terms with resurgent independence movements. Roger Makins, who later served as British ambassador to Washington in the mid-1950s, attempted to get some indication from the French Committee of National Liberation in Algiers regarding its position on postwar opium smoking in French Indochina. In response, the French promised at most to adhere to the "principle" of absolute suppression.[108]

In retrospect, it is clear that Britain and France, by engaging in considerable self-delusion about the dramatic changes on the horizon in the political structure of postwar Southeast Asia, were vainly trying to restore something of their imperial glory. Great Britain, as it turned out, was better prepared psychologically to cut its colonial losses, however difficult that was in the short term. France, though, wanted to find a middle way so that its presence in Indochina would not easily be eclipsed. One part of that effort after mid-1945 would involve nominally accepting the U.S. position on opium smoking and monopolies while continuing to act as before. In the cauldron of revolution and nationalism that marked much of Asia after the Second World War, such a transparent strategy was bound to fail.

In fairness to the often-maligned French, it must be asked whether other Western powers had sounder plans for pursuing their interests in postwar Asia. How, for example, were the British going to revive their economic position? Would they not, even more than during the war, have to link their fortunes to the security interests of the United States? Or could officials in London accept a greatly diminished role in Asia?

As for the United States, postwar security interests across the Pacific became entwined in various ways with the unexpected consequences of American programs for opium control and the fate of European colonies. Elizabeth Washburn Wright, a longtime, perceptive observer of the international opium scene, foresaw this eventuality perhaps as well as anyone else. Long before the surrender of Japan, she tried to prevent an administrative change in the State Department shifting jurisdiction of opium issues from the Far Eastern Division to the new Division of Labor Relations: "I do hope the Department will heed my appeal and will reconsider a move that could but weaken the power of the new drive about to be undertaken in the East in an attempt to protect thousands of American troops already in Asia and to forestall the possibility of opium infection to the thousands that will follow for months if not years to come—to whom in all likelihood will be left the final clearing up and restoring of order in Asia."[109]

Given the state of Sino-American relations in the autumn of 1944, it is noteworthy that this remarkably prophetic document should find its way into the papers of V. K. Wellington Koo. More Westernized than most of his compatriots, Koo accepted the need for an interdependent relationship with foreign powers. In the realm of opium control, he had worked closely at Geneva with Blanco, Fuller, and Anslinger in the 1930s (and with Elizabeth Wright earlier when she served as an assessor with the OAC). This experience convinced Koo that strict control was in the best interest of China. He did not mind that the United States led the way, but neither, for that matter, did Chiang Kai-shek and the Kuomintang hierarchy. "The opium problem," Koo wrote, "is, like peace, indivisible."[110]

This perspective supported the tendency in Washington to believe—erroneously, it turned out—that Chinese officialdom shared a common agenda regarding opium control,[111] even though China's special relationship with the poppy had become manifest again by the end of the war. While serving as ambassador in Washington after a stint in London, Koo deflected criticism of lax opium control by China while encouraging the United States to provide material assistance vital to his government's survival. In these important ways, then, Koo agreed with Elizabeth Wright that the mission of the United States in Asia following the war amounted to nothing less than acting as the guardian of order.

Conclusion

The days of sentimental attachment were nevertheless drawing to a close. Chiang was being held up to a critical standard that found him wanting, to say the least. On the eve of his departure from China, General Stilwell opined: "What they ought to do is shoot the G-mo and Ho [Ying-chin] and the rest of the gang." From Yenan, John Stewart Service wrote of the KMT's failure and the "unrealistic assumption that [Chiang] is China and that he is necessary to our cause." After barely one month in China, Major General Albert C. Wedemeyer termed Chiang and his followers "impotent and confounded." And at the end of November 1944, Churchill warned Roosevelt that Chiang's plan to remove his forces then operating in Burma would "jeopardize the success of the whole campaign."[112] The growing exasperation with Chiang roughly coincided with reports about the renewal of opium-related difficulties for his regime.

Regarding U.S. policy and China's domestic troubles, Theodore H. White and Annalee Jacoby wrote: "[W]e created the very thing we feared most, a huge organized mass of Asiatic peasants believing that America was their enemy and Russia their only friend."[113] Notwithstanding the journalistic hyperbole, White and Jacoby identified the central problem for the United States in the aftermath of war: How could Washington align itself with the burgeoning aspirations of Asian nationalism? When Roosevelt earlier proclaimed an anticolonial stance, he hoped to face the future aligned with the peoples of Asia. In the context of the emerging cold war and the requirements of American security policy, the several opium cultures in the region would not make the task any simpler for his successor.

EIGHT

Opium and Security Policy
in Postwar Asia through 1949

Having helped to preserve Allied security during the war, U.S. narcotics officials expected to concentrate on more routine matters in the postwar years. Indeed, they still perceived drug control as an important national security concern, but Harry J. Anslinger and his colleagues had no trouble adjusting to a somewhat lesser role in the policymaking process. That the advocates of opium control had found a niche within a rapidly changing security environment reveals a great deal about how they and other foreign policy officials viewed the world in which they operated.

The wave of the future in postwar Asia was one of nationalism. With few exceptions this meant, in the words of one U.S. diplomat, that "there are dynamic trends easily visible today which foreshadow the eventual dissolution of Western political domination" in much of Asia.[1] This alarming, prospective development seemed no small irony to policymakers in London and Washington who had envisioned a very different world. Churchill had paid obeisance to Roosevelt's Four Freedoms but made it clear that he would never preside over the destruction of the British Empire. Of the prime minister's relationship with the American people, Lord Halifax wrote that "he was expected, if not assumed, to cherish sentiments which the American mind, priding itself on its progressive vigour and virtue, must inevitably judge reactionary." But neither, to be sure, was it the intention of the United States simply to quit Asia and the Pacific at war's end. The pursuit of a revitalized international order precluded that possibility.[2]

To remain strategically entrenched across the Pacific carried with it risks for the foreign and security policies of both Western nations. One source of difficulty proved to be the nature of the Anglo-American union itself. The United States, through the acidulous person of General Joseph W. Stilwell, had not been inclined to work as closely as the British wished with Admiral Lord Louis

Mountbatten's South East Asia Command (SEAC). Where Americans saw "selfish imperialism" as Britain's primary motivation, Whitehall saw renewed responsibilities for economic welfare, defense, and political administration. The disparity in power between the two nations guaranteed, however, that the American opposition to empire would define the relationship until policymakers found the basis for an accommodation or one was imposed by outside events. In that sense, Britain's virtual bankruptcy after the war ironically appears as something of a godsend. Economic assistance helped forge over time a global partnership that was based on a more realistic appraisal of British security needs.[3]

This long-term consideration could not resolve the immediate question about what to do with colonial possessions. Roosevelt preferred the idea of a trusteeship prior to the bestowing of complete independence. The president discussed the idea with Churchill and Stalin, particularly as it pertained to French Indochina, when they met at Teheran. Moreover, the fate of India was never far from Roosevelt's mind—to Churchill's great consternation. At Yalta, the Big Three finally worked out a trusteeship formula that, in retrospect, seems to have circumscribed the future of European colonialism.[4]

The British did not see American objectives as altruistic. Roosevelt assumed, suspected Anthony Eden, that "former colonial territories, once free of their masters, would become politically and economically dependent upon the United States." Similarly, the French in Indochina grew restive in the summer of 1945 as they witnessed the reluctance of the American military mission to restore French sovereignty. Before the war, David Scott of the American Department in the Foreign Office doubted that the United States was capable of "thinking imperially." But R. A. Butler demurred and retorted: "I am certain she will be so thinking within a decade."[5] The wartime expansion of American power in Asia, it is safe to say, did nothing to inspire confidence at Whitehall about postwar alliance priorities across the Pacific.

Another urgent problem for the Western powers concerned the Nationalist-Communist dispute in China. Despite Britain's cautious wartime attitude, some Americans believed that London sought a return to a dominant economic position among Westerners there.[6] To officials in Washington who reassessed the situation after Roosevelt's death, the stakes in postwar China were far greater than just economic rewards; they involved larger questions of regional if not international security. With Stilwell's recall in November 1944, Isaiah Berlin, writing from Washington, had suggested that China's "extraordinary spell" over President Harry S. Truman's willingness to accommodate Chiang Kai-shek's government proved him a poor prophet.[7] This development portended as well the retention of American forces in Asia and, as Elizabeth Washburn Wright had feared, their concomitant exposure to opium.

To the extent that Western prestige in the Far East depended on the maintenance of political order, the West found itself at odds with Asian nationalism in mid-1945. Former colonial powers clung to an ethos of paternalism, suggesting that their lessons in self-government were not yet over. As for the United States, administration officials believed that self-determination must not conflict with nascent security imperatives resulting from tensions with the Soviet Union. In fact, the Office of Strategic Services proposed not the elimination, but the liberalization of colonial rule as a way "to check Soviet influence in the stimulation of colonial revolt." In such a policymaking environment, the nationalistic aspirations of colonial peoples played an admonitory role regarding the future of international relations in Asia, but the warnings were not easily heard in the West.[8]

For present purposes, attempts to place nationalistic aspirations within a decision-making calculus would have been more meaningful had policymakers taken into account how Asians themselves actually regarded opium. Certainly those perspectives were far from uniform. As the war drew to a close in the Asian theater, nowhere was the importance of opium for understanding the future any clearer than in Burma.

Prelude: Lessons from Upper Burma

Having employed tribes in guerrilla operations in Burma, Colonel William R. Peers and Dean Brelis of OSS Detachment 101 recounted the role of opium in their mission:

> Our decision to use opium was based on the fact that it would give our troops a certain amount of freedom, of buying power; we did not question it as just or unjust. . . . Simply stated, paper currency and even silver were often useless, as there was nothing to buy with money; opium, however, was the form of payment which everybody used. Not to use it as a barter would spell an end to our operations. . . . If opium could be useful in achieving victory, the pattern was clear. We would use opium.

To all under the command of Peers, Americans and Kachin Rangers alike, opium was just one more means to a vital end.[9] Likewise in western China, the United States, using opium as the medium of exchange, persuaded local farmers to protect navigational aids used to guide planes carrying military supplies to Chungking.[10] It was the situation in Burma, though, that captured the attention of prominent officials in Washington.

In late 1943, when Colonel William J. Donovan, head of the OSS, ordered the expansion of guerrilla operations to recover the area around Myitkyina, a contingent of Kachin Rangers serving with Detachment 101 assured the presence of opium in the operations.[11] Narcotics officials feared that American soldiers might smoke opium, which was by definition "smuggled" opium since Burma's opium-smoking dens were off limits to Allied personnel. Yet, as Richard Dunlop of Detachment 101 pointed out in his memoir, *Behind Japanese Lines*, opium was available to anyone who wanted to smoke it.[12]

What was occurring in Burma was significant for three reasons. First, Treasury Department officials felt that the British were violating the agreement of November 1943 by not cracking down on opium in Burma. Meanwhile, British authorities in SEAC and the War Office concluded that little could be done until after the war; thus, eating and smoking opium would continue. While Mountbatten accepted this assessment, he realized that anything other than a policy of suppression would be viewed "by ill-disposed critics as amounting to domestic economic protection" of an enterprise the British earlier had agreed to abandon.[13]

Second, Congress, hoping to pressure the colonial powers into implementing the agreement, passed the Judd Resolution in 1944 authorizing the president to ask all opium-producing nations to limit poppy cultivation to legitimate purposes. Great Britain, on behalf of Burma, was among those receiving a request from the State Department. L. Mainwaring Taylor of the Directorate of Civil Affairs in the War Office saw U.S. pressure as "misinformed American public sentiment . . . interfer[ing] with our policy," which "open[s] the door to similar interference in any other sphere of Imperial domestic policy." Only in 1946 did Britain agree to comply with the American request.[14]

Further pressure on London to get into line on opium control came when the United States asked Britain to participate in an international conference to write an opium limitation agreement. Because India and Burma were unprepared to restrict production to medical and scientific purposes, the Foreign Office rejected the idea, which it otherwise viewed sympathetically. Also, Commissioner Anslinger of the Federal Bureau of Narcotics informed the Kuomintang about British antiopium activities in Burma, an action that may have helped to undercut British efforts to recoup prewar prestige in China. In Anslinger's view, British arguments for a policy of gradualism were "worn out and untenable."[15]

The Burma situation was significant in a third way that went beyond the confines of Anglo-American relations. The persistence of several opium cultures indicated how nationalist or, in this case, tribal loyalties might hinder the realization of Western objectives. Simply put, expectations in Washington about postwar drug control had scant impact on those peoples of Burma who were accustomed to an autonomous existence in their daily lives. However, convinced of the importance of their efforts, U.S. policymakers could scarcely believe that the hill people would not soon share their antiopium position. Such was the strained logic of opium control policy.

The United States had long looked to source countries to solve its narcotics problems. Yet precious little opium from Southeast Asia had ever reached American shores. Moreover, OSS, State Department, and FBN officials were acutely aware of the difficulties the British would encounter in bringing opium control to the Shan States, the Kachin Hills, and Kengtung near the border with Thailand. Sino-Burmese animosity placed an additional obstacle in the path of control, making it more difficult to fashion a security policy for the region as a whole because of the marked potential for local conflict.[16] Stability at the Burma border became even less certain when Chiang Kai-shek forced Lung Yun out of power in October 1945. But again, considerations such as these had little impact on the making of U.S. narcotics or security policy for the region.

Japan as an American Success

Japan was the one place where the United States linked opium control and security imperatives without regard for British (or French) policy priorities or untimely interference from ethnolinguistic minorities. This opportunity grew out of U.S. strategic planning in 1944, which emphasized independence of action against Japan. Despite Soviet promises to enter the Pacific war after victory in Europe, civilian and military planners assumed that the United States would dominate the peace process.[17]

In characteristic style, Anslinger made clear in the autumn of 1945 his view of the Japanese and his intentions concerning drug control in occupied Japan: "I never trusted them, I don't trust them now, and I've yet to meet the man who can tell me why anyone should ever trust them in the future. Now that the war's over, somebody may find some good Japanese somewhere. Well, all I can say is that we'll still search them—to the bottoms of their soybean barrels and the insides of their shoes. There won't be any peace treaties with dope smugglers."[18]

Anslinger's nativist remarks were intended to keep the drug issue in the public eye as one aspect of postwar security problems in Asia. At the same time, the commissioner was too skilled a bureaucrat to stop at mere rhetoric, however uncompromising. While denouncing the Japanese narcotics record on the one hand, he also helped to shape a policy for occupation forces that would prevent Japan from threatening any nation's stability with narcotics in the foreseeable future. Years later he termed this endeavor one of the major accomplishments of his tenure in office. In a real sense, then, he did manage to "find some good Japanese somewhere."[19]

FBN and State Department officials waged their offensive against Japan and narcotics on several fronts. First, they joined with the Foreign Policy Association and the governments of Canada and China to continue the work of the OAC after the war. While the organization of the United Nations Economic and Social Council was under way, Anslinger and George A. Morlock made certain that its Commission on Narcotic Drugs (CND) would be guided by an American agenda.[20] At the CND's first meeting in November 1946, Anslinger called for the reestablishment of international and national drug controls, restrictions on raw narcotic materials, and the control of synthetic drugs. Colonel C. H. L. Sharman of Canada then raised the issue of narcotics control in Japan.[21] Having received a troubling report from occupation headquarters in Tokyo about drug problems, Anslinger probably gave the details to Sharman for his appraisal. Participants at the meeting urged the Permanent Central Opium Board to monitor Japanese narcotics transactions, a step that Major William H. Coles of the Home Office strongly endorsed.[22]

Second, the United States provided much of the information on which the International Military Tribunal for the Far East developed its case against Japan for using narcotics as a weapon of war. Doing so provided an additional means of restructuring Japanese politics and society so that Japan might ultimately take its place in the Western security regime in Asia. Anslinger laid out the steps necessary to hold Japan accountable for opium operations in the Greater East Asia Co-Prosperity Sphere: obtain opium export records from Bushire on the Persian Gulf and import certificates from Japan, get Japanese narcotics production data and compare the statistics with Drug Supervisory Body estimates, get Japanese government licenses for the manufacture of heroin in the Tientsin Concession, borrow from the Chinese a film taken in the factory district in Tientsin, inspect relevant OAC records, make M. R. Nicholson's dispatches available to the IMTFE, supply U.S. consular reports from posts in Manchuria, and discover whether there were unpublished League of Nations records.[23]

Some of the documents sought from Geneva did not exist, while many Japanese records had been lost in a fire following an air raid in May 1945. More promising was the discovery in Seoul of a 1943 report about opium supply and demand in the Japanese Empire. Administrators of several monopoly bureaus in Formosa, Kwantung, and Manchuria were then faced with inadequate supplies, the suggested remedy for which was temporarily to increase poppy growth in Chosen despite opposition by local authorities. Wayland L. Speer, a narcotics agent at occupation headquarters, sent a copy of the report to Anslinger and the International Prosecution Section, Narcotics Division, Supreme Commander for the Allied Powers (SCAP).[24]

The report's contents proved less damning than Anslinger and the war crimes tribunal would have liked. It disclosed that smuggling impaired the work of the monopolies—as it had often done no matter under whose jurisdiction they operated. Also, the registration of addicts for treatment was a slow and incomplete process, which indicated the enduring attraction of opium smoking to millions of Asians. Finally, the report contained a plan for phasing out opium production in Korea.[25] To an extent then, the report cast doubt on the assumption of U.S. officials and the IMTFE that Japan had deliberately sought to narcotize the inhabitants of the territories it occupied.

Nonetheless, the IMTFE included crimes involving opium in the particulars of its indictment against twenty-eight Japanese leaders. Specifically, opium came under the purview of Group One, pertaining to the perpetration of a conspiracy by the accused. Charging that successive Japanese governments brutally sought to weaken native populations throughout Asia, the indictment proclaimed:

> The Japanese Government secretly provided large sums of money, which, together with profits from the government-sponsored traffic in opium and other narcotics . . . were used by agents of the Japanese Government for all the above-mentioned [purposes]. . . . Further, revenue from the above-mentioned traffic in opium and other narcotics was used to finance the preparation for and waging of the wars of aggression set forth in this Indictment and to establish and finance the puppet governments set up by the Japanese Government in the various occupied territories.

The indictment asserted that Japan had violated international antiopium accords, including The Hague agreements of 1912 and 1913, the Second Geneva Convention of 1925, and the Manufacturing Limitation Convention of 1931.[26]

In its finding on issues of fact, the tribunal held that there had been a conspiracy to wage an aggressive war in East Asia, the western and southwestern Pacific, the Indian Ocean, and certain islands therein. Connected to the opium traffic in occupied lands were the Japanese army, the Foreign Ministry, and the Asian Development Board.[27] The tribunal's judgment did not specifically mention the charge of narcotization, but prosecutors believed it was subsumed within the charge of conspiracy. In its summation, the prosecution asserted that the "march of Japan through China brought with it, as it had earlier in Manchuria, the enforcement of the Japanese policy of narcotization in the occupied areas for the purpose of raising revenue for Japan's plans of aggression and of debauching the people to keep them subservient to the will and desire of Japan." As for the production of opium in Manchuria, Japan found it a convenient base for carrying on international drug-trafficking operations.[28]

The finding of guilt on the charge of conspiracy accorded nicely with American plans for Japan's role in postwar Asia. As a formerly aggressive nation on the road to reform, Japan, convinced of the probity of its new direction, could provide an instructive example to other Asian nations about how to redefine their own self-interest.[29] That the case of Japan might not be ideographic for, or even relevant to, other nations did not occur to policymakers in Washington. Thus, it scarcely mattered that the conspiracy charge and finding possessed severe legal and procedural defects. One of the dissenting justices, India's Radha Binod Pal, averred that "there is no direct evidence of this conspiracy or design."[30]

Anslinger and other officials nevertheless counted on a determination of conspiracy in order to link more closely drug control and broader policy objectives. First, they were able to incorporate concerns about opium into the overall design of security policy for the region. The occupation of Japan demonstrated how domestic regimes could adopt vigorous control programs, one purpose of which was to protect U.S. forces from drugs. Second, on its own terms, officials saw American-style narcotics control as a rational choice for public policy on opium by governments friendly to the United States.

How, given these considerations, did General Douglas MacArthur's command fashion a drug control policy in occupied Japan? Anslinger, not surprisingly, drew up a program of opium control under which poppy cultivation was prohibited. The office of the supreme commander would authorize all drug importation; exportation and manufacture of opiates was forbidden. The Supreme Command would dispose of existing stocks of narcotics except those for medical or scientific purposes, and detailed records of all narcotics-related activities were to be kept. These regulations were in place in Japan by mid-October 1945, allowing SCAP to create a system of centralized control. By

1948, a new Narcotics Control Law had taken effect in Japan, overseen by the Ministry of Welfare.[31] The centralized system worked so well that occupation authorities permitted the Japanese to process stocks of raw narcotics into medical drugs.[32]

As much as anything else, Anslinger and Speer wanted to head off the recurrence of smuggling. No later than March 1948 SCAP personnel were holding special drug control training schools in Tokyo for that purpose. The effort came none too soon, for illicit heroin then was making its way into Japan. SCAP records indicate that the heroin was of Asian origin but from an indeterminate source. The Center for Military History's monograph series on the U.S. occupation (written after 1950) flatly asserted that it was reaching Japan from the Chinese mainland "to finance [Communist] party activities."[33] The difference between the two accounts cannot be resolved, but the latter accorded well with the view of the opium situation in Asia that Anslinger would espouse in the 1950s.

Disappointment in China

Before Japan's drug control machinery was firmly in place, Anslinger's closeness to Victor Hoo Chi-tsai led him to hope that China might take the lead in a regional antiopium campaign.[34] Unfortunately for Hoo, Anslinger, Morlock, and China's friends at the Foreign Policy Association, the Kuomintang was in no position to do so. The resignation of an embittered Patrick Hurley as U.S. ambassador in December 1945 and the likelihood of an open civil war in China made it impossible for China to serve as a role model for the purpose of drug control.[35] U.S. consul Arthur Ringwalt, who had not always managed to keep from running afoul of Hurley, blamed Chiang for China's problems. The generalissimo, Ringwalt recalled, "was dumb, and his methods were not very clever. . . . He just built up his own little clique."[36]

Specifically concerning opium, Chiang's shortcomings should have raised misgivings among Americans about China's ability to keep its own house in order, let alone act as a guide for others. KMT opium laws were having little effect in Yunnan as the war neared an end. Missionaries protested to the authorities in Chungking but to no avail.[37] The province was "sodden with opium" as a result of the partial occupation by Japanese forces and because of continued planting of poppies by native tribes and Chinese. Provincial chairman Lung Yun profited from the business while cracking down on opium traders not in his favor. Increasingly, he presented an obstacle to plans for national economic rehabilitation, so it was not surprising when Chiang forced him out of office in October.[38]

The displacement of Lung Yun did not make his successor, Lu Han, any more tractable, since opium meant prosperity for the people of Yunnan. The KMT, again ensconced at Nanking, recognized the limits of its authority and encouraged the cultivation of opium in order to defray the costs of provincial administration. Granted its mild ethnocentricity, John Stewart Service's colorful depiction of Yunnan as "a screwball sort of place" accurately captured the perceptions of many Americans at the time. Opium caravans moved freely about the province, sometimes aided by generous bribes for Kuomintang inspectors.[39]

More promising for U.S. drug policy objectives was the public burning of nearly 1 million ounces of opium in Peiping in January 1946. Government officials invited foreign diplomats and Christian missionaries to witness the event. Alfred Dixon Heininger, who helped plan the burning, recalled the impression that a gust of wind made on the Chinese who were watching the conflagration: "They thought it was the opium devils ascending in the whirlwind." To Westerners in attendance, the operation symbolized the return of opium control to China, especially, they hoped, in the north.[40]

Unfortunately, the situation was far from being so clear-cut. Virtual anarchy defined the opium trade in southern Kweichow, many small factories were illegally producing morphine and heroin in the Shanghai area, and Tu Yueh-sheng was again making his presence felt in the business.[41] Moreover, getting reliable information about conditions in Manchuria was all but impossible and smuggling was resuming from China to the United States, possibly by way of military personnel in the Philippines. So concerned was Anslinger, who complained that "we are not getting any information from the Chinese and our own information leaves much to be desired," that he asked the State Department to place Melvin Hanks of U.S. Customs on the staff of General George C. Marshall. John Carter Vincent, head of the Division of Far Eastern Affairs, got Hanks appointed assistant Treasury attaché in China for the duration of the Marshall mission.[42]

By the time Hanks reached China, the internal situation had deteriorated despite Marshall's efforts. Marshall found the outlook for a peaceful resolution of China's troubles less than promising; Chiang's political and military machinations had worn out the patience of the Communists, who rejected his leadership and soon turned their anger on the United States and ultimately on Marshall himself.[43] A report prepared in the Central Bank of China in the autumn of 1946 made the case for major reforms if Communist influence among the people was to be contained. The report's description of areas held by the KMT revealed conditions like those that previously had led Chiang's government toward dependence on opium for revenue.[44]

From the embassy desk of Counselor W. Walton Butterworth, of whom Dean Acheson thought highly, came an alarming dispatch. "It is clear," Butterworth wrote, "that total consumption of opium in China each year is very large and that as a result the demand for opium and therefore the supply are very large." The message was inescapable: China was surrendering again to the allure of the opium poppy. Antiopium laws remained on the books but were not being enforced. Not only were government soldiers transporting opium, but also some generals were paying their troops with the forbidden drug. Perhaps 40 million Chinese used opium in one form or another, and that number showed no signs of decreasing.[45]

Other reports reaching Washington could easily have passed for recycled dispatches from the early to mid-1930s. They described a poppy belt extending from Kiangsi, Fukien, and Kwangtung to Sikang in which more than 215,000 acres were under cultivation; no reliable estimates were available for the extent of growth in Yunnan. Antiopium laws were termed "paper programs," while lax enforcement "brings into direct question the good faith of the opium suppression authorities." And where Kuomintang influence advanced in the north, dependence on opium revenues apparently went along.[46]

Government leaders in Nanking admitted the return of opium problems by announcing that they hoped to suppress the evil within two years. Revelations about worsening conditions and Nanking's lack of response must have caused Anslinger and Morlock great anxiety. One of the central parts of their carefully designed program for opium control in Asia was inexplicably, to their way of thinking, falling apart.[47] Hoping to change the situation, Anslinger appealed to Dr. T. H. Lew, then in charge of China's Opium Suppression Commission. As a result, the Ministry of the Interior, which housed the commission, set up an office in Shanghai to facilitate the exchange of information. Even so, Ambassador John Leighton Stuart, who tempered his usual support for the generalissimo with the knowledge that opponents had reason to doubt Chiang's "patriotism and nobility of character," termed the overall suppression effort "ineffective and irresponsible."[48] Claims that narcotics were reaching Korea from Manchuria, along with stories about "grave" conditions in Sikang, Szechwan, and Yunnan, starkly illustrated the eclipse of Kuomintang authority.[49]

While the Chinese situation was deteriorating, Hong Kong and Macao reemerged as international problems. The Portuguese colony especially offered a haven to opium smugglers. While smuggling of various goods also continued out of Hong Kong, the government seemed determined to combat the illegal opium trade; more than a ton of narcotics had been destroyed following the reoccupation of the colony from the Japanese.[50]

Hong Kong became important because authorities there and in Nanking accused one another of laxness in attacking the illicit opiate commerce. Noting an upswing in drug trafficking in mid-1947, U.S. consul general George D. Hopper, who knew Anslinger well, placed most of the blame on the poor enforcement of Chinese law. Anslinger, however, as he had in the prewar period, continued to see the British colony as a trouble spot. For his part, the governor of Macao sought to deflect criticism of his regime by claiming to have achieved control of smuggling, opium dens, and smoking—assertions that officials in Hong Kong strongly doubted. Hopper saw little sincerity in Macao's alleged antiopium actions, noting that "Macao has always lived by the smuggling trade, and continues to do so today."[51]

The primary task for Anslinger, though, was to extract better cooperation from his friends in Nanking. In the spring and summer of 1947, he tried to do so indirectly by requesting SCAP to submit samples of Asian opium, heroin, and morphine to the Federal Bureau of Narcotics in order to identify their country of origin. Then at the second session of the CND, he proposed that surplus medical supplies from the war, which China possessed in abundance, be destroyed to prevent their entry into illicit channels.[52]

Why did Anslinger take this particular course of action? At the same CND meeting, he openly criticized Mexico for tolerating, as he saw it, domestic opium cultivation and for failing to attack the ties between producers and underworld groups in the United States.[53] His circumspection regarding China resulted from his long association with Chinese officials; he expected them to act more in line with U.S. policy. Yet by late spring 1947, a KMT offensive against Mao Zedong's forces was weakening, notably in the Shansi-Hopei-Shantung-Honan Border Region. Also, popular resentment against the KMT had risen in the countryside, and the prospect of social reform enhanced the appeal of the Communists.[54] KMT pledges for reforms of its own, including an antiopium campaign, seemed empty by comparison.

Developments in China decidedly narrowed policy options for the United States. Secretary of State Marshall tried to buy time by sending the Wedemeyer Mission to evaluate the situation. Although a friend of China, Lieutenant General Albert C. Wedemeyer recognized the limits of what the United States could accomplish but called for a program of conditional military assistance within the framework of a government led by Chiang Kai-shek.[55]

Anslinger's actions regarding the dismal conditions in China in the summer of 1947 suggest that he may not have shared what John Lewis Gaddis calls the State Department's "strong sense of pessimism regarding the ability of the United States to influence events on the Asian mainland."[56] It is evident in retrospect that the commissioner badly misunderstood Chinese intentions. Acting on his interpretation of Chungking's antiopium campaigns of the late 1930s, he believed that the Kuomintang possessed both the will and the means to achieve fairly effective control over the internal opium trade.

Anslinger erred in his assessment of the enduring quality of the KMT's antiopium commitment. This misperception led him to think that forbearance was paying dividends when Hsia Ching-lin, China's representative to the CND, asked him in 1948 to discuss privately the illicit traffic out of China. The attachment in his belief system to a consistency that was so much at odds with the facts blinded Anslinger to the truth of China's lengthy relationship with opium. Even as Hsia was asking for the meeting, some high-ranking officials of the Kuomintang Army still in Manchuria were trafficking in opium.[57]

Indeed, Anslinger seemingly could not understand that Victor Hoo, V. K. Wellington Koo, and other Chinese with whom he dealt were far from representative of their government when it came to the issue of opium. Nelson Johnson had not suffered from such a liability; rather, he witnessed firsthand the importance of opium to the Kuomintang in time of need. Anslinger, though, clung to a distorted vision of the reliability of the KMT and thus averted the likely onset of extreme psychological stress. Even if he privately believed that officials in China were not interested in American-style opium control, and the evidence is silent on this issue, he was unable to incorporate that awareness into his policy calculations. Such a dramatic change would have amounted to a thorough reassessment of his belief system, probably forcing him to consider alternative courses of action not just in China but throughout Asia. With no ready way out of this dilemma, he adopted a strategy of defensive avoidance, or denial of the realities of the China situation, in order to cope with the inconsistencies generated by a deficient policy.

If Anslinger was not going to recommend a major revision in narcotics foreign policy, he had to find a way to explain the persistence of the illicit opium business in Asia. He needed to do so because the importance of China to his own objectives contrasted fundamentally with the lesser place then accorded Nanking in the deliberations over U.S. security policy for the region. At best, Japan would serve as a long-term model for antiopium programs in Asia; if Nanking could not provide a reliable example for other governments in the near term, then Anslinger and his colleagues had to explain why. That is, they needed a scapegoat.

The commissioner ultimately blamed the Communists for the failure of opium control in China. To do so, he had to make selective use of circumstantial evidence including allegations by the Opium Suppression Commission about poppy production and trade in Communist areas. Reports also pointed to a Communist need to earn revenue from opium, and there appeared unsubstantiated stories about Soviet-orchestrated trading of opium for strategic goods like tungsten (wolfram) and rubber as a means of bolstering Communist military activities.[58] In short, there existed material to build a case, whether factual or not, for Communist involvement with narcotics should the need to do so arise.

The collapse of the Kuomintang in 1949 gradually brought into alignment the perceptions of China held by Anslinger and other high-level policymakers. Previously, the FBN chief and major strategic planners, including Secretary of State Marshall, had retained some hope for the Kuomintang if it adopted economic and political reforms. Marshall largely shaped his views during his mission to China and listened carefully to arguments from Department of State experts such as John Carter Vincent. Even President Truman, at a press conference on 11 March 1948, called for the broadening of China's political base. In other words, U.S. officials were inclined to believe that reform, the substance of which they had rarely made explicit, could stem the tide of communism.[59]

The problem with this view was that the KMT leaders would not accept the literally radical social changes that might have preserved their authority. Yet corruption seemed rife in late Kuomintang China. Incredibly, Tu Yueh-sheng made an appeal for U.S. military and economic aid in exchange for trying to save Shanghai from the Communists.[60] Another problem for Americans was the image they had of themselves vis-à-vis the Chinese. In short, they could not believe that the Chinese would accept such an alien ideology as communism. Showing the resilience of the sentimental bond between the two nations, Secretary of State Dean Acheson wrote in the letter of transmittal with the "China White Paper" that the people of China "will throw off the foreign yoke" in favor of democratic individualism. Edwin W. Martin, who served throughout Asia before becoming the deputy director of the Office of Chinese Affairs, later observed that "we overestimated our own importance in China [and] the importance of the West as a whole."[61]

Acheson was not intensely interested in China; he focused primarily on preventing the extension of Soviet influence into Western Europe. Just the same, he and his advisers had to take into account the fact of Communist control and the trouble that meant for the Truman administration at home while they searched for a way to encourage a Sino-Soviet split. Their effort centered on the issues of trade, diplomatic recognition, and China's entry into the United Nations. To gain concessions from the United States, the Communist regime, in William W. Stueck's words, would have "to demonstrate its worthiness to enter the family of nations." For its part, Mao's regime resisted all overtures from the West suggesting the possible subversion of revolution in China.[62] Little room for accommodation existed between these two positions.

Ideological restraints also had a demonstrable impact on U.S. narcotics policy. Only weeks before the formal proclamation of the People's Republic of China on 1 October 1949, the New York Quinine and Chemical Works routinely applied for permission to import two one-pound samples of raw opium from Tsingtao; this request raised the likelihood of using opium from Communist China for American medical supplies. Anslinger summarily rejected the application and called for closer supervision of traditional smuggling channels between the mainland and Hong Kong and Japan.[63]

While the rejection of the firm's application to import opium samples appeared to be a normal decision by a governmental agency exercising proper jurisdiction, more was involved. Anslinger probably made his decision after hurried consultation with high State Department officials. So indicates a brief note in late December from Assistant Secretary of State Jack K. McFall to Senator Warren G. Magnuson of Washington.[64] As such, Anslinger's willingness to take a stand against communism, U.S. opium control policy in East Asia, and broader security policy considerations had finally coalesced. The Chinese could hardly prove themselves worthy of American largess by offering to supply narcotics to the West.

The situation doubtless reminded Anslinger of disputes with Japan in the 1930s in that an ostensibly legal commerce in drugs, as Japan had carried on, would obscure the reality of clandestine narcotics operations. The commissioner's anticommunism did not allow him to consider in an unbiased manner the offer to provide opium for medical purposes. His unflagging perception of the Communists as a threat to U.S. security interests—in this case, narcotics control—precluded him from dealing with the question on its merits and convinced him that negotiations with Beijing over drugs would be useless. Because of the cautious attitude of Acheson's State Department toward improving relations with China, policymakers at the highest levels of the administration were not greatly at odds with Anslinger about the dubious wisdom of dealing with Mao's regime and thereby prematurely conferring legitimacy on it. It was easier to follow policies supporting preconceived ideas than it was to change.[65] Similar limits also burdened America's narcotics policies in Southeast Asia in the immediate postwar years.

Opium and Nationalism in Southeast Asia

U.S. policy toward China had angered British officials on at least two counts. First of all, Washington seemed unduly suspicious of Great Britain's intentions in China, as though some variant of nineteenth-century economic domination were in the offing.[66] Moreover, Prime Minister Clement Attlee and Secretary Ernest Bevin of the Foreign Office could not understand how U.S. policy toward the Chinese civil war served the long-range strategic interests of either Western power. In that regard, the Anglo-American partnership gradually lost some of its relevance in Asia, differences over the specific case of China aside.[67] Whereas U.S. officials saw the hard realities of power and responsibility, Bevin and the Foreign Office feared the costs of naiveté or ignorance.

Bevin could have taken but small consolation in April 1949 when Acheson promised: "The U.S. henceforth will pursue a more realistic policy respecting China."[68] This admission came too late to overcome the negative effect of other differences between the two powers. Hong Kong remained a vital interest for Britain, yet Washington had not favored the return of British power after Japan's defeat. As we have seen, U.S. narcotics officials had long felt that opium control was largely a charade in the Crown Colony and ascribed this laxness to the presence of an opium-smoking monopoly along with graft and corruption in local officialdom. The British, however, blamed postwar problems with smuggling on the early demise of colonialism in the region.[69]

Probably more than any other issue, the fate of European colonies challenged the durability of the wartime Anglo-American partnership. Even by 1950, as British dependence on the United States to take the lead against communism increased, the two nations continued to disagree over the appropriate course to follow. For five years in Southeast Asia, as in China, Britain would watch with concern the evolution of U.S. security policy. Narcotics foreign policy as implemented by the Federal Bureau of Narcotics and the State Department would play a role in American security thinking and, in turn, contribute to Whitehall's misgivings about the growth of the United States as a regional power.

French Indochina

The future lines of disagreement were not evident in French Indochina at the end of the war. In talks with Charles de Gaulle in late August, Truman made it clear that he would not stand in the way of a French return to Indochina. Yet, with some Americans in Indochina working intimately with the movement for Vietnamese independence, Mountbatten saw a controversy in the making. "In fact," he informed the Joint Chiefs of Staff, "we shall find it hard to counter the accusations that our forces are remaining in the country solely in order to hold the Viet Namh [sic] Independence movement in check."[70]

In the summer of 1945, the OSS and a U.S. Army officer, probably Colonel Stephen Nordlinger, found widespread support for the Viet Minh League (VML) and apprehension over the return of French forces. The VML was prepared to accept, however, the emplacement of a French administration, under United Nations supervision, until independence. That concession was made in lieu of an American protectorate, which VML leaders hoped for but realized was impossible. Among the several prerequisites for the temporary return of French authority was a prohibition on the sale of opium.[71] Ho Chi Minh, leader of the VML, reiterated his opposition to the opium business in his well-known speech of 2 September 1945 proclaiming the independence of Vietnam. His government thereafter began to implement a thorough reform program, abolishing the hated opium and alcohol monopolies and prohibiting further use of the drugs. In an appeal to those Frenchmen of Indochina who were not enemies of Vietnam, he denounced the consumption of alcohol and opium as "disastrous calamities."[72]

Perhaps coincidentally, French authorities announced in September 1945—as they had promised U.S. officials in 1944 that they would do—their intention to suppress the smoking of opium, as had the British and the Dutch before them. Next, the French issued in mid-June 1946 a decree against the open sale of opium. Yet the outbreak of war with the VML in December drove the French to look at opium once again for its revenue potential. Large quantities of opium continued to be imported from Iran, notwithstanding the professed campaign against smoking, and at least one prominent official sought to reap the benefits of the clandestine sale of nearly four tons of opium to criminal interests in Cholon. Few persons were arrested or fined for buying or using opium.[73]

As the struggle for Indochina persisted through 1947 and into 1948, opium flowed into the French colony from Iran. This development troubled Anslinger, who believed to no avail that the Iranians had promised to cease poppy cultivation in 1946.[74] He responded by sending FBN agent William F. Tollenger, on assignment with SCAP in Tokyo, to investigate the situation. Tollenger's mission took him from Saigon to Haiphong. He was to gauge the extent of addiction, photograph alleged disintoxication centers, gather data on the sources of opium, estimate government revenue from the opium business, and provide an assessment of official attitudes regarding prohibition and law enforcement.[75]

French authorities, however, refused to cooperate with the investigation. As Tollenger reported, the inquiry disclosed:

> That the present government of French Indo-China is attempting, by means of the suppression of any and all information relative to the opium situation, by the hiding under fictitious accounts all revenues derived from opium, by means of emergency purchases of opium from external sources, by the total lack of effort to suppress the smoking of opium or of any budget for hospitalization in an effort to effect the cure for opium addiction, to maintain present revenues derived from opium as the greatest single source of revenue from any and all sources in French Indo-China at the expense of the opium addicted population.

French officials told U.S. consular personnel that "the High Commissioner [Emile Bollaert] . . . feels that it is up to the United States Government to forward a request direct to the French Government for data which would be helpful to the Narcotic Division of the United States Treasury."[76]

Bollaert's thinly disguised arrogance infuriated Anslinger. Soon after receiving Tollenger's report, he considered formally placing the matter before the CND. At length, and probably after consultation with Morlock, he decided not to subject the situation in French Indochina to the same notoriety as Mexico's opium difficulties had received the previous year. French representatives acknowledged to State Department officials that the entire affair bothered them greatly but feared that a public discussion would make things worse.[77]

Anslinger, it should be noted, held no brief for French colonialism. His opposition to opium smoking in the Far Eastern territories of European powers surely indicates an antipathy to empire. Embarrassing the French would not have caused him stress similar to that he experienced in the case of China. Playing down the Indochina situation shows that drug control was no isolated phenomenon in postwar foreign policy. Ever the skilled bureaucrat, he knew that his agency's interests would not be served if he took a strong stand and subsequently had to back down. He also had no philosophical trouble in deferring to more important policy considerations, even when doing so retarded progress in international drug control. Having recently refrained from pressuring Iran to curtail opium growth because the State Department did not want to place the young shah, Muhammed Reza Pahlevi, in a bad light, Anslinger certainly could do the same in the name of Franco-American amity.[78]

Moreover, France was crucially important to U.S. interests in Europe. A State Department policy statement on Indochina, prepared in September 1947, concluded that "we have an immediate interest in maintaining in power a friendly French government, to assist in the furtherance of our aims in Europe. This immediate and vital interest has in consequence taken precedence over active steps toward the realization of our [other] objectives in Indochina."[79] Dallas M. Coors, U.S. vice-consul at Saigon, indirectly echoed this perspective in a report on his own unproductive meetings with Saigon authorities: "[I] made it clear at the time that the interest of the United States was in the control of smoking and trade in opium and its derivatives in the United States, rather than in an effort to effect a change in Indochina's internal situation."[80]

The Indochina question did arise, however, at the third session of the CND in May 1948 when the French representative, Gaston Bourgois, whom Anslinger knew well from OAC meetings at Geneva, admitted that conditions in Indochina "made it impossible *so far* fully to apply measures of control." He likened the situation in Indochina to that brought about by the Japanese in China. Responding only briefly, Anslinger noted that progress against addiction "had been extremely slow."[81]

The State Department subsequently sent a detailed synopsis of Tollenger's report, as approved by the FBN chief, to Ambassador Jefferson Caffrey in Paris. Caffrey was instructed to ask French authorities to investigate at once the opium situation in Indochina.[82] Before he could act, Bollaert ordered the consumption of opium to be reduced by 20 percent annually through 1953, when the opium trade would finally cease; meanwhile, smokers could meet their needs by buying from the government monopoly. This step, which seemingly overrode the decree of June 1946 outlawing open sales of opium, evoked a strong American response. As a result, Caffrey received instructions to "inform the French government of the disappointment of your government over the enactment of the decree . . . and urge the French . . . to abolish the opium monopoly . . . and to carry out fully [the] declaration of 1944."[83]

While the language in the communication may have been somewhat less direct than Anslinger and the Treasury Department would have liked, the commissioner seems to have triumphed in a domestic bureaucratic skirmish. Viewed in an overall strategic context, his achievement cannot readily be explained. Not only was the United States in the autumn of 1948 indicating to Paris its willingness, under certain conditions, to provide some financial assistance for Indochina, but it was also trying to persuade the French that a European defense pact best served their security interests.[84] Given the unquestionably delicate nature of negotiations over these matters, how did Anslinger convince the State Department to make a strong overture to France about narcotics?

In short, Anslinger manipulated circumstances to his advantage. First, prewar supply routes for drugs leading from Iran, Turkey, and Lebanon through Marseilles were reappearing. And second, the traffic from Asia to North America was causing problems just as it had before the war. In this regard, Anslinger's understanding of the drug trade convinced him that Indochina might serve as a transshipment point for Chinese narcotics and as a point of origination for heroin produced from Laotian poppies. Nor was it off the mark to expect a degree of official connivance in the Indochinese trade. The dire need for revenue to fund the war against Ho Chi Minh's forces made that a likely prospect.

More important, though, Anslinger had worked hard to line up domestic support behind his narcotics control proposals. At the end of March, the House Committee on Appropriations had authorized the dispatch of a special agent for the FBN, George H. White, to report on the narcotics situation in an area extending from the Near East to Western Europe.[85] The inattentiveness of the French toward conditions at Marseilles, where illicit trafficking thrived, seemed to be indicative of their attitude regarding Indochina. Anslinger, it is fair to say, had cause to direct his ire against French officials in Southeast Asia or Europe. Domestic drug use was on the upswing by 1948, and foreign narcotics were reaching the country from areas under the legal jurisdiction of French authorities.[86]

Attempts to elicit cooperation against the opium business proved unavailing, however. Even as Caffrey was speaking to authorities in Paris, officials in Indochina were reportedly importing opium from the Near East in order to underwrite a currency stabilization scheme. The possibility that colonial administrators or, as it turned out after the Elysée Palace agreement of 8 March 1949, the emperor Bao Dai would rely on opium revenues to run the government greatly alarmed drug officials in Washington. Yet, as the Truman administration inexorably moved toward acceptance of the so-called Bao Dai solution in 1948–50, Anslinger's bureaucratic victory took on an increasingly

Pyrrhic appearance. Charles E. Reed II, chief of the Division of Philippine and Southeast Asian Affairs, knew well from consular experience in Saigon the link between opium and politics in Indochina, but his arguments against unconditional support for Bao Dai's return to power in Vietnam went unheeded.[87]

It remains one of the great ironies of the postwar era that Great Britain and the United States did not explore the possibility of a Ho Chi Minh alternative. An indirect appeal from Ho for assistance in the summer of 1949 fell on deaf ears in the Department of State, thereby thwarting any chance for an early abatement of drug trafficking from Indochina. Had the West worked out a modus vivendi with Ho, U.S. drug control officials could have accepted it, since Vietnam was less a threat to the integrity of global drug control than officials feared Communist China was. When Bao Dai became the only practicable alternative to the perpetuation of French colonial rule, pressure from Washington to bring the opium trade under control quietly dissipated. Anslinger, Morlock, and their colleagues were left with fragmentary evidence suggesting that unidentified anti-French forces in Vietnam may have occasionally paid for guns with opium. Given his anti-Communist convictions, Anslinger knew what to do with that kind of information when explaining the intractability of the narcotics traffic to Congress, his superiors, or the American people.[88]

As we shall see, when the commissioner did begin to blame Communist regimes for an increase in drug trafficking from Asia, he was neatly complementing recent developments in Anglo-American security policy. After 1948, a growing belief in the threat of Soviet-inspired communism throughout the region influenced policy deliberations by officials in Washington and London. Concern about Bao Dai as a legitimate representative of Vietnamese nationalism particularly came from the British, who hoped that France might interpret liberally the Elysée agreement if only to hasten support for him among dubious Asian nations.[89]

Just the same, the British were not inclined to stray too far from the lead of the United States on Indochina. If Indochina succumbed to communism, then British interests in Thailand and Burma would surely be in jeopardy. By the end of 1949, officials at the Foreign Office and the State Department agreed about the need to reduce Moscow's presumed influence in Southeast Asia—with Indochina as the starting point. The United States clearly outlined its position in National Security Council (NSC) document 48/2: "Particular attention should be given to the problem of French Indo-China and action should be taken to bring home to the French the urgency of removing the barriers to the obtaining by Bao Dai or other non-Communist nationalist leaders of the support of a substantial portion of the Vietnamese."[90]

Burma

Perceptions of a Communist threat also helped to bring into rough alignment by 1950 British and American policies toward Burma and Thailand. In Burma, though, the issue of opium briefly complicated that process. The final months of the Second World War saw Burmese nationalism run far ahead of British attempts to come to terms with it. Pressure from the Department of State in late December 1946 helped move Clement Attlee's Labour government toward talks with the Anti-Fascist People's Freedom League, producing an agreement on 27 January 1947 that pledged support for Burmese independence within one year.[91]

The United States wanted to assure the continuing process of Western influence without appearing to intrude in Burmese politics, yet communism remained a strong force within the country. Relations with China promised to be problematic as always, and the status of the hill tribes threatened to crack the facade of unity for the government of Aung San. The tragic assassination of the Burmese leader on 19 July brought Thakin Nu (U Nu) to the position of prime minister; he and Attlee signed a further agreement in October, and Burmese independence formally arrived on 4 January 1948.[92] Unfortunately, independence could neither assure the resolution of Burma's domestic and border problems nor clarify its relations with the West.

Political difficulties in Burma increased with U Nu's acceptance of a British military mission. Opponents of his regime, particularly the Communists, charged that the defense agreement compromised national sovereignty. In addition, corruption and gross inefficiency within the ruling officialdom exacerbated a deepening economic crisis that, in turn, widened the rift between the government and its strongest opponents.[93]

British officials anticipated these developments, if only inchoately, when the United States pressed for an end to opium smoking in the Far East. Burmese experts in the Foreign Office knew that "it [would be] difficult to get the Government of Burma to face squarely the issues involved." Nevertheless, by mid-1946 policymakers at Whitehall resigned themselves to travel down the road of progressive suppression since "we may expect [from the United States] unrelenting pressure irrespective of the difficulties that confront us." The interim governor, Sir Henry Knight, did not underestimate the job at hand. The hill tribes were unlikely to accept any form of opium control, and supplies would doubtless remain abundant in the Trans-Salween region. Meanwhile, restriction, however effective, would result in an enormous loss of revenue for the already financially strapped government.[94]

The debate over opium control in Burma underscored the tensions in Anglo-American relations. Somewhat miffed because of pressure from the FBN and the State Department, the Foreign Office pointedly remarked that opium suppression "must necessarily take time" and doubted that Washington appreciated such a fact.[95] That U.S. narcotics policy tended to be out of touch with conditions in Burma should not be surprising. As with their China policy, decision makers found it easier to cling to a position at variance with the reality of the situation than to reconsider their understanding of it. This myopia suggests that the United States wanted to supplant British influence in Burma, albeit in a less formal way.

Burma's uncompromising opposition to the continuation of a dependent relationship with the West should have resulted in Washington's deference, however grudging, to gradual movement toward opium suppression, particularly after early 1948 as security considerations began to impinge on other U.S. policy decisions. To act otherwise constituted the kind of interference in Burmese affairs that Aung San and his successors were trying to expunge from their relations with foreign powers. Moreover, Burma at that time was not closely linked to the global narcotics trade.

Pressure from Washington on the opium issue therefore amounted to an effort to redirect Burmese nationalism because of larger, regional strategic considerations. Thus, as domestic crises piled one on top of another in 1948, U.S. policymakers took an increasingly negative view of U Nu's brand of socialism as embodied in what they saw as an ill-conceived "leftist unity" program.[96] The socialist approach to opium suppression became clear, or so Washington believed, on 24 July. That day—in the midst of a resignation threat by U Nu over the handling of Burma's domestic insurgencies—the government decided to keep open one hundred official opium shops, hoping to curtail the influx of illegal opium from India, Yunnan, and rebellious sectors of the Shan States. Robert Lovett, the acting secretary of state, instructed the embassy in Rangoon to express Washington's disappointment with the plan.[97]

The problem was not simply the credibility of U Nu's antiopium commitment. Rather, rebellions by Communist factions, mutinies within the army, increasing tension between the government and the Karen minority (soon to become a full-scale revolt), and the daunting presence of thousands of Chinese in the border states rendered opium control plans meaningless. As was their wont, the Chinese smuggled considerable quantities of opium into Burma from Yunnan. Baptist missionaries stationed in Kengtung witnessed in late 1948 the growth and taxation of opium by the Chinese near the ill-defined border but could not determine whether the newcomers sided with the Kuomintang or the Communists.[98]

During 1949, events in Burma, as in French Indochina, more than ever before captured the attention of highly placed officials in Washington. This does not imply that Burma became a matter of vital importance to U.S. security. Just the same, the victory of the Communists in China infused the situation with an air of urgency even though the Burmese Communists suffered from serious internal divisions. Strategic thinking about Burma, contained in a Department of State Policy Planning Staff paper, PPS 51, persuaded the United States to encourage a more visible military and economic role for Great Britain while Washington reevaluated its own position on Burma's domestic and regional difficulties.[99]

Cables reaching the State Department after October 1948 indicated that the issue of opium might affect the ability of Britain and America to safeguard their interests. Unable to control opium production or trafficking near the border with China, in the Shan States, or in the Trans-Salween area, Rangoon was adhering to the line of least resistance and viewed the whole business as a financial and cultural matter to be addressed more seriously only after the extension of governmental authority. In the meantime, authorities derived revenue from opium by maintaining control over smoking during a period of gradual elimination.[100]

Given the traditional autonomy of the opium-producing regions near the Chinese and Thai borders, the imposition of centralized control would not be soon in coming from Rangoon or, for that matter, Bangkok. Cultivating opium approximated what James C. Scott refers to as the "weapons of the weak." That is, those who grew opium poppies did so as a means of defending their interests against outside forces of either a reactionary or progressive stripe. Cultivation sustained work habits, a sense of autonomy, and tribal ritual; in other words, it reinforced a culture. Their somewhat pristine way of looking at the external world enabled growers, while trying to earn a living, to make sense of that world while partly shielding themselves from it.[101]

Ascertaining who does or does not deal in opium at any given time is an uncertain business. Nonetheless, U.S. and British representatives learned enough from well-informed sources, often missionaries, to discern the nature of opium operations in Burma and Thailand. From Bhamo and Myitkyina near the China border to Kengtung State and northern Thailand, the Haw—refugees from Yunnan—evidently dominated the trade. Not only did the Haw produce opium, but also as entrepreneurs some Haw induced Karens and Kawa, or Wa, peoples to farm opium for them. The same could be said of the Meo, who came late to the opium fields of Kengtung and Thailand; they, too, called upon the agricultural skills of the Lahu and Karen to provide them with poppies for markets in Bangkok, Singapore, and beyond.[102]

The flight in 1949 of Kuomintang supporters, civilian and military, from China into Burma and Thailand made resolution of the opium question more difficult. It also threatened to undo efforts to secure a prominent place for Western interests in the balancing act that delimited Burma's foreign policy. The KMT, in the form of remnants of the Ninety-third Division, planned a triumphant return to China when the time was right. Meanwhile, the soldiers began to carve a niche in the Kengtung opium trade and also supplied weapons to rebellious forces in the Karen National Defense Organization (KNDO). Not only did the Rangoon government have to concern itself with the threat that the KNDO posed to domestic stability, but it also had to make certain that the presence of KMT troops did not elicit a military response from Beijing.[103] Thus, when Burma recognized the People's Republic of China on 16 December, it hardly came as a surprise.

Thailand

As the preceding pages suggest, opium also had some role to play in the formation of security policy vis-à-vis Thailand in the late 1940s. Understandably, London had not reacted favorably when Phibun Songgram's government declared war on the Allies. Britain sought to penalize Thailand by controlling its most vital resource, its rice crop, but pressure from Washington resulted in a less punitive approach so that by 1946 Thailand's sovereignty was assured. The next few years were marked by political instability and were therefore a time of increasing concern in the West over the emergence of pro-Communist elements. Less than six months after a military coup in November 1947, Phibun had regained power as prime minister. The fear of communism and the desire for stability appear to have been the determining factors in American recognition, over Ambassador Edwin F. Stanton's opposition, of Phibun's regime.[104]

While Britain maintained a prominent position in the Thai economy, the United States increasingly defined for Thailand a place in Western strategic policy in the early cold war.[105] Among those who kept close watch over events in Thailand were William J. Donovan, wartime head of the OSS, and Willis H. Bird, who worked with the OSS in China under Colonel Richard Pinkerton

Heppner—the chief of OSS in SEAC and a top aide to General Albert Wedemeyer. After the war, Bird, formerly an executive with Sears, Roebuck and Company and still a reserve colonel in military intelligence, ran an import-export house in Bangkok.

Following the November coup, Bird informed Donovan that he was trying to provide assistance to the Free Thai movement, which he felt merited American support. He implored Donovan: "Should there be any agency that is trying to take the place of O.S.S., and if they are more than a storage vault for odds and ends of information, please have them get in touch with us as soon as possible."[106] By the time Phibun returned as prime minister, Donovan was telling the Pentagon and the State Department that Bird was a reliable source whose information about growing Soviet economic activities in Thailand was credible.[107] In the early 1950s, Bird would become an important actor in clandestine operations in Thailand—some of which involved the opium trade.

Meanwhile, U.S. and British officials regarded the booming trade in opium in Thailand as a further threat to stability and, hence, to their security interests. In 1948, as the Foreign Office charted the movement of three hundred cases (27 tons) of opium from Iran to Bangkok, Anslinger told a session of the CND that "the traffic in opium is in full swing in Siam." Furthermore, the government was relying on the trade for 15 percent of its revenue and announced that it would purchase more opium from Iran despite the annual production in northern Thailand of more than 110,000 kilograms of raw opium.[108]

Notwithstanding earlier promises in 1946 to outlaw the smoking of opium and halt the illegal traffic, Thai authorities accomplished little. Concern in the United States became acute by the fall of 1949, when reports reached the State Department about the inroads communism was making within the Chinese community in Thailand as well as the involvement of the Thai army with opium. Since the army virtually controlled the nature of Thailand's security relationship with the West, foreign promotion of opium control had to take a back seat to other policy priorities.[109]

Although a Thai official working on United Nations matters in the Foreign Ministry blamed his country's difficulties with opium on Japanese wartime activities, which "had in general adversely affected the moral character of the Thai people," U.S. policymakers found his explanations disingenuous.[110] They did not realize, however, that their own plans to further opium controls had again foundered on the rough shoals of Asian nationalism and in the turbulent waters of national security policy. It was nearly impossible to bring pressure to bear on a government so dependent on its military forces for survival. The

Thai army was then seeking foreign assistance, thereby presenting an opportunity for a quid pro quo, but there is no indication that U.S. officials did much other than worry about the appeal of Communist aid to the Thais.[111]

One of the great American shibboleths after the war held that the United States sided with Asian nationalism. Underlying this belief was the assumption that nationalism in Asia would take on a pro-Western guise and, over time, more nearly accord with a reality embodying American values and institutions. This presumption was not wholly illusory since many Asian nationalists—from Sun Yat-sen to Gandhi to Aung San, U Nu, and others—had received Western-style educations and hence were conversant with, and by implication sympathetic to, Euro-American forms of government. (Where this perception left someone like Ho Chi Minh was not clear.) Yet this familiarity did not readily translate into cultural convergence in the daily operations of government.

Policymakers such as Morlock and Anslinger found it hard to comprehend this state of affairs. They interpreted antiopium declarations as a point of departure for an active suppression campaign, not as an invitation for negotiations between growers, users, traffickers, and the government. What they failed to appreciate about nationalism in Asia was that it had not become a commonly accepted societal phenomenon. Nationalism spoke more to the needs of the middle and working classes than to the daily rhythms of those tied to the soil. Consequently, competing perspectives in lands such as Thailand and Burma prevented the early adoption of nationalistic forms so dear to the West. Rupert Emerson captured the paradox U.S. policymakers overlooked when he observed that "nationalists are characteristically not found . . . in those parts of society which are most obviously representative of the heritage of the past, although these must furnish much of the claim to national distinctiveness."[112]

Coda: China at the Center

Cultural, political, and institutional restraints in Southeast Asia combined to make the junction of antiopium and security policies essentially meaningless. The more security considerations accommodated nationalistic sentiments, as in Burma and Thailand, the less likely was the adoption of opium control. Competing claims for nationalistic legitimacy and an enduring French presence in Indochina negated the chances of linking opium and security policy. Ho Chi Minh was an unacceptable risk and Bao Dai an unreliable leader on whom to base a policy of opium control in a security context. The Office of Intelligence and Research in the State Department asserted in January 1950 that "the fervor of nascent nationalism *might* have been considerably tempered if steps toward agricultural reform had been taken [by Bao Dai]."[113]

Therein lay an unexceptional truth and a substantial dilemma for Western policymakers. Opium control was impossible without improving the lot of the rural population, but the nationalists on whom the West was relying to serve its interests were not willing to accept fundamental agrarian reforms. The dilemma was that revolutionary nationalists like Ho Chi Minh were the most likely proponents of opium control. But since Ho was not about to seize power and bring Vietnam's opium traffic under control, we must look to the Chinese Communist party to understand the prospects for opium control in Asia in the late 1940s.

Even as the CCP tightened its grip on China, traditional dependence on opium persisted in the southwest, most notably in Yunnan. As always, bandits reaped whatever rewards they could from the opium trade, joined by army regulars and deserters who were fleeing to Kengtung.[114] Banditry was an essentially conservative, even reactionary phenomenon, most often aimed at little more than carving out a place in an alien world.[115] Although some shrewd bandits did align with the Communists, Mao's China played no verifiable role in the drug commerce of 1949.[116]

Indeed, KMT commanders were trying to make common cause with those bandits in Yunnan who opposed the Communists in order to preserve a foothold in the southwest. Payment for bandits and KMT troops came in the form of opium, the most negotiable commodity then available. Making a stand in Yunnan proved to be impossible, however; Lu Han successfully resisted an attempt to undercut his power and by mid-December had, in effect, thrown in his lot with the Communists.[117] The Central Intelligence Agency (CIA) had earlier discounted the ability of the KMT to maintain an outpost anywhere except on Taiwan because of both a lack of will and chronic graft and corruption.[118]

It therefore devolved to the Communists to bring about control over opium. For almost two decades in rural China, they had expunged opium from their midst as a matter of principle; it was now time to take the campaign to the cities as a matter of policy.[119] That the chances for success were good partly explains their rise to power. While the United States was trying to avert the fall of the Kuomintang just as foreign powers had attempted to prop up the Manchu dynasty many years before, the CCP built a base of support among the Chinese masses. Some observant Westerners understood what was happening but failed to locate its root deep in Chinese history.[120] Opium control became possible because the revolution had reestablished "a coherent *Chinese world view*," as Mark Mancall concludes. Though Marxist in form and ideology, the Communist regime was recognizable to those who would confer legitimacy on it.[121]

In viewing the world from the perspective of a widening rift with the Soviet Union, U.S. policymakers—including Morlock and Anslinger—were out of step with revolutionary nationalism in general and the Chinese Communists in particular. The Americans set down conditions under which they would deal with the CCP, but what they defined as acceptable international behavior, as seen in the assumptions then influencing security policy, all but precluded the Chinese from meeting such a standard.[122]

To be sure, there existed a level of misperception in Washington, as Dean Acheson essentially admitted when he acknowledged the unreality of U.S.-China policy. Those involved with drug control erred, too, in their evaluation of what they could accomplish. That the Communists were more likely to control opium growth and trafficking than non-Communist regimes contradicted long-held expectations about ideology and behavior. As a result, by the end of 1949 antiopium activity had become a virtual hostage to national security concerns. The irony was that American proponents of drug control found it relatively easy to accept that questionable situation.

NINE

In the Hills of Southeast Asia, 1950–1954

Narcotics officials in Washington all but abandoned the idea of opium control in Asia in the first half of the 1950s. Had they done so openly, that step would have constituted a bold move away from their traditional reliance on control at the source because of its limited results. With China serving as a convenient scapegoat, however, Harry Anslinger further entwined the Federal Bureau of Narcotics with U.S. security policy by accepting the need for clandestine operations in Burma and Thailand involving opium and narcotics. Publicly, at least, objectives had not been compromised; the United States took an active role at the 1953 United Nations Opium Conference.

Great Britain found little credibility in Anslinger's charges against China and believed that the involvement with opium by U.S.-supported KMT irregulars in Burma and Thailand harmed London's own regional security interests. Britain's reservations about U.S. narcotics control strategy showed in microcosm its uncertainty about some of the particulars of Washington's national security policy. The Americans, of course, were having troubles of their own protecting perceived strategic interests in Asia.

The Truman administration never successfully resolved its security dilemma. The problem was how to pursue major objectives without appearing to be an intervening or imperial power. Viewing security interests in East Asia and Southeast Asia through a quasi-European lens made the obstacles more insuperable and limited policy options.[1] Policymakers were often unable to imagine alternative courses when their actions ran afoul of the interests of their allies in Britain, their would-be associates in Burma and Thailand, and the Chinese Communists.[2] And, of course, raising the level of U.S. security concerns to the status of a vital interest after the outbreak of the Korean War further constrained the choices of those hoping to effect a change in the opium cultures of the region.

In the early months of 1950, U.S. authorities had no clear definition of salient Western objectives. For example, factions within the government did not fully agree about Japan's political and economic future.[3] Also, Washington and London anticipated an active American role in Southeast Asia, yet the British still felt that Washington might do Whitehall's bidding.[4] For their part, the U.S. chiefs of mission in the Far East acknowledged the need to cooperate with the British on major political and economic matters there.[5] Specifically regarding Indochina, M. Esler Dening, principal adviser on the Far East in the Foreign Office and formerly political adviser to Admiral Lord Louis Mount-batten, told Malcolm MacDonald, British high commissioner in Southeast Asia, that "we must hope that the United States, who alone can make any significant contribution, will respond favourably to French requests" for economic assistance.[6]

Despite Whitehall's antipathy to Bao Dai, recognition of his regime accompanied that of the United States in February. The threat of communism greatly colored Britain's decision: "This threat is of vital importance, both politically and economically, and can be countered only by a constructive policy which will offer hope of economic advance for the peoples of this region."[7] During tripartite talks at London in May, John D. Hickerson, the assistant secretary of state for United Nations affairs, saw the need for more than economic aid; Britain and France would also have to bolster regional political stability and military strength. The Truman administration had already committed itself to the dubious principle of extending military aid to Vietnam while reaffirming the basic Anglo-American belief that primary responsibility for dealing with the Indochina situation belonged to France.[8] An interdepartmental committee on assistance programs later revealed how important the associated states had become to Western security: "This country [sic] is the key to the control of the mainland of Southeast Asia. Its loss would represent a major strategic reversal for the United States and its allies."[9]

Opium and the proximity of the People's Republic of China (PRC) also influenced security considerations vis-à-vis Japan and Southeast Asia. Scattered reports about illicit opium traffic into Japan evoked fears of possible Chinese aggression, even though the opium was of uncertain origin. To U.S. narcotics officials, such indeterminacy meant only one thing: the Communist Chinese were trying to dump surplus opium from Manchuria and North China. The consulate in Hong Kong suggested that PRC leaders were seeking desperately needed revenue as well as trying to cause widespread demoralization throughout Asia with the help of opium.[10]

Alleged narcotics trafficking threatened American security objectives, but communism itself seemed even more menacing. Some officials, such as John Moors Cabot, viewed the PRC as little more than an advance agent for the Soviets; he once blustered that "we might as well face them in China as anywhere else." John M. Allison of the Office of Northeast Asian Affairs later wrote: "Monolithic communism was a reality in 1950." In dispatches that might fairly be termed "chatty," the first U.S. minister to Taipei, Karl Lott Rankin, who claimed to have "some feeling for the Red pattern," regretted that he could not have known China under better circumstances.[11]

Despite a willingness to consider recognition of the PRC under certain circumstances, several factors prevented President Truman and Secretary of State Acheson from following the British lead of January 1950. Backers of the Kuomintang in the United States, including Elizabeth Washburn Wright, were mobilized to uphold the Nationalist cause before the White House and the State Department. Wellington Koo rejoiced when Acheson chose Dean Rusk to replace W. Walton Butterworth as assistant secretary for Far Eastern affairs, since Rusk was opposed to recognition at the time.[12] Even more important than the political influence of the "China Lobby" in precluding recognition were Acheson's own perceptions of China. Because he was a key decision maker, the secretary's anticommunism, reinforced by his alarm over potential Communist adventurism following the signing in February of the Sino-Soviet treaty, along with Chinese and Russian recognition of Ho Chi Minh's government, made U.S. recognition unlikely. The start of the Korean War merely validated his judgment.[13]

Fears of PRC influence with Chinese minorities and Communist parties in Burma and Thailand led to an expanded American role there in the form of economic and limited military assistance.[14] After surveying economic conditions in Southeast Asia, the Griffin Mission, led by Robert A. Griffin of the Economic Cooperation Administration (ECA), argued that a U.S. aid program for Burma needed to rest on a foundation of confidence in the United States since Burma "cannot at all be taken for granted."[15] Officials in Washington reasoned that "a real effort must be made to keep it from falling under Communist domination because if Burma falls, all of Southeast Asia will be gravely imperilled." Western assistance might therefore enable the fiercely independent Rangoon government to become an important link in the anti-Communist chain in the region.[16]

The Griffin Mission did not have a comparable sense of urgency concerning Thailand; it recommended a modest military aid program for "[that] free and friendly government in the critical heart of Southeast Asia." The stability of the Bangkok regime led the U.S. embassy to expect some improvement in

Thailand's antiopium activity, although stories in the *Bangkok Post* were not nearly as sanguine.[17] Acheson's evaluation of Thailand, prepared for Truman in support of military assistance under Section 303 of the 1949 Mutual Defense Assistance Act, seemed to describe a different country altogether: "It is clearly apparent that unless Thailand is given military assistance it cannot hold out against communist pressure." Acheson submitted his report before the Griffin Mission had filed its own estimate of Thai stability; yet when the findings of the mission were known, he did not alter his position.[18] The secretary's consistency is perhaps best explained by a need to buttress the anti-Communist elements in his belief system, given the partisan attacks of the time against the administration, as well as by his growing exasperation with the PRC.

There remained an air of unreality in discussions about Western security interests in Southeast Asia in the spring of 1950. Realization of their mutual or individual goals depended on coming to terms with nationalism to forestall the onslaught of communism, or so Westerners believed. But the people of the region were mostly rural, politically out of step with central authority, and economically near or below a subsistence level of existence.[19] Hoping that such people would respond to the security imperatives of unknown or distrusted foreigners seems, in retrospect, little more than wishful thinking.

In a speech to the Naval War College in September 1950, Livingston T. Merchant, the deputy assistant secretary of state, framed the problem as well as anyone: "Thus with pride in their cultures, poor as a general rule, disillusioned with the West, disunited and disturbed internally—the intense nationalistic and revolutionary urge for independence as the answer to their problems is understandable." The question for the United States was how to promote popular non-Communist independence movements.[20] Until an answer was found, foreign and security policy goals were unattainable, including traditional antiopium objectives. In the final years of the Truman administration and the early years of Dwight D. Eisenhower's presidency, however, narcotics control officials pursued a revamped antidrug policy that was more congruent with the confines of existing security policy in the region.

The Indochina Avatar

Except for a few controversial forays into the interior of Mexico in the 1930s, proponents of drug control rarely got close to the source of illicit supplies. Consequently, effective control remained dependent on the good faith and capability of urban bureaucrats in producer countries. This decision-making strategy of making do with less than a satisfactory policy choice served the bureaucratic needs of Harry Anslinger, George A. Morlock, and their colleagues despite their failure to promote real control.[21]

As U.S. economic and military assistance began to flow into Indochina, conditions in the associated states virtually guaranteed more of the same strategy. The armed insurgency of the Viet Minh League against the French forecast continuing dependence by Bao Dai's regime on opium revenues. Gradually, certain extragovernmental elements in Saigon, identified by Alfred W. McCoy as French intelligence agencies, took over the Indochina opium business and came to depend on the Binh Xuyen gangsters of Cholon to run opium and narcotics operations and thus finance counterinsurgency activities against the Viet Minh.[22]

Government documentation is meager, but it appears that neither the Americans nor the British knew what was going on in Vietnam. Donald R. Heath, the U.S. minister at Saigon, reported periodic fluctuations in the price of opium on the black market but could not offer a good explanation for the changes.[23] British and American personnel in Bangkok uncovered evidence of extensive participation by Laotians in the regional drug trade, but a campaign of disinformation, presumably by French-backed traffickers, detailing the unlikely barter of guns for opium between government officials in Thailand and the Viet Minh obscured the importance of Laotian opium to French policy.[24] Heath lamented to Anslinger that it was impossible to describe the actual situation regarding opium in Vietnam.[25] This was surely true in one respect: the war against Ho's forces kept noncombatants largely confined to the cities. Even when Anslinger dispatched operatives to gather information from persons and places that were more or less off limits to diplomatic personnel, these agents were reduced at times to trading foulard ties and Zippo lighters for intelligence data of questionable value.[26]

Getting to the source, the poppy fields of Laos, was no easier logistically and no less dangerous in the early 1950s than it is today to enter the coca ranges of the Andes. To be sure, Anglo-American officials, relying on the accounts of missionaries and their own occasional trips to the fringes of opium-producing regions, knew well the proclivity of the Meo of Xieng Khouang province in Laos for farming opium poppies as readily as they grew rice. Britain's H. A. Graves described how he was beguiled by "Laotian charm" on a brief visit to Luang Prabang, a treatment that he found "in pleasant contrast to the rather sullen, or unanimated, character of the Vietnamese."[27] Alone, a few foreigners could neither destroy the opium planting and cultivation rituals of the Meo and other hill tribes nor interfere, even unknowingly, with the trafficking operations of the French in Saigon. And yet their paralysis indicates how the Indochinese situation serves as an archetype for understanding the limits of drug control in the context of security policy in Southeast Asia.

The ability of French intelligence to turn opium traffic in Vietnam to the service of a counterinsurgency program against the Viet Minh has a relatively straightforward explanation. In the first place, Operation X, as it was known, was kept extraordinarily secret. Second, a disinformation campaign by French intelligence made unlikely the discovery of how the operation worked. Indication of the spread of disinformation also came from Edmund A. Gullion, at the U.S. embassy in Saigon, who learned in June 1952 that Chinese battalions in Tonkin assisting the Viet Minh had encountered French-organized Meo counterguerrilla units. Gullion speculated that the Meo may have come upon an opium-foraging expedition by the Chinese and the Viet Minh. While that is conceivable, it is unlikely in view of the ideological opposition to reliance on opium by the Viet Minh and the PRC.[28] Indeed, the Chinese and the Viet Minh may have been looking for a way to rupture the Meo-French alliance.

Third, officials in Paris and Saigon, most of whom knew nothing about Operation X, could plead ignorance if Anslinger or anyone else asked probing questions about the narcotics traffic. In fact, the State Department asked Anslinger in April 1952 "to express interest in the opium situation in Indochina" at the forthcoming session of the Commission on Narcotic Drugs,[29] but nothing came of his inquiry since authorities in Saigon were closing opium-smoking detoxification centers. Accordingly, the commissioner could not charge French authorities with laxness in their antinarcotics efforts.

Anslinger's deference to other foreign and security policy goals in Franco-American relations further explains how the modification of U.S. antiopium objectives tacitly assisted Operation X.[30] The evolution during 1950 in Anglo-American thinking about security policy revealed the growing importance of Indochina to the fate of Southeast Asia. Rusk expressed the fear that "*present global commitments*" might make it impossible to "*counteract the immediate capability of Chinese forces to seize northern Indochina if World Communism so directs.*" Likewise in January 1951, John Paton Davies, Jr., then with the State Department's Policy Planning Staff, wondered whether "we may look forward to seeing our military forces deeply embroiled from Korea to Cambodia before Spring is over." A Foreign Office minute, also in January, concluded that "the present aggressive policy of the Chinese Government makes it more than ever necessary that a solution should be found which will prevent Indo-China from coming under Communist domination." Thus, as the security of Indochina and, hence, Western interests in Southeast Asia seemed in jeopardy, policymakers were prepared to accept novel forms of protection, including what Douglas S. Blaufarb calls "people's counterinsurgency."[31] Knowing what we do about Anslinger's actions as a bureaucrat and policymaker, there is no reason to believe he would have dissented from that strategy.

More and more the fate of Indochina became equated with the fate of the West. At the end of October, the Department of Defense flatly stated: "Present US policy toward IC is to support the anti-Commie forces in that area *by all means* short of commitment of US troops." At a tripartite foreign ministers' meeting at the Quai d'Orsay in late May 1952, René Pleven, the French defense minister, proclaimed: "If Indochina were defended purely for French interests, it would not be worth the effort." In reply, Acheson placed France's effort in Indochina "in the general international interest." Anthony Eden, once again at the Foreign Office after the return of Churchill to power in autumn 1951, concurred with his assessment.[32]

Finally, as we have seen, the inability of the West to respond effectively to revolutionary nationalism aided French intelligence as it utilized the opium trade in Vietnam to fund counterinsurgency activities. At least in the early 1950s, what Gabriel Kolko terms "revolutionary morality" was a tangible phenomenon among Viet Minh cadres who sought to expel from their homeland the French imperialists and their supporters. Americans recognized the paradox of promoting nationalism through the agency of a colonial power, but the ideological constraints of national security policy precluded an alternative course of action. Jean Letourneau, French high commissioner for Indochina, put the problem in its starkest terms: "No matter how much progress we make in the war, there is no real hope of convincing Asian people that we are working for their independence."[33] In such a situation, advocates of opium control could either reconsider or attempt to rationalize the irrelevancy of their policies. Anslinger chose the latter course.

The PRC as Scapegoat

The intensity of antiforeign sentiment in the wake of the Communist revolution ultimately destroyed, for example, the work of Christian missionaries in China. Hope in official Britain for better treatment than that accorded the United States was soon dashed.[34] If the British did not go as far as the Americans in stressing the Chinese threat, it was because they did not see Beijing as wholly subservient to Moscow. They also feared that preoccupation with the Far East would hamper U.S. defense of Western interests in Europe (and the Middle East) should the need arise.[35]

Fear of Communist expansion seemed warranted, though. Material assistance flowed steadily to the Viet Minh, and PRC forces were stationed not just near the Burma border but patrolled the Indochina frontier as well. Truman's decision to send a military assistance advisory group to Vietnam following the visit of the Melby-Erskine Mission in the summer of 1950 prefigured a CIA assessment of developments in Asia that found: "The Peiping regime will play an increasingly influential role in Asian affairs by virtue of its growing prestige and through the influence it exerts over Asian revolutionary movements."[36]

To Acheson, this meant that the PRC should be seen as more Communist than nationalist, a position that failed to impress Clement Attlee during his talks with Truman in December 1950. Even if Mao Zedong were not a Stalinist, as Attlee argued, Acheson believed that the stakes for Western security in Asia were too high to seek an accommodation with Beijing. More in line with American thinking, R. H. Scott, assistant under secretary of state for South Asian affairs in the Foreign Office, termed the PRC "an expansionist power and . . . a menace to Asia."[37]

Anslinger shared that perception and years later would write that the Communists were smuggling heroin out of China as early as 1948, ostensibly to Japan and the United States. He also charged the Communists with responsibility for the opium problems of Burma and Thailand.[38] As he told the CND in April 1953, the Communists had relied on the growth and sale of opium to finance their activities ever since they occupied Shensi in the 1930s. Subsequently, Anslinger blamed Beijing's Ministry of Finance under Bo Yibo for the narcotics traffic and implied that Deng Xiaoping played a similar role as Bo's successor.[39]

These allegations notwithstanding, the PRC issued decrees on 24 February and 1 November 1950 ordering an end to the domestic cultivation and use of opium. The first decree by Zhou Enlai, president of the Political Affairs Yuan, promised severe penalties for the transport, manufacture, and sale of opium in any form. Significantly, where ethnic minorities cultivated poppies, local circumstances were to dictate the pace of suppression.[40] Not at all verifiable are assertions that PRC officials tolerated opium use by the masses; it is more likely that being charged with crimes relating to opium constituted a great disgrace.[41]

The realities of the PRC's antiopium drive did not affect U.S. policy. As Anslinger prepared for the CND's fifth session, which met while the Attlee-

Truman talks were taking place, he was instructed to "strongly oppose any motion to unseat the representative of the Chinese National Government or any motion to seat [on the CND] a representative of the Chinese Communist regime."[42] In the weeks before the CND meeting, the PRC did explore the sale of five hundred tons of Jehol opium on the open market in Hong Kong to Imperial Chemical Industries (China) Ltd., but the offer was rejected. Whitehall discounted simultaneous U.S. allegations about opium trafficking, which threatened further damage to Sino-British relations, for lack of evidence.[43]

Anslinger may have seen the offer to sell opium as a ruse to cover a more nefarious trafficking operation. When sources of information on Taiwan continued making allegations against the Communists into the spring of 1951, U.S. officials were inclined to accept their accuracy despite the inconclusiveness of the evidence. As the State Department wired the consulate in Hong Kong: "This topic is of considerable interest and exploitable for propaganda reasons." Armed with what it considered damning information, the United States kept the PRC from replacing Taiwan on the CND at the April 1951 meeting—albeit on procedural rather than substantive grounds.[44]

The early skirmishing about China's involvement with illegal narcotics gave way to a frontal assault at the CND in May 1952. Anslinger charged that seizures in 1951 proved that the PRC was smuggling heroin into Japan through Hong Kong or North Korea. In prepared remarks, he declared: "Chinese Communists are planting opium poppies on a large scale in Jehol and are manufacturing heroin in Tientsin. The heroin is collected by the Central Financial and Economic Council in Peiping. This committee is assigned the duty of smuggling this heroin into foreign countries. . . . All heroin seized in Japan is attributed to China as the source." Just as Stuart Fuller had denounced Japan's involvement with narcotics trafficking to the Opium Advisory Committee in June 1938, so did Anslinger use every means at his disposal—his expertise, experience, and authority—to cast the Chinese as international outlaws on the subject of opium.[45]

Both Moscow and Beijing responded in the strongest possible terms. The Soviet Union called the charges "a baseless fabrication from start to finish," insisting that the PRC "has consistently and resolutely pursued a policy of the strictest prohibition of opium and other narcotic drugs." The PRC took the unusual step of sending a cable to the United Nations' secretary-general, Trygve Lie, categorically denying the American allegations.[46]

Available documentation does not permit final judgment about Beijing's responsibility for the Asian opium and narcotics trade in the early 1950s. Unclassified U.S. sources cast doubt on Anslinger's presumption of PRC culpability, however. In July 1952, he and Morlock requested the consulate at Hong Kong to transmit press reports from the mainland about opium. In reply, Julian F. Harrington detailed antinarcotics activity, which he compared to the earlier, vigorous KMT campaigns. Agitation against drugs appeared frequently in the Chinese press; interviews with persons leaving China confirmed its intensity and suggested that its scope was nationwide.[47]

Other considerations also question the validity of Anslinger's position on China and opium traffic. First, for more than a year after it had taken power, bandits and guerrillas who remained active in southern and western China kept Beijing from consolidating its rule there. As it had for untold years, opium played an important role in the political economy of the region near the Sino-Burmese border.[48] In contrast, even if the PRC had begun to transform the Chinese people's historic involvement with opium, critics averred that Mao Zedong and Zhou Enlai were not averse to weakening the West with narcotics—for reasons that went back to the first Opium War.[49] While that argument initially appears plausible, it fails because it implies that the CCP seized power without learning anything from the mistakes of the Kuomintang. A regime in China could not build a base of support on a foundation of opium poppies.

A further lesson taken from the experience of the Japanese army in the 1930s warned the Communist party about the dangers of making an accommodation with opium and narcotics. To promote suppression at home while engaging in narcotics trafficking abroad would inexorably lead the CCP to dependence on opium, politically and financially if not personally. Accordingly, in order to understand the intricacies of the opium trade in Burma and Thailand, we must turn our attention away from Beijing.

Taiwan and U.S. Security Policy

Dean Acheson could not turn his back on Chiang Kai-shek. While Attlee argued that "the UK [has] no sympathy with Chiang" or Formosa, the secretary believed with equal conviction that Beijing's aggression forced the United States and Great Britain to "link this problem [of Formosa] with the problems of Europe." That is, Taiwan could not be excluded from any credible strategy of containment.[50]

Chiang's advocates worked hard on his behalf to influence U.S. policy. While consul general at Hong Kong, Karl Lott Rankin—who admitted that he knew little about Taiwan—questioned the wisdom of those, including General

Omar Bradley, who felt the island was not strategically important. Rankin later derided those who had considered writing off, as he saw it, Korea, Indochina, and Taiwan but received a lecture for his troubles after making a similar suggestion to George F. Kennan. Kennan told Rankin that too friendly an association with Chiang would involve "our country in ventures far beyond its capabilities." By then, August 1950, Kennan's influence on State Department policy planning had waned and, despite warning that "we tend to assume that Asia might be ours to possess," his words fell on deaf ears.[51]

Ambassador Koo, of course, took every opportunity to convince the cautious Rusk that, if Taiwan were lost to the Communists, "the strategic defense of that area would be greatly affected."[52] Koo was far from alone in making the case for Taiwan as a strategic asset. Whiting Willauer, general manager and president of Civil Air Transport (CAT), and General Claire Lee Chennault, chairman of the board, were doing all they could to support Chiang; and, as William M. Leary has shown, their capabilities nearly matched their intentions. In May 1949, Thomas G. (Tommy) Corcoran, an adviser to President Roosevelt who shared with Willauer and Chennault an acute interest in the fate of Nationalist China, introduced Chennault to the head of the CIA, Rear Admiral Roscoe H. Hillenkoetter. After hesitating, the agency took an interest in CAT's plan to prevent the West from losing "the cold/hot war in the Far East," as Willauer put it. Rankin, not one of the State Department's China "dilettantes" but "a man of understanding, of force and action," would be an asset to the endeavor.[53]

With substantial funding from Taiwan, CAT by July 1950 was forming an international voluntary group similar to Chennault's American Volunteer Group of the Second World War. Chennault told Corcoran that he was prepared to train and outfit guerrilla units even in the most primitive locations. Rankin's former opposition to covert activities, because of the risk in dealing with "undisciplined and uncoordinated elements," soon vanished. Less than one week after Attlee's trip to the United States, Rankin found a place for "guerrilla movements" in the struggle against communism in Asia: "Our present position is too hazardous to permit overlooking any method which promises to help our cause." Rankin therefore supported Chennault's plans, recalling: "I had a high regard for his judgment and in this case I believe that his instinct was sound."[54]

Truman and Attlee had agreed, however, that a major war with China was out of the question. That being said, American policymakers sought to aid Chiang's government, a regime Livingston Merchant described as "rotten and beyond reclamation." Before the 17 January meeting of the National Security

Council, Chairman Bradley of the Joint Chiefs of Staff told Secretary of Defense George C. Marshall that the United States should employ "all appropriate means" to prevent the spread of communism in Asia. The NSC recommended an increase in Mutual Defense Assistance Program (MDAP) aid to Formosa as well as to Thailand and the provision of "all practicable covert aid to effective anti-communist guerrilla forces in China." While rendered less explicitly, these steps appear to be consistent with the policy toward, and courses of action in, Asia that Truman approved on 17 May as NSC 48/5.[55] Through covert operations the United States would exert what leverage it could against PRC expansionism without being able to control how the operations were conducted.

Foreign Aid, Covert Operations, and Opium Traffic

The Truman administration apparently did not try to return the Kuomintang to the mainland. Such schemes were left to the likes of Chennault and Willauer, who were disliked in Washington. In contrast, CAT's plans were welcomed by the China Lobby, which included the Committee to Defend America by Aiding Anti-Communist China. William J. Donovan served as vice-chairman of that particular organization, but it is not clear that he agreed with all of its efforts in support of Chiang.[56]

Just the same, the policy adopted by the National Security Council guaranteed that private interests would get involved in some way. The NSC sanctioned covert action against the PRC for several reasons. First, some aid was already reaching KMT forces in Burma, through the intercession of Formosa if not the CIA, months before the January 1951 NSC meeting.[57] Second, harassment of the PRC was intended to hasten a Sino-Soviet split, on the assumption that there were limits to Soviet assistance if China faced the prospect of armed conflict outside of Korea. Third, clandestine excursions into Yunnan promised the collection of intelligence data otherwise unavailable. Fourth, should the PRC act rashly by sending troops into Burma, the government in Rangoon might be forced to reassess its neutralist foreign policy position and move closer to the West. And fifth, in an indirect way, U.S. support for KMT forces would be seen favorably in Bangkok, which had long been suspicious of Burma's territorial ambitions. Whatever its rationale, covert activity meant trouble for opium control.

Even without a state of rebellion in producing areas, Rangoon would have had trouble curbing opium usage. Conditions in Burma and Thailand made it hard to understand how Anslinger could blame the opium business on the PRC. The Burmese Foreign Office acknowledged that the remote Kachin and Shan States produced "large quantities of opium."[58] Anslinger himself informed the CND that Burma was the likely place of origin for opium seized in Thailand. Even if China were the source for some of the opium, the FBN chief knew about the involvement of the Thai police with the traffickers. He even commended the Burmese for suggesting that the United Nations conduct an investigation of opium smuggling in Burma and Thailand, a step steadfastly resisted in Bangkok.[59] As the situation in Thailand worsened in the final year of the Truman presidency, the State Department instructed Anslinger to bring the matter to the attention of the CND.[60]

In retrospect, it is hard to separate opium-related events in Burma and Thailand from what was happening almost simultaneously in Vietnam and Laos. The lack of documentary evidence precludes a conclusion implying anything other than coincidence, but the similarities are no less striking. French intelligence was carrying out counterguerrilla operations as secretly as possible, just as U.S. support for General Li Mi's forces, though widely suspected, was known only to a few. On the eve of a meeting of foreign ministers in New York in September 1950, the British warned the State Department that KMT provocations against the PRC must stop or the inference could be drawn that the United States actively was supporting them.[61]

Attlee's government appealed to Washington for greater circumspection. The presence in Burma of KMT remnants, numbering more than ten thousand, heightened Anglo-American tensions. The Economic Cooperation Administration described the American task in Southeast Asia as "nothing less than that of taking the initiative in building a new order and stability . . . that is firmly oriented to the West." Harlan Cleveland of the ECA found the region to be an area of vital interest politically and of major importance for its strategic resources.[62] The Foreign Office, on the other hand, wanted what Eden would term in February 1952 a "confused and disturbing situation" in Burma cleared up as quickly as possible.[63]

Whitehall slowly began to mend its differences with Rangoon by playing down long-held sympathies for the Karens and by reassessing its view that the Left in Burma wanted to destroy Great Britain's economic interests.[64] Officials in Rangoon, of course, tried to take advantage of the divergent positions of London and Washington on the KMT issue. They insisted that the KMT forces threatened Burma's security and that they must leave. U.S. planners had dis-

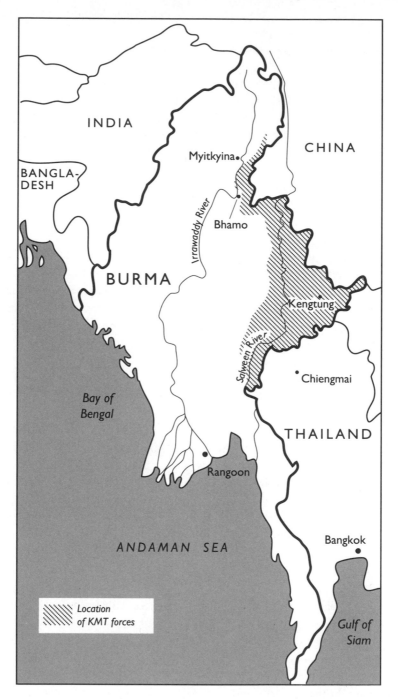

Map 3. Kuomintang Forces in Burma

cussed the KMT problem as early as mid-1950 as they prepared for the Melby-Erskine Mission, conceived in order to extend military assistance to Southeast Asia.[65] Acheson's subsequent, possibly disingenuous intercession with the Kuomintang through Rankin had no effect. A frustrated U.S. ambassador in Rangoon, David M. Key, underlined the security threat posed by Li Mi's forces; and Burma's ambassador, James Barrington, told Rusk and R. Austin Acly of the Office of Philippine and Southeast Asian Affairs that his government felt it had no recourse but to take its case to the United Nations.[66]

Acheson had participated from the start in the decision-making process relating to NSC 48/5, so he was familiar with the discussions about using covert operations against China's southern flank. Nonetheless, in February 1952 he sent a circular letter to U.S. representatives in London, Paris, New Delhi, Rangoon, Taipei, Hong Kong, and Bangkok declaring that, despite the rumors of American involvement, the "[KMT] problem [is] essentially one for BURM to solve." To side with Rangoon, he pointed out in a revealing passage, "WLD annoy CHI NATLS and raise charges that we are not (RPT not) sympathetic to anti COMMIE activities." Heath in Saigon and Rankin urged continued U.S. backing for the KMT troops.[67]

The ambiguity surrounding U.S. involvement with the KMT troubled diplomats in Asia. Yet, as was true in the case of French officials concerning the opium trade in Vietnam, lack of knowledge provided deniability for those who were left out of the decision-making process. Rankin, for one, argued that U.S. personnel in Rangoon and Bangkok should be fully informed.[68] In assessing relevant sources, deniability could not easily be distinguished from purposeful misinformation by top State Department officials. Representatives at Rangoon, London, and the United Nations were told "categorically to deny" to Burmese officials "that there is or CLD be in future any official or unofficial US GOVT connection whatsoever" with Li Mi's forces. In an appearance before the House of Commons, Eden wondered about the possibility of "deliberate distortion" but did not implicate the U.S. government directly in such a practice. The State Department's Office of Chinese Affairs in August 1952 concluded that "the present [and future] military usefulness of the KMT troops as an anti-Communist force is negligible at best."[69] Information about U.S.-KMT ties, it is fair to say, was provided on a need-to-know basis.[70]

The KMT irregulars, after several disastrous forays into Yunnan, were not capable of leading a successful uprising against the PRC from their sanctuary in Burma.[71] Of concern for present purposes is how the opium trade across the Burma-Thailand border helped sustain them. The Thais denied responsibility for the trade, but around Chiengmai and Chiengrai the KMT exchanged opium for food, clothing, arms, and ammunition, which often came from Bangkok.[72] Kokang and Kengtung states in Burma, with a lucrative trade controlled by the KMT, were awash in opium. CAT pilots may have transported opium from Kengtung to Thailand; General Phao Sriyanon, head of the Thai police, ordered that CAT flights, then under government contract, not be searched or interfered with.[73]

Albert B. Franklin, first secretary of the U.S. embassy at Rangoon, learned about the KMT and opium from U Aye Pe, the chief reporter for *New Times of Burma*, who had traveled through Kengtung. Franklin concluded that counterinsurgency operations were destined to fail since KMT forces were smoking opium to the point of addiction and would be no match, in Aye Pe's words, for "well-trained, non-opium-smoking Chinese communist troops." The unsuccessful KMT incursions into Yunnan during the summer of 1952 largely proved his point.[74] Nonetheless, Burmese-Western relations were being threatened by the opium traffic, which would continue unless Whitehall could persuade Bangkok and Washington to cut off supplies to Li Mi's forces. William J. Sebald, Key's successor, was concerned about the impact of KMT activities on Rangoon and maintained that the United States "has failed publicly in any way to guarantee the independence and sovereignty of Burma." The British, of course, heartily agreed.[75]

Thailand's participation in the KMT's opium operations becomes more explicable if viewed, first, in the light of overall U.S. strategic thinking about Southeast Asia. If the PRC tried to expand its influence into neighboring lands, then the Thais offered the last line of defense for Western interests. Thus, Ambassador Edwin F. Stanton and Prime Minister Phibun Songgram signed an agreement on 19 September 1950 for a Special Technical and Economic Mission (STEM).[76] Moreover, a report by the Melby-Erskine Mission argued for military assistance in the context of containment strategy: "Thailand approaches being the prototype of the kind of independent, gradually-developing, democratic nation which we wish to encourage in the Far East." As such, an agreement for military assistance was signed in mid-October to provide aid to the Thai army, navy, and air force.

Thailand was not, however, the kind of democratic nation that Washington ideally hoped to find in Southeast Asia. Failed coup attempts and an internal struggle for power dominated Thai politics in 1951. Out of the chaos, Phibun, Phao, and army commander General Sarit Thanarat solidified their respective positions by abrogating the 1949 constitution and by reinstating in February 1952 a revised version of the less democratic constitution of 1932.[77] Even in the midst of all the unrest, it was clear that Phao would profit in many ways. The State Department's Office of Intelligence and Research believed that Phao's gaining control of the inshore coastal patrols from the navy "will enable [him] and his clique to carry on opium smuggling operations."[78]

Seni Pramot, former prime minister and leader of the Free Thai movement in the United States during the Second World War, once termed General Phao the "worst man in the whole history of modern Thailand."[79] His ambition and ruthlessness served him well as the United States sought to secure a strategic foothold in Southeast Asia. Phao emerged as a willing guardian of America's security interests early in 1951. By the end of 1954, he was seen as an ally of considerable importance: "He has been a strong supporter of U.S. objectives in Thailand, has cooperated closely with U.S. agencies, and is a leading political figure."[80]

The agency with which Phao worked especially well was the CIA, and the individual with whom he associated most closely was Willis H. Bird. Bird ran the Sea Supply Company, the CIA's cover enterprise, and supplied arms to Li Mi's troops and Phao's police. Bird and Phao were in regular contact, and Li Mi visited them in Bangkok seeking money, arms, and other equipment.[81] However much the British accepted the importance of Thailand, they did not share the Truman administration's willingness to collaborate with Phao. Britain's ambassador at Bangkok, Geoffrey A. Wallinger, judged Phao "a formidable figure by any reckoning" but warned in September 1952 that "his power already far exceeds his understanding" of global politics. In other words, the United States would be well advised to keep a greater distance from the intrigues of Thai government leaders.[82]

Given the direction of U.S. policy, it was hardly possible to follow this admonition. By relying on General Phao as an instrument of security policy in order to ingratiate the United States with the Thais and to assist the KMT in Burma, officials had to tolerate his widely suspected involvement with opium.[83] It is possible to reconstruct how Phao operated. Thailand, he doubtless knew, was more important than Burma to U.S. security policy in Southeast Asia. If not, then why would Washington risk alienating Rangoon by aiding the KMT in the Shan States? Moreover, if the PRC attacked Burma as a result of Li Mi's forays into Yunnan, the Rangoon government would almost surely put aside its neutralist posture and align with Thailand and the West in opposing communism. Thus, if Phao helped smuggle MDAP aid to the Karens in their struggle against Rangoon, as he may have done, he was trying further to undermine Burmese neutralism and improve his standing with the KMT.

That he aided the Karen National Defense Organization is not clearly established, but he did assist Li Mi and thereby managed to bring order to the opium business.[84]

In relying partly for the success of containment policy in Southeast Asia on the Thais and KMT remnants, who were simultaneously compliant in opposing Communist expansion and intractable in conducting an illegal trade in opium, the United States placed itself in an untenable diplomatic position. With no easy way to resolve the uncontrollable consequences of covert action, administration officials practiced deception on a grand scale. More than a few times the Department of State sent cables like the following to its personnel in Europe and Asia:

> It has been stated officially by the DEPT on several occasions that these rumors are completely without foundation, and I [Acheson] wish to repeat that the US has never aided nor supported these [KMT] troops in any way and is not (RPT not) doing so now. . . . These rumors are typical of the absurd charges being circulated by the COMMIES in an effort to distract ATTN from their own aggressive schemes.[85]

In the same spirit, just as the Chinese Communists were impairing America's relations with Burma, so, too, were they smuggling opium in the Golden Triangle—or so Anslinger claimed and a January 1953 report from the U.S. consul at Chiengmai alleged. What Anslinger knew about the KMT, General Phao, and opium, aside from allegations in diplomatic cables and public rumors, is a matter of conjecture, but he surely was aware of the sorry state of affairs in Thailand. He had also known for some time and was in contact with William J. Donovan when the latter was ambassador to Thailand in 1953–54. Furthermore, it is clear that he had established a working relationship with the CIA by the early 1950s.[86]

The Truman administration left office with its Southeast Asian policy in disarray. Relations with Burma were barely cordial—U.S. policy depended on a regime in Thailand that abjured democracy—and covert support for Kuomintang forces had become a political and diplomatic liability. (Similarly, the situation in Indochina scarcely warranted much optimism.)[87] U.S. grand strategy, as defined in NSC 48/5 and implemented in Kengtung and at the Sino-Burmese border, was underwriting a flourishing opium trade in the Golden Triangle, the reasons for which the FBN and drug control officials in the Department of State could not publicly address. Accordingly, Anslinger blamed the PRC for orchestrating the annual movement of some two hundred to four hundred tons of opium from Yunnan to Bangkok. In short, U.S. antiopium strategy amounted to a subterfuge, the cynical bolstering of a failed policy.[88]

Southeast Asian drug policy may have had its domestic counterpart. Some Asian narcotics no doubt were reaching the United States, where, by most accounts, drug usage and addiction were increasing in the 1950s. Anslinger evidently underestimated the growth of use and addiction in order to show the ability of the Federal Bureau of Narcotics to handle the nation's drug problem. Yet even the FBN charted an increase in addiction, if only for budgetary purposes. To Anslinger, though, budgetary growth and the passage of the 1951 Boggs Act, which provided for mandatory sentences, would allow the FBN to deal with the unrepentant "young hoodlum addicts . . . who can[not] be deterred by copy-book maxims or reached by an educational program."[89] At home and abroad, he was shielding a deficient policy.

New Directions, Old Problems

President Dwight D. Eisenhower's administration sought to avoid the pitfalls of its predecessor's containment strategy in Asia. Secretary of State John Foster Dulles hoped to pressure the PRC in order to curb its expansionist tendencies and rupture its partnership with Moscow.[90] Not an easy task, it involved extricating Washington from dependence on Kuomintang irregulars and relying instead on Thailand as the ultimate protection for Western interests. Great Britain's interest in U.S. strategy remained essentially unchanged. Policymakers worried about the prospect of a close relationship between Beijing and the Viet Minh and saw Thailand as a buffer for Malaya.[91]

Ironically, when Eisenhower promised to unleash Chiang Kai-shek by removing the Seventh Fleet from the Formosan Straits, he raised expectations in Taipei both about U.S. aid for military operations against the mainland and additional supplies for General Li Mi's forces. Whatever else Eisenhower's announcement accomplished, it "aroused great apprehensions in Burma," as Oliver E. Clubb, Jr., later put it.[92] William Sebald worried that some officials still supported the KMT forces as "an exploitable political and military asset in our dealings with Communist China."[93] Sebald's fears proved unwarranted. The British with their abiding interest in Burma's security worked hard to conciliate the differences between Rangoon and Washington. Sir Roger Makins, British ambassador to the United States, was relieved to report in March that the Americans "were fully convinced that the continued presence of K.M.T. troops in Burma was very harmful."[94]

To be sure, the Eisenhower administration had reached that conclusion, though not quickly enough to please Rangoon. Walter Bedell Smith, previously director of central intelligence, who was now under secretary of state, told Koo and the State Department's John M. Allison, "It had formerly been thought that General Li with his troops could render some good service to the cause of freedom," but that expectation had been wrong. In Taipei, Li Mi pleaded with Foreign Minister George K. C. Yeh and Ambassador Rankin for continued U.S. support.[95]

Although events were passing Li Mi by, Burma's anger at U.S. support for the KMT troops boiled over before the Eisenhower administration could fashion an acceptable alternative policy. Not only did Rangoon terminate a technical cooperation accord, but also it made plans to take its case to the United Nations.[96] U.S. authorities responded by endeavoring both to expedite the removal of the now-expendable KMT forces and to deal with the consequences of their presence in Burma. For some officials, this ostensibly meant coming to grips with the expanded opium trade in the Golden Triangle.

No knowing observer would have imagined narcotics control to be a simple undertaking in 1953. The Thai army and police forces were rife with corruption and involved with opium at the highest levels. Elements among the KMT bands, whether loyal or only nominally subject to Taipei's authority, were engaged in lucrative arms and drug dealing. Making the prospect of opium control even dimmer, Phao was bringing new recruits into the business by enlisting into his operations Lisu tribesmen who regularly crossed into Burma from Yunnan. When they entered Thailand, they came under the control of the Thai police.[97]

Implicit condemnation of the KMT irregulars came and went at the United Nations, and elaborate plans for their evacuation were agreed on in Bangkok on 22 June by Taiwan, Burma, Thailand, and the United States. Nothing happened immediately thereafter because KMT leaders in Burma refused to accede to the agreement.[98] Sebald suspected, no doubt accurately, that KMT withdrawal from Burma would be a slow process at best because of the tremendous cost to both the KMT and Thai police in the form of lost revenue from the opium trade.[99]

While Sebald accurately assessed the situation, there was more at stake in the timing of the evacuation for Nationalist China than the loss of opium revenue for a few thousand troops. For Chiang to assist with the removal of Li Mi's forces, he had to believe that Washington was not abandoning him strategically. Philip W. Bonsal of the Office of Philippine and Southeast Asian

Affairs took up Chiang's cause at the time of the talks in Bangkok, declaring that "regardless of the number of these 'foreign forces' actually evacuated, . . . Free China's prestige must be preserved." During a conversation with Admiral Arthur Radford, chairman of the Joint Chiefs of Staff (JCS), Chiang promised to give the withdrawal of forces priority attention; yet despite Chiang's commitment, evacuation was slow in coming.[100]

Upgrading Thailand's place in strategic planning coincided with the effort to remove Li Mi's forces. Sharing America's antipathy to the PRC brought the regime in Bangkok $56 million in military assistance in 1953. The question facing Washington was how best to prevent the advance of communism in Thailand, especially after the Viet Minh's move into Laos in April. Dulles noted: "Thailand is an essential element in the front against the advance of communism in Southeast Asia."[101] A reconstituted, activist National Security Council recommended to Eisenhower on 6 May that training, advice, and aid to Thai armed forces be increased forthwith. The president authorized the action and instructed special assistant C. D. Jackson to prepare a study about the feasibility of using Thailand as a base for psychological warfare.[102]

Part of the plan to draw the two nations together included the naming of a new ambassador. Jackson's Psychological Strategy Board (PSB) welcomed the interest in the post of former OSS chief William J. Donovan. "Nevertheless," Jackson told Walter Bedell Smith, "the special character of the jobs we envision quite properly extends beyond the geographical boundaries of that particular country." By July, the board had a proposal ready for the NSC, entitled "U.S. Psychological Strategy with Respect to the Thai Peoples of Southeast Asia" (PSB D-23). The proposal designated Thailand as a base for overt and covert paramilitary operations against communism; in the second phase of the program, Thailand would serve as the base for similar operations throughout the whole of Southeast Asia.[103]

Indeed, the PSB did not shy away from discussing the two problems most likely to impede the spread of Western influence: nationalism and corruption. There were no easy ways to deal with them. "We must learn eventually to associate ourselves with Asian nationalism," especially at the village level, the PSB declared. As for corruption, uncontrollable missions must be prevented; and yet graft, "which is commonplace among high Thai officials," will not soon disappear. Nonetheless, the PSB deemed the program of such importance that it recommended implementation without undue delay. The JCS, on the other hand, questioned the need for a plan as elaborate as PSB D-23. In its view, U.S. strategy in the region should focus on aid for Indochina. Further interagency talks followed, and on 9 September the NSC approved Phase I of PSB D-23; Phase II would be initiated on recommendation of the Operations Coordinating Board, which replaced the PSB.[104]

As a less elaborate program took shape, some in the administration found Donovan's approval as ambassador all the more important. Dulles termed the nomination most urgent; it was designed "to accomplish a particular purpose in this very sensitive area." Donovan himself believed that the president and Walter Bedell Smith favored the implementation of a psychological strategy in Thailand. As Smith told national security adviser Robert Cutler, even after the decision to delay Phase II of PSB D-23, Donovan, who would report to Smith, was appointed to set up a base in Thailand to expand psychological operations to nearby areas; he "is quietly to assume command and direction" of activities there.[105] This interpretation of the NSC meeting of 9 September doubtless pleased Jackson, who had worried that "very little is going to be done in order to produce our kind of world if every single U.S. move has got to be watered down to the lowest common denominator."[106]

Donovan's appointment as ambassador was welcomed in Bangkok despite the OSS's earlier support for the Free Thai movement. The Eisenhower administration's emphasis on Thailand's importance to Western security interests had taken care of that.[107] For PSB D-23 to succeed, though, Donovan had to remove the KMT remnants as an issue in regional affairs. He had earlier found much to admire in Li Mi's forces, but by mid-1953 changes in strategy had rendered them an obstacle to U.S. goals. An exchange of letters between Eisenhower and Chiang Kai-shek and Donovan's deftness in arranging the details for troop evacuation soon took the issue out of the public eye. CAT's agent in Bangkok, Willis Bird, agreed to airlift troops out of the Burma-Thailand border area beginning in November.[108]

Meanwhile, the matter of the KMT and opium reappeared. Robert W. Rinden, U.S. political officer at Taipei, wanted a rapid evacuation in order to prevent the leakage of information about the KMT's opium business. Indeed, on the eve of the first airlift from Monghsat, it was not clear how thorough the removal would be because of KMT and Thai involvement with the traffic. Thus, it is significant that Phao briefly refused to permit Burmese observers into the evacuation area.[109] Sebald wondered whether Taipei ordered those who stayed behind to continue "nefarious operations in Burma and Thailand including [the] opium smuggling racket."[110] Phao, of course, would still oversee the trade. As we shall see, his importance to U.S. security policy served to undermine an American-led opium conference held earlier that year at the United Nations.

In Indochina as in Thailand, Dulles did not want to be associated with the presumably defensive containment policy of Truman and Acheson. He therefore searched for a way to prevent Indochina's fall to the Viet Minh. His variant of containment was meant to intimidate the PRC and align the United States with nationalism in Southeast Asia. Yet try as the Eisenhower administration might to devise an appropriate strategy, it remained dependent on what the French forces could accomplish on the ground. In early 1953, Donald Heath conceded that the defeat of the Viet Minh was impossible in the near term.[111]

His assessment seemed on target when Viet Minh moved into Laos in April, a development long feared in Washington, Paris, and Saigon.[112] The possible loss of Laos portended grave strategic difficulties; Eisenhower feared that "we [would] likely . . . lose the rest of Southeast Asia and Indonesia. The gateway to India, Burma and Thailand would be open." Moreover, the Viet Minh would create in Laos a center for resistance against the French and their allies among ethnic Tai tribes.[113]

Of lesser import, but equally consequential for certain elements in Saigon, including French commander General Raoul Salan and French intelligence, was the potential loss of access to the opium fields of Laos. By mid-May, though, the Viet Minh had withdrawn, and loyal Meo tribesmen presented the bulk of the opium crop, which they had harvested and hidden just before the offensive. We already know that opium funded counterinsurgency activities; it also fattened the bank accounts of some officials, probably including General Salan, who had coauthorized Operation X. Laos was like a second home to him, he related: "I know it like the back of my hand, and a very good thing too."[114]

The Viet Minh may have seized nearly fifteen tons of Laotian opium, however. Speculation held that Ho Chi Minh's forces would exchange the opium for military and medical supplies from the PRC. Yet it seems more likely in view of the PRC's antiopium campaigns that the Viet Minh bartered the opium for supplies on the black market from Chinese and Vietnamese traders. The U.S. chargé in Vientiane went so far as to predict that Viet Minh disruption of Meo opium production and distribution might affect the conduct of the Indochina struggle itself.[115] And in a way it did.

The invasion of Laos directly threatened the survival of French counterinsurgency operations in northern Vietnam. Without Meo opium from Laos, the Meo of northwestern Tonkin, who also traded with the French, would have been difficult to deal with. Through the intercession of the hated White Tai leader, Deo Van Long of the Tai Federation, the Tonkin Meo had long sold their opium to the French at a nominal price. Given the right opportunity, they and the Black Tai minority would have joined forces with the Viet Minh against the French and Deo Van Long. That chance came in late November after French troops reoccupied Dien Bien Phu in the heart of Black Tai country and prepared to make a stand against the Viet Minh.[116]

The battle for Dien Bien Phu was still in the future, though, when Lieutenant General Henri Navarre replaced Salan in May. Navarre's appointment gave the United States, via the O'Daniel Mission, a pretext to call for changes in French military strategy. Lieutenant General John W. O'Daniel, commander of the U.S. Army, Pacific, encouraged Navarre to act more aggressively; he and Heath responded favorably to the resultant Navarre Plan.[117] Colonel Edward G. Lansdale, the O'Daniel Mission's expert on psychological and guerrilla warfare, discovered while looking into counterinsurgency activities in northwestern Tonkin and Laos that the French were involved with opium production and trafficking. He met with Colonel Maurice Belleux, who had authorized Operation X for the Service de Documentation Extérieure et du Contre-Espionage, at Cap Saint Jacques, a major transit point for Laotian opium. Lansdale later told Alfred W. McCoy that when he suggested an investigation was in order, his superiors told him to drop the idea—presumably because of the embarrassment the revelations would cause French authorities.[118]

Lansdale also may have ferreted out evidence linking French opium operations with the Binh Xuyen of Saigon's Cholon district. Binh Xuyen control of Cholon's vice rackets was widely known among foreign diplomats who transmitted reports of varying accuracy regarding the organization's activities. The British, for example, believed that payoffs by the Binh Xuyen had helped make Bao Dai an incredibly wealthy man, while also bringing them some respectability. On the other hand, a U.S. intelligence assessment more accurately described their plunder-and-profit operations under Le Van Vien's leadership. Lansdale, of course, became better acquainted with the Binh Xuyen when he returned to Vietnam to assist Ngo Dinh Diem.[119]

In retrospect, it seems remarkable that high-ranking U.S. officials of differing political persuasions found their nation's security at stake in a part of the world about which they knew so little and over which they exerted scarcely any influence. Compounding their dilemma, they assumed that they could design a foreign policy strategy to cope with the perceived threat. In December 1953, Eisenhower and Dulles met at Bermuda with Eden, Churchill, who had formed his second government in October 1951, and French foreign minister Georges Bidault. Without a prior agenda, as Lloyd C. Gardner concludes,

"Bermuda proved to be a contentious meeting, the least satisfactory of any Western get-together in the middle years of the Cold War." Strain still plagued the Anglo-American relationship over how best to drive the Chinese away from the now-Stalinless Soviets. Little was said at Bermuda about Indochina but for a few words of bland praise for the heroic French effort, which Churchill tried to turn into a testimonial to colonialism. For his part, Eden left the meeting with further misgivings about U.S. strategy in Asia.[120] Concurrent assessments about progress by Navarre in Vietnam tended to be pessimistic.[121]

The Futility of Opium Control

On the international level in 1953, far removed from the realities of the opium trade in Southeast Asia, the United States perfunctorily continued to promote the cause of opium control. As before, the People's Republic of China served as a convenient scapegoat for the commissioner of narcotics, who again charged that Beijing permitted, even encouraged, narcotics trafficking out of Tientsin and Canton. The avenues of export for narcotics presumably went through Thailand and Hong Kong to the rest of the Pacific area, Europe, and America.[122]

Anslinger had dominated all aspects of U.S. drug policy for more than a decade. As we have seen, however, his evaluation of the drug situation in Asia was often based on questionable information and rarely rendered to fellow decision makers in an unbiased fashion. Reaction against his misrepresentations had set in by 1953 in regard to both domestic and foreign policy. The House of Delegates of the American Bar Association had condemned the mandatory sentencing provisions of the 1951 Boggs Act, and some in Washington were questioning the data on which Anslinger based his charges against the PRC. One of the commissioner's supporters later disclosed that in August 1953 the Pentagon found the allegations "a gross exaggeration." These seeds of doubt were not uniform within the government, though, for copies of Anslinger's remarks were made available to the CIA and other intelligence units at the time.[123]

The United Nations Opium Conference convened soon after the close of the CND session. Thirty-four nations sent representatives, including Burma, Nationalist China, and Vietnam; Thailand sent an observer who did not have voting privileges. The conference adopted the first international protocol to limit the production of, wholesale trade in, and nonmedical use of opium.

Anslinger served as the chief U.S. delegate, with Morlock as his expert adviser. In a postmortem on the conference, the State Department expressed satisfaction with its outcome.[124]

However historic the accord, it stood no chance of being implemented in Southeast Asia. The volatile political situation there, an unabating reliance on opium as a means to a greater end (be it economic, military, or strategic), and the persistence of cultures tied to the poppy exposed the hollowness of the agreement. No more authentic than fool's gold, it promised to frustrate those narcotics control officials in the major powers who were not privy to the machinations being carried on in the name of security. For Thailand, the 1953 accord was simply an irrelevancy. In fact, the Thai representative at the April CND session had admitted that his country could not afford to give up the revenue from the opium business.[125]

Whenever the opportunity arose throughout the remainder of 1953, Anslinger castigated the PRC for trafficking in narcotics. As the French were retaking Dien Bien Phu in November, without regard for the validity of his evidence, he told a Senate inquiry into teenage addiction that heroin trafficking "is exclusively a Red Chinese operation." Indeed, the PRC was allegedly forcing poor farmers to grow opium in order to pay taxes and then shipping manufactured narcotics to Japan and the West through a receptive Hong Kong.[126]

The commissioner and other U.S. policymakers, it should be recalled, had long found suspect the efforts of antinarcotics officials in Hong Kong. Furious about the charges, the Home Office, Foreign Office, and Colonial Office decided to speak with Anslinger directly rather than work through the State Department, since, as J. H. Walker of the Home Office put it, he "would undoubtedly so resent this step that not merely would we almost certainly get no information of any value but our relations with him might be permanently worsened." Importantly, Frank McGrath, the U.S. Treasury attaché at Hong Kong, had no evidence lending credence to the charges. One report to the South East Asia Department from Bangkok averred that "even the International authorities engaged in fighting opium traffic [do not] know who are the principals in the opium business."[127]

Anslinger quietly acknowledged that some of his information was unverifiable, an admission that explains Wayland Speer's quick fact-finding trip to Asia prior to the 1954 session of the CND.[128] Walker, convinced that Nationalist China was Anslinger's source of information about the PRC, feared that he would make little headway about Hong Kong with the FBN chief, who "has strong motives for emphasizing the responsibilities of other countries for illicit traffic in the United States and for attributing this traffic to Communist sources."[129]

Yet Walker worried needlessly because the PRC was still Anslinger's main target. Thus, when Anslinger learned that Hong Kong had a good antinarcotics record, he dropped the Crown Colony from his litany of accusations regarding drug trafficking in Asia. The traffic remained, however, "an insidious, calculated scheme of the Chinese Communist regime to obtain operating funds and . . . spread the debauchery of narcotic addiction among the free nations."[130] Once again, Anslinger's bureaucratic dexterity served him well; muting his critique of Hong Kong had enabled him to avert the most serious challenge yet to his domination of U.S. drug policy.

As I have argued, Anslinger apparently tolerated narcotics trafficking by the KMT and Phao in the name of national security. Although conclusive evidence is lacking, he must have believed that this otherwise objectionable activity would be temporary in nature. Hence, even perfunctory work at the Commission on Narcotic Drugs could set the stage for later substantive action against opium. In that light, he joined with the British and others at the CND's ninth session to consider the creation of a United Nations–sponsored opium control bureau at Bangkok. The idea got nowhere, largely as a result of disputes over the role of Nationalist China and the possible inclusion of the PRC, which Walker advocated despite doubting that Beijing would be willing to participate.[131]

British officials reasonably feared that locating the proposed bureau in Bangkok would help Phao facilitate the illicit traffic. It is hard not to believe that the proprietors of the hotel Heng Lak Hung eagerly awaited the emplacement of a regional opium bureau in Bangkok. Journalist Richard Hughes recalled: "It was a cheap but most respectable inn. Room service was obligatory. There was no main dining room on [any] of the four floors. It was the biggest opium den in the world."[132] How much grander it would have been had its owners been able to compromise a major antiopium agency.

Nowhere in Southeast Asia did effective opium control appear on the horizon in 1954. The futility that was evident at the United Nations and in Thailand pervaded Burma and Indochina as well. Opium smuggling across the Burma-Thailand border near Chiengmai revived tensions in Rangoon's relations with Bangkok and Washington.[133] Strategic planners in the United States continued to curry favor with Bangkok, as evidenced in NSC 5405 of 16 January, which authorized increased assistance "if a serious deterioration of the situation in either Indochina or Burma appears imminent."[134] In practical terms, this meant that the United States would provide additional funding for

Thai defense efforts as part of an incipient regional defense pact. And, as we have seen, General Phao's star continued to rise as a protector of U.S. security interests.[135]

Meanwhile, disquieting reports surfaced concerning opium traffic into the Saigon area even after the fall of Dien Bien Phu.[136] Wayland Speer, whom Anslinger had again sent to Asia, reported that the PRC and the Viet Minh were largely responsible for the opium found around Saigon, which local officials were selling for personal gain. Speer, it seems, got his information from French security police. Rumors in Saigon indicated that the Viet Minh controlled the Laotian opium crop, although the illicit trade was in the hands of professional smugglers.[137]

To make use of this information, Anslinger, as was his wont, resorted to distortion if not outright falsification of unverifiable information. It mattered little to him that the PRC took the unusual step of publicly denying any connection with drug trafficking. At the tenth session of the CND in 1955, he brushed aside Beijing's denial as mere propaganda: "Actual conditions in Southeast Asia and other free countries refute this unsupported denial and clearly prove that the Communist regime of Mainland China is pouring opium, morphine, and heroin out through the Province of Yunnan to augment the already existing lines of traffic out of Tientsin, Tsingtao and Canton."[138]

Conclusion

The real story, of course, was far different from that told by the FBN chief. Nevertheless, his misrepresentation of the PRC's antiopium record contributed to the development of U.S. security policy early in Eisenhower's administration. That is, Anslinger and other decision makers who were responsible for shaping narcotics foreign policy saw to it that their objectives complemented existing strategic goals.

The limits of this endeavor became apparent in 1954. The administration, working through Ambassador Donovan, hoped to put something other than rhetoric into PSB D-23. At an NSC meeting on 11 March, Robert Cutler praised Donovan, who "had done exactly what the State Department had asked him to do, and had made great progress in Thailand."[139] Donovan, who was about to leave Bangkok after one year of duty, observed that his successor would have the "methods and means, including the unconventional, . . . to sustain Thailand's determination to resist and to weaken the aggressive capabilities of the enemy."[140] The British, meanwhile, accepted the need for a common policy with the United States but hoped to prevent Phao from becoming involved in the affairs of other Southeast Asian nations.[141] As we know, the Americans were unprepared to control Phao in mid-1954, let alone to hold him accountable for his involvement with opium.

Administration officials had built up Thailand as a bastion of U.S. policy in Southeast Asia. Yet when the French position in Vietnam fell apart, faith in Bangkok soon diminished and concern over Western security interests intensified.[142] Just the same, Secretary Dulles cautioned on 12 May, after the French defeat at Dien Bien Phu, that he would not make Indochina a symbol for all of Southeast Asia.[143] Dulles, of course, was far from being able to chart the region's future. The British, who realized how little could be accomplished in the short term, refused to commit themselves to the collective defense of Indochina, preferring not to act until after the upcoming talks at Geneva.[144]

The United States had failed to find a coherent anti-Communist strategy in Southeast Asia. Containment by indirection through Thailand, one course essayed by the Eisenhower administration, created more problems than it solved. Not only was the quest for security in jeopardy, but Anglo-American relations were also in disrepair. For nearly fifty years, the two nations had tried to create an international order in Asia that would preserve their individual and common interests. Defining the makeup of that order became all but impossible in the mid-1950s.

Perhaps it was too much to expect any nation to formulate a broad policy protecting Western interests, especially after October 1949. While that may be so, U.S. officials denied that more than a fine tuning of security policy was necessary. Their antipathy to communism restricted policy options, as did their inability to come to terms with traditional opium cultures. At length, they accepted and even suborned opium and narcotics trafficking as the ironic cost of seeking security in a dangerous world that they had helped to create.

Culture, Drug Lords, and Strategy

Opium played a significant role in Sino-Western relations for more than a century. The affinity of millions of Chinese for opium directly affected the security of foreign interests in China. That is, opium not only defined the rhythms of daily life in much of the country, but it also dramatically influenced the way in which many Chinese viewed their own society and partly defined how they reacted to the economic and missionary presence of foreigners in their land. By seeing the external world—whether at the national or international level—through a lens colored by opium smoke, some 20 percent of the Chinese people at any one time managed in a comprehensible way to exist within, if not understand, that alien world. Accepting the reality and importance of a culture of opium in China allows us to understand that the historical Sino-Western relationship has been vastly more complex than most Westerners imagined.

China's poppy culture was not restricted to the habit of smoking. Especially in the time of Yuan Shih-k'ai, a narcotics culture also developed in China. Access to morphine was easy; it came from Great Britain and the United States by way of Japan. By the time the British and the Americans were prepared to quit the morphine trade, Japanese, Koreans, and others were ready to fill the gap with a product produced locally. Thus, even as the brief promise of Yuan Shih-k'ai's presidency was fading, some Chinese and Japanese were locked in a struggle for the drug appetites of the Chinese masses. Heroin apparently had become the narcotic of choice by the 1930s, and Japanese purveying of the drug resulted in condemnation from the West.

Sir John Jordan ruefully acknowledged the obloquy that adhered to the reputation of His Majesty's Government for participating in the drugging of the Chinese. In truth, the British vessels that plied the Indian opium trade were only intermediaries; the British themselves had no power to force anyone to smoke opium. Yet the captains of the ships and entrepreneurs in London realized that the brown mud carried in the holds of ships was a product the Chinese were inclined to receive. Jonathan D. Spence has aptly written of the many Chinese youngsters who grew up in homes where opium was smoked as a matter of course. They could, he observed, "join in the debates about the harmfulness of opium addiction with melancholy satisfaction." This activity alone, however, could not alter the habits of the many Chinese who smoked "to escape from the anguish of the times."[1]

Opium as an anodyne meant instability for Chinese social and economic relationships. Liberal reformers and revolutionaries alike recognized the power that flowed from the ability to provide opium to willing consumers. Antiopium activists in the 1920s had no chance of putting their programs into effect because of the economic importance of opium to warlords and, later, the Kuomintang. Even before the Long March began, the Communists determined that real opium control must come to China. By virtually all accounts, they reached their goal not long after seizing power in October 1949. Despite charges to the contrary by U.S. officials, it is highly likely that poppy cultivation declined dramatically as well. Nonetheless, allegations persisted that drugs from the People's Republic of China were making their way to Korea, Japan, Hong Kong, and the West itself as a conscious foreign policy strategy on the part of Beijing. Available evidence does not support this conclusion. It therefore ought to be relegated to the array of misperceptions of the PRC held by U.S. policymakers that served to prolong a hostile relationship.

Cultures closely linked to opium also flourished in Southeast Asia, having been established long before reformers in the West took notice.[2] And as in China, some Westerners endeavored to profit from the opium habit. No less a figure than Ho Chi Minh decried the readiness of the French to poison Indochinese peasants with alcohol and opium. Heavy taxes exacted from peasants who were often coerced to grow poppies provided nationalist leaders with fertile ground in which to sow the seeds of revolt.[3] Elsewhere in Southeast Asia, in what is now known as the Golden Triangle, autonomous hill tribes rejected nationalist appeals and maintained their traditional association with opium.

An unusual concatenation of events led to the emergence of several kinds of opium lords in Southeast Asia. Growers, traffickers, and their protectors combined to bring a previously unknown, though crude, order to the region's drug business. The Japanese appear to have failed in a similar attempt during the Second World War, but struggles for power in the postwar decade assisted rather than deterred movement toward a kind of rationalization. Touby Lyfoung and Deo Van Long organized cultivation and trafficking in northeastern Laos and Tonkin, respectively. In working through them to rescue a dying empire as the Viet Minh revolt spread, the French fed conflicts among hill people that only hastened the demise of the empire while leaving Indochina in thrall to opium.[4] At the same time, U.S. support for the Kuomintang irregulars of General Li Mi spawned a new era for the opium trade in Burma and Thailand. In short order, opportunistic individuals or groups, such as General Phao Sriyanon and the Binh Xuyen, came forward to protect and profit from the illicit commerce.

These developments bear witness to just how unlikely were the prospects for opium control in Southeast Asia in the decade after 1945. More than that, they explain why, for example, officials like Harry J. Anslinger needed the PRC as a scapegoat after 1949. As Tokyo had been in the 1930s, Beijing was summarily judged guilty of narcotics trafficking. Drug policy failure was made understandable in this way to the informed American public, and high officials in the Truman and Eisenhower administrations found support for their own perceptions of the Chinese threat. In mixing security policy and opium, U.S. policymakers abetted the growth of corruption in Thailand in much the same way as France had done around Saigon. In the process, they also politicized the work of the Commission on Narcotic Drugs at the United Nations.

American officials knew that their cold-war strategy in Southeast Asia suffered from serious weaknesses. It was conceived in haste and subordinated effective crisis management to the fears of the moment. (The occasional strains in relations with Great Britain served as a stark reminder of those debilities.) Thus, Li Mi's forces became expendable in a remarkably short time. That ill-conceived clandestine operation has left an enduring legacy; remnants of the KMT irregulars still grow opium for the illicit traffic. They and others, including elements in the Burmese Communist party, transship opium and heroin through the south of China. The situation evoked such alarm in Beijing in the late 1980s that the Drug Enforcement Administration was advising the PRC on how to cope with the matter.[5]

The deference of drug control strategy in Southeast Asia to greater security policy considerations was not an isolated occurrence. Although the evidence is less conclusive, a similar situation apparently occurred in Iran in the late 1940s. The Afghan rebels of the 1980s, too, were no strangers to the opium and heroin trade of Southwest Asia. And numerous sources of varying credibility have confirmed suspicions about the drug trafficking activities of that now-deposed double or triple agent, Panamanian General Manuel Antonio Noriega.[6] In sum, claims by the U.S. government that international narcotics control is a foreign policy priority of the first rank do not stand up well under close scrutiny.

Ultimately, there are deeper reasons for the shortcomings of U.S. drug control strategy. The drug problem is at bottom a demand problem. Choosing to take drugs is exactly that, an individual choice. To be sure, it is a choice made in a larger context—one in which the drug consumed provides welcome relief against the vagaries of daily life. In that sense, the drug problem has no final solution in the West or anywhere else. But something is terribly amiss when national security policy in the leading nation in the battle against drugs suborns the spread of illicit narcotics trafficking. Inevitably, more people will fall victim to the ravages of addiction. Recognition by the U.S. Congress in the 1988 Anti-Drug Abuse Act of the signal importance of demand cannot quickly compensate for such long-term contradictions in security policy.

Inadequacies in drug control policy did not result from an initial absence of strategy. They have historical roots in a poorly conceived strategy that approximated what international relations scholars and policymakers call "compellence." Beginning with the 1909 meeting at Shanghai, U.S. narcotics experts, far more than their counterparts from other nations, insisted on immediate control at the source and concerted action against the illicit traffic in drugs. That is, in general terms the goal was to put a halt to ongoing objectionable practices.[7] Officials in Washington assumed, and still do in some situations, that failure to enforce U.S. objectives amounted to a failure of political will. In those places where corruption and graft abounded, that presumption doubtless held true. The departure of the American delegation from the Geneva opium conference in 1925 remains the classic example of such a perception and how it can impair the policymaking process.

If daily life for some is often a contingent existence, then it is especially so for most growers of raw narcotic materials and small-time drug traffickers. To them, control at the source and related antinarcotics measures constitute a kind of cultural warfare: such measures deny the legitimacy of how they make sense of the world around them. U.S. drug control officials have rarely appreciated the possible consequences of their intended actions on other cultures.

In a related vein, the baleful ecological and sanitary side effects of unchecked demand reveal the deadly arrogance of organized traffickers and drug consumers. Societal destruction of this kind in the late 1980s in the coca regions of Peru's Upper Huallaga Valley resembled the agricultural loss and human devastation that accompanied the forced production of opium in parts of China in the 1930s. The only difference is that in the case of China, demand was essentially a domestic phenomenon.

U.S. narcotics foreign policy has also tended to overlook the economic importance of drugs to producer nations or to those countries through which drugs pass. For them, effective drug control has the potential to disrupt accustomed economic and social relationships and perhaps foster political unrest. Groups whose identification partly rests on a drug culture often see themselves in a passive, autonomous role vis-à-vis the national government. The hill tribes of the Golden Triangle exemplify this relationship. In effect, the enforcement of American-style narcotics control might be construed as violating a nation's sovereignty by promoting unwelcome changes.

There is no easy way to overcome the dilemmas created by a drug control strategy that has focused inordinately long on the issue of supply and deferred to dubious security concerns. In addition to giving greater attention to the problem of demand, a starting place would be to move toward cultural understanding. A start can be made by examining the making of narcotics foreign policy and the complex process of implementation. Western actions against opium in Asia in the first half of the twentieth century, particularly on the part of the United States, disclose a pattern of misperception, willful or not, of the immensity of the task.

Policymakers must endeavor to set aside preexisting beliefs about the intentions and behavior of producing peoples and nations. They need to try to appreciate the worldview, the culture, of others.[8] The most frequently suggested ways to reduce the supply of drugs propose a combination of crop substitution and income replacement. Since these proposals offer only a remote chance for success in the short term, advocates of drug control must accept the limits of foreign policy and adopt a more sophisticated strategy. To do less is to ignore the many dimensions of the historical obstacles to narcotics control.

NOTES

Abbreviations

ACSI	Assistant Chief of Staff Intelligence (G-2) Files
AID	Agency for International Development
AIPDF	Army Intelligence Project Decimal File
BGCA/WC	Billy Graham Center Archives, Wheaton College
BL/CU	Butler Library, Columbia University
CA	Division [Office] of Chinese Affairs
CBMS	Conference of British Missionary Societies [Conference of Missionary Societies in Great Britain and Ireland]
CF, OF	Central Files, Official File
CIA	Central Intelligence Agency
CMH	Center for Military History
CMOHP	China Missionaries Oral History Project, Butler Library, Columbia University
CND	United Nations Commission on Narcotic Drugs
CNH	Center for Naval History, Washington, D.C.
CO	Colonial Office
COHP	Chinese Oral History Project of the East Asia Institute, Butler Library, Columbia University
C & R	Warren F. Kimball, ed., *Churchill and Roosevelt: The Complete Correspondence*
DBFP	Foreign Office, *Documents on British Foreign Policy*
DDEL	Dwight D. Eisenhower Library, Abilene, Kans.
DS	U.S. Department of State
DSC	Defense Supplies Corporation
DT	U.S. Department of the Treasury
ECA	Economic Cooperation Administration
FBN	Federal Bureau of Narcotics, U.S. Department of the Treasury
FEA	Foreign Economic Administration
FO	Foreign Office
FPA	Foreign Policy Association, New York, N.Y.
FRUS	U.S. Department of State, *Foreign Relations of the United States*

FSP	Foreign Service Post
GUB	Government of the Union of Burma
H.C. Deb.	House of Commons, Debates
HIWRP	Hoover Institution on War, Revolution, and Peace, Palo Alto, Calif.
HO	Home Office
HSTL	Harry S. Truman Library, Independence, Mo.
IMTFE	International Military Tribunal for the Far East
IWM	Imperial War Museum, London
JCS	Joint Chiefs of Staff
JFD	John Foster Dulles
KMT	Kuomintang
MD/LC	Manuscript Division, Library of Congress
MHI	Military History Institute, U.S. Army, Carlisle Barracks, Pa.
ML/PU	Mudd Library, Princeton University
NA	National Archives, Washington, D.C.
NAMP	National Archives Microfilm Publication
NSC	National Security Council
OAC	Opium Advisory Committee, League of Nations
OCB	Operations Coordinating Board
OHRO	Oral History Research Office, Butler Library, Columbia University
OIC	Opium Investigation Committee, Philippine Commission
OIR	Office of Intelligence and Research, U.S. Department of State
OPM	Office of Production Management
OSANSA	Office of the Special Assistant for National Security Affairs
OSS	Office of Strategic Services
PL/PSU	Pattee Library, Pennsylvania State University
P.R.	Political Report
PRO	Public Record Office, Kew, Richmond
PSA	Office of Philippine and Southeast Asian Affairs
PSF	President's Secretary's File
R & A	Research and Analysis
RFC	Reconstruction Finance Corporation
RG	Record Group
s., ser.	series
SACSEA	Supreme Allied Commander for South-East Asia
SCAP	Supreme Commander for the Allied Powers
SCAP AG	Supreme Commander for the Allied Powers, Adjutant General
SEAD	South-East Asia Division, Foreign Office
SOAS/UL	School of Oriental and African Studies, University of London
S-SGR	Security-Segregated General Records
UN	United Nations
USMC	U.S. Marine Corps

WNRC   Washington National Records Center, Suitland, Md.
WO   War Office
WPB   War Production Board

Preface

1. The earlier book is Walker, *Drug Control in the Americas.* Reins, "China and the International Politics of Opium," discusses some of the same issues with which I am concerned, but the author did not evaluate his source material with a sufficiently critical eye.

2. Walker, "Drug Control and the Issue of Culture in American Foreign Relations."

3. Spencer and Navaratnam, *Drug Abuse in East Asia;* House Select Committee on Narcotics Abuse and Control, *Report of a Study Mission,* 1–2. The best treatment of money laundering is Kwitny, *The Crimes of Patriots.*

4. House Select Committee on Narcotics Abuse and Control, *Report of a Study Mission,* 2.

5. House Committee on Foreign Affairs, *Narcotics Review in Southeast/Southwest Asia,* 2–4, 10.

6. Westermeyer, *Poppies, Pipes, and People;* White, "Laos Today" and "The Poppy—For Good and Evil," 170–73; Crooker, "Opium Production in North Thailand."

Chapter One

1. Kaku Sagataro, "The Opium Question in China: Introductory Remarks," 1916, Hornbeck Papers, box 93, HIWRP. Katu also served as the civil governor of Formosa and was the Japanese delegate to the Geneva opium conferences of 1924–25. In 1924 he penned a defense of Japan's opium policy: *Opium Policy in Japan.*

2. Wakeman, *The Fall of Imperial China,* 125; Owen, *British Opium Policy,* 8–16.

3. Fay, *The Opium War,* 42–43; Wakeman, *The Fall of Imperial China,* 19–28, 127–28; Fairbank, *The Great Chinese Revolution,* 63–67.

4. Wakeman, *The Fall of Imperial China,* 126; Fairbank, *Trade and Diplomacy,* 48–53, 57–63.

5. Fay, *The Opium War,* 44–49.

6. Wu, *The Chinese Opium Question,* 18; Wakeman, *The Fall of Imperial China,* 126.

7. Spence, "Opium Smoking in Ch'ing China," 150–51; Fairbank, *Trade and Diplomacy,* 68–71; Wu, *The Chinese Opium Question,* 19.

8. Fay, *The Opium War,* 54–55; Wakeman, *The Fall of Imperial China,* 127–28; Teng, *The Taiping Rebellion,* 28; Fairbank, *Trade and Diplomacy,* 67 (quotation).

9. Fay, *The Opium War,* 45–46; Wakeman, *The Fall of Imperial China,* 128; Fairbank, *Trade and Diplomacy,* 76–78.

10. Walker, *Drug Control in the Americas*, 1, 3–4, 9–11.

11. On opium as an anodyne in China, see Spence, "Opium Smoking in Ch'ing China," 144–46; Fay, *The Opium War*, 48–49; Fairbank, *Trade and Diplomacy*, 137, 226; Chang, *Commissioner Lin*, 31, 176–79, 189–95; Mancall, *China at the Center*, 99–100.

12. Wakeman, *The Fall of Imperial China*, 39–40, 121–29; Mancall, *China at the Center*, 97–98. See also Wakeman, "The Canton Trade and the Opium War," 163–212.

13. Morse, *The International Relations of the Chinese Empire*, 1:171–297; Fay, *The Opium War*, 128–29, 138; Chang, *Commissioner Lin*, 92–94, 120–21, 126–28.

14. Wakeman, *The Fall of Imperial China*, 131–33; Chang, *Commissioner Lin*, 128–79. Lin's letter to Queen Victoria appears in Teng and Fairbank, *China's Response to the West*, 24–27. See also Fay, *The Opium War*, 80–81, 142–61; Slade, *Narrative of the Late Proceedings and Events in China*.

15. Chang, *Commissioner Lin*, 192–205; Fay, *The Opium War*, 175–79, 194–95; Ridley, *Lord Palmerston*, 247–57.

16. Wakeman, *The Fall of Imperial China*, 135; Chang, *Commissioner Lin*, 208–12.

17. Fay, *The Opium War*, 267–78, 281; Fairbank, *Trade and Diplomacy*, 79–81.

18. Wakeman, *The Fall of Imperial China*, 134–38; Fairbank, *Trade and Diplomacy*, 90–104; Fay, *The Opium War*, 361–63; Mancall, *China at the Center*, 115–19.

19. Teng and Fairbank, *China's Response to the West*, 28.

20. Fairbank, *Trade and Diplomacy*, 86–90; Wakeman, *The Fall of Imperial China*, 141–46.

21. Occurring as the monopoly of the British East India Company ended, the Napier Mission constituted an attempt to force Ch'ing officials to open China's ports to all foreign merchants selling opium. On British politics and free-trade foreign policy under Palmerston, see Ridley, *Lord Palmerston*, 186, 248–49, 285–86. Other than on the commitment to free trade, the anticolonial radicals had little in common with the foreign minister. Concerning free trade and foreign policy, especially as it related to the Anti-Corn–Law League and Richard Cobden, one of its more influential members, see Spall, "Reform Ideas of the Anti-Corn–Law Leaguers," 233–37.

22. Fay, *The Opium War*, 89–94, 97 (quotation).

23. Ibid., 41–42, 157; Fairbank, *Trade and Diplomacy*, 226; Hunt, *The Making of a Special Relationship*, 7–15.

24. Fairbank, *Trade and Diplomacy*, 229–40. By revising slightly their response to the traffic in opium, British consuls seemed to be employing what Irving Janis and Leon Mann have characterized as a pattern of unconflicted change. Janis and Mann, *Decision Making*, 25–29 and especially 55, 71–73.

25. Mancall, *China at the Center*, 112–20; Fairbank, *The Great Chinese Revolution*, 83, 92–95, 106.

26. Fairbank, *Trade and Diplomacy*, 240–43.

27. Morse, *The Trade and Administration of China*, 21; Wakeman, *Strangers at the Gate*, 159; Teng, *The Taiping Rebellion*, 243.

28. Oliphant, *Elgin's Mission to China and Japan*, 1:17–25, 91–114; Teng, *The Taiping Rebellion*, 243.

29. Morse, *The International Relations of the Chinese Empire*, 1:539–56; Wakeman, *The Fall of Imperial China*, 157–59; Teng, *The Taiping Rebellion*, 244, 267–69.

30. Jen, *The Taiping Revolutionary Movement*, 444–45; Teng, *The Taiping Rebellion*, 284–316; Morse, *The International Relations of the Chinese Empire*, 2:90–111. See also Gregory, *Great Britain and the Taipings*, 160–65.

31. Wakeman, *The Fall of Imperial China*, 163–74; Teng, *The Taiping Rebellion*, 390–400.

32. Jen, *The Taiping Revolutionary Movement*, 445.

33. Oliphant, *Elgin's Mission to China and Japan*, 2:278–81; Wu, *The Chinese Opium Question*, 57; Teng, *The Taiping Rebellion*, 259–63; Hunt, *The Making of a Special Relationship*, 21–24.

34. Mancall, *China at the Center*, 139–41, 145–60, 184–85; Wakeman, *The Fall of Imperial China*, 185–86, 189–95.

35. Spence, "Opium Smoking in Ch'ing China," 160–61, 164–67.

36. Bruner, Fairbank, and Smith, *Entering China's Service*, 268.

37. Wakeman, *The Fall of Imperial China*, 171–72, 177–78.

38. Spence, "Opium Smoking in Ch'ing China," 170–71.

39. Ibid., 151, 154.

40. Fairbank, Bruner, and Matheson, *The I.G. in Peking*, 2:letters 1019, 1023–24, 1052, 1059–60, 1062, 1070; Spence, "Opium Smoking in Ch'ing China," 171–72; Morse, *The Trade and Administration of China*, 373.

41. Hsu, "Late Ch'ing Foreign Relations," 84; Hao and Wang, "Changing Chinese Views of Western Relations," 161–66; Teng and Fairbank, *China's Response to the West*, 100 (quotation). On Li Hung-chang, see Wakeman, *The Fall of Imperial China*, 185–95. For Li's denunciation of the opium situation in China, see Wu, *The Chinese Opium Question*, 60.

42. A. Williamson, *Journeys in North China*, 1:17–18, indicates a growing intolerance of foreigners for their part in the opium traffic. See also Wu, *The Chinese Opium Question*, 110; Spence, "Opium Smoking in Ch'ing China," 151, 153. On the domestic and foreign policy origins of the Anglo-Oriental Society for the Suppression of the Opium Trade, a major antiopium organization, see Berridge and Edwards, *Opium and the People*, 174, 176.

43. *Records of the General Conference of the Protestant Missionaries of China*, 314–16, 322, 324 (quotation), 329; A. Williamson, *Journeys in North China*, 2:66.

44. Morse, *The Trade and Administration of China*, 368–69. Enforcement of the Sino-American accord was another matter altogether. See also Wu, *The Chinese Opium Question*, 109, 132–35; Owen, *British Opium Policy*, 311, 314–19, 326.

45. Wu, *The Chinese Opium Question*, 134–35 (quotation, 135), 141, 152–53; Owen, *British Opium Policy*, 319–20; John Morley, *Recollections*, 2:172, 202–3. Around 1890, India was realizing about 18 percent of its revenue from the opium trade. Parssinen, *Secret Passions*, 11.

46. Mancall, *China at the Center*, 158–68, 184–85; Hunt, *The Making of a Special Relationship*, 187–88; Esherick, *The Origins of the Boxer Uprising*.

47. Chang, "Intellectual Change and the Reform Movement," 283–91; Kung, "Cultural Revolution in Modern Chinese History," 236–40.

48. Chang, "Intellectual Change and the Reform Movement," 312–16; Teng and Fairbank, *China's Response to the West*, 164 (quotation).

49. Wakeman, *The Fall of Imperial China*, 210–16; Teng and Fairbank, *China's Response to the West*, 170 (quotation). See also Morse, *The Trade and Administration of China*, 380–81.

50. *FRUS, 1906*, 357–58.

51. A. Smith, *The Uplift of China*, 215 n. 1.

52. Cameron, *The Reform Movement in China*, 139–43; International Anti-Opium Association, *The War against Opium*, 18; Morse, *The International Relations of the Chinese Empire*, 3:436. This evidence suggests that the General Conference of Missionaries of China was premature in 1890 when it determined that the Chinese could not take the first step toward opium control. *Records of the General Conference of the Protestant Missionaries of China*, 350. Cf. A. Taylor, *American Diplomacy and the Narcotics Traffic*, 21–22, 28–31.

53. OIC, *Use of Opium and Traffic Therein*, 52–55. For further discussion, see Cameron, *The Reform Movement in China*, 140–41; Owen, *British Opium Policy*, 327–28; A. Taylor, *American Diplomacy and the Narcotics Traffic*, 31–44.

54. Morse, *The International Relations of the Chinese Empire*, 3:437. The text of the edict appears in Morse, *The Trade and Administration of China*, app. F. Cf. *FRUS, 1906*, 366–69.

55. Cameron, *The Reform Movement in China*, 143–45; *FRUS, 1907*, 149, 152, 161; Owen, *British Opium Policy*, 333–37.

56. Cameron, *The Reform Movement in China*, 146. The China Centenary Missionary Conference of 1907 went on record with its willingness to help bring opium control to China. *China Centenary Missionary Conference Records*, 387–90.

57. Hatano, "The New Armies," 369; Morse, *The Trade and Administration of China*, 373–78; Kapp, *Szechwan and the Chinese Republic*, 4.

58. Wright, "Introduction: The Rising Tide of Change," 14; Cameron, *The Reform Movement in China*, 146–50. Resistance to opium edicts appeared to be popularly based. Bastid-Bruguiere, "Currents of Social Change," 598.

59. Morse, *The International Relations of the Chinese Empire*, 3:437–38; FO, *The Opium Trade*, 1:III, January–June 1911, no. 183 and enclosure (for the final text of the 1911 agreement). Regarding antiopium activity, see FO, *The Opium Trade*, 1:I, January–June 1910, nos. 21, 25; II, July–December 1910, no. 155.

60. OIC, *Use of Opium and Traffic Therein*, passim; *FRUS, 1906*, 361–63; Zabriskie, *Bishop Brent*, 101–3; *China Centenary Missionary Conference Records*, 760.

61. *FRUS, 1907*, 144, 146.

62. Ibid., 159, 162–63, 165–66.

63. A. Taylor, *American Diplomacy and the Narcotics Traffic*, 53–58, 61–62; *FRUS, 1908*, 100–102.

64. A. Taylor, *American Diplomacy and the Narcotics Traffic*, 65–80.

65. Ibid., 65, 74–75.

66. *FRUS, 1909*, 102–3.

67. FO, *The Opium Trade*, 1:II, July–December 1910, no. 63 and enclosure.

68. Ibid., I, January–June 1910, no. 41 and enclosures; III, January–June 1911, nos. 69, 108 and enclosure, 201; IV, nos. 60–61, 91 and enclosures, 102.

69. Ibid., II, July–December 1910, no. 80; IV, July–December 1911, nos. 117, 180.

70. Wakeman, *The Fall of Imperial China*, 97–120.

71. A. Taylor, *American Diplomacy and the Narcotics Traffic*, 97–120. Two more meetings were held to clarify procedures for ratification and implementation of the convention.

72. FO, *The Opium Trade*, 2:V, January–June 1912, no. 81.

73. Nish, *The Anglo-Japanese Alliance*, 142, 365, 369, 372–77.

74. Nish, *Alliance in Decline*, 81–82, 99–105, 392–93; Lowe, *Great Britain and Japan*, 58–88, 99–117.

75. OIC, *Use of Opium and Traffic Therein*, 24–28, 68, 73.

Chapter Two

1. MacKinnon, *Power and Politics in Late Imperial China*, 13–14, 16–21; Wakeman, *The Fall of Imperial China*, 229–32. Yuan's inherent conservatism earned him the support of foreign powers at the height of the revolution in 1911. See E. Young, "Yuan Shih-k'ai's Rise to the Presidency," 428–33.

2. E. Young, *The Presidency of Yuan Shih-k'ai*, 52–55; MacKinnon, *Power and Politics in Late Imperial China*, 35–45, 138–79.

3. *FRUS, 1906*, 365–66, and *1907*, 151–53.

4. MacKinnon, *Power and Politics in Late Imperial China*, 167.

5. FO, *The Opium Trade*, 2:VI, July–December 1912, no. 113 enclosure 1.

6. Ibid., no. 150.

7. Ibid., V, January–June 1912, nos. 89, 118 (quotation).

8. E. Young, *The Presidency of Yuan Shih-k'ai*, 127, 169; FO, *The Opium Trade*, 2:VI, July–December 1912, no. 124. See also Nish, *Alliance in Decline*, 8, 188–89. In all provinces where opium grew extensively, suppression meant a dramatic loss of local revenue. On the eve of the revolution, unions of growers had formed to resist anti-

opium decrees in western Hunan and Hupei. Esherick, *Reform and Revolution in China*, 109, 114.

9. FO, *The Opium Trade*, 2:VI, July–December 1912, nos. 1, 59 and enclosure; Kapp, *Szechwan and the Chinese Republic*, 8.

10. FO, *The Opium Trade*, 2:V, January–June 1912, no. 64; VI, July–December 1912, no. 144.

11. Ibid., VI, July–December 1912, no. 89.

12. Ibid., 3:VII, 1913, no. 12 and enclosures. For a discussion of this final point as it related to the situation in Kwangtung and Kiangsi, see E. Young, *The Presidency of Yuan Shih-k'ai*, 91–92, 111.

13. FO, *The Opium Trade*, 3:VII, 1913, no. 51 (for conditions at the Burma-China border); 1:IV, July–December 1911, no. 157 (for Indochina); 2:VI, July–December 1912, nos. 36, 46; OIC, *Use of Opium and Traffic Therein*, 15, 36, 229ff.

14. Woodis, *Ho Chi Minh*, 13–14.

15. E. Young, *The Presidency of Yuan Shih-k'ai*, 120–33; *FRUS, 1913*, 124, 127; Ch'en, *Yuan Shih-k'ai*, 163–68; Sheridan, *China in Disintegration*, 47–54.

16. *FRUS, 1913*, 219.

17. E. Young, *The Presidency of Yuan Shih-k'ai*, 123–28, 134, 180; Lowe, *Great Britain and Japan*, 103, 127–29, 132–43. On U.S. policy and the consortium, see Pugach, *Paul S. Reinsch*, 70–71, 79; *FRUS, 1913*, 143–44, 170–73, 175–77, 180–82.

18. *FRUS, 1913*, 188; E. Young, *The Presidency of Yuan Shih-k'ai*, 126, 181, 199–200. The issue was larger than the security of the loan. Ch'en, *Yuan Shih-k'ai*, 158.

19. Pugach, *Paul S. Reinsch*, 54, 124–27; E. Young, *The Presidency of Yuan Shih-k'ai*, 172–76, 220–22. For Goodnow's role in Yuan Shih-k'ai's decision, see *FRUS, 1915*, 46–58. For reports on reaction to the restoration, see *FRUS, 1915*, 62, 69–70.

20. Mancall, *China at the Center*, 201–2.

21. *British Documents on the Origins of the War*, enclosure in no. 497 and app. I; Nish, *Alliance in Decline*, 105, 155–58. The Foreign Office still hoped that the alliance with Japan might curb rather than encourage Japanese adventurism.

22. *FRUS, 1915*, 84, 93–95, 111, 146, 159–70; Link et al., *The Papers of Woodrow Wilson*, 32:139, 322–24, 520–21, 531. Cf. Grey, *Twenty-Five Years*, 2:103–5. See also Gardner, *Safe for Democracy*, 83–84.

23. Sheridan, *China in Disintegration*, 50–56.

24. On the limited capacity of the salt tax to provide revenue, see E. Young, *The Presidency of Yuan Shih-k'ai*, 241.

25. FO, *The Opium Trade*, 3:IX, January–November 1915, nos. 21–22, 38 enclosure 5. A comparable arrangement was made with an opium combine in Hong Kong. Ibid., X, January–September 1916, no. 3 enclosure 2.

26. Ibid., X, January–September 1916, no. 8, and 4:XI, 1917, nos. 14, 18 enclosure 2.

27. Ibid., 4:XI, 1917, no. 31 and enclosures 3, 4, and 6, no. 41 and enclosures.

28. Bashford, *China: An Interpretation*, 336–37, 418–29; Board of Foreign Missions, *Annual Report . . . 1917*, 191 (Bashford's quotation); Denby, *China and Her People*, 2:21. On Denby, see Hunt, *Frontier Defense and the Open Door*, 23–29.

29. Board of Foreign Missions, *Annual Report . . . 1907*, 163 (for Fukien), 230 (for Szechwan); *Annual Report . . . 1908*, 162 (for Fukien); Schlesinger, "The Missionary Enterprise and Theories of Imperialism," 360–73; *Annual Report . . . 1918*, 222–23 (quotation).

30. Link et al., *The Papers of Woodrow Wilson*, 33:23–26, 31–37 (quotation, 35).

31. *FRUS, 1917*, 260–66, 268, 273; Nish, *Alliance in Decline*, 223–24, 258, 261. Cf. Gardner, *Safe for Democracy*, 217–24.

32. MacMurray to DS, 26 August 1918, and Page to the secretary of state, 14 September 1918, RG 59, 893.114/174, NA; FO, *The Opium Trade*, 4:XII, 1918, nos. 16–17, 19. Neither British nor American representatives could ascertain the precise amount of opium in question. Figures ranged from 1,200 to 1,700 chests, a difference of some 33 tons! The number was likely more than 1,500 chests. Had the stocks of opium been disposed of when first offered to the government, at least another 400 chests, or nearly 27 tons of opium, would not have reached China.

33. Paul S. Reinsch to DS, 25 November 1918, RG 59, 893.114/185, NAMP, M329, roll 113, NA. See also *North China Herald*, 28 September 1918.

34. International Anti-Opium Association, *The War against Opium*, i–ii.

35. Ibid., ii–iii; Thomas Sammons to Reinsch, 18 January 1919, RG 59, 893.114/206, NAMP, M329, roll 114, and V. K. Wellington Koo to Mrs. Hamilton Wright, 20 November 1918, RG 59, 893.114/185, NAMP, M329, roll 113, NA.

36. FO, *The Opium Trade*, 4:XIV, 1919, no. 13.

37. Sammons to Reinsch, 18 January 1919, RG 59, 893.114/206, NAMP, M329, roll 114, NA; LaMotte, *Peking Dust*, 125–26, 237 (second quotation).

38. Reinsch to DS, 27 January 1919, RG 59, 893.114/213, NAMP, M329, roll 114, NA; Pugach, *Paul S. Reinsch*, 122–39, 252–55 and passim.

39. Sammons to DS, 5 February 1919, RG 59, 893.114/215, and Reinsch to DS, 24 February 1919, RG 59, 893.114/219, NAMP, M329, roll 114, NA.

40. A. Taylor, *American Diplomacy and the Narcotics Traffic*, 142–44; *FRUS: Paris Peace Conference, 1919*, 552–53, 567–69, 595.

41. Morphia was then the British word for morphine. Morse, *The Trade and Administration of China*, 379–80. Morse claimed that one ounce of morphine would give between 1,000 and 2,000 injections. China legally imported 195,133 ounces in 1902. See E. Williams, *China Yesterday and Today*, 459–63; Parssinen, *Secret Passions*, 145–52.

42. Regarding Tsingtao, see News Bulletin, 20 September 1914, Peck Papers, box 3, HIWRP; *North-China Daily News*, 26 August 1915; FO, *The Opium Trade*, 3:X, January–September 1916, no. 2; 4:XI, 1917, nos. 17, 20, 27, 30, 37, 44–46.

43. Mrs. Hamilton Wright to DS, 8 June 1917, RG 59, 893.114/157, and Baker to DS, 27 July 1918, RG 59, 893.114/179, NAMP, M329, roll 113, NA; *North-China Daily News,* 17 December 1918.

44. Willys R. Peck memorandum to Reinsch, 21 November 1918, and Peck to DS, 6 July 1919, Peck Papers, box 3, HIWRP; FO, *The Opium Trade,* 4:XIII, 1919, no. 11. See also Nish, *Alliance in Decline,* 253 n. 11, 255, 258 (on Soejima), 265 (on Hara Kei). Morphine injections cost about five cents apiece.

45. Egerton, *Great Britain and the Creation of the League of Nations,* 164, 168; FO, *The Opium Trade,* 4:XIII, 1919, no. 16; XV, January–June 1921, nos. 6, 78 and enclosures, 79 and enclosures. Charges of trafficking in morphine against some Westerners and the Japanese caused considerable furor in certain quarters in the West; in the *Literary Digest:* "A Chinese Charge against Japan," 20, and "Poisoning the Chinese," 30; and in *Millard's Review of the Far East* (published in Shanghai): "Great Britain, America, and the China Opium Problem," 320–24, which concluded: "The white race can't escape the responsibility and the consequences of forcing the drug evil on the subject and backward races of Asia" (p. 324).

46. G. C. Hanson to Reinsch, 12 October 1918, RG 59, 893.114/192, and Sammons to Reinsch, 16 January 1919, RG 59, 893.114/202, NAMP, M329, roll 113, NA; FO, *The Opium Trade,* 4:XIV, 1920, no. 20 and enclosure.

47. FO, *The Opium Trade,* 4:XIII, 1919, no. 16 and enclosure; Reinsch to DS, 29 April 1919, RG 59, 893.114/231, NAMP, M329, roll 114, NA.

48. Sheridan, *China in Disintegration,* 57–59, 78–87, and *Chinese Warlord,* 105; Nathan, *Peking Politics,* 25 (for the changes in government).

49. Sheridan, *Chinese Warlord,* 26; Note by Nelson T. Johnson, 25 January 1919, RG 59, 893.114/192, NAMP, M329, roll 113, NA; Nathan, *Peking Politics,* 60–62.

50. The discussion on nationalism, Sun Yat-sen, and the role of the warlords as quasi-agents of nationalism is based on O. Edmund Clubb, *Twentieth-Century China,* 65–67, 100–107; Wilbur, *Sun Yat-sen,* passim; Sheridan, *China in Disintegration,* 96–106, and *Chinese Warlord,* 121–23.

51. The United States and Great Britain watched with interest the vain attempt at national reconciliation. *FRUS, 1919,* 328–33, 354–57.

52. Billingsley, *Bandits in Republican China,* 17–43; Board of Foreign Missions, *Annual Report . . . 1920,* 57. Authorities put pressure on peasants throughout Fukien to plant opium. Land taxes for poppy growing were assessed even if peasants chose not to plant. See Board of Foreign Missions, *Annual Report . . . 1924,* 35, 41–42.

53. FO, *The Opium Trade,* 4:XV, January–June 1921, nos. 93, 98 and enclosures; International Anti-Opium Association, *The War against Opium,* 61 and 75 (quotations).

54. FO, *The Opium Trade,* 4:XVI, July–December 1921, nos. 6 and enclosure, 7 and enclosure.

55. Ibid., XV, January–June 1921, no. 11.

56. M. S. Myers to DS, 28 October 1922 (RG 59, 893.114/421), 5 February 1923

(RG 59, 893.114/434), and 12 July 1923 (RG 59, 893.114/454), NAMP, M329, roll 115, NA.

57. Woodhead, *China Year Book, 1921–22*, 790–93, and *1923*, 887–92. Rev. Arthur Sowerby prepared the section on opium for 1921–22 and Dr. Graham Apsland did likewise for 1923; both belonged to the International Anti-Opium Association. See also P. Stewart Heintzleman to Jacob Gould Schurman, 26 March 1923, RG 59, 893.114/441, and C. J. Spiker (Chungking) to Schurman, 26 April 1923, RG 59, 893.114/449, NAMP, M329, roll 115, NA; Billingsley, *Bandits in Republican China*, 126–27.

58. International Anti-Opium Association, *Annual Report*, 103; FO, *The Opium Trade*, 4:XVII, January–June 1922, no. 40 and enclosure; A. E. Carleton (Amoy) to DS, 24 November 1922, RG 59, 893.114/423, NAMP, M329, roll 115, NA.

59. *Peking & Tientsin Times*, 27–29 June 1922; Stuart J. Fuller to DS, 2 February 1923, RG 59, 893.114/430, NAMP, M329, roll 115, NA.

60. William Phillips to Schurman, 15 May 1923, RG 59, 893.114/435, Schurman to DS, 20 February 1923, RG 59, 893.114/436, and International Anti-Opium Association to Schurman, 14 February 1923, RG 59, NAMP, M329, roll 115, NA.

61. Lester L. Schnare to Schurman, 13 February 1923, RG 59, 893.114/437, Samuel Sokobin to DS, 18 January 1924, RG 59, 893.114/473, Edward Bell (Peking) to DS, 26 November 1923, RG 59, 893.114/464, and Schurman to DS, 5 April 1924, RG 59, 893.114/487, ibid.

62. *Central China Post*, 16 August 1923; John R. Putnam (Foochow) to General Sun Ch'uan-fang, *Tuli* of Fukien, 26 November 1923, RG 59, 893.114/472, NAMP, M329, roll 115, NA.

63. OAC, *Minutes of the Sixth Session*, 42; International Anti-Opium Association, *Annual Report*, 5–6.

64. Clarence E. Gauss to DS, 24 February 1925, RG 59, 893.114/522, NAMP, M329, roll 115, NA.

65. FO, *The Opium Trade*, 5:XXI, 1924, no. 20.

66. Ibid., no. 16.

67. A. Taylor, *American Diplomacy and the Narcotics Traffic*, 171–72; League of Nations, *First Geneva Opium Conference*, 115–16.

68. A. Taylor, *American Diplomacy and the Narcotics Traffic*, 187–90.

69. League of Nations, *Second Geneva Opium Conference*, 1:201–4.

70. FO, *The Opium Trade*, 5:XXII, 1925, nos. 1, 3; A. Taylor, *American Diplomacy and the Narcotics Traffic*, 208–9.

71. *The Reminiscences of Herbert L. May*, 18, OHRO. About Representative Stephen G. Porter, who led the walkout, May was even harsher. Porter's interest in opium, May averred, "was not only on the humanitarian side but also because it was a good subject for publicity in the newspapers" (ibid., 16).

72. Minutes of the Executive Committee, FPA, 14 December 1922, 7 May 1924, 3

March and 7 April 1926; *The Reminiscences of Herbert L. May*, 18–19, 26–29, OHRO.

73. Porter to MacMurray, 26 May 1925, RG 59, 493.11/1159, Memorandum by Johnson, 9 April 1926, RG 59, 493.11/1233, and White Cross International Anti-Narcotics Society of Seattle to Secretary of State Frank B. Kellogg, 27 July 1927, RG 59, 893.114/535, NAMP, M329, roll 115, NA. On extraterritoriality, see Borg, *American Policy and the Chinese Revolution*, 58–60.

74. Cross Oral History, CMOHP, 1:10.

75. Jefferson Caffrey to DS, 20 September 1924, RG 59, 511.4A2/103, NA; A. Taylor, *American Diplomacy and the Narcotics Traffic*, 181–83, 203–4. On Anglo-Japanese relations generally, cf. Hosoya, "Britain and the United States in Japan's View of the International System," 10–11, and Nish, "Japan in Britain's View of the International System," 30–33.

76. For a discussion of the appropriateness of a monopoly for handling morphine, see International Anti-Opium Association, *Morphia and Narcotic Drugs in China.*

77. The State Department feared that it might unwittingly find itself in the undesirable position of putting pressure on Great Britain and Japan if, for example, indemnity funds went for antiopium activities. Johnson to DS, 10 April 1926, RG 59, 493.11/1233, NA.

78. See, for example, Ikei, "Ugaki Kazushige's View of China," 199–200, 212–14.

79. *The Reminiscences of K'ung Hsiang-hsi*, 58, COHP. On the opium business in Sun's China, see FO, *The Opium Trade*, 5:XXI, 1921, nos. 18, 22; Wilbur, *Sun Yat-sen*, 277–78.

Chapter Three

1. Barnhart, *Japan Prepares for Total War*, 9, 22–28.

2. Louis, *British Strategy in the Far East*, 6–9, 43.

3. Borg, *American Policy and the Chinese Revolution*, 20–46, 145–53.

4. Sheridan, "The Warlord Era," 291–303, 315–17. See Ch'i, *Warlord Politics*, 150–78, on the near-anarchic economic conditions of the mid-1920s, and Wilbur, *The Nationalist Revolution in China*, for a thorough portrayal of warlord conflict and the rise of the Kuomintang.

5. Board of Foreign Missions, *Annual Report . . . 1925*, 106. The Kiangsi Conference noted that the opium traffic persisted under government auspices and that Christian action was having little impact.

6. MacMurray to Grew, 12 February 1927, Peck Papers, box 3, HIWRP.

7. FO, *The Opium Trade*, 5:XXII, 1925, no. 7.

8. Ibid., no. 10 and enclosure 1.

9. Ibid., XXII, 1925, no. 14.

10. Ibid., no. 18 enclosures 1 and 2, no. 19; XXIII, 1926, no. 2 enclosure.

11. Ibid., no. 4 and enclosure.

12. Ibid., XXII, 1925, no. 8.

13. Ibid., XXIII, 1926, no. 20.

14. Ibid., 6:XXIV, 1927, nos. 6, 9. See also Janis and Mann, *Decision Making*, 56–57, 70, 73; Lebow, *Between Peace and War*, 108.

15. FO, *The Opium Trade*, 6:XXIV, 1927, no. 11 and enclosure. As in the case of Malaya, officials had little recourse other than to adopt a temporary "satisficing" policy; on this strategy as used by political scientists, see Lebow, *Between Peace and War*, 108–11.

16. FO, *The Opium Trade*, 6:XXIV, 1927, no. 5.

17. For a discussion of the importance of the United States to British policy in East Asia, see Louis, *British Strategy in the Far East*, 27, 48. For general summaries of U.S. policy toward China and Japan at the time, see Cohen, *America's Response to China*, 107–22; Neu, *The Troubled Encounter*, 116–31.

18. FO, *The Opium Trade*, 5:XXIII, 1926, no. 21; 6:XXIV, 1927, no. 1.

19. Ibid., 5:XXIII, 1926, no. 10. Lord Robert Cecil doubted whether opium smoking raised a question of international importance. Ibid., no. 12 and enclosure.

20. Ibid., 6:XXIV, 1927, no. 2; *FRUS, 1926*, 250–54.

21. Generally, see Nish, "Japan in Britain's View of the International System," 30–32; cf. Hosoya, "Britain and the United States in Japan's View of the International System," 7–15, which emphasizes Tokyo's effort to maintain a system of cooperation after the Washington Conference.

22. *The Reminiscences of Li Tsung-jen*, 1:chap. 17, p. 11, COHP. Sun Yat-sen is quoted in Lo, "A Review of the People's Anti-Opium Movement," 25. Recollections about Sun's opposition to opium are in the *North China Herald*, 10 November 1928. On Li Tsung-jen, see Sheridan, *China in Disintegration*, 70–72; Wilbur, *The Nationalist Revolution in China*, 50–53, 57, 97–99.

23. The four military leaders are identified in Ch'i, *Warlord Politics*, 166 n. 1, 200–201. See also Wilbur, *The Nationalist Revolution in China*, 29, 49–53, 57; O. Edmund Clubb, *Twentieth-Century China*, 140, 143, 149; Sheridan, *Chinese Warlord*, 240–41.

24. Sheridan, *China in Disintegration*, 164–77.

25. FO, *The Opium Trade*, 5:XXII, 1925, no. 13.

26. *The Reminiscences of Herbert L. May*, 29, OHRO.

27. Sidney Barton (Shanghai) to Miles Lampson (Peking), 1 December 1927, and British consulate (Tsinan) to Lampson, 22 November 1927, FO 228/3680, PRO; Barton to Lampson, 9 December 1927, FO 228/3888, PRO; Edwin S. Cunningham (Shanghai) to DS, 12 December 1927, RG 59, 893.114/602, NAMP, M329, roll 115, NA; *The Reminiscences of K'ung Hsiang-hsi*, 63, COHP.

28. Douglas Jenkins (Canton) to MacMurray, 26 November 1928, RG 59, 893.114/638, NAMP, M329, roll 115, NA; S. F. Groton (Shanghai) to FO, 27 April, 12 July 1928, FO 228/3888, PRO.

29. Garfield Huang to Alfred Sao-ke Sze, 10 May 1929, RG 59, 893.114 Narcotics/45, and DS to DT, RG 59, 893.114 Narcotics/15, NAMP, M329, roll 116, NA; *North*

China Herald, 15 September 1928. See also Lo, *The Opium Problem in the Far East*, 27–43.

30. "Editorial: On the Way to Absolute Prohibition" (this issue of the National Anti-Opium Association journal contains a copy of the manifesto put forward by the conference: "The Opium Policy of the Chinese National Government" [see pp. 2–7]); Lo, *The Opium Problem in the Far East*, 27–37; *North China Herald*, 10 November 1928; C. F. Garstin (Shanghai) to British minister (Peking), 21 November 1928, FO 228/3886, PRO.

31. Brenan (Shanghai) to F. Ashton-Gwatkin (FO), 25 June 1928, FO 228/3888, PRO. See also Ferdinand Mayer (Peking) to DS, 17 March 1928, RG 59, 893.114/613, NAMP, M329, roll 115, NA.

32. FO, *The Opium Trade*, 6:XXV, 1928, no. 10; XXVI, 1929, no. 6, which is a long memorandum concerning the opium problem in the Far East; Lampson to Arthur Henderson, 15 July 1929, FO 228/4051, PRO (quotation).

33. Memorandum of a conversation between Kellogg and Sze, 17 May 1928, Johnson Papers, memoranda files, box 48, MD/LC (for the U.S. response to the Tsinan Incident); Huang to Sze, 10 May 1929, RG 59, 893.114 Narcotics/45, NAMP, M329, roll 116, NA (quotation). The United States and China signed a treaty in July 1928 granting tariff autonomy; thereafter, as Warren I. Cohen concludes, America was "China's principal friend." Cohen, *America's Response to China*, 115, 121–22.

34. Sokobin (Foochow) to MacMurray, 25 May 1929, RG 59, 893.114 Narcotics/39, NAMP, M329, roll 116, NA; G. S. Moss (Foochow) to Lampson, 28 August 1928, FO 228/3888, PRO; Jenkins to MacMurray, 1 April 1929, RG 59, 893.114 Narcotics/28, NAMP, M329, roll 116, NA. Men looked "almost like living corpses" in the Amoy district. P. Grant Jones to Lampson, 15 December 1930, FO 228/4292, PRO. On KMT troubles with Kwangsi, see O. Edmund Clubb, *Twentieth-Century China*, 152–55; Eastman, "Nationalist China during the Nanking Decade," 124–27.

35. David Berger to DS, 14 June 1929, RG 59, 893.114 Narcotics/44, NAMP, M329, roll 116, NA.

36. Wilbur, *The Nationalist Revolution in China*, 82–108; Louis, *British Strategy in the Far East*, 163. The Nanking Incident involved looting of the British, American, and Japanese consulates by Nationalist soldiers with the loss of several lives.

37. Sheridan, "The Warlord Era," 318–19.

38. *The Reminiscences of K'ung Hsiang-hsi*, 72, COHP; Cohen, *The Chinese Connection*, 140.

39. *The Reminiscences of Li Tsung-jen*, 2:chap. 25, pp. 2, 4, COHP.

40. Confidential report on opium traffic in Shanghai by Garstin, 24 September 1929, FO 228/4051, PRO; Jenkins to DS, 16 March 1931, RG 59, 893.114 Narcotics/208, NA (on the 1925 agreement).

41. Barton to Lampson, 1 December 1927, FO 228/3680, PRO (for the phrase "trinity of scoundrels"); Coble, *The Shanghai Capitalists*, 28–41; Tien, *Government and*

Politics in Kuomintang China, 48; Wu Tien-wei, "Chiang Kai-shek's April Twelfth Coup of 1927," 149–57. More generally, see Wang, "Tu Yueh-sheng."

42. FO, *The Opium Trade*, 6:XXVI, 1929, nos. 6 sec. 6, 9 and enclosure, 16 enclosure 2. On the activities of Tu Yueh-sheng, see Marshall, "Opium and the Politics of Gangsterism."

43. Garstin to Lampson, 25 April 1929, and Lampson to FO, 11 July 1929, FO 228/4051, PRO; Cunningham to DS, 16 September 1929, RG 59, 893.114 Narcotics/ 69, NAMP, M329, roll 116, NA; Lee, "Opium and Extraterritoriality"; Delevingne to George A. Mounsey, 4 April 1929, FO 228/4051, PRO.

44. Lampson to Henderson, 15 July 1929, FO 228/4051, PRO.

45. Coble, *The Shanghai Capitalists*, 35–36; Etō, "China's International Relations," 112–13; Iriye, "Japanese Aggression and China's International Position," 498.

46. *The Reminiscences of Herbert L. May*, 31, OHRO.

47. Chutiyutse, "Japan and the Opium Scourge in China."

48. FO, *The Opium Trade*, 6:XXV, 1928, nos. 1, 14 and enclosure; M. E. Dening (Dairen) to John Tilley (Tokyo), 15 November 1927, and Dening to FO, 25 May 1928, FO 228/3887, PRO; Mounsey to Delevingne, 20 July 1928, FO 228/3886, PRO; Sheridan, "The Warlord Era," 304–6, 317; Etō, "China's International Relations," 113–14; Myers (Mukden) to Johnson, 16 March 1931, RG 59, 893.114 Narcotics/210, NA. See also the article by Edgar Snow, *New York Herald Tribune*, 15 December 1929. For further information on Chang Tso-lin and opium, see McCormack, *Chang Tso-lin in Northeast China*, 105–6, 197, 201. McCormack finds that the Young Marshal did indulge in opium in the hard times of 1927–28 (p. 210).

49. Delevingne to Mounsey, 11 July 1928, FO 228/3886, PRO. On Satō, see Barnhart, *Japan Prepares for Total War*, 48.

50. M. D. Perrins to Mounsey, 20 July 1928, FO 228/3886, Tilley to Henderson, 8 November 1929 (enclosing Baron Shidehara to Tilley, 31 October 1929), FO 228/ 4290, and Tilley to FO, 4 October 1930, FO 228/4292, PRO; *FRUS, 1929*, 390–93. For more on Japan and the narcotics traffic, see Lo, *The Opium Problem in the Far East*, 48–53.

51. Edwin L. Neville (Tokyo) to DS, 1 October 1928, RG 59, 893.114/633, NAMP, M329, roll 115, NA; British embassy (Tokyo) to British legation (Peking), 14 June 1929, FO 228/4049, PRO; FO, *The Opium Trade*, 6:XXVI, 1929, no. 8 and enclosures. The coping strategy of defensive avoidance seems to describe Tokyo's action. See Janis and Mann, *Decision Making*, 57–60; Lebow, *Between Peace and War*, 110. Even before Shidehara returned to power, it was clear that the Washington system could not readily protect China. Moreover, the turbulent internal situation, with its dual threat to vital Japanese interests in the form of communism and nationalism, made it likely that Japan would seize an early opportunity to protect its interests north of the Great Wall. Jansen, "Introduction: The Manchurian Incident," 130–31; Jervis, "Deterrence Theory Revisited," 314–17 (on the place of intrinsic interests in the policymaking process).

52. FO, *The Opium Trade*, 6:XXVII, 1930, nos. 28 and enclosure, 52 and enclosure. See also "Editorial: The Shaping of a Treaty."

53. "China Famine Relief, 1928," Kemmerer Papers, box 80, ML/PU; Frank P. Lockhart (Hankow) to MacMurray, 23 April 1929, RG 59, 893.114 Narcotics/31, NAMP, M329, roll 116, NA; Woodhead, *China Year Book, 1928*, 529–35. In Shensi between 1928 and 1934, perhaps one-third of the population starved to death while poppy planting continued, even being paid for indirectly by famine relief aid. See Marshall, "Opium and the Politics of Gangsterism," 24–25; *North-China Daily News*, 16 October 1930; DS to DT, 6 August 1931, RG 59, 893.114 Narcotics/272, NA.

54. "China Famine Relief, 1928," Kemmerer Papers, box 80, ML/PU; A. Young, *China's Nation-building Effort*, 12–25, 33.

55. A. Young, *China's Nation-building Effort*, 16–17, 31; *Bankers' Weekly* (China), January 1928 [in translation], Kemmerer Papers, box 58, ML/PU. See also Public Credit Reports and Papers (typescript), chap. viii, "The Foreign Debt of the Chinese Government"; chap. x, "The Present Financial Incapacity of the Chinese Government"; chap. xi, "The Potential Financial Capacity of the Chinese Government"—all in Kemmerer Papers, box 71.

56. A. Taylor, *American Diplomacy and the Narcotics Traffic*, 183, 189, 271. For a critical appraisal, see Eisenlohr, *International Narcotics Control*, 119–21.

57. British embassy (Tokyo) to FO, 4 August 1928, and British consulate (Nanking) to Lampson, 22 September 1928, FO 228/3886, PRO; League of Nations, *Control of Opium Smoking in the Far East: Note by the Secretary General*, 2.

58. Dai [secretary, National Anti-Opium Association], *The Commission of Inquiry and Opium Monopoly*, 1–8.

59. Ashton-Gwatkin to Delevingne, 17 November 1928, FO 228/4290, PRO; League of Nations, Commission of Enquiry, *Report to the Council*, 10–11, 14–15, 19, 24 (quotation).

60. League of Nations, Commission of Enquiry, *Report to the Council*, 25, 32, 37, 57–58 (for the situation in Burma), 77–83 (for Siam), 85–86 (for Indochina), 90–93 (for Hong Kong), 95–97 (for Macao), 135 (quotation).

61. Langdon (Dairen) to William R. Castle, Jr. (Tokyo), 7 April 1930, RG 59, 500.C1197/376, and Neville to DS, 6 May 1930, RG 59, 500.C1197/379, NA; FO, *The Opium Trade*, 6:XXVII, 1930, no. 28 and enclosure.

62. League of Nations, Commission of Enquiry, *Report to the Council*, 138–45 (quotation, 138).

63. A. Taylor, *American Diplomacy and the Narcotics Traffic*, 275; FO minute, 18 March 1931, FO 371/15526, and Minute by N. H. H. Charles, 10 September 1931, FO 371/15527, PRO.

64. FO memorandum on the Bangkok conference, 12 May 1931, FO 371/15527, PRO.

65. FO minute, 18 March 1931, FO 371/15526, PRO. The manufacturing limitation convention of 1931 was intended to prevent the accumulation of an excessive supply

of raw materials. It also made binding the estimates of legitimate narcotics requirements on the nation submitting them. Walker, *Drug Control in the Americas*, 53–55, 61–63, 70–73; A. Taylor, *American Diplomacy and the Narcotics Traffic*, 233–63.

66. Caldwell's memorandum of a conversation, 26 November 1930, RG 59, 500.C1197/422, and Memorandum by Caldwell, 20 April 1931, RG 59, 511.4R1/4, NA; A. Taylor, *American Diplomacy and the Narcotics Traffic*, 250, 277; Stimson to Caldwell, 5 November 1931, RG 59 511.4R1/59, NA (quotation); LaMotte, "'Limiting' Drug Manufacture."

67. FO minute, 15 January 1932, FO 371/16252, PRO; Report by Caldwell on the Bangkok conference, RG 59, 511.4R1/81, NA; FO, *The Opium Trade*, 6:XXIX, 1932, no. 1.

68. Caldwell to Johnson, 22 September 1930, Johnson Papers, general correspondence, box 13, MD/LC; Buhite, *Johnson*, 46–50 (on extraterritoriality and Anglo-American relations).

69. Walker, *Drug Control in the Americas*, 63–70; Musto, *The American Disease*, 206–14; Anslinger and Oursler, *The Murderers*, 3–24; Spinelli, *Dry Diplomacy*, 112, 133–34 (for Anslinger's experience with international liquor control); Kinder, "Foreign Fear and the Drug Specter," chap. 2. Anslinger's belief system is not easily characterized. In the idiom of motivational psychology, what could be seen as an unmotivated bias concerning foreign threats to American security later approximated a highly motivated bias that served to rationalize questionable policies. Generally, see Jervis, "Perceiving and Coping with Threat," 18–33 and chaps. 8–9 infra.

70. Mrs. Hamilton Wright to Anslinger, 28 April 1931, RG 59, 893.114 Narcotics/233, NA; A. Taylor, *American Diplomacy and the Narcotics Traffic*, 274.

71. Seymour Lowman to DS, 6 April 1932, RG 59, 500.C1197/515, and Fuller to DS with a report on the fifteenth session of the OAC, 14 September 1932, RG 59, 500.C1197/538, NA.

72. Eastman, *The Abortive Revolution*, 1; Liu, "Short Visit to Shanghai and Nanking," July–August 1928, contained in Roger S. Greene to M. K. Eggleston, 16 August 1928, Liu Jui-heng Papers, box 15, and *The Reminiscences of Dr. Wu Kuo-cheng*, 16, COHP.

73. *Shanghai Evening Post and Mercury*, 2–4 March 1931; *Ta-kung-pao*, 7 February 1931 [in translation], RG 59, 893.114 Narcotics/206, NA.

74. Memorandum of a conversation between Johnson and Bert Hall, aviation adviser to the Nanking government, 2 May 1930, RG 59, 893.114 Narcotics/125, Culver B. Chamberlain to DS, 10 May 1930, RG 59, 893.00 P.R. Yunnan/18, DS to DT for Anslinger, 21 March 1931, RG 59, 893.114 Narcotics/201, and Lockhart to Stimson, 31 October 1930, RG 59, 893.114 Narcotics/166, NA.

75. Lockhart to Johnson, 9 May 1930, RG 59, 893.114 Narcotics/115, Lockhart to DS, 6 March 1931, RG 59, 893.00 P.R. Hankow/35, and Stimson to DT for Anslinger, 1 December 1931, RG 59, 893.114 Narcotics/293, NA.

76. *North China Herald*, 12 August 1930; Lockhart to DS, 2 October 1930, RG 59, 893.00 P.R. Chungking/28, and Lockhart to Johnson, 12 December 1930, RG 59,

893.114 Narcotics/178, NA. See also Kapp, *Szechwan and the Chinese Republic*, 37, 40–41, 46–47.

77. Putnam (Amoy) to DS, 13 January 1931, RG 59, 893.00 P.R. Amoy/37, Gordon L. Burke to Johnson, 4 December 1931, RG 59, 893.00 P.R. Foochow/47, and Burke to Johnson, 4 May 1932, RG 59, 893.00 P.R. Foochow/52, NA.

78. Cunningham to DS, 12 February 1930 (RG 59, 893.00 P.R. Shanghai/21) and 3 March 1930 (RG 59, 893.114 Narcotics/105) NA; FO, *The Opium Trade*, 6:XXVII, 1930, no. 43 and enclosure; *Shanghai Evening Post and Mercury*, 16 March 1931.

79. Myers to Johnson, 13 March 1930, RG 59, 893.114 Narcotics/107, NA; O. Edmund Clubb, *Twentieth-Century China*, 172; Myers to Johnson, 9 June 1930 (RG 59, 893.114 Narcotics/130) and 16 March 1931 (RG 59, 893.114 Narcotics/210) NA.

80. John Carter Vincent to DS, 15 May 1931, RG 59, 893.00 P.R. Mukden/48, and DS to DT for Anslinger, 19 May 1931, RG 59, 893.114 Narcotics/239, NA.

81. B. G. Tour (Mukden) to Lampson, 22 February 1930, FO 228/4295, PRO; *North-China Daily News*, 4 December 1930; *Shanghai Evening Post and Mercury*, 10 March 1931; "Extraterritoriality and the Japanese Dope Trade in Manchuria."

82. Minute by F. K. Roberts regarding drug control in foreign concessions in China, 9 November 1931, FO 371/15525, PRO; Lampson to FO, 12 March 1930, FO 228/4290, PRO; MacMurray to Arthur Bullard, 17 April 1929, MacMurray Collection, box 102, ML/PU.

83. S. R. Penn to Anslinger, 3 July 1930, RG 59, 893.114 Narcotics/142, NA; OAC, *Minutes of the Thirteenth Session*, 166–71, and *Minutes of the Fourteenth Session*, 178–82.

84. *Shanghai Evening Post and Mercury*, 18 March 1931.

85. Johnson's memorandum of a conversation with C. T. Wang, 26 February 1931, and with T. V. Soong, 12 March 1931, Johnson Papers, memoranda files, box 51, MD/LC; Wu Lien-teh, "Opium Problem Reaches Acute Stage." H. G. W. Woodhead favored a monopoly in place of the existing system. *Shanghai Evening Post and Mercury*, 18 March 1931.

86. Cunningham to DS, 4 August 1931, RG 59, 893.00 P.R. Shanghai/38, and Berger (Swatow) to Johnson, 10 September 1931, RG 59, 893.00 P.R. Swatow/46, NA; Coble, *The Shanghai Capitalists*, 114–15. Douglas Jenkins, U.S. consul general at Shanghai, believed that Hu Han-min defected from the Kuomintang in opposition to the monopoly proposal. Jenkins to DS, 16 March 1931, RG 59, 893.114 Narcotics/208, NA.

87. Young to Edwin W. Kemmerer, 9 January 1931, Kemmerer Papers, box 88, ML/PU; Stanley K. Hornbeck to Johnson, 22 June 1931, Johnson Papers, general correspondence, box 16, MD/LC; Iriye, *After Imperialism*, 294–99.

88. *The Reminiscences of Herbert L. May*, 32 (quotation), 42, OHRO. The Mukden Incident involved officers of the Kwantung Army who blew up property of the South Manchurian Railway and used that as a pretext to attack Chinese forces.

Chapter Four

1. Louis, *British Strategy in the Far East*, 172–79 (quotation, 173).

2. Wheeler, *Prelude to Pearl Harbor*, 187–93; Wilson, *American Business and Foreign Policy*, 216–23; Iriye, *After Imperialism*, 300–301; Perkins to MacMurray, 8 January 1932, MacMurray Collection, box 123, ML/PU.

3. Buhite, *Johnson*, 62–65; Johnson to Kellogg, 12 January 1932, Johnson to Grew, 7, 13 June 1932, and Grew to Johnson, 6 July 1932, Johnson Papers, general correspondence, box 17, MD/LC.

4. Young to Kemmerer, 20 October, 19 September 1931, Kemmerer Papers, box 88, ML/PU; Greene to Max Mason, president, Rockefeller Foundation, 4 February 1932, Liu Jui-heng Papers, pt. 2, COHP.

5. Lockhart to Soong, 18 July 1931, and Kuo Min News Agency, 12 October 1931, Young Papers, box 55, HIWRP.

6. On the complex bandit situation in Manchuria after the Mukden Incident, see Billingsley, *Bandits in Republican China*, 218–25. See also F. Lockhart to DS, 2 December 1931, RG 59, 123W212/73, NA. On Anglo-American differences in response to the situation in Manchuria, see Louis, *British Strategy in the Far East*, 181–98; Thorne, *The Limits of Foreign Policy*, especially 225–72.

7. Prentiss B. Gilbert (Geneva) to DS, 29 January 1932, RG 59, 893.114 Narcotics/315, enclosing Anti-Opium Information Bureau, Press Note no. 32, 22 January 1932, NA.

8. C. D. Meinhardt (Tsinan) to DS, 2 February 1932, RG 59, 893.114 Narcotics/323, and Myers to Johnson, 21 April 1932, RG 59, 893.114 Narcotics/342, NA; Johnson to Karl Bickel, United Press Associations, 18 August 1932, Johnson Papers, general correspondence, box 17, MD/LC.

9. Johnson to Stimson, 9 September 1921, RG 59, 893.114 Narcotics/405, NA; Nakamura, "Japan's Economic Thrust into North China," 225; Grew to DS, 2 December 1932, RG 59, 893.114N16 Manchuria/2, and 9 December 1932, RG 59, 894.00 P.R./60, NA.

10. Johnson's memorandum of a conversation with Upton Close (Joseph Washington Hall), 30 August 1932, Johnson Papers, memoranda files, box 32, MD/LC; O. Edmund Clubb, *Twentieth-Century China*, 172; Close, "Jehol: A Struggle Colored with Opium."

11. Johnson to Hornbeck, 13 September 1932, and Johnson to Bertram D. Hulen, National Press Club, Washington, 15 November 1932, Johnson Papers, general correspondence, box 17, MD/LC; Hornbeck memorandum, 14 February 1933, Hornbeck Papers, box 259, HIWRP.

12. Johnson to Henry K. Norton, 9 March 1933, and Johnson to Hulen, 10 March 1933, Johnson Papers, general correspondence, box 20, MD/LC; Shimada, "Designs on North China," 18, 27–36. See also Johnson to MacMurray, 3 December 1932, MacMurray Collection, box 128, ML/PU.

13. Johnson to Hulen, 10 March 1933, Johnson Papers, general correspondence, box 20, MD/LC; Johnson to DS, 29 March 1933, RG 59, 893.00 P.R./65, NA (quotation).

14. *Peking & Tientsin Times*, 18 May 1933; Shimada, "Designs on North China," 12, 31–32. The Tangku truce followed Japan's conquest of Jehol and temporarily ended hostilities with China.

15. IMTFE, *Judgment*, pt. B, chap. V, "Japanese Aggression against China: Narcotics in China," 1:530, 644–45, FO 648, IWM.

16. RG 59, 500.C1197/6001/2, with Anti-Opium Information Bureau, Communiqué no. 20, 15 May 1933: "Illicit Narcotics Increased in China since 1928," NA.

17. *Peking & Tientsin Times*, 8 September 1931.

18. F. Lockhart to Johnson, 16 February 1932, RG 59, 893.114 Narcotics/325 (for the report on Feng), Burke to Johnson, 4 May 1932, RG 59, 893.00 P.R. Foochow/52, and Lynn W. Franklin to Johnson, 1 July 1932, RG 59, 893.00 P.R. Amoy/58, NA; H. I. Harding (Foochow) to E. M. B. Ingram (Peking), 26 September 1932, FO 371/16251, PRO; Burke to Johnson, 2 August 1933, RG 59, 893.00 P.R. Foochow/67, NA. British records concur in their assessment of events in Fukien. See A. J. Martin (Foochow) to Lampson, 21 February 1933, FO 676/156, and E. W. P. Mills (Amoy) to Lampson, 28 July 1933, FO 371/17170, PRO.

19. DS to FBN, 26 June 1932, RG 59, 893.114 Narcotics/352, and Johnson to DS, 6 July 1932, RG 59, 893.114 Narcotics/369, NA; *Peking & Tientsin Times*, 4 May 1932; Johnson to Stimson, 6 July 1932, RG 59, 893.114 Narcotics/370, NA. Chinese forces, sent to do battle with opium bandits, joined their foes on occasion to profit from the drug trade. Hanson (Harbin) to DS, 23 March 1932, RG 59, 893.114 Narcotics/336, NA.

20. Memorandum of a conversation in Far Eastern Affairs with Kemmerer, 21 May 1931, RG 59, 893.51-A/56, NAMP, LM63, roll 122, Fuller's memorandum of a conversation with Anslinger, 5 March 1931, RG 59, 893.114 Narcotic Laws/45, and Stimson conversation with Sir Arthur Salter, director, League of Nations Financial Section, 6 June 1931, RG 59, 893.50-A/19, NAMP, LM63, roll 109, NA; Johnson to Fuller, 4 September 1931, Johnson Papers, general correspondence, box 15, MD/LC.

21. Perkins to DS, 13 March 1931, RG 59, 893.114 Narcotic Laws/51, Perkins to DS, 18 March 1931, RG 59, 893.114 Narcotic Laws/55, and Fuller to Caldwell, 16 June 1931, RG 59, 893.114 Narcotic Laws/60, NA.

22. Walter A. Adams (Hankow) to Johnson, 14 November 1933, RG 59, 893.00 P.R. Hankow/78, and Fuller's report on the sixteenth session of the OAC, 28 August 1933, RG 59, 500.C1197/609, NA.

23. Nish, "Japan in Britain's View of the International System," 38, 42–43; *DBFP*, 2d ser., vol. 11, no. 50; Cohen, *America's Response to China*, 130–38.

24. Memorandum by Anslinger, 21 June 1933, RG 59, 500.C1197/607, Hornbeck to Secretary of State Cordell Hull, 27 May 1933, RG 59, 500.C1197/607, and Fuller's

report on the sixteenth session of the OAC, 23 August 1933, RG 59, 500.C1197/615, NA.

25. Fuller's report on the sixteenth session of the OAC, 23 August 1933, RG 59, 500.C1197/615, Fuller to Hull, 10 May 1933, RG 59, 893.114N16 Manchuria/21, Hull to Fuller, 11 May 1933, RG 59, 893.114N16 Manchuria/25, Phillips to Charles C. Hart, 4 April 1933, RG 59, 893.114 Narcotics/203, and Grew to Hull, 19 July 1933, RG 59, 893.114 Narcotics/215, NA.

26. Anslinger to Fuller, 29 March 1933, RG 59, 893.114 Narcotics/72, Memorandum by Fuller, 15 April 1933, RG 59, 893.114 Narcotics/73, and F. Lockhart to DS, 8 May 1933, RG 59, 893.114 Narcotics/80, NA.

27. Fuller's report on the seventeenth session of the OAC, 9 January 1934, RG 59, 500.C1197/655, and Gilbert to DS, 27 January 1934, RG 59, 500.C1197/660, NA; OAC, *Minutes of the Seventeenth Session*, 14–17.

28. Fuller's report on the seventeenth session of the OAC, 9 January 1934, RG 59, 500.C1197/655, NA.

29. OAC, *Minutes of the Seventeenth Session*, 13, 17; Gilbert to DS, 27 January 1934, RG 59, 500.C1197/660, NA.

30. Nish, "Japan in Britain's View of the International System," 38, 42–43; *DBFP*, 2d ser., vol. 11, no. 497.

31. Lampson to FO, 7 February 1933, FO 371/17169, FO minute, 10 March 1933, FO 371/17168, Military attaché (Peking) to Lampson, 27 November 1933, FO 676/130, Herbert Phillips (Canton) to British legation (Peking), 7 January 1934, FO 371/18078, and H. Phillips to Sir Alexander Cadogan, 19 March 1934, FO 371/18199, PRO; O. Edmund Clubb, *Twentieth-Century China*, 183–84; Eastman, *The Abortive Revolution*, 102–39.

32. *The Reminiscences of Herbert L. May*, 58, OHRO (May described Fuller's predecessor, John Kenneth Caldwell, as "a timid individual"); Fuller to U.S. legation, 4 September 1933, RG 59, 893.114 Narcotics/534, NA; E. W. Allen, "Japanese Drug Trade Poisoning North China"; Memorandum of a conversation by Eugene H. Dooman, 7 September 1933, RG 59, 893.114 Narcotics/538, and Johnson to Hull, 24 October 1933, RG 59, 893.114 Narcotics/574, NA. For more about E. W. Allen, see Liu to Peck, 18 September 1933, RG 59, 893.114 Narcotics/565, Peck to Johnson, 7 November 1933, RG 59, 893.114 Narcotics/581, and Gauss to U.S. consular officers in China, 1 May 1934, RG 59, 893.114 Narcotics/737, NA.

33. Johnson to Fuller, 4 September 1931, Johnson Papers, general correspondence, box 15, MD/LC; Irving S. Brown, Treasury representative (Shanghai), to the commissioner of customs, 28 September 1932, RG 59, 893.114 Narcotics/528, NA; *North China Herald*, 4 October 1933.

34. Anslinger, "The Chinese Story," typescript, [1947–49?], Anslinger Papers, box 1, HSTL.

35. A. I. Ward and Stuart Allen to DS, 4 June 1932, RG 59, 893.114 Narcotics/356,

and Memorandum by Ward, 5 October 1932, RG 59, 893.114 Narcotics/417, NA; Gillin, *Warlord*, 116–17, 125–40.

36. Burke to Johnson, 4 May 1932, RG 59, 893.00 P.R. Foochow/52, and 16 May 1932, RG 59, 893.114 Narcotics/349, and Burke to DS, 4 October 1932, RG 59, 893.00 P.R. Foochow/57, NA.

37. Charles S. Reed II to DS, 12 June 1933, RG 59, 893.114 Narcotics/513, NA.

38. O. Edmund Clubb, *Twentieth-Century China*, 183–84, 194–202.

39. Eastman, "Nationalist China during the Nanking Decade," 130–34.

40. M. R. Nicholson, Treasury attaché (Shanghai), to Customs, 15 June 1931, RG 59, 893.114 Narcotic Laws/67, and Adams to DS, 4 June 1932, RG 59, 893.114 Narcotics/354, with *New Hankow Daily News*, 3 June 1932 [in translation], NA.

41. *Shanghai Evening Post and Mercury*, 27 July 1932; *Peking & Tientsin Times*, 27 June 1932.

42. Peck to Stimson, 24 June 1932, RG 59, 893.114 Narcotics/358, NA; *Peking & Tientsin Times*, 21 June 1932; Johnson to Stimson, 6 July 1932, RG 59, 893.114 Narcotics/370, NA.

43. George M. Graves, "The Opium Problem in Central China," 29 September 1932, RG 59, 893.114 Narcotics/419, and *Shih-chieh jih-pao* (Peking), 25–26 September 1932 [in translation], in RG 59, 893.114 Narcotics/407 and Narcotics/414, NA.

44. DS to FBN with Hankow consular report, 1 December 1933, RG 59, 893.114 Narcotics/580, and Report from Hankow, 21 December 1933, RG 59, 893.00 P.R. Hankow/78, NA; *Ta-kung-pao* [in translation], 9 September 1933 (in RG 59, 893.114 Narcotics/580) and 8 October 1933 (in RG 59, 893.114 Narcotics/591) (quotation), NA.

45. Johnson to Lattimore, 6 January 1934, Johnson Papers, general correspondence, box 23, MD/LC.

46. Fuller to H. G. W. Woodhead, 17 March 1934 (box 23), and Blanco to Fuller, 10 January 1934 (box 22), ibid.; Fuller to Johnson, 29 January 1934, RG 59, 893.114 Narcotics/625, NA. On the general situation in North China, see Shimada, "Designs on North China," 65–75.

47. Johnson to Moorehead, 14 July 1931 (box 16), and Johnson to Fuller, 21 March 1934 (box 22), Johnson Papers, general correspondence, MD/LC.

48. Johnson to Hornbeck, 31 May 1934, box 23, ibid. More generally, see Buhite, *Johnson*, 89–95.

49. *The Reminiscences of Li Huang*, 446–47, 469, and *The Reminiscences of Chang Fa-k'uei*, 392, 394 (quotation), 432, COHP.

50. Sheridan, *Chinese Warlord*, 142; *The Reminiscences of Yi-yun Shen Huang*, 412–14, 423 and 426 (quotations), COHP.

51. *DBFP*, 2d ser., vol. 20, no. 77.

52. Ibid., vol. 11, app.

53. Cadogan to Sir John Simon, 2 June 1934, FO 371/18200, PRO; Louis, *British Strategy in the Far East*, 185.

54. *DBFP*, 2d ser., vol. 20, no. 77, minuted 5 March 1934.

55. Iriye, "Japanese Aggression and China's International Position," 511; Shimada, "Designs on North China," 75–91; Barnhart, *Japan Prepares for Total War*, 116; Borg, *The United States and the Far Eastern Crisis*, 46–99; Iriye, "The Role of the United States Embassy in Tokyo," 108–14; Heinrichs, *American Ambassador*, 199–203, 218.

56. *DBFP*, 2d ser., vol. 20, nos. 122, 107. See also Cadogan to Vansittart, 29 April 1934, Cadogan Papers, FO 800/293, PRO.

57. Grew, *Turbulent Era*, 2:957–62, and *Ten Years in Japan*, 128–31 (quotation, 130).

58. *DBFP*, 2d ser., vol. 11, app.

59. Ch'en, "The Communist Movement," 198–208; Eastman, *The Abortive Revolution*, 86, 120–27; Borg, *The United States and the Far Eastern Crisis*, 196–200. U.S. officials knew little about communism in China, relying largely on Edmund Clubb's dispatches, the most famous of which later appeared in print. O. Edmund Clubb, *Communism in China*.

60. Salisbury, *The Long March*, 106–8, 181; Chang Kuo-t'ao, *Autobiography*, 317–19; Snow, *Red Star over China*, 190, 311; Perry, *Rebels and Revolutionaries*, 181, 211; *The Reminiscences of Chang Fu-k'uei*, 394–95, COHP.

61. O. Edmund Clubb, *Communism in China*, 23; Clubb to DS, "The Opium Traffic in China," 24 April 1934, RG 59, 893.114 Narcotics/738, NA (quotation).

62. Koo to secretary general, League of Nations, 1 May 1934, Koo Papers, box 8, BL/CU.

63. Memorandums by Fuller, 15 March 1934, RG 59, 500.C1197/671, and 15 April 1935, RG 59, 500.C1197/856 (quotations—emphasis in original), NA.

64. OAC, *Minutes of the Eighteenth Session*, 54, 58–61, 63–69; Fuller's report on the eighteenth session of the OAC, 13 August 1934, RG 59, 500.C1197/756, NA.

65. Memorandum of a conversation with Hoo, 18 July 1934, Johnson Papers, memoranda files, box 54, MD/LC; Johnson to Hull, 28 July 1934, RG 59, 893.114 Narcotics/822, NA.

66. Eastman, *The Abortive Revolution*, 13–14, 66–70, and "Nationalist China during the Nanking Decade," 146.

67. Thomson, *While China Faced West*, 154–74.

68. *Peiping Chronicle*, 11 May 1934; Compilation of monthly consular political reports (March 1934), RG 59, 893.114 Narcotics/729, NA; *Central China Post*, 6 June 1934.

69. *Shanghai Evening Post and Mercury*, 29 December 1934 (quotation); P. R. Josselyn (Hankow) to DS, 15 October 1935, RG 59, 893.114 Narcotics/1390, NA; *Peking & Tientsin Times*, 20 February 1935; Compilation of monthly consular political reports (March 1935), RG 59, 893.114 Narcotics/1120, NA. See also *North China Herald*, 21 November 1934, for a favorable report on the New Life Movement; Kapp, *Szechwan and the Chinese Republic*, 116–18.

70. National Christian Council of China, Biennial Report, 1933–35, CBMS, E/T. China 2, box 348, SOAS/UL.

71. Thomson, *While China Faced West*, 167; Eastman, "Nationalist China during the Nanking Decade," 143–45, and *The Abortive Revolution*, 31–84; Marshall, "Opium and the Politics of Gangsterism," 21–22, 25, 30–34; Peck to Gauss, 23 January 1935, RG 59, 893.114 Narcotics/1024, NA.

72. Clubb to DS, "The Opium Traffic in China," 24 April 1934, RG 59, 893.114 Narcotics/738, NA; Tien, *Government and Politics in Kuomintang China*, 60–71.

73. Records of Major James F. Moriarty, USMC, China Repository, CNH; *Shanghai Evening Post and Mercury*, 2 June, 29 December 1934; Peck to DS, 11 June 1934, RG 59, 893.00 P.R. Nanking/76, and George Atcheson (Tientsin) to DS, 7 September 1934, RG 59, 893.00 P.R. Tientsin/75, NA; *Peking & Tientsin Times*, 20, 28 February 1935; Compilation of monthly consular political reports (March 1935), RG 59, 893.114 Narcotics/1120, NA.

74. FO, *The Opium Trade*, 6:XXX, 1933–36, no. 10; DS to FBN with report (9 October 1934), "The Opium Problem in China," RG 59, 893.114 Narcotics/909, NA.

75. Fuller's report on the nineteenth session of the OAC, 9 February 1935, RG 59, 500.C1197/819, and Johnson to Hull, 21 March 1936, RG 59, 893.114 Narcotics/1547, NA; FO, *The Opium Trade*, 6:XXX, 1933–36, no. 18.

76. Fuller's report on the nineteenth session of the OAC, 9 February 1935, RG 59, 500.C1197/819, Fuller's report on the twentieth session of the OAC, 27 July 1935, RG 59, 500.C1197/885, and Phillips to Geneva for Fuller, 9 November 1934, RG 59, 893.114 Narcotics/894, NA.

77. G. E. Mitchell to British consulate general (Shanghai), 16 September 1935, FO 676/206, PRO; Sir Robert H. Clive (Tokyo) to Anthony Eden, 2 April 1936, and Unsigned FO minute, 7 May 1936, FO 371/20294, PRO.

78. *DBFP*, 2d ser., vol. 20, no. 342. Jervis, *Perception and Misperception in International Politics*, 212, has informed my discussion of perceptual biases.

79. FBN, *Traffic in Opium and Other Dangerous Drugs for . . . 1933*, 5, 7, 35, and *for . . . 1934*, 6–7; *Washington Herald*, 18 July, 10 September 1934; R. Walton Moore to U.S. legation (Peiping), 4 September 1934, RG 59, 893.114 Narcotics/827, and Anslinger to Fuller (Geneva), 14 November 1934, RG 59, 893.114 Narcotics/897, NA. See also William H. Coles (HO) to G. V. Kitson, 29 June 1935, FO 371/19370, PRO. There is some evidence that the illicit traffic from China actually declined in 1934. See Nicholson to Customs, 23 April 1935, RG 59, lot file 55 D 607, box 15, "Wong Sui" folder, NA.

80. Nicholson to Customs, 17 October 1934 (RG 59, 893.114 Narcotics/917), 13 March 1935 (RG 59, 893.114 Narcotics/1008), and 18 April 1935 (RG 59, 893.114 Narcotics/1130), NA; Marshall, "Opium and the Politics of Gangsterism," 27–28.

81. Gauss to DS, 10 September 1934, RG 59, 893.00 P.R. Nanking/79, Nicholson to Customs, 18 October 1934, RG 59, 893.114 Narcotics/910, and Peck to Gauss, 20 October 1934, RG 59, 893.114 Narcotics/911 (quotation), NA.

82. On Chinese opposition to Chiang's policy by a local KMT office in Shanghai, see Nicholson to Customs, 30 November 1935, RG 59, 893.114 Narcotics/1388, NA; *Shanghai Evening Post and Mercury*, 25 October 1935.

83. Gauss to DS, 8 November 1934, RG 59, 893.114 Narcotics/913, Josselyn to DS, 13 June 1935, RG 59, 893.00 P.R. Hankow/97, and Nicholson to Customs, 20 March 1935, RG 59, 893.114 Narcotics/1101, NA. See Nicholson's summary of the operations in Nicholson to Customs, 14 June 1935, RG 59, 893.114 Narcotics/1231.

84. Adams to DS, 9 April 1934, RG 59, 893.00 P.R. Hankow/83; Service Oral History, 1:110, HSTL.

85. *North China Herald*, 10 January 1934; Reed (Yunnanfu) to Hull, 13 March 1934, RG 59, 893.114 Narcotics/698, NA; Harding to Cadogan, 6 June 1934, FO 371/18199, PRO.

86. Nicholson to Customs, 11 April 1935 (RG 59, 893.114 Narcotics/1115) and 10 April 1935 (RG 59, 893.114 Narcotics/1138), NA; Snow, *Red Star over China*, 198–99.

87. DT to DS with Nicholson's reports, 3 November 1935, RG 59, 893.114 Narcotics/1340, NA.

88. Nicholson to Customs, 19 March 1935 (RG 59, 893.114 Narcotics/1100), 26 April 1935 (sent to Anslinger—RG 59, 893.114 Narcotics/1139), and 14 April 1935 (RG 59, 893.114 Narcotics/1118), NA; DS to Anslinger, 18 July 1935, RG 59, 893.114 Narcotics/1208, NA; Lary, *Region and Nation*, 197.

89. Eastman, "Nationalist China during the Nanking Decade," 148–49; Tien, *Government and Politics in Kuomintang China*, 70; J. W. O. Davidson to Cadogan, 30 April 1935, FO 371/19303, PRO; Kapp, *Szechwan and the Chinese Republic*, 116–17; Nicholson to Customs, 24 December 1935, RG 59, 893.114 Narcotics/1455, NA.

90. Wei, *Shanghai*, 3, 235–36 (first quotation); Sues, *Shark Fins and Millet*, 68–69. See also Wang, "Tu Yueh-sheng," passim.

91. Nicholson to Customs, 27 March 1934 (RG 59, 893.114 Narcotics/713) and 23 April 1935 (RG 59, 893.114 Narcotics/1156), NA; *China Press Weekly*, 11 May, 15 June 1935.

92. Cunningham to DS, 2 August 1935 (RG 59, 893.00 P.R. Shanghai/82) and 17 October 1935 (RG 59, 893.114 Narcotics/1359), NA; Brenan to the British embassy, 21 October 1935, FO 371/19367, PRO. The most accessible popular source concerning Tu Yueh-sheng is Seagrave, *The Soong Dynasty*.

93. *Peking & Tientsin Times*, 7 April 1935.

94. Nicholson to Customs, 4 March 1935, RG 59, 893.114 Narcotics/1072, NA; *Peiping Chronicle*, 5 March 1935; Nicholson to Customs, 23 May 1935, RG 59, 893.114 Narcotics/1131, NA (quotation).

95. *Peiping Chronicle*, 5 March, 9 April 1935; Berger to DS, 15 August 1935, RG 59, 893.00 P.R. Tientsin/86, NA. For an earlier report on the competition over which opium would find a market in North China, see *Ta-kung-pao*, 8 September 1934 [in translation], in RG 59, 893.00 P.R. Tientsin/76, NA.

96. Lockhart to DS, 9 March 1934, RG 59, 893.114 Narcotics/680, and Compilation of monthly consular political reports (April 1934), RG 59, 893.114 Narcotics/762, NA; *Japan Chronicle*, 22 May 1935; *North-China Daily News*, 18 January 1935 (quotation).

97. *Ta-kung-pao*, 15 July 1934 [in translation], in RG 59, 893.114 Narcotics/845, NA.

98. *The Reminiscences of Chang Fa-k'uei*, 448, COHP.

99. Fuller to U.S. consulate (Geneva), 24 July 1934, RG 59, 893.114 Narcotics/788, and Nicholson to Customs, 29 April 1935, RG 59, 893.114 Narcotics/1137, NA.

100. Shimada, "Designs on North China," 98, 102–28.

Chapter Five

1. Barnhart, *Japan Prepares for Total War*, 35–48; Shimada, "Designs on North China," 135–202; Mancall, *China at the Center*, 276.

2. Memorandum by Hornbeck, 9 May 1933, in Nixon, *Roosevelt and Foreign Affairs*, 1:103–7.

3. Thomson, "The Role of the Department of State," 82, 86–88; Burns, "Hornbeck," 92–94, 11; cf. Thorne, *The Limits of Foreign Policy*, 86–87, 389–91; *FRUS, 1935*, 832 (quotation). See also Ferrell, *American Diplomacy and the Great Depression*, 38, 130–31, for an indication of Hornbeck's influence in the Hoover administration.

4. Memorandum by Hornbeck, 26 February 1934, in Nixon, *Roosevelt and Foreign Affairs*, 1:660.

5. *FRUS, 1935*, 856–57, 863. Joseph Grew agreed with Hornbeck about the need for a stronger navy. For Grew's defense of the open door, see Heinrichs, *American Ambassador*, 186, 219, 224.

6. Pelz, *Race to Pearl Harbor*, 69, 77, 94, 150–51, 160–64; Dallek, *Roosevelt and American Foreign Policy*, 76–77; *FRUS, 1935*, 828.

7. *DBFP*, 2d ser., vol. 20, nos. 216, 222, 304, 313; *FRUS, 1935*, 836 (quotation).

8. Davis to Roosevelt, 31 October and 14 December 1934, in Nixon, *Roosevelt and Foreign Affairs*, 2:250–54, 316 (quotation).

9. 303 H.C. Deb. 5s., 24 June 1935, 815; *DBFP*, 2d ser., vol. 20, no. 321.

10. Shimada, "Designs on North China," 154.

11. Cadogan to Vansittart, 29 April 1934, Cadogan Private Papers, FO 800/293, PRO; Johnson to Hull, 31 March 1936, RG 59, 893.114 Narcotics/1547, with Stilwell's analysis of the narcotics situation, NA. See also Tuchman, *Stilwell and the American Experience in China*, 154.

12. The generalizations in this paragraph are largely based on Feuerwerker, "Economic Trends."

13. *The Reminiscences of Ho Lien*, 156–57, COHP; Young, "Outline of a Program of Financial Reform for China," Chen Private Papers, box 1, BL/CU.

14. Young, "Outline of a Program of Financial Reform for China," Chen Private Papers, box 1, BL/CU. On the U.S. silver policy, see Borg, *The United States and the Far Eastern Crisis*, 121–37; *The Reminiscences of K'ung Hsiang-hsi*, 90–91, COHP; A. Young, *China's Nation-building Effort*, 210–15, 223–29. *The Reminiscences of Ch'en Kuang-fu*, 76, COHP, credits the Bank of China with staving off financial destruction.

15. Cadogan to Charles Orde, 25 March 1935, FO 371/19365, PRO; Atcheson to U.S. legation, 12 June 1935, RG 59, 893.00 P.R. Nanking/88, NA.

16. Young, "Outline of a Program of Financial Reform for China," Chen Private Papers, box 1, BL/CU.

17. A. Young, *China's Nation-building Effort*, 194, 201–3, 207–11.

18. *The Reminiscences of K'ung Hsiang-hsi*, 86, 89, 91–95, COHP; Coble, *The Shanghai Capitalists*, 192–94.

19. *The Reminiscences of Ch'en Kuang-fu*, 75–78, and *The Reminiscences of K'ung Hsiang-hsi*, 91–92, COHP; Louis, *British Strategy in the Far East*, 227–31; Trotter, *Britain and East Asia*, 148–61; Endicott, *Diplomacy and Enterprise*, 102–28. Still useful in providing a framework of understanding about the British role in China's monetary reconstruction is Gull, *British Economic Interests in the Far East*, 155–58. On Britain and a positive economic role for Japan in China, see Cadogan to Sir Victor Wellesley, 30 August 1934, FO 676/171, PRO.

20. 307 H.C. Deb. 5s., 5 December 1935, 336–37; *The Reminiscences of Ch'en Kuang-fu*, 69, 77 (quotation), COHP.

21. *The Reminiscences of Ch'en Kuang-fu*, 67–69, COHP; Coble, *The Shanghai Capitalists*, 172–92. The government probably sparked the crisis by hoarding bank notes.

22. Fuller's statement to the twenty-first session of the OAC, 28 May 1936, RG 59, 500.C1197/976, NA; Coble, *The Shanghai Capitalists*, 195–96; Sues, *Shark Fins and Millet*, 57; Selle, *Donald of China*, 294–95.

23. A. Young, *China's Nation-building Effort*, 263; Coble, *The Shanghai Capitalists*, 195–96.

24. O. Edmund Clubb, *The Witness and I*, 6, 39, 45; Gauss to DS, 6 June 1936, RG 59, 893.00 P.R. Shanghai/92, NA. In June 1935, the United States raised the status of the legation to that of an embassy. Under the influence of Hirota's conciliatory policy toward China, Japan had announced the same change in May. The Foreign Office followed suit. Buhite, *Johnson*, 99–100.

25. Peck to DS, 12 August 1936, RG 59, 893.114 Narcotics/1687, and Nicholson to Customs, 23 October 1936, RG 59, 893.114 Narcotics/1765, NA.

26. Copy of a speech by Wang Ching-wei at the 1934 National Financial Conference, Young Papers, box 51, HIWRP; *North China Herald*, 2 December 1936.

27. Nicholson to Customs, 20 May 1937 (RG 59, 893.114 Narcotics/1975) and 9 June 1937 (RG 59, 893.114 Narcotics/2009), NA.

28. Cochran and Hsieh, *One Day in China*, 167–68, 183.

29. Gauss to DS, 16 February 1937, RG 59, 893.114 Narcotics/1886, NA. For information on opium exports from Iran, see Josephine Roche to DS, 14 July 1937, RG

59, 891.114 Narcotics/262, and Moore to Cornelius Van H. Engert, 25 September 1937, RG 59, 891.114 Narcotics/263, NA.

30. Gauss to Johnson, 18 May 1937 (RG 59, 893.114 Narcotics/1971), 3 June 1937 (RG 59, 893.00 P.R. Shanghai/104—quotation), and 24 June 1937 (RG 59, 893.114 Narcotics/2014), NA. See also Gauss to DS, 22 June 1937, RG 59, 893.114 Narcotics/2013, NA.

31. Johnson to DS, 3 July 1937, RG 59, 893.114 Narcotics/2015, and Gauss to Johnson, 6 July 1937, RG 59, 893.114 Narcotics/2039, NA.

32. Nicholson to Customs, 10 July 1937, RG 59, 893.114 Narcotics/2025, and Gauss to Johnson, 15 July 1937, RG 59, 893.114 Narcotics/2042, NA.

33. *North-China Daily News*, 4 July 1937. Rural debt may have been as high as Y900 million by mid-1937.

34. Chang Kuo-t'ao, *Autobiography*, 325–29; Harding (Yunnanfu) to Cadogan, 5 October 1934, WO 106/5371, PRO; Holleman Oral History, CMOHP, 19, 27, 61–62.

35. Nicholson to Customs, 28 December 1935, RG 59, 893.114 Narcotics/1455, and Fuller's statement to the twenty-first session of the OAC, 28 May 1936, RG 59, 500.C1197/976, NA. For the situation in Yunnan, see Nicholson to Customs, 6 October 1936, RG 59, 893.114 Narcotics/1718, NA.

36. J. N. Behrens to FO, 21 May 1935, WO 106/5371, PRO; *Peiping Chronicle*, 1 March 1936; Gillin, *Warlord*, 216–17; Shimada, "Designs on North China," 152.

37. 307 H.C. Deb. 5s., 5 December 1935, 337; Shimada, "Designs on North China," 141–44, 153–61.

38. *North China Herald*, 27 June 1934; Hanson to Johnson, 18 February 1934 (RG 59, 893.114N16 Manchuria/73) and 28 February 1934 (RG 59, 893.114N16 Manchuria/76), Cabot Colville to Johnson, 7 April 1934, RG 59, 893.114N16 Manchuria/90, and Myers to DS, 17 May 1934, RG 59, 893.114N16 Manchuria/93, NA. On Japan's racial attitudes toward Asians and others, see, for example, Hashikawa, "Japanese Perspectives on Asia," 329–31, 334–36, 338, 340, 352; Dower, *War without Mercy*, 7–8, 47; Ienaga, *The Pacific War*, 3–12, 153, 156–59.

39. Adams to DS, 22 November 1934, RG 59, 893.114N16 Manchuria/136, and Nicholson to Customs, 18 February 1935 (RG 59, 893.114N16 Manchuria/147) and 8 May 1935 (RG 59, 893.114N16 Manchuria/164), NA.

40. Nicholson to Customs, 10 March 1935, RG 59, 893.114N16 Manchuria/162, NA.

41. IMTFE, *Proceedings*, 20309–20, 20323–50, FO 648, IWM. For a different view of Namba, see Brackman, *The Other Nuremberg*, 193–94.

42. *Japan Advertiser*, 12–13 June 1937; *Peking & Tientsin Times*, 7, 12 June 1937; Caldwell to Hull, 25 June 1937, RG 59, 893.114 Narcotics/2016 (quotation). On the action by the Foreign Ministry in 1936, see Grew to Hull, 25 June 1936, RG 59, 893.114 Narcotics/226, Caldwell to Hull, 25 June 1937, and DS to FBN, 15 June 1937, RG 59, 893.114 Narcotics/1979, NA.

43. Memorandum by Robert S. Wood (Tientsin) of a conversation with Dr. Ernest

H. Clay, 7 May 1936, RG 59, 893.114 Narcotics/1600, NA; *China Weekly Review,* 18 April 1936; Nicholson to Customs, 4 June 1936 (RG 59, 893.114 Narcotics/1641), 9 July 1936 (RG 59, 893.114 Narcotics/1653), 30 July 1936 (RG 59, 893.114 Narcotics/1683), 12 November 1936 (RG 59, 893.114 Narcotics/1745), and 17 April 1937 (RG 59, 893.114 Narcotics/1950), NA.

44. Berger to DS, 29 December 1936, RG 59, 893.114 Narcotics/1842, NA.

45. Johnson to Hull, 21 March 1936, RG 59, 893.114 Narcotics/1547, NA. As with many such reports received in the State Department, this one was routinely passed to Anslinger at the FBN.

46. Johnson to Hull, 20 April 1936, RG 59, 893.114 Narcotics/1579, NA.

47. Johnson to Hull, 3 June 1936, RG 59, 893.114 Narcotics/1624, NA; Minute by E. L. Hall-Patch, 23 March 1937, FO 676/326, PRO.

48. Clive to Eden, 19 June 1934, FO 676/234, General Staff (Intelligence) to WO, 18 March 1937, WO 106/5375 (quotation), and Knatchbull-Hugessen to Lord Brabourne, 20 November 1936, Knatchbull-Hugessen Private Papers, FO 800/297, PRO.

49. Johnson to Thomas W. Lamont, 5 September 1935 (box 27), Hornbeck to Johnson, 14 August 1935 (box 26), and Johnson to Hornbeck, 9 October 1936 (box 26), Johnson Papers, general correspondence, MD/LC.

50. Johnson to Malcolm D. Simpson, 3 August 1936, box 30, ibid.

51. Following his stint as ambassador in China, Sir Alexander Cadogan returned to the Foreign Office to serve as deputy under secretary of state. In an interview with U.S. chargé Ray Atherton, Cadogan reiterated his belief that the West would not extend active military support to China in the event of a conflict with Japan. Memorandum by Atherton, 13 July 1936, Hornbeck Papers, box 181, HIWRP. See also Dilks, *The Diaries of Sir Alexander Cadogan,* 6–12.

52. Johnson to DS, 7 April 1936, RG 59, 893.114N16 Manchuria/215, and Memorandum by Gauss, 16 February 1937, RG 59, 893.114 Narcotics/1886, NA.

53. On concern over the spread of addiction among Japanese citizens, see Joseph W. Ballantine to DS, 17 February 1936, RG 59, 893.114 Narcotics/1641, and Langdon to Johnson, 4 September 1936, RG 59, 893.114N16 Manchuria/225, NA.

54. On political legitimacy in the Chinese context, see Johnson, *Peasant Nationalism and Communist Power,* ix, 1–30; Selden, *The Yenan Way,* 79, 155–57, is also helpful. On Vietnam, see McCoy, *The Politics of Heroin in Southeast Asia.*

55. [Mao Zedong], *Selected Works of Mao Tse-tung,* 1:160.

56. Ibid., 255.

57. Knatchbull-Hugessen to FO, 13, 18 December 1936, FO 676/232, PRO; Lockhart to DS, 5 January 1937, RG 59, 893.114 Narcotics/1809, and Sokobin to U.S. embassy, 5 February 1937, RG 59, 893.00 P.R. Tsingtao/107, NA. In the short term, Chiang Kai-shek seemed to overcome the potential humiliation of the Sian Incident. Eastman, *The Abortive Revolution,* 267–70. But cf. Selden, *The Yenan Way,* 116–20; O. Edmund Clubb, *Twentieth-Century China,* 202–10.

58. Crowley, *Japan's Quest for Autonomy*, 279–82; Shimada, "Designs on North China," 129–34.

59. Johnson to Norton, 10 January 1936, Johnson Papers, general correspondence, box 30, MD/LC.

60. Endicott, *Diplomacy and Enterprise*, 138–41, 145–49; Shimada, "Designs on North China," 144–45, 161–67; *DBFP*, 2d ser., vol. 20, no. 557; Knatchbull-Hugessen to William Kirkpatrick, 19 February 1937, Knatchbull-Hugessen Private Papers, FO 800/297, PRO.

61. Endicott, *Diplomacy and Enterprise*, 146–49; Trotter, *Britain and East Asia*, 189–99; Crowley, *Japan's Quest for Autonomy*, 316–22; 321 H.C. Deb. 5s., 24 March 1937, 2876; Borg, *The United States and the Far Eastern Crisis*, 254–56. In Tokyo, Grew seems to have responded to Satō's efforts with studied circumspection. Grew, *Ten Years in Japan*, 206–7.

62. Shimada, "Designs on North China," 199–202; IMTFE, *Proceedings*, 3890–92, 4820–50, FO 648, IWM.

63. Ella M. Jacobson to Customs, 19 May 1936, RG 59, 893.114 Narcotics/1618, and Nicholson to Customs, 1 May 1936 (RG 59, 893.114 Narcotics/1603) and 5 June 1936 (RG 59, 893.114 Narcotics/1641), NA.

64. Lary, *Region and Nation*, 190–91, 196–99; Nicholson to Customs, 14 October 1936, RG 59, 893.114 Narcotics/1743, NA.

65. Nicholson to Customs, 25 February 1936 (RG 59, 893.114 Narcotics/1524) and 2 March 1936 (RG 59, 893.114 Narcotics/1527), and Jacobson to Customs, 27 March 1936, RG 59, 893.114 Narcotics/1554, NA.

66. *North China Herald*, 2 September 1936; Shewmaker, *America and the Chinese Communists*, 106–9, 248–49.

67. Marshall, "Opium and the Politics of Gangsterism," 29–30; Nicholson to Customs, 9 November 1934, RG 59, 893.114 Narcotics/927, Compilation of monthly consular political reports (October 1934), Foochow, RG 59, 893.114 Narcotics/933, and Nicholson to Customs, 30 November 1936, RG 59, 893.114 Narcotics/1819, NA.

68. Phillips to Johnson, 14 August 1936, RG 59, 893.114 Narcotics/1674, Nicholson to Customs, 17 March 1937, RG 59, 893.114 Narcotics/1921, and H. H. Dick (Amoy) to Johnson, 6 July 1937, RG 59, 893.00 P.R. Amoy/118, NA.

69. 321 H.C. Deb. 5s., 15 March 1937, 1612–13.

70. Nicholson to Customs, 26 September 1935, RG 59, 891.114 Narcotics/244, NA; Cadogan to Vansittart, 29 April 1934, Cadogan Private Papers, FO 800/293, PRO; Nicholson to Customs, 25 May 1937, RG 59, 893.114 Narcotics/1981, NA.

71. DS to DT, 5 June 1937, RG 59, 893.114 Narcotics/1959, and Johnson to DS, 9 January 1937, RG 59, 893.00 P.R./130, NA; *China Weekly Review*, 9 January 1937. For a review of the penalties for opium and narcotics offenses, see Nicholson to Customs, 12 August 1936, RG 59, 893.114 Narcotics/1717, NA.

72. Monnet B. Davis (Shanghai) to DS, 7 February 1936, RG 59, 893.114 Narcotics/

1484, and Peck to Hull, 6 April 1936, RG 59, 893.114 Narcotics/1561, NA; *China Weekly Review*, 28 January 1937.

73. Gauss to Hull, 8 April 1937, RG 59, 893.114 Narcotics/1935, NA; Tien, *Government and Politics in Kuomintang China*, 24; Eastman, "Nationalist China during the Nanking Decade," 122; Sues, *Shark Fins and Millet*, 89. For Shanghai's addict population, see Jacobson to Customs, 29 April 1936, RG 59, 893.114 Narcotics/1592, NA. Few observers dissented from Kan's assessment of China's antiopium record. For one view more charitable to Chiang, see Josselyn to DS, 30 June 1937, RG 59, 893.114 Narcotics/2017, NA. With more than 2 million inhabitants, Shanghai may have been home to 150,000 drug addicts.

74. Fuller's report on the twenty-first session of the OAC, 22 September 1936, RG 59, 500.C1197/997, and Atherton to DS, 19 April, 15 May 1936, RG 59, 500.C1197/967, NA.

75. Fuller's statement to the twenty-first session of the OAC, dated 28 May 1936, RG 59, 500.C1197/976, and Fuller's report on the twenty-first session of the OAC, 22 September 1936, RG 59, 500.C1197/997, NA.

76. *Shanghai Evening Post and Mercury*, 22 May 1936; *North-China Daily News*, 22–23 May 1936.

77. Fuller's report on the twenty-first session of the OAC, 22 September 1936, RG 59, 500.C1197/997, NA.

78. Ibid. The official OAC minutes, which Fuller termed "mediaeval," are in OAC, *Minutes of the Twenty-first Session*.

79. Grew to Hull, 25 June 1936, RG 59, 894.114 Narcotics/218, NA.

80. Fuller to Johnson, 1 October 1935, Johnson Papers, general correspondence, box 26, MD/LC.

81. Blanco to Koo, 14 January 1937, Koo Papers, box 10, BL/CU; Nicholson's report to Customs, 25 March 1937, RG 59, 893.114 Narcotics/1934, NA.

82. Chiang's order is contained in Nicholson to Customs, 15 July 1937, RG 59, 893.114 Narcotics/2045, NA.

83. Memorandum by Hornbeck, 24 August 1935, RG 59, 500.C1197/894 1/2, NA.

84. Memorandum by Fuller, 29 July 1937, RG 59, 500.C1197/1110, and Gauss to Johnson, 6 July 1937, RG 59, 893.114 Narcotics/2039, NA; OAC, *Minutes of the Twenty-second Session*, 58 (quotation). Gauss disagreed with Fuller's commendation of China.

85. *South China Morning Post*, 4 June 1937.

86. *Peiping Chronicle*, 5 (quotation) and 13 June 1937; *Peiping News*, 16 June 1937.

87. Anslinger to Harold N. Graves, assistant secretary of the Treasury, 2 June 1937, RG 59, 894.114 Narcotics/264, NA.

88. OAC, *Minutes of the Twenty-second Session*, 62–63; John W. Bulkley (Customs) to George A. Morlock, 4 June 1937, RG 59, 500.C1197/1079, NA; *Peiping Chronicle*, 4 June 1937; Fuller to Hull, 7 June 1937, RG 59, 500.C1197/1081, NA.

89. Bulkley to Morlock, 10 June 1937, RG 59, 500.C1197/1087, and Nicholson to Customs, 12 June 1937, RG 59, 500.C1197/1094, NA. For the contradiction, see n. 70 supra.

90. Memorandum by Hornbeck, 7 September 1934, Hornbeck Papers, box 93, HIWRP; Moore to Fuller, 16 April 1937, RG 59, 500.C1197/1059C, and Fuller to DS, 12 June 1937, RG 59, 500.C1197/1088, NA.

91. Grew to Wilson, 13 May 1937, in Grew to Johnson, 17 May 1937, Johnson Papers, general correspondence, box 31, MD/LC.

92. FO memorandum to Knatchbull-Hugessen, 31 March 1937, FO 676/326, PRO; Crowley, *Japan's Quest for Autonomy*, 320–22. Grew's letter to Wilson, n. 91 supra, suggests a comparable evaluation of Hayashi's policies.

93. Knatchbull-Hugessen to Cadogan, 29 June 1937, Knatchbull-Hugessen Private Papers, FO 800/297, PRO.

94. *Shanghai Evening Post and Mercury*, 7 and 9 (quotation) July 1937; *North-China Daily News*, 9 and 16 July 1937.

95. Nicholson to Customs, 7 June 1937, RG 59, 893.114 Narcotics/1992, NA.

96. Smedley, *The Great Road*, 43, 82, 446. For a provocative interpretation of the relationship between the CCP and Chinese peasants that helps explain how opposition to opium by both groups contributed to the growth of revolution, see Thaxton, *China Turned Rightside Up*, 47–51, 116, 220–30.

97. Knatchbull-Hugessen to FO, 29 July 1937, FO 676/327, PRO.

Chapter Six

1. 326 H.C. Deb. 5s., 21 July 1937, 2182–83; Hull, *Memoirs*, 1:531–34 (quotation, 534).

2. Nixon, *Roosevelt and Foreign Affairs*, 2:256.

3. Knatchbull-Hugessen, *Diplomat in Peace and War*, 118–27; Craigie, *Behind the Japanese Mask*, 42.

4. Kennedy, *The Rise and Fall of the Great Powers*, 318–19.

5. Dallek, *Roosevelt and American Foreign Policy*, 137–40; Borg, *The United States and the Far Eastern Crisis*, 334–36; Rock, *Chamberlain and Roosevelt*, 147, 166, 171; *FRUS, 1937*, 100 (quotation). See also Leutze, *Bargaining for Supremacy*, which shows how Japan's disavowal of limits on naval construction in 1936 helped bring Britain and America closer together strategically.

6. Lee, *Britain and the Sino-Japanese War*, 18–22, 46–49; Craigie, *Behind the Japanese Mask*, 49–50; Endicott, *Diplomacy and Enterprise*, 171 (quotation).

7. Trotter, *Britain and East Asia*, 203–4; Lee, *Britain and the Sino-Japanese War*, 46–49; Kennedy, *The Rise and Fall of the Great Powers*, 320. Kennedy aptly terms the British Empire "overstretched."

8. *DBFP*, 2d ser., vol. 21, no. 159 n. 2. For a discussion of relations with the United States in Asia, see ibid., nos. 151, 194.

9. Adams, *Economic Diplomacy*, 171–87 (Pierson's quotation, 178); *FRUS, 1936*, 614 (Johnson's quotation). On China's economic situation, see generally A. Young, *China's Nation-building Effort*, 408–30.

10. Barnhart, *Japan Prepares for Total War*, 80–85; Iriye, "Japanese Aggression and China's International Position," 516–19.

11. Crowley, *Japan's Quest for Autonomy*, 322–42; Hata, "The Marco Polo Bridge Incident," 248–68.

12. Garver, "Chiang Kai-shek's Quest for Soviet Entry," 303. Chiang is quoted in a report by the League of Nations Assembly in *FRUS, Japan: 1931–1941*, 1:393.

13. Office Reports of the FPA, Opium Research Committee, 13 March, 24 November, 21 December 1936; 15 January, May 1937.

14. Merrill, "The Opium Menace in the Far East," 303–4.

15. Blanco to Koo, 9 February, 17 March (quotation) 1937, Koo Papers, box 10, BL/CU. For a report on China's antiopium efforts, see *New York Times*, 10 January 1937.

16. Koo to Merrill, 15 May 1937, and Merrill to Koo, 8 June 1937, Koo Papers, box 10, BL/CU.

17. Hoo to Teh Chuan (Alfred C. K. Sze), 11 May 1937, Hoo Papers, box 7, BL/CU; Office Reports of the FPA, Opium Research Committee, November 1937.

18. Chien to Hoo, 29 May 1937, and Chien to Blanco, 29 May 1937, Koo Papers, box 10, BL/CU.

19. Office Reports of the FPA, Opium Research Committee, May, November 1937; FBN, *Traffic in Opium and Other Dangerous Drugs for . . . 1936*, 16, and *for . . . 1937*, 14, 16. See also Merrill, *Japan and the Opium Menace*.

20. *The Reminiscences of Ch'en Kuang-fu*, 85 (quotation), 98, *The Reminiscences of Li Huang*, 550, and *The Reminiscences of Wu Kuo-cheng*, 386, 391, COHP.

21. Garver, "Chiang Kai-shek's Quest for Soviet Entry"; O. Edmund Clubb, *China and Russia*, 306–18; Mancall, *China at the Center*, 278–84.

22. Hornbeck to Graves, 20 September 1937, Hornbeck Papers, box 93, HIWRP; Grew to DS, 6 July 1937 (RG 59, 894.114 Narcotics/282) and 30 July 1937 (RG 59, 894.114 Narcotics/297), NA.

23. FO, *The Opium Trade*, 6:XXXI, 1937–41, no. 2; Howard Bucknell (Geneva) to DS, 28 September 1937, RG 59, 500.C1197/1121 (Hoo's quotation), and Langdon to DS, 27 September 1937, RG 59, 893.114N16 Manchuria/253, NA.

24. DS memorandum to DT, 16 February 1938, RG 59, 500.C1197/1137, NA.

25. Nicholson's reports on Tientsin and Peiping in Nicholson to Customs, 12 July 1937, RG 59, 893.114 Narcotics/2045, NA.

26. *North-China Daily News*, 31 October 1937.

27. *The Reminiscences of K'ung Hsiang-hsi*, 108–9, COHP. On Imai, see Boyle, *China and Japan at War*, 175–76, 202–5. Mukden consulate general political report for August, 10 September 1937, RG 59, 893.114 Narcotics/2121, NA.

28. Hata, "The Marco Polo Bridge Incident," 272; Usui, "The Politics of War," 323–25; Boyle, *China and Japan at War*, 54, 130–32.

29. Caldwell to DS, 3 September 1937, RG 59, 893.00 P.R. Tientsin/112, and Lockhart to DS, 16 December 1937, RG 59, 893.114 Narcotics/2159, NA; *Peking & Tientsin Times*, 1 January 1938.

30. On Western concern, see Allan Archer (Peking) to Viscount Halifax, 1 July 1938, FO 371/22194, PRO; Boyle, *China and Japan at War*, 84–86; IMTFE, *Judgment*, pt. B, chap. V: "Japanese Aggression against China: Narcotics in China," 1:771–74, FO 648, IWM.

31. U.S. consulate general (Harbin) to DS, 12 October 1937, RG 59, 893.114 Narcotics/2098, and John Paton Davies, Jr. (Mukden) to DS, 22 November 1937, RG 59, 893.114N16 Manchuria/262, NA. The compilation of information on narcotics for January 1938 (RG 59, 893.114 Narcotics/2215, NA) indicates a revival of unease regarding the situation at Mukden.

32. Gauss to DS, 9 July 1937, RG 59, 893.00 P.R. Shanghai/105, Fuller's memorandum, 7 September 1937, RG 59, 893.114 Narcotics/2072, and Gauss to Johnson, 17 September 1937, RG 59, 893.00 P.R. Shanghai/118, NA.

33. Nicholson to Customs, 12 and 14 July 1937, RG 59, 893.114 Narcotics/2045, and Irving N. Linnell to DS, 8 December 1937, RG 59, 893.00 P.R. Canton/118, NA.

34. *North China Herald*, 14 July 1937; *Manchester Guardian*, 9 October 1937.

35. Robert S. Ward to DS, 20 September 1937 (RG 59, 893.00 P.R. Foochow/115) and 1 November 1937 (RG 59, 893.00 P.R. Foochow/117), and Nicholson to Customs, 27 September 1937, RG 59, 893.114 Narcotics/2125, NA.

36. Hoo to Koo, 4 August 1937, Hoo Papers, box 7, HIWRP; Office Reports of the FPA, Opium Research Committee, November 1937.

37. Borg, *The United States and the Far Eastern Crisis*, 399–441 (Roosevelt's quotation, 407); Lee, *Britain and the Sino-Japanese War*, 62–78; Hull, *Memoirs*, 1:550–56; Craigie, *Behind the Japanese Mask*, 50–52.

38. This point is best developed in Reynolds, *The Creation of the Anglo-American Alliance*, 27–32.

39. A. L. Warnshuis, Foreign Missions Conference of North America, to Secretaries of Missions Boards with work in China, 8 September 1937, in CBMS, E/M.1, box 330, SOAS/UL; Cross Oral History, CMOHP, 2:131–32.

40. Far East Committee Minutes, 1937–40, CBMS, E/M.2, box 331, SOAS/UL.

41. G. B. Moss (Hankow) to R. G. Howe (Peking), 15 November 1937, Knatchbull-Hugessen Papers, FO 800/297, PRO.

42. Lowe, "Great Britain's Assessment of Japan," 459–60; Grew, *Ten Years in Japan*, 222–31; *DBFP*, 2d ser., vol. 21, nos. 245, 258; Crowley, *Japan's Quest for Autonomy*, 342–78 (quotation, 350).

43. Eden, *Facing the Dictators*, 614–45; James, *Eden*, 171–95; Harvey, *The Diplomatic Diaries of Oliver Hardy*, 66–73, 92–98 (quotation, 71); Dilks, *The Diaries of Sir*

Alexander Cadogan, 45–54; Lowe, *Great Britain and the Origins of the Pacific War*, 32–38; Rock, *Chamberlain and Roosevelt*, 55–77, 81–83. The *Panay* crisis occurred in late 1937, when the Japanese sunk an American gunboat and a war scare briefly ensued.

44. MacDonald, *The United States, Great Britain, and Appeasement*, 50–75; Leutze, *Bargaining for Supremacy*, 19–25, 30; Pelz, *Race to Pearl Harbor*, 197–98.

45. *DBFP*, 2d ser., vol. 21, no. 497; Memorandum by Swire of a meeting of the China Association, 14 January 1938, Inverchapel Papers, FO 800/299, PRO.

46. Minute by M. J. R. Talbot, 31 May 1938, FO 371/22194, PRO.

47. Strong to Fuller, 11 April 1938, RG 59, 893.114 Narcotics/2211, NA.

48. Ibid.; DS to DT with a memorandum by Gauss, 19 August 1939, RG 59, 893.114 Narcotics/2607, and Nicholson to Customs, 24 October 1939, RG 59, 893.114 Narcotics/2657.5, NA.

49. Johnson to Roy Howard, 25 January 1938, and Johnson to Charles Hodges, 2 February 1938 (unbound correspondence, box 34), Johnson to Lamont, 8 February 1938, and Johnson to William Allen White, 9 February 1938 (general correspondence, box 35), Johnson Papers, MD/LC. British records paint a similar picture. See British embassy (Shanghai) to Halifax, 14 April 1938, FO 371/22155, and "Economic Position of the Japanese Empire," a report by Edmund Stinnes, 8 August 1938, in Inverchapel Papers, FO 800/299, PRO.

50. Clark Kerr to Halifax, 31 August 1938, FO 371/22195, PRO. On Halifax, see Barnett, *The Collapse of British Power*, 472; Harvey, *The Diplomatic Diaries of Oliver Harvey*, 100.

51. Caldwell to DS, 4 March 1938, RG 59, 893.00 P.R. Tientsin/118, NA; Archer to FO, 19 December 1948, FO 676/394, PRO.

52. Caldwell to DS, 9 June 1938, RG 59, 893.00 P.R. Tientsin/121, NA; *Peking & Tientsin Times*, 1 September 1938; Caldwell to DS, 4 October 1938 (RG 59, 893.114 Narcotics/2347) and 3 November 1938 (RG 59, 893.114 Narcotics/2363—quotation), and Nicholson to Customs, 1 July 1939, RG 59, 893.114 Narcotics/2618.5, NA.

53. Minute by J. P. E. C. Henniker-Major, 31 January 1939, FO 371/23576, PRO.

54. 342 H.C. Deb. 5s., 22 December 1938, 3204 (quotation). See also 336 H.C. Deb. 5s., 16 May 1938, 9; FO, *The Opium Trade*, 6:XXXI, 1937–41, no. 3.

55. DS to U.S. embassy (London), 1 August 1928, RG 59, 893.114 Narcotics/2302, NA.

56. Parssinen, *Secret Passions*, 220 (quotation); A. Taylor, *American Diplomacy and the Narcotics Traffic*, 227.

57. James, *Eden*, 196n; Moorehead to Halifax, 12 April 1938, Hornbeck Papers, box 305, HIWRP.

58. Davies to DS, 3 February 1938, RG 59, 893.114N16 Manchuria/275 (first quotation), and Davies to U.S. embassy, 10 March 1938, RG 59, 893.114N16 Manchuria/288, NA; Davies, *Dragon by the Tail*, 179 (second quotation). That addicts do not make good revolutionaries was not lost on either Mao Zedong or Ho Chi Minh.

59. Johnson to Malcolm D. Simpson, 24 February 1938, and Johnson to Lamont, 18 August 1938 (quotation), Johnson Papers, general correspondence, box 35, MD/LC.

60. See Morlock's comments on Langdon to DS, 1 May 1939, RG 59, 893.114N16 Manchuria/336, NA.

61. Langdon to DS, 15 September 1938 (RG 59, 893.00 P.R. Mukden/130), 15 October 1938 (RG 59, 893.00 P.R. Mukden/131), and 10 November 1938 (RG 59, 893.114N16 Manchuria/316), NA.

62. Langdon to DS, 17 December 1938 (RG 59, 893.00 P.R. Mukden/133) and 14 January 1939 (RG 59, 893.114N16 Manchuria/323), NA.

63. Langdon to DS, 1 May 1939, RG 59, 893.114N16 Manchuria/336, NA.

64. IMTFE, *Proceedings*, 3890–92, 4731–40, FO 648, IWM; Butow, *Tojo and the Coming of War*, 109–10, n. 9.

65. Langdon to DS, 1 May 1939, RG 59, 893.114N16 Manchuria/336, NA; Minute by Henniker-Major, 25 January 1939, and Oswald White to Clark Kerr, 27 January 1939, FO 371/23584, PRO. Comparable developments were taking place around Harbin. See George R. Merrell (Harbin) to DS, 6 September 1938, RG 59, 893.114N16 Manchuria/313, and H. Merrell Benninghoff (Harbin) to DS, 4 January 1938, RG 59, 893.00 P.R. Harbin/120, NA.

66. Boyle, *China and Japan at War*, 110–16.

67. Johnson to Lamont, 21 April 1938 (general correspondence, box 35), and Johnson to Hull, 27 May 1938 (unbound correspondence, box 34), Johnson Papers, MD/LC.

68. Lee, *Britain and the Sino-Japanese War*, 95, 113–20; *Memoirs of John Kenneth Caldwell*, 80, HIWRP; Lowe, "Britain and the Opening of the War in Asia," 103–7.

69. John M. Allison (Nanking) to Johnson, 18 March 1938, RG 59, 893.114 Narcotics/2221, NA; British embassy (Shanghai) to FO, 26 August 1938, FO 371/22155, PRO.

70. Miner S. Bates, "An Open Letter on Narcotic Problems in Nanking," 22 November 1938, in Hornbeck Papers, box 93, HIWRP. See also R. L. Smyth (Nanking) to DS, 23 November 1938, RG 59, 893.114 Narcotics/2352, NA; Allen Price (Nanking) to Clark Kerr (Shanghai), 25 November 1938, FO 371/23576, PRO.

71. Memorandum by Morlock, 26 May 1938, RG 59, 500.C1197/1195, NA. On the problems arising from restricted perceptions like Morlock's, see Jervis, *Perception and Misperception in International Politics*, 212, 216. Reliable evidence indicates that the need for revenue was the moving force behind the opium policy of the Reformed Government. See Merrill, *Japan and the Opium Menace*, 54, 58–59; Minute by Henniker-Major, 12 January 1939, FO 371/23576, PRO; Clubb to DS, 12 May 1939, RG 59, 893.114 Narcotics/2569, NA; Boyle, *China and Japan at War*, 292–97.

72. Nicholson to Customs, 21 October 1938, RG 59, 893.114 Narcotics/2379, and Jacobson to Customs, 25 November 1938, RG 59, 893.114 Narcotics/2393, NA.

73. Jacobson to Customs, 10 December 1938 (RG 59, 893.114 Narcotics/2399) and

19 January 1939 (RG 59, 893.114 Narcotics/2450), NA; Sues, *Shark Fins and Millet,* 98–99.

74. Lockhart to DS, 21 June 1938, RG 59, 893.114 Narcotics/2287, Nicholson to Customs, 8 July 1938 (RG 59, 893.114 Narcotics/2308) and 29 July 1938 (RG 59, 893.114 Narcotics/2349 1/2), Gauss to DS, 7 November 1938, RG 59, 893.114 Narcotics/2364, and Jacobson to Customs, 16 December 1938 (RG 59, 893.00 P.R. Shanghai/125) and 27 July 1939 (RG 59, 893.114 Narcotics/2609.5), NA.

75. Jacobson to Customs, 24 April 1939, RG 59, 893.114 Narcotics/2544, NA; Boyle, *China and Japan at War,* 160–61; Usui, "The Politics of War," 337–38; Gauss to DS, 1 March 1939, RG 59, 893.114 Narcotics/2489, NA; FO, *The Opium Trade,* 6:XXXI, 1937–41, no. 4 and enclosure.

76. Lee, *Britain and the Sino-Japanese War,* 140–48; Craigie, *Behind the Japanese Mask,* 60–61; Usui, "The Politics of War," 330–36.

77. See n. 48 supra; Clark Kerr to Halifax, 31 August 1938, FO 371/22195, PRO.

78. Memorandum by Hamilton, 13 May 1938, RG 59, 893.114 Narcotics/1182, NA.

79. Memorandum by Morlock of a conversation with Colonel Strong, 4 May 1938, RG 59, 500.C1197/1183, and DS to Fuller, 14 May 1938, RG 59, 500.C1197/1187A, NA.

80. Memorandum by Morlock, 13 May 1938, RG 59, 500.C1197/1190, and Hull to DT, 12 March 1938, RG 59, 500.C1197/1156, NA; Anslinger and Tompkins, *The Traffic in Narcotics,* 8–9.

81. Hull to Fuller (Paris), 5 May 1938, RG 59, 500.C1197/1181A, and Hull to Fuller (Geneva), 14 May 1938, RG 59, 500.C1197/1182, NA.

82. Moore to Langdon, 25 February 1938, RG 59, 893.114N16 Manchuria/269, and Langdon to DS, 4 August 1938, RG 59, 893.114N16 Manchuria/307, NA.

83. *FRUS, Japan: 1931–1941,* 1:463–64; Grew, *Ten Years in Japan,* 244. The United States, however, was not prepared to mediate an end to the Sino-Japanese conflict—as Great Britain had proposed.

84. Hornbeck to Cadogan, 15 April 1938, Hornbeck Papers, box 174, HIWRP; Fuller to DS, 4 May 1938, RG 59, 500.C1197/1177, NA.

85. British embassy (Peking) to FO, 24 February 1938, FO 371/22194, PRO; Memorandum by Nigel B. Ronald to U.S. embassy (London), 16 April 1938, RG 59, 500.C1197/1176, NA; Lee, *Britain and the Sino-Japanese War,* 138 (quotation).

86. Paul W. Meyer (Kunming) to Johnson, 4 April 1938, RG 59, 893.00 P.R. Yunnan/113, NA; Major James M. McHugh, USMC, to Johnson, 23 August 1938, Johnson Papers, general correspondence, box 35, MD/LC; Boyle, *China and Japan at War,* 201–2, 210–11.

87. OAC, *Minutes of the Twenty-third Session,* 46–49.

88. Ibid., 49–51.

89. Fuller's report on the twenty-third OAC session, 30 August 1938, RG 59, 500.C1197/1244, NA; Wilkins, "The Role of U.S. Business," 361.

90. Fuller to DS, 14 June 1938, RG 59, 500.C1197/1203, NA.

91. Grew to DS, 22 June 1938, RG 59, 500.C1197/1209, NA—Fuller received a copy of this dispatch; Hamilton to Fuller, 24 June 1938, with Anslinger's remarks, RG 59, 500.C1197/1213A, NA.

92. Fuller's report on the twenty-third session of the OAC, 30 August 1938, RG 59, 500.C1197/1244, NA; *North-China Daily News*, 25 June 1938; *Shanghai Evening Post and Mercury*, 28 June 1938.

93. Fuller's report on the twenty-third session of the OAC, 30 August 1938, RG 59, 500.C1197/1244, NA.

94. Grew to DS, 11 August 1938, RG 59, 500.C1197/1240, NA.

95. Heinrichs, *American Ambassador*, 258–63 (quotation, 260); *FRUS, Japan: 1931–1941*, 1:611–19.

96. Usui, "The Politics of War," 336–38; *FRUS, 1938*, 48–53.

97. Memorandum by Fuller, 16 September 1938, and Moore to Grew, 12 September 1938, RG 59, 500.C1197/1240, NA.

98. Memorandum by Fuller, 16 September 1938, RG 59, 500.C1197/1258, NA—Grew received a copy of this memorandum; Koo's speech, Koo Papers, box 13, BL/CU. For additional information, see Bucknell to DS, 17 August 1938, RG 59, 500.C1197/1243, NA.

99. Bucknell to Fuller, 31 October 1938, RG 59, 500.C1197/1270, NA; Usui, "The Politics of War," 338–44, 348–52; Bucknell to DS, 2 November 1938, RG 59, 500.C1197/1267, NA.

100. OAC, *Minutes of the Twenty-third Session*, 60; Memorandum by Welles, 29 July 1938, RG 59, 893.114 Narcotics/2298, NA.

101. Usui, "The Politics of War," 349–54; Lee, *Britain and the Sino-Japanese War*, 147–61; Dilks, *The Diaries of Sir Alexander Cadogan*, 116, 119; Clark Kerr to British consulate (Hankow), 29 December 1938, FO 676/394, PRO.

102. British aide-mémoire to DS, 4 January 1939, RG 59, 893.114 Narcotics/2389, NA; FO, *The Opium Trade*, 6:XXXI, no. 5 and enclosure; DS to Grew, 16 February 1939, RG 59, 893.114 Narcotics/2457, NA.

103. Grew to DS, 14 April 1939, RG 59, 893.114 Narcotics/2531, NA; *FRUS, 1939*, 438.

104. 342 H.C. Deb. 5s., 22 December 1938, 3201 (first quotation), 3203; 350 H.C. Deb. 5s., 31 July 1939, 1967 (second quotation).

105. 344 H.C. Deb. 5s., 20 February 1939, 12.

106. Lee, *Britain and the Sino-Japanese War*, 169–73; Reynolds, *The Creation of the Anglo-American Alliance*, 58–62; Leutze, *Bargaining for Supremacy*, 36–41.

107. Lee, *Britain and the Sino-Japanese War*, 192–204 (quotation, 201); Jones, *Shanghai and Tientsin*, 172–80. For more on the sensitive nature of Anglo-Japanese relations and London's growing strategic dependence on the United States, see Clifford, *Retreat from China*, 128–35; Haggie, *Britannia at Bay*, 153–59.

108. This conclusion derives from attribution theory in social psychology. For dis-

cussion, see Larson, *Origins of Containment*, 34–39; Stein, "Building Politics into Psychology," 255–57; Jervis, *Perception and Misperception in International Politics*, 239–40, 319–29. More generally, see Nisbett and Ross, *Human Inference*.

109. Thomson, Stanley, and Perry, *Sentimental Imperialists*, 189.

110. Fuller to DS, 17 May 1939, RG 59, 500.C1197/1328, NA; OAC, *Minutes of the Twenty-fourth Session*, 34–37 (for Hoo), 37–42 (for Fuller).

111. Dr. Forbes Tocher, Ichang Municipal Council, to Rev. A. S. Kidd, 24 January 1938, CBMS, E/T.51, box 397, SOAS/UL; "Aspects of Life in Chungking, 1938–1941," Weil Papers, CNH. On the frequent link between expected behavior and inferences drawn therefrom that may be more plausible than conclusive, see Jervis, *Perception and Misperception in International Politics*, 181–82.

112. Langdon to DS, 22 May 1939, RG 59, 893.114N16 Manchuria/355, Merrell to Peck, 27 April 1939, RG 59, 893.114N16 Manchuria/342, Merrell to DS, 5 July 1939, RG 59, 893.00 P.R. Harbin/128, Sokobin to Johnson, 7 December 1938, RG 59, 893.114 Narcotics/2414, and Sokobin to DS, 18 July 1939, RG 59, 893.114 Narcotics/2581, NA.

113. Lee, *Britain and the Sino-Japanese War*, 204.

Chapter Seven

1. 351 H.C. Deb. 5s., 3 October 1939, 1829; Reynolds, *The Creation of the Anglo-American Alliance*, 46–47; Memorandum of a conversation between Lothian and Welles, 21 November 1939, in Hornbeck Papers, box 181, HIWRP.

2. Halifax to Lester, 18 January 1940, FO 371/24673, PRO; Lowe, "Britain and the Opening of the War in Asia," 107–8, and *Great Britain and the Origins of the Pacific War*, 103–19.

3. Davies, *Dragon by the Tail*, 196; P. R. Josselyn to Peck, 9 March 1939, in Johnson Papers, general correspondence, box 36, MD/LC.

4. Unsigned memorandum, "Political and Economic Conditions in the Occupied Areas of East Asia," n.d. [probably late 1939], RG 59, CA, box 7, NA. See also George, *Presidential Decisionmaking in Foreign Policy*, 71–72.

5. Grew, *Ten Years in Japan*, 302–3; *FRUS, 1940*, 262, 285–87.

6. *Christian Science Monitor*, 12 July 1938.

7. FO Minute, 21 March 1940, FO 371/24747, PRO.

8. Opium Research Committee, FPA, to Hull, 11 November 1939, in Hornbeck Papers, box 305, HIWRP; Office Reports of the FPA, December 1939.

9. Hornbeck to W. Cameron Forbes, 12 February 1940, RG 59, 894.114 Narcotics/374, NA.

10. Lowe, *Great Britain and the Origins of the Pacific War*, 120–27; Boyle, *China and Japan at War*, 289–305; Bunker, *The Peace Conspiracy*, 211–34, 250–51; *FRUS, 1940*, 265–67, 270–72, 309–10, 446–48.

11. *FRUS, 1940*, 446–48; Dallek, *Roosevelt and American Foreign Policy*, 269–71; Boyle, *China and Japan at War*, 304; Eastman, "Nationalist China during the Sino-Japanese War," 568, 604–5; *The Reminiscences of Ho Lien*, 440, COHP.

12. Schaller, *The U.S. Crusade in China*, 43; *FRUS, 1940*, 472–73, 476.

13. Blanco, "Narcotics as a Weapon of War," 30 January 1940, in RG 59, 800.114N16/653, NA.

14. Kinder, "Bureaucratic Cold Warrior," 178; Anslinger and Tompkins, *The Traffic in Narcotics*, 8–10.

15. Anslinger to DS, 10 December 1940, RG 59, 893.114 Narcotics/2854, NA.

16. Nicholson to Customs, 8 May 1940, RG 59, 893.114 Narcotics/2787, NA.

17. Ibid.; Lockhart to DS, 22 December 1939, RG 59, 893.114 Narcotics/2686, Nicholson to Customs, 24 February 1940, RG 59, 893.114 Narcotics/2731, and Lockhart to DS, 5 February 1940, RG 59, 893.114 Narcotics/2713, NA; W. Stark Toller (Canton) to British embassy (Shanghai), 20 February 1940, FO 371/24747, PRO.

18. Gauss to DS, 15 March 1940, RG 59, 893.00 P.R. Shanghai/137, Richard P. Butrick (Shanghai) to DS, 4 April 1940, RG 59, 893.114 Narcotics/2756, and Nicholson to Customs, 30 July 1940, RG 59, 893.114 Narcotics/2813, NA.

19. J. W. O. Davidson (Hankow) to Clark Kerr, 12 February 1940, and A. J. Martin (Tsingtao) to Clark Kerr, 20 January 1940, FO 371/24747, PRO; Carl O. Hawthorne (Tsinan) to DS, 4 February 1941, RG 59, 893.114 Narcotics/2918, NA.

20. Caldwell to Johnson, 7 March 1940, RG 59, 893.00 P.R. Tientsin/142, and Samuel J. Fletcher (Tientsin) to Johnson, 11 July 1940, RG 59, 893.114 Narcotics/2802 (for indications of poppy cultivation in Inner Mongolia), NA; A. A. L. Tuson (Peking) to Clark Kerr, 9 October 1940, FO 371/28075, PRO; Smyth (Peiping) to DS, 30 October 1940, RG 59, 893.114 Narcotics/2841, NA.

21. Merrell to DS, 7 November 1939, RG 59, 893.00 P.R. Harbin/132, and Langdon to DS, 29 December 1939 (RG 59, 893.114N16 Manchuria/367) and 12 February 1940 (RG 59, 893.114N16 Manchuria/363—quotations), NA.

22. Statement by Garvan, received 1 September 1941, CBMS, E/T.51, box 397, SOAS/UL; Heininger Oral History, CMOHP.

23. IMTFE, *Proceedings*, 2657–69, FO 648, IWM.

24. Ibid., 4760–79. The prosecution also entered DS monthly reports into the official record. Ibid., 4784–4804. See also Brackman, *The Other Nuremberg*, 195.

25. IMTFE, *Proceedings*, 4805, 4954–96 (quotation, 4973), FO 648, IWM.

26. Feis, *The Road to Pearl Harbor*, 122. The chapter from which the quotation is taken is aptly entitled, "We Draw Closer to Britain." In Tokyo, Grew saw Japanese actions as an integral part of the larger world problem that was forcing the United States and Great Britain closer together. Grew, *Ten Years in Japan*, 330–39.

27. On the stalemate in China, see Usui, "The Politics of War," 406–22; Boyle, *China and Japan at War*, 289–305. See also Schroeder, *The Axis Alliance and Japanese-American Relations*, 24–25; Jervis, *Perception and Misperception in International Politics*, 168.

28. Reynolds, *The Creation of the Anglo-American Alliance*, 133–41. More than a peripheral consideration in the minds of policymakers in London and Washington was the effort Japan was making to extend its influence into Indochina and the Netherlands East Indies. Colonel Charles Hines, U.S. Army, secretary, Army and Navy Munitions Board, to RFC, 7 October 1940, RG 234, Minutes, RFC, 1:31, and Milo Perkins, executive director, Board of Economic Warfare, to William L. Clayton, deputy federal home loan administrator, 10 January 1942, RG 234, Minutes, RFC, 2:77–78, NA.

29. Jacobson to Customs, 8 May 1941, RG 59, 893.114 Narcotics/3030, Philip M. Davenport to DS, 3 May 1941, RG 59, 893.114 Narcotics/3034, Myers to DS, 28 July 1941, RG 59, 893.114 Narcotics/3070, and Jacobson to Customs, 28 July 1941, RG 59, 893.114 Narcotics/3074, NA. Tu may have provided the requested opium. Jacobson to Customs, 18 August 1941, RG 59, 893.114 Narcotics/3074, NA.

30. Merrill, *Japan and the Opium Menace*, annex II; Morlock, cover note, 13 November 1941, in Carl H. Boehringer (Tokyo) to DS, 3 September 1941, RG 59, 893.114 Narcotics/3103, NA.

31. Grew to DS, 5 September 1941, RG 59, 893.114 Narcotics/3081, and Boehringer to DS, 19 September 1941, RG 59, 893.114 Narcotics/3102, NA.

32. A. A. E. Franklin (Chungking) to Clark Kerr, 2 April 1941, FO 371/28075, and H. I. Prideaux-Brune (Kunming) to Clark Kerr, 27 February 1940, FO 371/24747 (quotation), PRO.

33. Prideaux-Brune to Clark Kerr, 30 December 1940, FO 371/28075, PRO. In some districts of Yunnan, cotton farming replaced opium cultivation. U.S. consulate (Kunming) to DS, 1 March 1940, RG 59, 893.114 Narcotics/2763, NA.

34. Thaxton, *China Turned Rightside Up*, 116.

35. Merrill, *Japan and the Opium Menace*, annex I.

36. Johnson to DS, 8 April 1941, RG 59, 893.114 Narcotics/2949, and Morlock to Chungking, 6 May 1941, RG 59, 893.114 Narcotics/2983, NA.

37. Troy L. Perkins (Kunming) to DS, 28 May 1941, RG 59, 893.114 Narcotics/3000, and Perkins to DS, 27 September 1941, RG 59, 893.114 Narcotics/3106, NA.

38. Gauss to DS, 24 October 1941, RG 59, 893.114 Narcotics/3123, NA.

39. O. Edmund Clubb, *Twentieth-Century China*, 237–38; Van Slyke, "The Chinese Communist Movement during the Sino-Japanese War," 658–71. The New Fourth Army Incident amounted to a Communist-Kuomintang battle for public favor in central China. The Communist New Fourth Army lost many men but, with some justification, could charge that Chiang's forces were trying to undermine the united front against Japan.

40. *FRUS, 1940*, 473.

41. *FRUS, 1941*, 477–78, 491–92.

42. Ibid., 534–35 (first quotation); Woodward, *British Foreign Policy in the Second World War*, 2:114–17. In general, see Clifford, *Retreat from China*, 155–58; Haggie, *Britannia at Bay*, 197–211.

43. [Mao Zedong], *Selected Works of Mao Tse-tung*, 2:391.

44. Ibid. (18 March 1941), 2:459 (quotation); Rosenberg and Young, *Transforming Russia and China*, 167–78.

45. Reynolds, *The Creation of the Anglo-American Alliance*, 280–85; DT press release, 26 January 1942, RG 56, FBN, 1941–50 file.

46. Anslinger's remarks to the eighth session of the CND, April 1953, in Anslinger Papers, box 1, PL/PSU.

47. OIC, *Use of Opium and Traffic Therein*, passim.

48. FO, *The Opium Trade*, 6:XXV, 1928, nos. 22–23 and especially 24; 6:XXVI, 1929, no. 6.

49. DS to Anslinger, 12 January 1933, RG 59, 893.114 Narcotics/54, Quincy F. Roberts (Saigon) to DS, 24 March 1933, RG 59, 893.114 Narcotics/57, and Fuller to American legation (Peking), 14 August 1934, RG 59, 893.114 Narcotics/812, NA.

50. Roberts to DS, 20 March 1935, RG 59, 851G.114 Narcotics/70, Arthur J. Campbell (Hong Kong) to Nicholson, 3 April 1936, RG 59, 851G.114 Narcotics/75, Fuller's report on the twenty-first session of the OAC, 22 September 1936, RG 59, 500.C1197/997, Political report from the consulate in Saigon, 9 January 1937, RG 59, 851G.114 Narcotics/78, and Roberts to DS, 18 January 1938, RG 59, 851G.114 Narcotics/95, NA. Regarding opium as a highly valuable cash crop for the Meo, see Halpern and Kunstadter, "Laos: Introduction," 238, 248; Barney, "The Meo of Xieng Khouang Province, Laos," 283–84; Westermeyer, *Poppies, Pipes, and People*, 25–28.

51. Peter H. A. Flood (Saigon) to DS, 2 April 1940, RG 59, 851G.114 Narcotics/111, and Political report from the consulate in Saigon, 10 February 1941, RG 59, 851G.114 Narcotics/119, NA.

52. FO, *The Opium Trade*, 6:XXVI, 1929, no. 6; *The Reminiscences of Herbert L. May*, 69, OHRO.

53. DS to Fuller, 16 June 1938, RG 59, 500.C1197/1207, NA, Fuller's report on the twenty-third session of the OAC, 30 August 1938, RG 59, 500.C1197/1244 (Fuller's quotation), Herbert C. Pell (Lisbon) to DS, 14 June 1938, RG 59, 500.C1197/1218, and DS to Fuller, 24 June 1938, RG 59, 500.C1197/1213A (Anslinger's quotation), NA. Nicholson feared, of course, that the Japanese might extend their opium regime into South China with the help of corrupt officials at Macao.

54. Jacobson to Customs, 29 December 1938 (RG 59, 893.114 Narcotics/2428) and 4 January 1939 (RG 59, 893.114 Narcotics/2431), and Pell to DS, 31 March 1939, RG 59, 500.C1197/1309, NA.

55. Jacobson to Customs, 10 December 1938, RG 59, 893.114 Narcotics/2425, and Memorandum by Morlock, 7 March 1939, RG 59, 500.C1197/1302, NA. See also Miners, *Hong Kong under Imperial Rule*.

56. DS aide-mémoire, 30 January 1939, RG 59, 846G.114 Narcotics/271, NA, and FO 371/23576, PRO; Addison E. Southard (Hong Kong) to DS, 3 August 1938, RG 59, 846G.114 Narcotics/253, NA; Anslinger to Coles, 6 January 1939, FO 371/23576, PRO.

57. Minutes by Henniker-Major, 2–3 March 1939, FO 371/23576, PRO.

58. Minute by Henniker-Major, 2 March 1939, ibid.

59. H. Ashley Clarke (FO) to Sir Ronald Lindsay (Washington), 28 August 1939, FO 371/23577, PRO; V. A. L. Mallet to Hornbeck, 12 September 1939, RG 59, 846G.114 Narcotics/294, NA.

60. OIC, *Use of Opium and Traffic Therein*, 113–23; FO, *The Opium Trade*, 6:XXIX, 1932, no. 1; J. Crosby (Bangkok) to Simon, 22 January 1935, FO 371/19370, PRO.

61. Buker Interviews, BGCA/WC; Memorandum by W. T. Annam (Burma Office), 4 April 1945, FO 371/50654, PRO.

62. Lowe, *Great Britain and the Origins of the Pacific War*, 138–53; Hata, "The Army's Move into Northern Indochina," 155–68.

63. Nagaoka, "The Drive into Southern Indochina and Thailand," 218–40; *FRUS: Japan, 1931–1941*, 2:315–17; *C & R*, 1:225; Lowe, *Great Britain and the Origins of the Pacific War*, 208, 223, 236–39; Barnhart, *Japan Prepares for Total War*, 207–14; Thorne, *Allies of a Kind*, 71; Schroeder, *The Axis Alliance and Japanese-American Relations*, 80–81.

64. FO minute, 22 May 1941, J. M. Troutbeck to Clarke, 31 May 1941, and Troutbeck to S. I. James (CO), 8 November 1941 (quotation), all in FO 371/28074, PRO; Decoux, *A La Barre de L'Indochine*, 148–56, 235–36; Jones, Borton, and Pearn, *The Far East*, 26–27.

65. "Strategic Survey of Indo-China," 14 March 1942, RG 59, OSS, R & A, no. 719, 4, 9 (first two quotations), and OSS, Special Intelligence Operations, RG 226, OSS Files, entry 106, June 1944, box 48 (final quotation), NA.

66. *Washington Star*, 19 January 1942; L'Association culturelle pour le Salut du Viêt-Nam, *Témoignages et Documents*, II-5, II-6; McCoy, *The Politics of Heroin in Southeast Asia*, 76–78.

67. Anslinger to John D. Goodloe, 8 January 1942, and Fred J. Stock, Health Supplies Sec., OPM, to Howard C. Sykes, chief, Stockpile and Shipping Imports Branch, OPM, 19 December 1941, RG 234: RFC, DSC: "Commodity Procurement Files: Opium, Part I," NA; Clayton to Perkins, 15 January 1942, RG 169: FEA, Records of the Office of the Administrator, box 753, WNRC; Goodloe to Clayton, 14 January 1942, RG 234: RFC, DSC, Minutes, 2:81, and Morris S. Rosenthal, Bureau of Economic Warfare, to Secretary of Commerce Jesse Jones, 5 May 1943, RG 234: RFC, DSC: "Drugs and Chemicals: Opium folder," box 5, NA; Directive no. 10, 6 October 1942, RG 179: WPB, Policy Documentation File, 533.7 O, NA.

68. Davies, *Dragon by the Tail*, 234; *New York Times*, 5 September 1942; Vincent (Chungking) to DS, 18 March 1943, RG 59, 893.114 Narcotics/3144, NA.

69. "The Guerrilla Front in North China," 21 May 1943, RG 59, OSS, R & A, no. 892, 9, NA; Report on East Hopei and western Shantung, 9 February 1944, RG 319, AIPDF, 1941–45, box 330, WNRC.

70. "Programs of Japan in China," Part III: "Northern Coast," 21 April 1945, RG 59, OSS, R & A no. 3049, 220, NA. On Wang Ching-wei's regime and antiopium activities, see IMTFE, *Proceedings*, 39, 324–25, FO 648, IWM.

71. IMTFE, *Proceedings*, 12087–89, 35525, 35755–67, 36446, and *Judgment*, Annexes, app. A, sec. 4, "Methods of Corruption and Coercion in China and Other Occupied Territories," 66–67, FO 648, IWM; Boyle, *China and Japan at War*, 307.

72. John W. Russell (British embassy) to DS, 28 March 1945, RG 59, 893.114 Narcotics/3–2845, NA; Hammer, *The Struggle for Indochina*, 14–23, 26–29; Lebra, *Japanese-trained Armies in Southeast Asia*, 134–40; OSS: Special Intelligence Operations, RG 226, OSS Files, entry 106, June 1944, box 48, NA; Patti, *Why Viet Nam?* 128–29; OSS: Special Intelligence Operations, RG 226, OSS Files, entry 106, 20 December 1943, box 48, and Gauss to DS, 22 December 1943, RG 59, 851G.114 Narcotics/125, NA.

73. *C & R*, 1:369; Shai, *Britain and China*, 11–15; Willmott, *Empires in the Balance*, 409, 431–35; Spector, *Eagle against the Sun*, 336, 340; Eden, *The Reckoning*, 367–68.

74. "Social Conditions, Attitudes, and Propaganda in Burma with Suggestions for American Orientation toward the Burmese," 6 April 1942, RG 59, OSS, R & A, no. 272, NAMP, M1221, Intelligence Reports, 1941–61, NA.

75. Romanus and Sunderland, *Stilwell's Mission to China*, 110–11; Thorne, *Allies of a Kind*, 60, 206; Lebra, *Japanese-trained Armies in Southeast Asia*, passim; Thorne, *The Issue of War*, 114–16, 150–51.

76. "Japanese Administration of Burma," 10 July 1944, RG 59, OSS, R & A, no. 2015, NA.

77. *Washington Post*, 26 June 1944; "Request for Information on Opium," 2 August 1944, RG 59, OSS, R & A, no. 2441, NAMP, M1221, Intelligence Reports, 1941–61, NA. For an intimate look at OSS Detachment 101's involvement with opium, the Kachins, and the Japanese, see Dunlop, *Behind Japanese Lines*, 26, 33–34, 142, 191, 325–26.

78. *C & R*, 1:365, 277–78 (quotations). Generally, see Shai, *Britain and China*, 11–20; Feis, *The China Tangle*, 3–13, 37–44; Thorne, *Allies of a Kind*, 170–97. Thorne sees a convergence of American and British sympathy for China; with the defeat of Japan, Anglo-American differences over China were sure to reappear.

79. Sainsbury, *The Turning Point*, 165–216; Schaller, *The U.S. Crusade in China*, 149–53; Thorne, *Allies of a Kind*, 307–12; Louis, *Imperialism at Bay*, 279–83; Eden, *The Reckoning*, 493.

80. Eastman, *Seeds of Destruction*, 5, 10–31.

81. Schaller, *The U.S. Crusade in China*, 232–40; Miles Papers, chap. 27, folder 5, box 32, CNH.

82. Perkins to DS, 21 July 1942, RG 59, 893.114 Narcotics/3156, and Atcheson (Chungking) to DS, 9 July 1943, RG 59, 893.114 Narcotics/3168, NA.

83. Horace H. Smith to Atcheson, 27 August 1943, RG 59, 893.114 Narcotics/3169, and Gauss to DS, 25 October 1943, RG 59, 893.114 Narcotics/3170, NA; Eastman, *Seeds of Destruction*, 43.

84. William F. McGovern, "Smuggling between Free and Occupied China," 30 November 1943, and Report by Lieutenant Colonel Edward G. Barlow, 17 January 1944,

RG 319, AIPDF, 1941–45, box 323, WNRC. See also Colonel M. B. DePass, Jr., "Report on Central Government Authority in Yunnan Province," 7 April 1943, ibid.; White, *The Stilwell Papers*, 238; Romanus and Sunderland, *Stilwell's Command Problems*, 56–57.

85. Colonel Charles G. Mettler, "Report on Political and Military Situation in Sikang and Ninghsia Provinces," 2 November 1943, Mettler, "Report on Yunnan," 10 March 1944, and First Lieutenant Alida C. Mayer, "Report on Northwestern Szechwan Province and Eastern Sikang," 13 April 1944, RG 319, AIPDF, 1941–45, box 33, WNRC.

86. George A. Wallinger to Eden, 31 January 1945, FO 371/50647, PRO.

87. Atcheson to DS, 4 September 1943, RG 59, 893.00/15134, NA; Kahn, *The China Hands*, 1.

88. Stein, *The Challenge of Red China*, 31–35, 46–48, 75–76, 182–83; Forman, *Report from Red China*, 9–10, 192; Shewmaker, *America and the Chinese Communists*, 158–71.

89. Report by Edward E. Rice, 23 February 1944, RG 59, 893.114 Narcotics/3174, NA; Romanus and Sunderland, *Stilwell's Command Problems*, 316–40, 371–76; Spector, *Eagle against the Sun*, 365–81; Eastman, *Seeds of Destruction*, 28–29, 137–44; Reardon-Anderson, *Yenan and the Great Powers*, 21–32.

90. Eastman, *Seeds of Destruction*, 29; Mettler, "Report from Yunnan," 10 March 1944, RG 319, AIPDF, 1941–45, box 330, WNRC; Ady Oral History, CMOHP; Report by Ludden, 2 February 1945, RG 226, OSS Files, entry 99, box 68, NA.

91. Wallinger to Eden, 31 January 1945, FO 371/50647, PRO; Russell to DS, 28 March 1945, RG 59, 893.114 Narcotics/3–2845, and U.S. embassy (Chungking) to DS, 26 March 1945, RG 59, 893.114 Narcotics/3–2645, NA.

92. Thorne, *The Issue of War*, 47–48. On the policy dilemmas brought about by China's inability to meet Western expectations, reduced though they were in the final year of the war, see Schaller, *The U.S. Crusade in China*, 192–229, 251–70; Feis, *The China Tangle*, 208–367. Tsou, *America's Failure in China*, 176–236, is particularly good on the incongruity of American images of China late in the war. To be sure, formulating an appropriate China policy was also a function of domestic politics in the United States. Chern, "The Politics of American China Policy," 631–47. Despite American predominance, Great Britain exhibited considerable interest in China's political battle. Woodward, *British Foreign Policy in the Second World War*, 4:526–30, 534–40.

93. *C & R*, 1:557. On Roosevelt's anticolonialism, see Hess, "Franklin Roosevelt and Indochina"; LaFeber, "Roosevelt, Churchill, and Indochina"; Thorne, "Indochina and Anglo-American Relations"; Louis, *Imperialism at Bay*; Sbrega, "The Anticolonial Policies of Franklin D. Roosevelt."

94. Kinder and Walker, "Stable Force in a Storm," 908–11, 920; Kinder, "Bureaucratic Cold Warrior," 172–77; Moorehead, "International Narcotics Control"; May, "The Tasks of the Permanent Central Opium Board," 337; Bruun, Pan, and Rexed, *The Gentlemen's Club*, 14–15.

95. Memorandum by Herbert L. May of a meeting in Anslinger's office, 4 December

1942, dated 19 January 1943, RG 59, 893.114 Narcotics/3163, NA; Minutes, FPA board of directors, 28 October, 16 December 1942.

96. Memorandum of a meeting held in Anslinger's office, 13 January 1943, RG 59, 893.114 Narcotics/3163, NA.

97. British embassy (Washington) to FO, 10 February 1943, and FO to British embassy, 18 February 1943, FO 371/34545, PRO.

98. Delevingne to S. W. Harris (HO), 28 February 1943, and FO to British embassy, 4 March 1943, ibid.

99. Minutes of a meeting held in Anslinger's office, 17 March 1943, RG 59, 890.114 Narcotics/5, NA; Woodward, *British Foreign Policy in the Second World War*, 4:510–15; Bruun, Pan, and Rexed, *The Gentlemen's Club*, 127.

100. Minutes of a meeting held in Anslinger's office, 17 March 1943, RG 59, 890.114 Narcotics/5, NA; Halifax to Eden, 26 April 1943, FO 371/34545, PRO.

101. Halifax to Eden, 26 April 1943, and Roberts to the under secretary of state, CO, 15 June 1943, FO 371/34545, PRO.

102. Memorandum by Morlock, "Suppression of Opium Smoking in the Recaptured Areas of the Southwest Pacific," 26 March 1943, Hull to Frank Knox, Henry Stimson, and Henry Morgenthau, Jr., 26 June 1943, Stimson to Hull, 7 July 1943, and Knox to Hull, 8 July 1943, RG 59, 890.114 Narcotics/6–11, NA.

103. Morgenthau to Hull, 23 July 1943, RG 59, 890.114 Narcotics/12, Atcheson to DS, 10 August 1943, RG 59, 890.114 Narcotics/13, and Chinese embassy (Washington) to DS, 4 May 1944, RG 59, 890.114 Narcotics/59, NA. On the likely negative reception of Chinese troops as an occupying force, see Patti, *Why Viet Nam?* 281–82, 284–93; Hess, *The United States' Emergence as a Southeast Asian Power*, 85–89; Thorne, *Allies of a Kind*, 190, 309–10.

104. Aide-mémoire, 21 September 1943, RG 59, 890.114 Narcotics/19, and Anslinger to Morlock, 12 August 1943, RG 59, 890.114 Narcotics/16, NA; J. J. Paskin (CO) to under secretary of state (CO), 11 August 1943, and Memorandum by A. L. Scott (FO), 7 September 1943, FO 371/34545, PRO; Annam to W. J. Thorogood (CO), 19 October 1943, FO 371/34546, PRO.

105. Government of the Netherlands to DS, 4 November 1943, RG 59, 890.114 Narcotics/35, and British embassy to DS, 6 November 1943, RG 59, 890.114 Narcotics/44, NA; FO to British embassy (Washington), 31 October 1943, and Paskin to M. S. Williams, 21 October 1943, FO 371/34546, PRO.

106. Esterline and Esterline, *"How the Dominoes Fell,"* 217–20; Steinberg, *In Search of Southeast Asia*, 394–96; Kunstadter, "Burma: Introduction," 76–77; La Raw, "Toward a Basis for Understanding the Minorities in Burma," 129–31, 135–45.

107. Hornbeck to Secretary of State Edward Stettinius, 30 November 1943, Hornbeck Papers, box 93, HIWRP; Annam to Williams, 29 October 1943, and Minute by Williams, 26 November 1943, FO 371/34546, PRO.

108. Roger Makins, Office of the British Representative with the French Committee of National Liberation (Algiers), to Rene Massgli, commissioner for foreign affairs, 10

November 1943, and Massgli to Harold Macmillan, 3 January 1944, FO 371/39366, PRO.

109. Wright to Green H. Hackworth, 4 September 1944, in Koo Papers, box 54, BL/CU.

110. Memorandum on the limitation of the cultivation of the opium poppy by international agreement, 25 September 1944, ibid.

111. On the decision-making fallacies of centrality and commonality, see Jervis, *Perception and Misperception in International Politics*, 212, 216.

112. White, *The Stilwell Papers*, 327; Esherick, *Lost Chance in China*, 161–62 (Service's quotation); Davies, *Dragon by the Tail*, 373 (Wedemeyer's quotation); *C & R*, 3:423.

113. White and Jacoby, *Thunder out of China*, 242.

Chapter Eight

1. Quoted in Thorne, *The Issue of War*, 184.

2. Halifax, *Fulness of Days*, 273–74.

3. Ziegler, *Mountbatten*, 241–42, 247; Woodward, *British Foreign Policy in the Second World War*, 4:515–17 (quotation). On images and expectations, see Jervis, *Perception and Misperception in International Politics*, 181–82, 191. On the continuity of Anglo-American tension, see Anderson, *The United States, Great Britain, and the Cold War*, 1–32; Ovendale, *The English-speaking Alliance*, 3–21.

4. Bohlen, *Witness to History*, 140–41; Louis, *Imperialism at Bay*, 283–86, 448–65; *C & R*, 1:373–74, 3:419–21, 424–25; Woodward, *British Foreign Policy in the Second World War*, 4:531–33.

5. Eden, *The Reckoning*, 593; Hammer, *The Struggle for Indochina*, 129–30. Scott and Butler are quoted in Reynolds, *The Creation of the Anglo-American Alliance*, 266.

6. Shai, *Britain and China*, 69; Woodward, *British Foreign Policy in the Second World War*, 4:525–26; Thorne, *Allies of a Kind*, 546–63; *FRUS, 1944*, 697, 726.

7. Schaller, *The U.S. Crusade in China*, 285–93; J. Blum, *The Price of Vision*, 519–22; *Washington Dispatches* (Great Britain), 447.

8. Thorne, *The Issue of War*, 190, 195–96 (quotation, 196), and "Indochina and Anglo-American Relations," 90–96; Herring, "The Truman Administration and the Restoration of French Sovereignty in Indochina."

9. Peers and Brelis, *Behind the Burma Road*, 64; Dunlop, *Behind Japanese Lines*, 259–62, 265–79, and passim; B. Smith, *The Shadow Warriors*, 261.

10. Schoenbaum, *Waging Peace and War*, 91–92. I am indebted to John Garofano for bringing this detail to my attention.

11. Report by Theater Officer (Stilwell) on the Far East, RG 226, entry 99, 31 August 1943, box 52, and William J. Donovan, Special Report for March 1944, RG 226, entry 99, May 1944, box 56, NA; Peers and Brelis, *Behind the Burma Road*, 114–15.

12. Memorandum by Annam, 4 April 1945, and Annam to Major C. M. Logan (WO), 18 April 1945, FO 371/50654, PRO; Stimson to Morgenthau, 9 March 1945, RG 59, 845C.114 Narcotics/2–2145, NA.

13. Lieutenant Colonel L. Mainwaring Taylor (WO) to G. W. Harrison (FO), 14 August 1944, and Mountbatten to L. S. Amery (Burma Office), 12 October 1944, FO 371/40510, PRO.

14. *Congressional Record*, 1944, pp. 5325, 6472–73, 6710, 6713; Moorehead, "International Narcotics Control"; Taylor to Harrison, 10 May 1944, FO 371/39366 (quotation), and Mountbatten to Amery, 21 August 1944, FO 371/40510, PRO; Anslinger to Morlock, 22 August 1946, and Clayton to Trygve Lie, 28 August 1946, RG 59, 501.BD Narcotics/8–2246, NA.

15. FO memorandum on the opium traffic, 2 August 1945, FO 371/50647, PRO; Anslinger to Hoo, 16 May 1945, with a copy of the British note to DS (dated 24 April 1945) and enclosing a proposed U.S. response, undated, Hoo Papers, box 2, HIWRP. See also British embassy to DS, 24 April 1945, RG 59, 845C.114 Narcotics/4–2445, NA; DS to FO regarding opium policy in Burma, 8 August 1945, FO 371/50654, PRO.

16. Morlock to DS, 4 July 1945, RG 59, 845C.114 Narcotics/4–2445, NA; Reports on "The Strategic Value of the Shan States" and "Chinese in Burma during the War," both dated 27 December 1944, RG 226, OSS Files, box 770, NA.

17. Iriye, *Power and Culture*, 187–88; Feis, *Contest over Japan*, 6–9; Truman, *Year of Decisions*, 432; Schaller, *The American Occupation of Japan*, 6–19.

18. Anslinger quoted in Albert Q. Maisel, "Getting the Drop on Dope," *Liberty Magazine*, 24 November 1945, in Hoo Papers, box 2, HIWRP.

19. Bureau Accomplishments and Current Problems (December 1952), Narcotics Section, Snyder Papers, box 86, HSTL.

20. Moorehead to Stettinius, 7 April 1945, RG 59, 500.CC/4–745, NA; Hoo to Anslinger, 1 October 1945, and Anslinger to Hoo, 26 January 1945, 23 April 1946, Hoo Papers, box 2, HIWRP; Memorandum by Morlock, 7 March 1946, RG 59, 501.BD Narcotics/3–746, NA. Despite Elizabeth Wright's misgivings, the opium work of the State Department was transferred in 1945 from the Division of Far Eastern Affairs to the Division of International Labor, Social, and Health Affairs. Key personnel also made the switch.

21. Fred M. Vinson to James F. Byrnes, 19 March 1946, RG 59, 501.BD Narcotics/3–1946, President Harry S. Truman to Anslinger, 17 May 1946, RG 59, 501.BD Narcotics/5–1546, and Memorandum by Morlock, 12 April 1946, RG 59, 501.BD Narcotics/4–1246, NA; Memorandum by Sharman, 11 March 1947, FO 371/67642, PRO. See also the overview contained in "Control of Narcotic Drugs: U.N. to Assume Existing Functions."

22. Memorandum on narcotics control activities in Japan by General Headquarters, SCAP, 10 May 1946, RG 331, SCAP AG, box 462, WNRC; DS to Anslinger, 22 November 1946, RG 59, 501.BD Narcotics/11–2246, and Anslinger's report on the first session of the CND, 1 April 1947, RG 59, 501.BD Narcotics/4–147, NA. See also Coles

to J. T. Fearnley (FO), 15 January 1948, FO 371/72907, PRO. For a similar sentiment by the CND, see "Old and New Narcotic Perils," 364.

23. Herbert E. Gaston to Morlock with a memorandum by Anslinger, 16 October 1945, RG 59, 894.114 Narcotics/10–1645, NA.

24. DS to U.S. consulate (Geneva), 16 October 1945, ibid.; Brigadier General B. M. Fitch to the Imperial Japanese Government, 19 May 1946, Central Liaison Office to SCAP, 24 May 1946, Lieutenant Colonel William A. Glass, Jr., Civil Administration, to SCAP, 11 March 1946 (with the report), and Memorandum by Speer, 9 April 1946, all in RG 331, SCAP AG, box 462, WNRC.

25. Glass to SCAP, 11 March 1946, RG 331, SCAP AG, box 462, WNRC.

26. IMTFE, *Indictment*, app. A: Summarized Particulars, sec. 4: "Methods of Corruption and Coercion in China and Other Occupied Territories," and app. B: Articles of Treaties Violated by Japan, FO 648, IWM. See also Brackman, *The Other Nuremberg*, 190–95.

27. IMTFE, *Judgment*, pt. B, chap. 4: "Japanese Aggression against China," 644–47, 771–75, FO 648, IWM.

28. IMTFE, *Proceedings*, 39178–89, 39309 (quotation), FO 648, IWM.

29. Generally, see Schaller, "Securing the Great Crescent."

30. Minear, *Victors' Justice*, 125–34 and passim; Pal, *International Military Tribunal for the Far East*, 557–58 (quotation).

31. Anslinger to Morlock, 12 October 1945, RG 59, 894.114 Narcotics/10–1245, NA; Speer memorandums, 6 June 1937 (box 523), 3 January 1946 (box 462), and Colonel H. W. Allen to AG (War Department), 25 January 1946 (box 462), RG 331, SCAP AG, WNRC; RG 319, CMH Monograph Series, box 535, 8–5 AA7 V5 C1: *Public Health*, VIII: *Political and Social*, chap. 17, "Narcotics," NA.

32. Anslinger to Speer, 21 May 1947, and Speer memorandum, 6 June 1947, RG 331, SCAP AG, box 523, WNRC. By this time, Speer was heading the Narcotics Control Branch of SCAP's Public Health and Welfare Sec.

33. SCAP memorandum, 10 June 1947 (box 523), and General Headquarters, SCAP, to Anslinger with *Annual Report of Japan on the Traffic in Opium and Other Dangerous Drugs*, 25 March 1950 (box 659), ibid.; RG 319, CMH Monograph Series, box 535, 8–5 AA7 V5 C1: *Public Health*, NA. For antismuggling endeavors carried out by the FBN at the end of the war, see *Atlanta Constitution*, 19 August 1945.

34. For an indication of the cordial relations among Chinese and American narcotics experts, see Moorehead to Hoo, 1 April 1946, Hoo Papers, box 2, HIWRP.

35. Buhite, *Hurley and American Foreign Policy*, 253–81; Peck, "America and the Chinese Revolution," 328–30, 334–44; Pepper, *Civil War in China*, 7–41; Melby, *The Mandate of Heaven*, 14–48.

36. Ringwalt Oral History, HSTL. See also Kahn, *The China Hands*, 145–46.

37. Report by Lieutenant Colonel Gerald Church, 9 March 1945, no. 131858, and report on Yunnan opium by Church, 12 March 1945, no. 131863, RG 319, Army Staff, ACSI, WNRC.

38. Langdon to Patrick J. Hurley, 20 February, 18 July 1945, and Memorandum by Philip D. Sprouse of a conversation with Lung Yun, 22 September 1945, RG 84, FSP, Kunming, S-SGR, 1944–49, box 3, 1945, WNRC.

39. "China: Lu Han's Replacement of Lung Yun as Governor of Yunnan," 10 November 1945, RG 59, R & A, no. 3275, NAMP, M1221, Intelligence Reports, 1941–61, and Stanley A. McGeary (Kunming) to DS, 16 September 1946, RG 59, 893.114 Narcotics/9–1646, NA; Service Oral History, 1:109, HSTL. Even after the departure of Lung Yun, rumors abounded that caves around Yunnan still held his opium.

40. Heininger Oral History, CMOHP, 33; Harry E. Stevens to DS, 28 January 1946, RG 59, 893.114 Narcotics/1–2846, NA.

41. Langdon to DS, 1 May 1945, RG 84, FSP, Kunming, S-SGR, 1944–49, box 4, 1946, and Report by L. H. Barton, drug analyst, Shanghai Municipal Council, 21 November 1945, no. 219336, RG 319, Army Staff, ACSI, both in WNRC; Miles, *A Different Kind of War*, 508–9, 531–33.

42. Memorandum by Speer, 16 April 1948, RG 331, SCAP AG, box 574, WNRC; Anslinger to Vincent, 18 June 1946, RG 59, 102.19602/5–1546, NA.

43. Pogue, *Marshall*, 107–34; Gallicchio, *The Cold War Begins in Asia*, 130–35; Ferrell, *Off the Record*, 78–80; Reardon-Anderson, *Yenan and the Great Powers*, 151–55, 157–59.

44. Frank M. Tamanga, Central Bank of China, to Soong, chairman, Executive Yuan (Nanking), 10 October 1946, Soong Papers, box 25, HIWRP.

45. Acheson, *Present at the Creation*, 144–45 (for praise of Butterworth); Butterworth to DS, 20 September 1946, RG 59, 893.114 Narcotics/9–2046, NA.

46. John Leighton Stuart to DS, 14 July 1947, RG 84, FSP, Shanghai, General, box 16, 1947, WNRC.

47. Morlock's memorandum of a conversation with Dr. Szeming Sze, 29 August 1946, RG 59, CA, box 4, NA; Stuart to DS, 11 July 1947, RG 84, FSP, Shanghai, General, box 16, 1947, WNRC.

48. Chinese Ministry of Foreign Affairs to U.S. embassy, 28 July, 30 August 1947, RG 59, 893.114 Narcotics/9–1247, NA; Stuart, *Fifty Years in China*, 120; Stuart to DS, 14 July 1947, RG 84, FSP, Shanghai, General, box 16, 1947, WNRC. Supporting Stuart's assessment were reports about Manchuria. See Angus Ward (Mukden) to DS, 18 July 1947, RG 59, 893.114 Narcotics/7–1847, NA.

49. Monthly Report (February 1947), Narcotics Sec., dated 5 March 1947, RG 331, SCAP AG, box 523, Report by Major Robert B. Eckvall, assistant military attaché (Kunming), 8 July 1947, no. 381552, RG 319, Army Staff, ACSI, and Harold C. Roser, Jr., to Nanking, 21 July 1947, RG 84, FSP, Kunming, S-SGR, box 5, 1947, all in WNRC.

50. U.S. Naval Intelligence report on Macao, 23 May 1947, RG 84, FSP, Hong Kong, S-SGR, box 3, 1947, Report on racketeers in Hong Kong, 13 August 1946, RG 84, FSP, China, Hong Kong consulate, S-SGR, 1946–49, box 2, 1946, and Report for May 1947 by George D. Hopper, U.S. consul general (Hong Kong), 10 June 1947, RG 84, FSP,

Hong Kong, S-SGR, box 3, 1947, all in WNRC. Authorities in Macao had abolished opium smoking in July 1946.

51. Report by Hopper, 7 July 1947 (box 4, 1947), Hopper's political report for October 1947, 5 November 1947 (box 3, 1947), Anslinger to Hopper, 26 March 1946 (General Records, 1936–49, box 115, 1946), Report by Hopper on Macao, 4 November 1946 (General Records, 1936–49, box 115, 1946), and Hopper to DS, 21 April 1948 (box 8, 1948) (quotation), RG 84, FSP, Hong Kong, S-SGR, WNRC.

52. Memorandum by Speer, 21 May 1947, RG 331, SCAP AG, box 523, WNRC; DS to Nanking, 22 September 1947, RG 59, 893.114 Narcotics/7–947, NA.

53. Anslinger's report on the second session of the CND, dated 12 September 1947, RG 59, 501.BD Narcotics/9–1247, NA.

54. Pepper, "The KMT-CCP Conflict," 758–70, and *Civil War in China*, 346.

55. Stueck, *The Road to Confrontation*, 46–52; Gaddis, *The Long Peace*, 75–78; Cohen, "The United States and China since 1945," 134; Buhite, "'Major Interests,'" 425–32.

56. Gaddis, *The Long Peace*, 75. The subsequent analysis is based on Jervis, *Perception and Misperception in International Politics*, 24–31, 120–216. See also Janis and Mann, *Decision Making*, 45–75.

57. Thomas F. Power, Jr., for Hsia Ching-lin, to Anslinger, 1 May 1948, RG 84, U.S. Mission to the UN, 1945–49, box 85, NA. See also n. 48 supra.

58. Fulton Freeman to DS, 19 July 1947, RG 59, 893.114 Narcotics/7–1947, NA; Hopper to DS, 21 April 1948 (box 8, 1948), and Davis (Shanghai) to Stuart, 2 September 1947 (box 3, 1947), RG 84, FSP, Hong Kong, S-SGR, WNRC; Hopper to Davis, 9 September 1947, RG 84, FSP, Shanghai, General Records, box 16, 1947, and George M. Abbott (Saigon) to James E. McKenna (Hong Kong), 5 June 1948, RG 84, FSP, Hong Kong, S-SGR, box 6, 1948, WNRC. H. Merrell Benninghoff, consul general at Dairen, categorically denied allegations of Soviet involvement in the drug trade. Benninghoff to Stuart, 30 August 1947, RG 59, 893.114 Narcotics/8–3047, NA. See also Kinder, "Bureaucratic Cold Warrior," 182. There were some allegations about smuggling by the Communists. See Walter P. McConaughy (Shanghai) to DS, 12 September 1949, RG 59, 893.114 Narcotics/9–1249, and Smyth to DS, 6 June 1949, RG 59, 893.114 Narcotics/6–349, NA. In November 1990 charges resurfaced concerning Communist involvement with opium traffic during the Chinese civil war. The Associated Press reported that in *White Snow, Red Blood*, a book by Lt. Col. Zhang Zhenglu about the siege of Changchun, published in August 1989 and later banned in China, the author claims that an army division under the current vice president, Wang Zhen (not named in the book), carried on a profitable trade in opium. See *Honolulu Star-Bulletin*, 22 November 1990.

59. Pepper, "The KMT-CCP Conflict," 774–83; Stueck, *The Road to Confrontation*, 17–18, 36–37; G. May, *China Scapegoat*, 153–55; *The China White Paper*, 273; Cohen, "Acheson, His Advisers, and China," 14; E. May, *The Truman Administration and China*, 45–46; Melby, *The Mandate of Heaven*, 247–53.

60. *The Reminiscences of Ho Lien*, 435–37, COHP; Martin Oral History, 35–37, HSTL; John Moors Cabot to Butterworth, 6 February 1948, Cabot Papers, reel 12: China, 1947–48, DDEL; H. D. Robinson to Cabot, 2 December 1948, and Cabot to Stuart, 3 December 1948, RG 84, FSP, Shanghai, General Records, box 29, 1948, WNRC. For information on Tu after the war, see Wang, "Tu Yueh-sheng," 447–55.

61. Lebow, *Between Peace and War*, 207; *The China White Paper*, xvi; Martin Oral History, 58, HSTL.

62. Stueck, *The Road to Confrontation*, 120–24 (quotation, 123); Cohen, "Acheson, His Advisers, and China," 34–42; Goldstein, "Chinese Communist Policy toward the United States," 235–36, 253–54, 261–70. See also NSC document 48/2 in *FRUS, 1949*, 1218–19.

63. Memorandum by Morlock, 20 September 1949, RG 59, 893.114 Narcotics/9–1649, and Clubb to DS, 29 October 1949, RG 59, 893.114 Narcotics/10–2949, NA.

64. McFall to Magnuson, 16 December 1949, RG 59, 893.114 Narcotics/12–1249, NA.

65. Lebow, *Between Peace and War*, 106; Jervis, *Perception and Misperception in International Politics*, 128–30, 135–42, 196. Both Lebow and Jervis discuss irrational consistency and flexibility in policymaking.

66. Shai, *Britain and China*, 69–73, 153–55; Watt, "Britain and the Cold War in the Far East," 101–3; Bullock, *Bevin*, 31.

67. Ovendale, "Britain and the Cold War in Asia," 121–23; Bullock, *Bevin*, 31, Watt, "Britain and the Cold War in the Far East," 92–93, 101.

68. *FRUS, 1949*, 1138–41.

69. Bullock, *Bevin*, 31; Watt, "Britain and the Cold War in the Far East," 99–100; Gardner, *Approaching Vietnam*, 37, 60–62; Hopper to DS, 21 April 1948, RG 84, FSP, Hong Kong, S-SGR, box 8, 1948, WNRC.

70. Hess, *The United States' Emergence as a Southeast Asian Power*, 160–63, 181–82; Rose, *Roots of Tragedy*, 50–52; Herring, "The Truman Administration and the Restoration of French Sovereignty in Indochina," 101–12; SACSEA (Mountbatten) to JCS, 2 October 1945, RG 218, Chairman's File, Admiral William D. Leahy, 1942–48, box 4, NA (I am indebted to Bob Buzzanco for this citation).

71. Chen, *Vietnam and China*, 99–105, 115–32; Sprouse to DS, 27 September 1945, RG 84, FSP, Kunming, S-SGR, box 3, 1945, WNRC; Sainteny, *Histoire d'une Paix Manquée*, 177–79, 181–84, 259–63.

72. [Ho Chi Minh], *Selected Works* 2:11–13, 30–35, 3:17–21, 36–39; Patti, *Why Viet Nam?* 251–52, 296.

73. Anslinger's report on the first session of the CND, 1 April 1947, RG 59, 501.BD Narcotics/4–147, Reed (Saigon) to DS, 25 June 1946, RG 59, 851G.114 Narcotics/6–2546, and Reed to DS, 13 June 1947, RG 59, 851G.114 Narcotics/6–1347, NA. On the importation of more than 48,000 kilograms of Iranian opium in one shipment in 1945 before the Japanese assumed full control of Indochina, see A. G. Ardalan, CND

representative from Iran, to the secretary-general of the UN, 18 June 1949, RG 59, 501.BD Narcotics/7–649, NA.

74. Coles to H. K. Matthews, UN Department (FO), 9 February 1948, FO 371/72908, PRO; U.S. Mission to the UN to DS, 30 November 1946, RG 59, 501.BD Narcotics/11–3046, NA; Hammer, *The Struggle for Indochina*, 201–31.

75. Anslinger to Tollenger, 7 January 1948, RG 84, FSP, Bangkok, General Records, box 81, 1948, WNRC.

76. Report by Tollenger, 16 March 1948, RG 59, 851G.114 Narcotics/3–1648, NA.

77. Division of Western European Affairs to Morlock, 4 May 1948, RG 84, U.S. Mission to the UN, 1945–49, box 85, NA.

78. On the connection between Iran, opium control, and security policy, see Walker, "Drug Control and the Issue of Culture in American Foreign Relations," 376–77.

79. Rotter, *The Path to Vietnam*, 84–93; *FRUS, 1948*, 49.

80. Coors to DS, 21 April 1948, RG 59, 851G.114 Narcotics/4–2148, NA.

81. "Summary Record of the Third Session of the Commission on Narcotic Drugs, 3 to 22 May 1948," RG 59, 501.BD Narcotics/2–1649, especially pp. 117–19 (emphasis added).

82. Willard L. Thorp (for the secretary of state) to Caffrey, 7 June 1948, RG 59, 851G.114 Narcotics/6–748, NA.

83. Minutes, FPA board of directors, 28 October 1948; E. H. Foley to DS, 21 October 1948, and William Sanders, acting director for UN Affairs, to Caffrey, 6 November 1948, RG 59, 851G.114 Narcotics/10–2148, NA.

84. *Pentagon Papers*, 1:32–33; Leffler, "The United States and the Strategic Dimensions of the Marshall Plan," 289–94.

85. Acting Secretary of State Robert Lovett to Certain Diplomatic Officers, 5 April 1949, RG 59, 102.196/4–549, NA. This document includes Morlock's memorandum on congressional action regarding White's trip for the FBN. For a report by White detailing an active Indochinese role in the heroin trade at Marseilles, see White to Anslinger, 22 June 1948, RG 59, 102.196/6–2248, NA. It is worth noting that White submitted his report between the CND's meeting and the Treasury Department's appeal to officials at the State Department to approach the French government. For general information on similar, subsequent missions by Garland H. Williams, see Lovett to Certain Diplomatic Officers, 24 December 1948, RG 59, 102.196/12–2448, NA. On opium in Laos, see "Summary Record of the Third Session of the Commission on Narcotic Drugs," RG 59, 501.BD Narcotics/2–1649, p. 119, NA.

86. Musto, *The American Disease*, 230. Anslinger's success as a bureaucrat fits comfortably into the analysis of organizational interests developed by Halperin, *Bureaucratic Politics and Foreign Policy*. More generally, see G. Allison, *Essence of Decision*, 67–100, 144–84.

87. Stuart to DS, 16 November 1948, RG 59, 893.114 Narcotics/11–1548, and Foley to DS, 21 October 1948, RG 59, 851G.114 Narcotics/10–2148, NA; Hess, *The United States' Emergence as a Southeast Asian Power*, 313–32.

88. Hess, *The United States' Emergence as a Southeast Asian Power*, 179–83, 193–96, 325–27; R. Blum, *Drawing the Line*, 108–10; *Pentagon Papers*, 1:33–34; *FRUS, 1949*, 92; U.S. consulate (Hanoi) to DS, 8 April 1948, RG 84, FSP, Hong Kong, S-SGR, box 6, 1948, WNRC. On the Viet Minh and opium, see McAlister, "Mountain Minorities and the Viet Minh," 817–35.

89. *FRUS, 1949*, 76–79, 84–86, 1207; Ovendale, "Britain and the Cold War in Asia," 125–29, and "Britain, the United States, and the Cold War in South-East Asia."

90. Ovendale, *The English-speaking Alliance*, 171, and "Britain and the Cold War in Asia," 128–29; Buhite, *Soviet-American Relations in Asia*, 202–3; *FRUS, 1949*, 1215–20 (quotation).

91. Tinker, *The Union of Burma*, 116–23; Hess, *The United States' Emergence as a Southeast Asian Power*, 261–67; Thorne, *Allies of a Kind*, 607–12.

92. Tinker, *The Union of Burma*, 23–33; Cady Oral History, 21, 59–60, HSTL.

93. "Summary of Communist Activities in Southeast Asia," 24 June 1948 (box 8), and "Needs for United States Economic and Technical Aid in Burma: Report No. 3 of the United States Economic Survey Mission to Southeast Asia," 23 March–4 April 1950 (box 9), Melby Papers, HSTL; Tinker, *The Union of Burma*, 32–40; Steinberg, *In Search of Southeast Asia*, 394–97; Cady, *The History of Post-War Southeast Asia*, 44–45, 66–68.

94. FO to the Burma Office, 27 September 1946, enclosing Secretary of State for Burma to the Governor of Burma, 13 July 1946, and Governor of Burma to the Secretary of State for Burma, 28 August 1946, FO 371/59609, PRO.

95. British embassy to DS, 12 November 1946, RG 59, 845C.114 Narcotics/11–1246, NA; British embassy to FO, 12 November 1946, FO 371/59612, PRO.

96. Hess, *The United States' Emergence as a Southeast Asian Power*, 269–70.

97. R. Austin Acly (Rangoon) to DS, 24 August 1948, RG 59, 845C.114 Narcotics/8–2488, and Lovett to U.S. embassy (Rangoon), 3 November 1948, RG 59, 845C.114 Narcotics/11–348, NA.

98. Tinker, *The Union of Burma*, 34–39; GUB to British embassy (Nanking), 14 November 1946, FO 371/59212, PRO; Rev. M. Vincent Young to U.S. consulate (Kunming), 23 November 1948, RG 84, FSP, Kunming, General Records, 1938–49, box 81, and Acly to Butterworth, 1 July 1948, RG 84, FSP, Rangoon, Confidential File, box 5, 1948, WNRC.

99. *FRUS, 1949*, 1128–30, 1132; Hess, *The United States' Emergence as a Southeast Asian Power*, 346–48; R. Blum, *Drawing the Line*, 105, 110, 112–13.

100. Memorandum by James B. Lindsay (Rangoon), 22 November 1948, RG 59, 845C.114 Narcotics/11–2248, NA; U.S. embassy (Rangoon) to DS, 28 June, 22 July 1949, RG 84, FSP, Rangoon, Confidential File, box 6, 1949, WNRC.

101. Scott, *The Weapons of the Weak*, xvi, 23, 29–36, 289–303, and *The Moral Economy of the Peasant*, 197–203.

102. Edwin F. Stanton (Bangkok) to DS, 5 October 1949, RG 84, FSP, Hong Kong, S-SGR, box 10, 1949, WNRC; R. H. Bushner (Bangkok) to Sir Geoffrey Thompson,

14 December 1949, FO 991/25, PRO. See also Kunstadter, Introduction to *Southeast Asian Tribes*, 35–36; Geddes, "The Tribal Research Centre, Thailand," 567–68; cf. Mote, "The Rural 'Haw' of Northern Thailand," 487–94.

103. Stanton to DS, 5 October 1949, RG 84, FSP, Hong Kong, S-SGR, box 10, 1949, WNRC; Tinker, *The Union of Burma*, 39–48.

104. Ovendale, "Britain and the Cold War in Asia," 121, 125; Cady Oral History, 12, 17, 21, HSTL; Hess, *The United States' Emergence as a Southeast Asian Power*, 251–61; Gaddis, *The Long Peace*, 90.

105. *FRUS, 1949*, 1132, 1188–89, 1195, 1201; Rinehart, "Historical Setting," 30–33.

106. Patti, *Why Viet Nam?* 26–27, 66, 71, 485, 545 n. 29; Bird to Donovan, 20 December 1947, Donovan Papers, box 73a, MHI.

107. Bird to Donovan, 5 April 1948, and Donovan to Major General Alfred M. Gruenther, JCS, Pentagon, and to Lovett, DS, 14 April 1948, Donovan Papers, box 73a, MHI.

108. British consulate (Khorramshahr) to British embassy (Teheran), 3 April 1948, FO 371/72909, PRO; Statement by Anslinger to the third session of the CND, 12 May 1948, RG 59, 501.BD Narcotics/6–2448, NA; Ingram, *Economic Change in Thailand*, 143, 179, 184–87.

109. Norman B. Hannah's report on political events in Thailand, October 1949, 15 November 1949 (box 19), Stanton to DS, 12 September 1949 (box 18), and John F. Stone to DS, 28 November 1949 (box 18), RG 84, FSP, Bangkok, Confidential File, 1949, WNRC.

110. Bushner's memorandum of a conversation with Prince Moruchao Wongmaship Chayangkun, 11 April 1949, RG 84, FSP, Bangkok, Confidential File, box 18, 1949, WNRC.

111. Quarterly Military Survey, 1 June 1949, by Colonel Elliot G. Thorpe, military attaché (Bangkok), RG 59, PSA Records, Country Files, box 19, NA.

112. Emerson, *From Empire to Nation*, 188–200 (quotation, 195).

113. "The Problem of Agrarian Reform in Indochina," 27 January 1950, RG 59, OIR Report no. 4994.4, NA (emphasis added).

114. LaRue R. Lutkins (Kunming) to DS, 10 December 1948, RG 59, 893.114 Narcotics/12–1048, NA; Lutkins to DS, 10 February 1949, RG 84, FSP, Kunming, S-SGR, box 6, 1948–49, and U.S. embassy (Rangoon) to DS, 6 May 1949, RG 84, FSP, Rangoon, Confidential File, box 6, 1949, WNRC.

115. Billingsley, *Bandits in Republican China*, 4–11, 126–28, 177, 263–65, 269–70.

116. Lutkins to DS, 10 February 1949, RG 84, FSP, Kunming, S-SGR, box 6, 1948–49, WNRC. Burma doubted the existence of an alliance between bandits and Chinese Communists in the drug trade. See memorandum by Reed, 16 May 1949, RG 59, PSA Records, Country Files, box 6, WNRC.

117. See the series of reports from the U.S. vice-consul at Kunming, LaRue R. Lutkins, dated 16 March, 8 April, 17 July, 2 September, and 9 November 1949, 11 Janu-

ary 1950, RG 84, FSP, Kunming, S-SGR, box 6, 1948–49, WNRC; Lewis Clark (Canton) to DS, 19 August 1949, RG 59, 893.114 Narcotics/8–1949, NA.

118. "Survival Potential of Residual Non-Communist Regimes in China," 19 October 1949, RG 319, ORE 76–49, CIA, Intelligence Document Files, WNRC.

119. Vogel, *Canton under Communism*, 31–32, 67–68.

120. Both White and Jacoby (*Thunder out of China*, 314) and Belden (*China Shakes the World*, 463–66), while recognizing the bond between the Communists and the majority of the Chinese people, see the creation of a "new" element in China's politics.

121. Mancall, *China at the Center*, 330–32, 337–39, 356–60 (quotation, 338—emphasis added).

122. Tucker, *Patterns in the Dust*, 192.

Chapter Nine

1. Statement of Anslinger before the Senate Special Committee to Investigate Organized Crime in Interstate Commerce, 27 March 1951, RG 46, Records of the U.S. Senate Judiciary Committee, Subcommittee on Narcotics, 85 Cong., box 37, NA. On Truman's China policy, see Tucker, *Patterns in the Dust*, 189–94.

2. On the failure of imagination in policymaking and the relationship of beliefs and predispositions to perceptions of threat, see Jervis, "Perceiving and Coping with Threat," 13–15, 18–22. For a discussion of the Chinese Communists and threat perception, see Tsou, *America's Failure in China*, 561–64, 576–80.

3. Gardner, *Approaching Vietnam*, 80–84; Schaller, *The American Occupation of Japan*, 246–50; Borden, *The Pacific Alliance*, 115–42.

4. Gardner, *Approaching Vietnam*, 84; FO minute by L. C. Glass, 2 March 1950, FO 371/83122, PRO.

5. On a meeting at Bangkok in February 1950, see *FRUS, 1950,* 6:18–19.

6. Dening to MacDonald, 3 March 1950, FO 371/83644, PRO; *FRUS, 1950,* 3:1598–99; Acheson, *Present at the Creation*, 323–34.

7. *FRUS, 1950,* 3:1632–33; Monthly reports from Hanoi and Haiphong for January–February 1950, FO 959/70, PRO.

8. *FRUS, 1950,* 1:216–17. Hickerson's views were consistent with those of the State-Defense Study Group as expressed in its famous paper, NSC 68. See also Spector, *Advice and Support*, 102–11; *FRUS, 1950,* 3:945, 990–92, 1018–20.

9. *FRUS, 1950,* 1:438–39.

10. Anslinger to Morlock, 12 April 1950, RG 59 894.53/4–1250, and James R. Wilkinson to DS, 21 November 1950, RG 59, 893.53/11–2150, NA.

11. Cabot to Butterworth, 6 February 1948, Cabot Papers, reel 12, DDEL; J. Allison, *Ambassador from the Prairie*, 123; Rankin to Butterworth, 12 August 1949 (box 12), 15 January 1950 (box 14), Rankin Papers, ML/PU; Tucker, *Patterns in the Dust*, 200.

12. Minute by Dening, 6 May 1950, FO 371/83018, PRO; Ovendale, *The English-*

speaking Alliance, 185–210; Tucker, *Patterns in the Dust*, 38–39, 177–78; Martin, *Divided Counsel*, 100–145, which shows the difficulties attendant to the issue of recognition; Notes of a conversation with Dean Rusk, 20 April 1950, Koo Papers, box 180, BL/CU; Schoenbaum, *Waging Peace and War*, 205–6.

13. Cohen, "Acheson, His Advisers, and China," 37–42. The analysis for this point follows Jervis, "Perceiving and Coping with Threat," 18–19, 22, 24–27. It is highly probable that motivated biases, reflecting Acheson's needs as a decision maker, merged with the unmotivated biases comprising the strong opposition to communism in his belief system. For more on the activities of the China Lobby, see Bachrack, *The Committee of One Million*, 36–48; Koen, *The China Lobby in American Politics*. See also Martin Oral History, 59, HSTL.

14. CIA, "Communist Influence in Burma," 11 January 1950, PSF, Intelligence File, box 527, HSTL; James Bowker (Rangoon) to FO, 24 February 1950, and Minute by R. H. Scott, 2 March 1950, FO 371/83122, PRO; Willard Galbraith, memorandum on Burma, 22 December 1949, RG 59, Lot File 57 D 472, NA; John F. Root to Scott, 1 March 1950, FO 371/83122, PRO.

15. Report no. 3 of the U.S Economic Survey Mission to Southeast Asia, "Needs for United States Economic and Technical Aid in Burma," Melby Papers, box 9, HSTL.

16. "Chinese Communist Influence in Burma, 1949–1951," 15 April 1952, RG 59, OIR 5480.1, NAMP M1221, Intelligence Reports, 1941–61, NA; *FRUS, 1950*, 3:1000 n. 12 (quotation), 6:233–35, 240–44.

17. Galbraith, "Problem Paper: Military Aid for Thailand," 27 January 1950, RG 59, Lot File 57 D 472, NA; Report no. 4 of the U.S. Economic Survey Mission to Southeast Asia, "Needs for United States Economic and Technical Aid in Thailand," Melby Papers, box 9, HSTL; Stanton to DS, 4 October 1949, RG 84, FSP, Bangkok, Confidential File, box 18, 1949, WNRC; *Bangkok Post*, 20 April 1950.

18. Acheson's memorandum to Truman, 9 March 1950, RG 59, Lot File 57 D 472, NA; Acheson, *Present at the Creation*, 394; *FRUS, 1950*, 3:945.

19. *FRUS, 1950*, 3:935–36; "Postwar Regional Economic Problems of the Far East," 25 August 1949, RG 59, OIR 5028 (PV), NA.

20. Speech by Merchant, 12 September 1950, Merchant Papers, box 1, ML/PU.

21. On the benefits and shortcomings of "satisficing," see Janis and Mann, *Decision Making*, 25–35.

22. McCoy, *The Politics of Heroin in Southeast Asia*, 95, claims that the government abandoned opium as a source of revenue as it significantly reduced the incidence of opium smoking. That conclusion may not be wholly accurate. Donald R. Heath, the U.S. minister at Saigon, believed that officials were obtaining nearly 10 percent of all customs revenues from the opium trade in 1952; in Cambodia the figure was slightly higher. Heath to DS for Anslinger, 27 February 1952, RG 59, 851G.53/2–2752, NA. On the incorporation of the Indochinese opium trade into French paramilitary activities, see McCoy, *The Politics of Heroin in Southeast Asia*, 90–98, 110–18.

23. Heath to DS for Anslinger, 27 February 1952, RG 59, 851G.53/2–2752, NA.

24. French report on arms smuggling in Indochina, received by the War Office, 20 July 1950, and R. Whittington (Bangkok) to J. Dalton Murray (SEAD), 1 November 1950, FO 371/83654, PRO.

25. Heath to DS for Anslinger, 27 February 1952, RG 84, FSP, Saigon, Confidential File, box 14, 1950–52, WNRC.

26. Anslinger to Morlock, 3 May 1950, RG 59, 102.14/5–350, NA, requesting a special passport for George H. White to visit France, Italy, Egypt, Hong Kong, Macao, Thailand, and Indochina to confer with local offices in the hope of promoting more vigorous action against opium. See also Charles W. Lewis, Jr. (Istanbul) to DS for Anslinger from Charles Siragusa, 7 August 1950, RG 59, 102.14/8–750, NA.

27. Irvin and Sawyer Interviews, BGCA/WC; Memorandum [1950?] of a visit to the Kingdom of Laos by Coors, in Donovan Papers, box 75b, MHI; McCoy, *The Politics of Heroin in Southeast Asia,* 78–85; Dommen, *Conflict in Laos,* 15–17; Graves to Eden, 20 March 1952, FO 959/136, PRO. For more on Laos in the maelstrom of international and Indochinese politics around 1950, see Dommen, *Conflict in Laos,* 36–38; Adams, "Patrons, Clients, and Revolutionaries," 100–120.

28. Gullion to DS, 26 June 1952, RG 59, 751G.5/6–2652, NA. Gullion felt that the SDECE (Service de Documentation Extérieure et du Contre-Espionage) was behind the counterinsurgency activity of the Meo.

29. Position paper by Durward V. Sondifer, deputy assistant secretary of state, 15 April 1952, RG 59, 340.1 AH/4–1552, NA.

30. Restricted access to documents makes it impossible to ascertain whether any U.S. officials knew about Operation X. While it cannot be known with certainty what Anslinger or Morlock would have done had they possessed such knowledge, it is clear that in other instances they had no trouble relegating narcotics control policy to a secondary place when larger security concerns intervened.

31. *FRUS, 1950,* 3:1148, 6:135; Memorandum by Rusk, 15 December 1950, RG 59, PSA Records, box 8 (emphasis in original); *FRUS, 1951,* 1:19 (Davies's quotation); FO minute, 23 January 1951, FO 959/110, PRO; Blaufarb, *The Counterinsurgency Era,* 128–37. More generally on Anglo-American thinking about security policy, see Spector, *Advice and Support,* 111–21; Gardner, *Approaching Vietnam,* 97–101.

32. *FRUS, 1951,* 6, pt. 1:115 (emphasis added); *FRUS, 1952–1954,* 13:159, 161. From Paris, Oliver Harvey wrote Eden: "Politically Indo-China is now at the heart of Europe." Harvey to Eden, 19 November 1952, FO 959/122, PRO. For a contrasting view, see CIA, "Consequences to the US of Communist Domination of Mainland Southeast Asia," 13 October 1950, ORE 29–50, PSF, Intelligence File, box 257, HSTL.

33. Kolko, *Anatomy of a War,* 49–51; [Ho Chi Minh], *Selected Works* 3:116–18, 165–70, 332–43; Richard M. Bissell, Jr., head of ECA, to William C. Foster, 19 July 1951, RG 286, AID, ECA, Country Subject Files, 1950–51, box 2, WNRC; *FRUS, 1952–1954,* 13:199 (quotation).

34. Rev. E. Bruce Copeland, "The People's Republic of China and the Christian Church," 17 February 1950, CBMS, E/M.2, Far East Committee Minutes, 1950–53,

box 331, SOAS/UL. The Far East Committee reported favorably at its May 1950 meeting the content of Zhou Enlai's "How Shall the Church Go Forward," 23 June 1950, ibid. See also Varg, *Missionaries, Chinese, and Diplomats*, 303–18; H. R. Williamson, *British Baptists in China*, 188–99, 337–60. Returning missionaries later described in vivid terms their troubles with the PRC. See Victoria, *Nun in Red China*; McCammon, *We Tried to Stay*; Greene, *Calvary in China*; Martinson, *Under the Red Dragon*. For the difficulties the British encountered, see Martin, *Divided Counsel*, 119–26, 139–50.

35. *FRUS, 1950*, 3:1657–69.

36. Chen, *Vietnam and China*, 213–27; *Pentagon Papers*, 1:82–85, 373–74; Kalicki, *The Pattern of Sino-American Crises*, 5, 33; Spector, *Advice and Support*, 111–21, 123–26; *FRUS, 1951*, 1:203–5 (quotation).

37. *FRUS, 1950*, 3:1714, 1727–29, 1732–33; *FRUS, 1951*, 6 pt. 2:1656 (quotation). For more on the Truman-Attlee talks, see Acheson, *Present at the Creation*, 478–85; Attlee, *As It Happened*, 280–83, which is far less revealing; F. Williams, *A Prime Minister Remembers*, 235–40. Privately, Truman called the British position on Asia "fantastic." Ferrell, *Off the Record*, 203. See also Mayers, *Cracking the Monolith*, 92–96; Foot, *The Wrong War*, 103–5, 109–23.

38. Anslinger, "The Red Chinese Dope Traffic." This article appeared in his penultimate year as FBN chief.

39. Anslinger's remarks at the eighth (15 April 1953) and seventeenth (8 May–1 June 1962) sessions of the CND, Anslinger Papers, box 1, PL/PSU. Anslinger and others frequently repeated this basic anti-Communist allegation for diverse audiences. See Anslinger and Tompkins, *The Traffic in Narcotics*, 76–83; Deverall, *Red China's Dirty Drug War*, 140–50; Hamberger, *The Peking Bomb*, 49–61.

40. "Review of the Illicit Narcotic Traffic in the United States in 1949," 5 April 1950, RG 59, 340.1 AH/4–550, NA (narcotics were readily available in major cities throughout Asia); British embassy to FO, 10 March 1950, FO 371/88823, PRO; British consulate general (Canton) to SEAD, 17 June 1950, and FO minute, 11 July 1950, FO 371/83540, PRO. For information concerning temporary measures taken by the PRC in 1949 against opium, see British embassy to Far Eastern Department, FO, 14 December 1949, FO 371/88823, PRO. The government adopted a brief amnesty period in order to discourage cultivation, manufacture, traffic, and use.

41. Martinson, *Under the Red Dragon*, 100; Victoria, *Nun in Red China*, 43; Meisner, *Mao's China*, 90–91.

42. Wilkinson to DS, 21 November 1950, RG 59, 893.53/11–2150, NA. I obtained a sanitized version of this document through a Freedom of Information Act request from RG 319, AIPDF, WNRC; I read the unsanitized version earlier in DS records. See also Hickerson to Anslinger, 1 December 1950, RG 59, 340.1 AH/12–150, NA.

43. "Offer for Sale in China of Five Hundred Tons of Opium," UN, CND, 5th sess., provisional agenda item 13, RG 59, 340.1 AH/11–350, NA; Samuel Hoare (FO) to J. S. H. Shattuck, 3 November 1950, FO cover minute, 15 November 1950, and FO to UN delegation, 8 November 1950, FO 371/88826, PRO.

44. Robert W. Rinden (Taipei) to DS, 19 April 1951, RG 59, 893.53/4–1951, and DS to U.S. consulate (Hong Kong), 27 January 1951, RG 59, 893.53/1–2751 (quotation); British delegate to the UN to FO, 12 April 1951, FO 371/95594, PRO.

45. Anslinger's remarks are contained in Walter M. Kotschnig to Hickerson, RG 59, 340.1 AH/5–1952, NA. The commissioner again blamed most of Southeast Asia's opium problems on the Communists in China. The Viet Minh received some of the blame for conditions in Indochina.

46. Records of the fourteenth session of the UN Economic and Social Committee, 27 May 1952, RG 59, 340.1 AH/7–1152 (quotation), and U.S. Mission to the UN to DS, 15 July 1952, RG 59, 894.53/7–1552, NA.

47. Anslinger to Morlock, 11 July 1952, and Morlock to U.S. consulate (Hong Kong), 11 July 1952, RG 59, 340.1 AH/7–1152, NA; Harrington to DS, 4 November 1952, RF 59, 893.53/11–452, NA. A report reaching the State Department not long after Harrington's dispatch, in which the Japanese Ministry of Welfare rekindled fears of Chinese aggression with narcotics, was deemed to be "probably true." John M. Steves (Tokyo) to DS, 18 December 1952, RG 59, 893.53/12–1852, NA.

48. "Preliminary Observations: Chinese Resistance Movement," unsigned memorandum, 10 August 1950, RG 59, CA, box 17, NA; Clubb's memorandum of a talk with D. A. Greenhill, British embassy, 26 April 1951, RG 59, PSA, box 6, NA; Moseley, *The Consolidation of the South China Frontier*, 20–26, 33–39.

49. Hamberger, *The Peking Bomb*, 77–116, 143–48; Deverall, *Red China's Dirty Drug War*, 125–69. Anslinger and Tompkins, *The Traffic in Narcotics*, 95–99, denies the reality of the antiopium campaign within China; the FBN chief later modified this position, however. See also Anslinger and Oursler, *The Murderers*, 228.

50. *FRUS, 1950,* 3:1721 and 1733–34 (quotations); Gaddis, *Strategies of Containment,* 101–3, and *The Long Peace,* 80–89.

51. Rankin to Fulton Freeman, 23 November 1949 (box 12), Rankin to Rusk, 1 November 1950 (box 14), Rankin to Kennan, 30 June 1950 (box 15), and Kennan to Rankin, 9 August 1950 (box 14), Rankin Papers, ML/PU.

52. Notes of a conversation with Rusk, 20 April 1950, Koo Papers, box 180, BL/CU.

53. Leary, *Perilous Missions,* 8–9, 14–19, 70–73; Whiting Willauer to Louise Willauer, 1 May 1950, and Willauer to Corcoran, 6 January 1950, Willauer Papers, box 14, ML/PU (quotations).

54. Chennault to Corcoran, 18 July 1950, Willauer Papers, box 14, ML/PU; Rankin to Merchant, 9 December 1949 (box 13), and Rankin to "Dear Friend," 14 December 1950 (box 14), Rankin Papers, ML/PU—the latter intimate correspondent remains unidentified. See also R. Taylor, *Foreign and Domestic Consequences of the KMT Intervention in Burma,* 39–40; Rankin, *China Assignment,* 99–100.

55. *FRUS, 1950,* 3:1762; "Estimate of a Princeton Graduate Interested in the Far East," 18 July 1951, Merchant Papers, box 1, ML/PU; NSC Meeting no. 80, 17 January

1951, NSC 101: "A Report to the National Security Council by the Secretary of Defense on Courses of Action Relative to Communist China and Korea," 12 January 1951, and NSC 101/1: "A Report to the National Security Council by the Executive Secretary on U.S. Action to Counter Chinese Communist Aggression," 15 January 1951, Truman Papers, PSF, HSTL: NSC Meeting no. 80 (NSC 101/1 changed "Nationalist guerrilla forces" to "anti-communist guerrilla forces"); *FRUS, 1951*, 6 pt. 1:34–38, 52, 7:1538, 1598–1605.

56. Koen, *The China Lobby in American Politics*, 53–54. William D. Pawley told Koo that Chennault was out of favor with the administration "because he had been playing his hand too conspicuously." Notes of a conversation with Pawley, 22 March 1951, Koo Papers, box 184, BL/CU. This discussion took place two months after the NSC had approved covert operations against China.

57. GUB, *Kuomintang Aggression against Burma*, 20; Weekly Intelligence Digest: Burma, "KMT Troops in Burma—A Chronology," 17 July 1951, RG 59, Lot File 57 D 472, NA; Notes of a conversation with Rusk, 27 July 1950, Koo Papers, box 180, BL/CU. At that early date, Rusk spoke with Koo about getting KMT forces, growing in number, out of Burma. *New York Times*, 25 May 1951.

58. CND, *Abolition of Opium Smoking in the Far East*; Henry B. Day (Rangoon) to DS, 5 June 1950, RG 59, 890B.53/6–550, NA.

59. CND, *Summary Record of the Fifth Session*.

60. Sondifer's position paper for the seventh session of the CND, 15 April 1952, RG 59, 340.1 AH/4–1552, and Kotschnig to Hickerson, 19 May 1952, RG 59, 340.1 AH/5–1952, NA.

61. *FRUS, 1950*, 3:1161.

62. Ibid., 6:233, 235; FO to British embassy (Bangkok), 21 June 1951, FO 371/92141, PRO; *FRUS, 1951*, 6 pt. 2:1656; ECA, Office of the Assistant Administrator for Programs, "Economic Aid to Asia," 27 March 1951, RG 286, AID, ECA, Country Subject Files, 1950–51, box 1, WNRC (quotation). For a staff study on NSC 48/5 regarding the PRC's threat to the region, see *FRUS, 1951*, 6 pt. 1:59.

63. 495 H.C. Deb. 5s., 5 February 1952, 826. R. H. Scott feared that it might be too late to allay Rangoon's uncertainty about Anglo-American intentions. Minute by Scott, 21 September 1951, FO 371/92143, PRO.

64. U.S. embassy (Rangoon) to DS with a report on political trends in Burma for July 1952, 16 July 1952, RG 59, 790B.00/9–1652, NA; R. Taylor, *Foreign and Domestic Consequences of the KMT Intervention in Burma*, 5–7.

65. *FRUS, 1950*, 6:107, 110; Rotter, *The Path to Vietnam*, 207.

66. *FRUS, 1950*, 6:246–47; British embassy (Rangoon) to FO, 14 August 1950, FO 959/72, PRO; Key to DS, RG 59, 790B.00/6–2051, and Memorandum of a conversation with Barrington, 2 October 1951, RG 59, Lot File 57 D 472, box 1, NA.

67. Acheson's circular letter, 4 February 1952, and Heath to DS, 4 February 1952, RG 59, 790B.00/2–452, NA. For a dispatch regarding rumors in Rangoon charging

the United States with aiding the KMT irregulars, see Albert B. Franklin (Rangoon) to DS, 26 February 1952, with clippings from *The Nation* (Rangoon), 22–24 February 1952, RG 59, 790B.00/2–2652, NA.

68. Rankin to Merchant, 31 May 1951, Rankin Papers, box 16, ML/PU; Richard L. Speaight (Rangoon) to FO, 7 May 1951, FO 371/92140, PRO; Cady Oral History, 63–64, and Martin Oral History, 82, HSTL; vanden Heuval telephone interview.

69. James E. Webb, acting secretary of state, to various representatives, 15 September 1951, RG 59, 790B.00/9–1951 (first quotation—the same communication, from Rusk to Key, is in *FRUS, 1951*, 6 pt. 1:289–90, and see also Leary, *Perilous Missions*, 247 n. 15); 495 H.C. Deb. 5s., 5 February 1952, 826 (Eden's musings); W. O. Anderson (CA) to PSA, 1 August 1952, RG 59, 790B.00/8–152, NA.

70. Cady Oral History, 60, HSTL; vanden Heuval telephone interview; MacDonald to FO, 1 September 1951, FO 371/92142, Memorandum by Murray, 22 January 1952, FO 371/101008, and Minute by Scott, 1 February 1952, FO 371/101009, PRO; Allison to Matthews, 1 August 1952, RG 59, 790B.00/8–152, NA, in which Allison wrote that "all agencies of our Government" ought to help bring an end to KMT activities in Burma; McConaughy to Allison, 29 August 1952, RG 59, 790B.00/8–2952, NA.

71. GUB, *Kuomintang Aggression against Burma*, 13–14; Oliver E. Clubb, *The Effect of Chinese Nationalist Military Activities in Burma*, 5–6, 14–16, and *The United States and the Sino-Soviet Bloc in Southeast Asia*, 85–86; British embassy (Bangkok) to Murray, 27 February 1952, FO 371/101173, PRO; *London Sunday Observer*, 2 March 1952. In October 1950, the CIA put greater faith in Li Mi's troops. See CIA, "Consequences to the US of Communist Domination of Mainland Southeast Asia," WNRC. General Omar N. Bradley, chairman, JCS, to the secretary of defense, 18 April 1952, RG 59, Lot File 55 D 282, discusses the PRC's concern about the Yunnan-Burma border. On the links between the CIA and the CAT, see Leary, *Perilous Missions*, 129–43; Prados, *Presidents' Secret Wars*, 67–77.

72. William T. Turner (Bangkok) to DS, 27 November 1950, RG 59, 892.53/11–2750, and Monthly political report for September 1951 by Robert Anderson (Bangkok), 29 October 1951, RG 59, 792.00/10–2951, NA; George M. Widney to U.S. embassy (Bangkok), 17 January 1952, RG 84, FSP, Chiengmai, box 1, WNRC.

73. Day to DS, 11 February 1952, RG 59, 790B.00/2–1152, NA; British embassy (Bangkok) to Murray, 27 February 1952, FO 371/101173, PRO; Whiting Willauer to Louise Willauer, 15 August 1951, Willauer Papers, box 15, ML/PU. For information helping to corroborate CAT ties with the Thai government and the CIA, see *The Bulletin* (CAT), 5 (January 1952), 8–9; copy in Willauer Papers, box 16.

74. Franklin to DS, 16 May 1952, RG 59, 790B.00/5–1652, NA; Oliver E. Clubb, *The Effect of Chinese Nationalist Military Activities in Burma*, 14–15; R. Taylor, *Foreign and Domestic Consequences of the KMT Intervention in Burma*, 10–14.

75. FO memorandum regarding KMT troops in Burma, 19 May 1952, FO 371/101012; Sebald, "Burma Diary," 19–20 (quotation), 475–76 n. 21, Sebald Papers, HIWRP; 499 H.C. Deb. 5s., 28 April 1952, 499.

76. *FRUS, 1950*, 3:1664; Stanton to DS, 22 September 1950, RG 286, AID, ECA, Productivity and Technical Assistance Division, Office of the Director, box 34, WNRC.

77. Galbraith, "Problem Paper: Politico-Military Objectives and Policies Relating to MDAP in Thailand," 11 September 1950, RG 59, Lot File 57 D 472, NA; Whittington to FO, 22 September, 26 October 1950, FO 371/84399, PRO; Mungkandi, "Thai-American Relations in Historical Perspective," 12–15; Rinehart, "Historical Setting," 32–33; Girling, *Thailand*, 108–10; Esterline and Esterline, *"How the Dominoes Fell,"* 252–55; Soonthornojana, "The Rise of United States–Thai Relations," 78.

78. "Questions and Answers on the Title III Programs, Thailand," 15 June 1951, RG 59, 792.5-MSP/6–1551, and "The Attempted Thai Coup (June 29, 1951)," 5 July 1951, OIR 5569, NAMP, M1221, Intelligence Reports, 1941–61, NA.

79. Seni Pramot is quoted in Warner, *The Last Confucian*, 282.

80. Ibid., 282–84; McCoy, *The Politics of Heroin in Southeast Asia*, 132–41; McGehee, *Deadly Deceits*, 26; *FRUS, 1952–1954*, 12:740 (quotation).

81. FO to British embassy (Washington), 27 September 1951, FO 371/92142, PRO. British records are indispensable for uncovering the link between the CIA, the Thai government, the KMT—and opium. See in the PRO, for example, Sir Oliver Franks to FO, 4 October 1951, FO 371/92143; E. H. Jacobs-Larkcom (Tamsui) to Murray, 1 November 1952, and Minute by S. J. L. Olver (SEAD), 18 January 1952, FO 371/101008; FO to Wallinger, 10 May 1951, FO 371/92140; Tamsui consulate to FO, 15 August 1951, FO 371/92141, in which CAT pilot Steve Kusak is reported to have claimed that he landed supplies in Yunnan. See also Day to DS, 30 November 1951, RG 59, 790B.00/11–3051, NA.

82. *FRUS, 1951*, 6 pt. 1:98; Wallinger to Eden, 10 September 1952, FO 371/101168, PRO.

83. For evidence of some frustration with the intrigues of Thai politics by U.S. officials in Bangkok, see Charles N. Sprinks to DS, 30 June 1952, RG 59, 792.5-MSP/6–3052, NA. Regarding allegations about Phao and opium, see *FRUS, 1952–1954*, 12:22; vanden Heuval telephone interview.

84. Aaron Brown (Bangkok) to DS, 28 July 1952, RG 59, 790B.00/2–2852, and John H. Ohly to Edwin M. Martin (DS) and Frank Nash (Defense Department), 12 August 1952, RG 59, 792.5-MSP/8–1252, NA. John F. Melby admitted that the Truman administration could do little about Phao's alleged misuse of MDAP aid because of the strategic and economic importance of Thailand to U.S. policy. Melby to Philip W. Bonsal, 14 August 1952, RG 59, 792.5-MSP/8–1452, NA. For more on Phao and opium, see Widney to DS, 3 October 1952, RG 59, 792.00/10–352, NA.

85. Acheson to U.S. embassy (Rangoon), repeated to Bangkok, Taipei, London, and Paris, 21 January 1952, RG 59, 790B.00/1–2152, NA.

86. Widney to DS, 8 January 1953, RG 59, 792.00/1–853, NA; vanden Heuval telephone interview. On Anslinger and the CIA, see Marks, *The Search for the "Manchurian Candidate,"* 87–90. Some U.S. military officials in Burma blamed the problems there on Chinese Communist infiltration of KMT forces. Major C. E. Toury, British

Services Mission (Rangoon) to Major A. I. Forestier-Walker (WO), 20 February 1953, FO 371/106684, PRO.

87. Spector, *Advice and Support*, 161; Gardner, *Approaching Vietnam*, 123; Sebald, "Burma Diary," 84, Sebald Papers, HIWRP.

88. Anslinger, "The Opium of the Peoples [sic] Government," 759–63, Anslinger Papers, box 4, HSTL.

89. Musto, *The American Disease*, 230–34; Lindesmith, *The Addict and the Law*, 99–124; Statement of Anslinger before the Senate Special Committee to Investigate Organized Crime in Interstate Commerce, 27 March 1951, RG 46, Records of the U.S. Senate Judiciary Committee, Subcommittee on Narcotics, 85 Cong., box 37, NA.

90. Gaddis, *The Long Peace*, 171–77.

91. Porter, *Britain and the Rise of Communist China*, 49, 133–35; Eden, *Full Circle*, 91–96; Memorandum by J. G. Tahourdin (SEAD) of a meeting with Arthur Ringwalt, 7 May 1953, FO 371/106890, PRO.

92. Notes of conversations with John M. Allison, 2–3 February 1953, Koo Papers, box 187, BL/CU; Sebald, "Burma Diary," 119, Sebald Papers, HIWRP; Oliver E. Clubb, *The United States and the Sino-Soviet Bloc in Southeast Asia*, 86.

93. Sebald, "Burma Diary," 127–28, Sebald Papers, HIWRP.

94. *FRUS, 1952–1954*, 12:122–24; Minute by Tahourdin, 28 February 1953, FO 371/106684, and Makins to FO, 6 March 1954, FO 371/106685, PRO.

95. Notes of a conversation with Allison and Smith, 6 March 1953, and Record of a conference at Foreign Minister George Yeh's house, 2 March 1953, Koo Papers, box 144, BL/CU. Regarding Rankin, Sebald felt that he was "being led by the nose by the Chinese and . . . his heart is not in it for finding a speedy solution to the KMT matter." "Burma Diary," 141, Sebald Papers, HIWRP.

96. Cady, *The United States and Burma*, 211; Sebald, "Burma Diary," 144–49, 154, Sebald Papers, HIWRP; *FRUS, 1952–1954*, 12:74–81, 84–94; Speaight to FO with monthly political report for March 1953, 8 April 1953, FO 371/106677, PRO.

97. Geoffrey Wallinger to Eden with a report by the military attaché, 12 February 1953, FO 371/106909, PRO; Notes of a conversation with Allison and Smith, 6 March 1953, Koo Papers, box 144, BL/CU; Sprinks to DS, 6 May 1953, RG 59, 792.00/5–653, NA. On the development of the opium business near the Burma-Thailand border, see Crooker, "Opium Production in Northern Thailand," 69–75, 80–84, 88; Soonthornojana, "The Rise of United States–Thai Relations." Soonthornojana does not mention Phao and the KMT in his discussion of U.S.-Thai relations in the early 1950s.

98. Oliver E. Clubb, *The Effect of Chinese Nationalist Military Activities in Burma*, 19–32; R. Taylor, *Foreign and Domestic Consequences of the KMT Intervention in Burma*, 44–47; *New York Times*, 23 June 1953; Trager, Wohlgemuth, and Kiang, *Burma's Role in the United Nations*, 9–12.

99. Sebald, "Burma Diary," 242–43, Sebald Papers, HIWRP.

100. Howard P. Jones (Taipei), Joint Weeka 21, 22 May 1954, RG 59, 794A.00(W)/5–2253, Bonsal to W. Bradley Connors, 2 June 1953, RG 59, 690B.9321/6–253, and

Jones's memorandum of a meeting between Chiang and Radford, 18 June 1953, RG 59, 611.90/6–1853, NA.

101. Randolph, *The United States and Thailand*, 15; Dulles to Secretary of Defense Charles E. Wilson, 25 April 1953, RG 59, 792.5-MSP/4–2553, NA.

102. Anderson Oral History, DDEL; Record of action by the NSC at its 143d meeting, 5 June 1953, Ann Whitman File, NSC Series (box 1), and 143d meeting of the NSC, 5 June 1953 (box 4), DDEL; *FRUS, 1952–1954*, 12:671–77.

103. C. D. Jackson to Smith, 25 May 1953, Jackson Records (box 6), and PSB D-23, 2 July 1953, White House Office, OSANSA: Records, 1952–61, NSC Series, Policy Papers Subseries (box 3), Eisenhower Papers, DDEL.

104. PSB D-23, 2 July 1953, White House Office, OSANSA: Records, 1952–61, NSC Series, Policy Papers Subseries, box 3, Eisenhower Papers, DDEL; JCS memorandum to the secretary of defense, 16 July 1953, Jackson Records (box 1), and 161st meeting of the NSC, 9 September 1953, Ann Whitman File, NSC Series (box 4), DDEL; *FRUS, 1952–1954*, 12:677–91.

105. Dulles to Senator Alexander Wiley, 29 July 1953, Dulles Papers, JFD Chronological Series, box 4, DDEL; Donovan to Smith, 10 August 1953, Donovan Papers, box 137b, MHI; Memorandum by Cutler for Smith, 10 September 1953, White House Office, OSANSA: Records, 1952–61, NSC Series, Briefing Notes Subseries (box 16), and Smith to Cutler, 11 September 1953 (box 16), Eisenhower Papers, DDEL.

106. Jackson to Smith, 18 August 1953, Jackson Records, 1953–54, box 6, DDEL.

107. Gordon C. Whitteridge (Bangkok) to Tahourdin, 23 July 1953, FO 371/106890, PRO; *FRUS, 1952–1954*, 12:679–80. According to Wise and Ross, *The Invisible Government*, 133, Rangoon may not have been pleased with the appointment. In fact, the British were uneasy about Donovan's assignment. Sebald, "Burma Diary," 345, Sebald Papers, HIWRP.

108. "Guerilla [*sic*] Activities in China," undated [February 1952?] assessment, Donovan Papers, box 11b, MHI; Eisenhower to Chiang Kai-shek, 28 September 1953, and Chiang Kai-shek to Eisenhower, 9 October 1953, in Koo Papers, box 144, BL/CU; Donovan to DS, 29 October 1953, RG 84, FSP, Taipei, box 3, WNRC.

109. S. M. Black (Tamsui) to FO, 9 October 1953, FO 371/106691, and R. F. G. Sarell (Rangoon) to MacDonald, 2 November 1953, FO 371/106892, PRO; *New York Times*, 9 November 1953; McCoy, *The Politics of Heroin in Southeast Asia*, 139; Paul H. Gore-Booth (Rangoon) to FO, 16 November 1953, FO 371/106693, PRO.

110. *FRUS, 1952–1954*, 12:173. Donovan, too, seems to have doubted Taipei's commitment to the evacuation. Donovan to DS, 23 November 1953, RG 84, FSP, Taipei, box 3, WNRC; Wallinger to FO, 29 November 1953, FO 371/106694, PRO.

111. Gardner, *Approaching Vietnam*, 123–26, 135–37; *FRUS, 1952–1954*, 13:356, 359.

112. *FRUS, 1952–1954*, 13:429–30, 468–69, 490–91, 512.

113. Ibid., 519 (quotation); Robert McClintock (Saigon) to DS, 25 March 1953, RG 59, 751G.5/3–2553, NA.

114. McClintock to DS, 14 May 1953, RG 59, 751G.00/5–1453, and Paul J. Strum (Hanoi) to DS, 16 May 1953, RG 59, 751G.00/4–1653, NA. See also McCoy, *The Politics of Heroin in Southeast Asia*, 96.

115. M. G. L. Joy (Saigon) to FO, 10 June 1953, and British legation (Saigon) to SEAD, 3 July 1953, FO 371/106801, PRO; *Le Monde*, 29 May 1953; Lloyd M. Rives (Vientiane) to DS, 17 July 1953, RG 59, 851H.53/7–1753, NA.

116. McCoy, *The Politics of Heroin in Southeast Asia*, 96, 102–6; McAlister, "Mountain Minorities and the Viet Minh," 803–7, 810–28.

117. Spector, *Advice and Support*, 174–75; *FRUS, 1952–1954*, 13:628; Heath to DS, 9 July 1953, RG 59, 751G.5/7–953, NA; *FRUS, 1952–1954*, 5:1597–98, 1689. See also Report of Joint U.S. Military Mission to Indochina, 15 July 1953, RG 59, 711.5851G/7–1553, NA.

118. Report of the Joint U.S. Military Mission to Indochina, 15 July 1953, RG 59, 711.5851G/7–1553, especially 146–56, NA; McCoy, *The Politics of Heroin in Southeast Asia*, 96, 102. Lansdale, *In the Midst of Wars*, 109–13, is misleading on the issue of opium in Laos.

119. Graves to FO, 27 January 1953, FO 371/106789, PRO; "Major Non-Communist Political Parties and Religious Armed Groups in the State of Vietnam," 28 September 1953, RG 59, OIR 6431, NA; Lansdale, *In the Midst of Wars*, 147–48.

120. *FRUS, 1952–1954*, 5:1809–11, 1817, 1828–29; Gardner, *Approaching Vietnam*, 150; James, *Eden*, 374–75.

121. Compare O'Daniel's fairly positive follow-up report of 19 November in RG 59, 711.5851G/11–1953, NA, with Spector, *Advice and Support*, 179–81.

122. Anslinger's remarks at the eighth session of the CND, 1 April 1953, Anslinger Papers, box 1, PL/PSU.

123. Musto, *The American Disease*, 230–32; DS to Harrington, 27 April 1953, RG 59, 340.1 AH/4–2753, and Harold G. Kissick to Anslinger, 7 May 1953, RG 59, 340.1 AH/7–753, NA; Rodney Gilbert to Donovan, 20 January 1953, Donovan Papers, box 9a, MHI (quotation). In September 1954 Gilbert, an ardent critic of the PRC, wrote an article, entitled "Dope from Red China," for the *American Legion Magazine*, which the Committee of One Million reprinted and distributed.

124. May, "Narcotic Drug Control," 498, 523–29; *Yearbook of the United Nations*, 484–88; Memorandum by Dulles to Eisenhower, 11 May 1953, RG 59, 340.1 AH/5–1153, and Memorandum by Kotschnig, 24 June 1953, RG 59, 340.1 AH/6–2453, NA. By September 1954, the United States had ratified the opium protocol.

125. J. H. Walker (HO) to CO, 8 March 1954, FO 371/112505, PRO.

126. *Yearbook of the United Nations*, 475–76; *Washington News*, 23 November 1953 (quotation); *South China Morning Post*, 25 November 1953; Morlock to Ruth E. Bacon (Bureau of Far Eastern Affairs), 8 January 1954, RG 59, 102.14/1–854, NA. For more charges by Anslinger against the PRC, see Morlock, "Recent Developments in the International Control of Narcotics," 367–68; Senate, Subcommittee of the Committee on Foreign Relations, *Hearing on International Opium Control*, 8–9.

127. Walker to H. F. Bartlett (CO), 14 January 1954, and Governor's office (Hong Kong) to the secretary of state for colonies, 14 December 1953, FO 371/112506, PRO; British embassy (Bangkok) to SEAD, 20 November 1953, FO 371/106920, PRO.

128. F. R. MacGinnis (Washington) to SEAD, 15 January 1954, and MacGinnis to UN Department, FO, 22 January 1954, FO 371/112506, PRO.

129. Minute by Bartlett, 21 January 1954, ibid.; Chen Hsien-chiu, director, Taiwan Provincial Police, to [George] Kung-chao Yeh, minister of foreign affairs, 15 June 1954, RG 84, FSP, Taipei, box 9, WNRC; Walker to Miss D. G. Hallet (CO), 2 February 1954, FO 371/112506, PRO.

130. Anslinger's remarks at the ninth session of the CND, 4 May 1954, RG 46, Records of the U.S. Senate Judiciary Committee, Subcommittee on Narcotics, 85 Cong., box 29, NA. Following his address, the FO minuted: "Mr. Anslinger is adopting a more reasonable attitude over the Hong Kong question. Mr. Walker has no doubt been able to make good use of the evidence from Hong Kong of the deplorable lack of cooperation from the Americans." FO minute, 4 May 1954, ibid.

131. John P. Weitzel, special assistant to the secretary of the Treasury, to Bernard M. Shanley, special counsel to the president, 14 April 1954, CF, OF, box 600, Eisenhower Papers, DDEL; Bartlett to FO, 10 February 1954, Walker to Bartlett, 19 February 1954, and CO minute, 23 February 1954, FO 371/112505, PRO.

132. Humphrey Trevelyan (Peking) to Colin T. Grave (FO), 11 October 1954, FO 371/112506, PRO; Hughes, *Foreign Devil*, 249.

133. Gerald Warner (Bangkok) to DS, 4 February 1954, RG 59, 792.00/2–454, and Rufus Z. Smith (Chiengmai) to DS, 8 March 1954, RG 59, 790B.00/3–854, NA; Sebald, "Burma Diary," 409–10, 519–20 n. 35, Sebald Papers, HIWRP; Political report for March 1954, 18 May 1954, RG 59, 790B.00/5–1854, NA; British embassy (Bangkok) to SEAD, 30 June 1954, FO 371/111967, and FO minute, [?]August 1954, FO 371/111968, PRO.

134. Elmer B. Staats (OCB) to James S. Lay, Jr., executive secretary, NSC, 15 July 1954, White House Office, NSC Staff: Papers, 1948–61, OCB, Central Files Series, box 55, Eisenhower Papers, DDEL.

135. *FRUS, 1952–1954*, 12:704–8, 738–40.

136. McClintock to DS, 18 May 1954, RG 59, 851G.53/3–1854, NA.

137. Anslinger to Morlock, 10 August 1954, enclosing Speer to Anslinger, 7 July 1954, RG 59, 851G.53/8–1054, and Francis E. Melvy (Saigon) to DS, 28 September 1954, RG 59, 851G.53/9–2854, NA.

138. Anslinger's remarks at the tenth session of the CND, 18 April–13 May 1955, RG 46, Records of the U.S. Senate Judiciary Committee, Subcommittee on Narcotics, 85 Cong., box 29, NA.

139. Memorandum by John E. MacDonald, executive secretary, OCB, 18 January 1954, Jackson Records, and Memorandum by Kenneth P. Landon, chairman, OCB working group on PSB D-23, 17 January 1954, box 1, DDEL; Sebald, "Burma Diary," 375–76, 391, Sebald Papers, HIWRP; Wallinger to Eden, 18 January 1954, FO 371/

112261, PRO; 188th meeting of the NSC, 11 March 1954, Ann Whitman File, NSC Series, box 5, DDEL (quotation).

140. Donovan to Eisenhower, 17 May 1954, Donovan Papers, box 137b, MHI. In agreeing to take the post in Thailand, Donovan limited his term to one year.

141. Note on the situation in Indochina and Siam following the Geneva settlement by the Office of the Commissioner-General for the United Kingdom in Southeast Asia, 7 August 1954, box 9b, ibid.

142. *Senate Foreign Relations Committee (Historical Series)*, 51, 112–13; *FRUS, 1952–1954*, 12:713–20.

143. *Senate Foreign Relations Committee (Historical Series)*, 269, 274–75.

144. Ibid., 269; Gardner, *Approaching Vietnam*, 275, 277; Kahin, *Intervention*, 48–50. That Eisenhower and Dulles tended to hold Great Britain responsible for exacerbating the Western situation in Indochina shows how stress impairs the cognitive abilities of policymakers. See George, *Presidential Decisionmaking in Foreign Policy*, 49. Anti-British feeling ran high in the American popular press. See "Editorial: Mr. Attlee's Friends."

Conclusion

1. Spence, *The Gate of Heavenly Peace*, 125, 246.

2. Spencer and Navaratnam, *Drug Abuse in East Asia*, 8–19.

3. Popkin, *The Rational Peasant*, 136.

4. McCoy, *The Politics of Heroin in Southeast Asia*, 78 and passim.

5. *Washington Post*, 13 June, 6 December 1988; House, Committee on Foreign Affairs, *Narcotics Review in Southeast/Southwest Asia*, 7–8.

6. Walker, "Drug Control and the Issue of Culture in American Foreign Relations," 371; House Committee on Foreign Affairs, *Narcotics Review in Southeast/Southwest Asia*, 6–7, 11–12, 15, 44–45, 94; *New York Times*, 7 September 1988; Lifschultz, "Bush, Drugs, and Pakistan"; Walker, *Drug Control in the Americas*, 216–20.

7. Compellence is a variant of the strategy of deterrence. It shares similar assumptions about the roots of adversarial relationships and how they should be handled. In that sense, compellence suffers from the same liabilities as deterrence. See, especially, the work of Lebow and Stein; George and Smoke, *Deterrence in American Foreign Policy*.

8. Jervis, *Perception and Misperception in International Politics*, 409–10.

BIBLIOGRAPHY

This bibliography is organized as follows:

A. Manuscript Sources
B. Published Official Documents
C. Newspapers
D. Books, Monographs, and Other Published Documents and Papers
E. Articles and Dissertations

A. *Manuscript Sources*

Official Documents

Great Britain
  Kew, Richmond
    Public Record Office
      Foreign Office
        FO 228: China: Embassy and Consular Archives: Correspondence Series I
        FO 371: General Correspondence: Political
        FO 676: China: Embassy and Consular Archives: Correspondence Series II
        FO 800: Private Collections: Ministers and Officials
          #293: Private Papers of Sir Alexander Cadogan
          #297: Private Papers of Sir Hughe Knatchbull-Hugessen
          #299: Private Papers of Lord Inverchapel (Sir Archibald Clark Kerr)
        FO 959: Indochina: Embassy and Consular Archives: Correspondence
        FO 991: Thailand: Embassy and Consular Archives
      War Office
        WO 106: Directorate of Military Operations and Intelligence

  London
    Imperial War Museum
      Foreign Office
        FO 648: International Military Tribunal for the Far East

United States
  Abilene, Kansas
    Dwight D. Eisenhower Library
      Dillon Anderson Oral History
      The Diplomatic Papers of John Moors Cabot (microfilm)
      John Foster Dulles Papers, 1951–59
        Chronological Series
      Dwight D. Eisenhower Papers
        Central Files, Official Files
        White House Office, NSC Staff: Papers, 1948–61, Operations Coordinating
          Board, Central Files Series
        White House Office, Office of the Special Assistant for National Security
          Affairs: Records, 1952–61, NSC Series: Policy Papers Subseries and Brief-
          ing Notes Subseries
      C. D. Jackson Records, 1953–54
      Ann Whitman File
        NSC Series
  Carlisle Barracks, Pennsylvania
    Military History Institute, U.S. Army
      William J. Donovan Papers
  Independence, Missouri
    Harry S. Truman Library
      Harry J. Anslinger Papers
      John F. Cady Oral History
      Edwin W. Martin Oral History
      John F. Melby Papers
      Arthur R. Ringwalt Oral History
      John Stewart Service Oral History (copy from the Bancroft Library, University
        of California, Berkeley)
      John W. Snyder Papers
      Harry S. Truman Papers
        President's Secretary's File, Intelligence File
        President's Secretary's File, Subject File
  Suitland, Maryland
    Washington National Records Center
      Record Group 84: Foreign Service Posts of the Department of State
      Record Group 169: Foreign Economic Administration
        Records of the Office of the Administrator, General Records
      Record Group 286: Agency for International Development, Economic Coop-
        eration Administration
        Office of the Deputy Administrator, Country Subject Files, 1950–51

Productivity and Technical Assistance Division, Office of the Director,
  Country Subject Files, 1949–52
Record Group 319: Army Intelligence Project Decimal File, 1941–45
Record Group 319: Army Staff, Assistant Chief of Staff for Intelligence (G-2)
  Files
Record Group 319: Central Intelligence Agency, Intelligence Document Files
Record Group 331: Supreme Commander for the Allied Powers
  Adjutant General's Section, Operations Division, Mail and Records Branch
Washington, D.C.
  Center for Naval History
    China Repository
    Vice Admiral Milton E. Miles, USN, Papers
    Thomas Eliot Weil Papers
  Manuscript Division, Library of Congress
    Nelson Trusler Johnson Papers
  National Archives
    Record Group 46: Records of the U.S. Senate Judiciary Committee, Subcom-
      mittee on Narcotics
    Record Group 56: Department of the Treasury
      General Records, Federal Bureau of Narcotics, 1941–50
    Record Group 59: Department of State
      Division [Office] of Chinese Affairs
      Division [Office] of Philippine and Southeast Asian Affairs
      General Records of the Department of State, Decimal Files
      Lot File 55 D 282: Records of the Assistant Secretary of State for Far East-
        ern Affairs (John Moore Allison), 1950–52
      Lot File 55 D 607: Division of Far Eastern Affairs, Name File of Suspected
        Narcotics Traffickers, 1907–42
      Lot File 57 D 472: Records Relating to the Mutual Assistance Program (Far
        East), 1949–54
      Research and Analysis Branch, Intelligence Reports, 1941–61
      ———, Office of Intelligence and Research
      ———, Office of Strategic Services
    Record Group 84: U.S. Mission to the United Nations, 1945–49
    Record Group 179: Combined Production and Resources Board
    Record Group 179: War Production Board
      Policy Documentation File
    Record Group 218: Joint Chiefs of Staff
      Chairman's File, Admiral William D. Leahy, 1942–48
    Record Group 226: Office of Strategic Services Files
    Record Group 234: Reconstruction Finance Corporation, Defense Supplies
      Corporation

Record Group 319: Army Staff, Army Chief of Staff
Intelligence, Intelligence Document Files
Record Group 319: Center for Military History Monograph Series

Private Collections

Great Britain
London
School of Oriental and African Studies, University of London
Conference of Missionary Societies in Great Britain and Ireland (CBMS)

United States
New York, New York
Butler Library, Columbia University
K. P. Chen Private Papers
China Missionary Oral History Project, Claremont Graduate School (copy)
Merrill Steele Ady Oral History
Rowland McLean Cross Oral History
Alfred Dixon Heininger Oral History
Dr. Clarence H. Holleman Oral History
Chinese Oral History Project of the East Asia Institute
Liu Jui-heng Papers
The Reminiscences of Chang Fa-k'uei
The Reminiscences of Ch'en Kuang-fu (K. P. Chen)
The Reminiscences of Ho Lien (Franklin L. Ho)
The Reminiscences of K'ung Hsiang-hsi (H. H. Kung)
The Reminiscences of Li Huang
The Reminiscences of General Li Tsung-jen
The Reminiscences of Dr. Wu Kuo-cheng (K. C. Wu)
The Reminiscences of Yi-yun Shen Huang
V. K. Wellington Koo Papers
Oral History Research Office
The Reminiscences of Herbert L. May
Foreign Policy Association
Minutes of the Executive Committee
Office Reports

Palo Alto, California
Hoover Institution on War, Revolution, and Peace
The Memoirs of John Kenneth Caldwell
Victor Hoo Chi-tsai Papers
Stanley K. Hornbeck Papers

Willys R. Peck Papers
William J. Sebald Papers
   "Burma Diary (1952–1954): Some Unlearned Lessons in Southeast Asia"
T. V. Soong Papers
Arthur N. Young Papers

Princeton, New Jersey
   Seeley G. Mudd Library, Princeton University
      Edwin W. Kemmerer Papers
      John V. A. MacMurray Collection
      Livingston T. Merchant Papers
      Karl Lott Rankin Papers
      Whiting Willauer Papers

University Park, Pennsylvania
   Pattee Library, Pennsylvania State University
      Harry J. Anslinger Papers

Wheaton, Illinois
   Billy Graham Center Archives, Wheaton College
      The Reverend Raymond Bates Buker, Jr., Interviews
      The Helen Irvin and Malcolm Maurice Sawyer Interviews

Other

William J. vanden Heuval telephone interview with author, 12 January 1989

B. *Published Official Documents*

Burma

Government of the Union of Burma. Ministry of Information. *Kuomintang Aggression against Burma*. Rangoon, 1953.

Great Britain

British Documents on the Origins of the War, 1898–1914. Edited by G. P. Gooch and Harold Temperly. Vol. 10, *The Last Years of Peace*, pt. 2. London: His Majesty's Stationery Office, 1938.
Foreign Office. *Documents on British Foreign Policy, 1919–1939*. 2d ser., vol. 11, *Far Eastern Affairs, October 13, 1932–June 3, 1933*. Edited by W. N. Medlicott, Douglas Dakin, and M. E. Lambert. London: Her Majesty's Stationery Office, 1970.

————. *Documents on British Foreign Policy, 1919–1939.* 2d ser., vol. 20, *Far Eastern Affairs, May 20, 1933–November 5, 1936.* Edited by W. N. Medlicott and Douglas Dakin, assisted by Gillian Bennett. London: Her Majesty's Stationery Office, 1984.

————. *Documents on British Foreign Policy, 1919–1939.* 2d ser., vol. 21, *Far Eastern Affairs, November 6, 1936–July 27, 1938.* Edited by W. N. Medlicott and Douglas Dakin, assisted by Gillian Bennett. London: Her Majesty's Stationery Office, 1984.

————. *The Opium Trade, 1910–1941.* FO 415: Correspondence Respecting Opium, PRO. 6 vols. Wilmington, Del.: Scholarly Resources, 1974.

Parliamentary Debates, House of Commons, Official Report, 5th ser.

Washington Dispatches, 1941–1945: Weekly Political Reports from the British Embassy. Edited by H. G. Nicholas. Chicago: University of Chicago Press, 1981.

League of Nations

Advisory Committee on the Traffic in Opium and Other Dangerous Drugs (Opium Advisory Committee). *Minutes of the Sixth Session Held at Geneva, August 4–14, 1924.* C.397.M.146.1924.XI. Geneva, 1942.

————. *Minutes of the Thirteenth Session Held at Geneva, January 20–February 14, 1930.* C.121.M.39.1930.XI. Geneva, 1930.

————. *Minutes of the Fourteenth Session Held at Geneva, January 9–February 7, 1931.* Vol. 1. C.88.M.34.1931.XI. Geneva, 1931.

————. *Minutes of the Seventeenth Session Held at Geneva, October 30–November 9, 1933.* C.661.M.316.1933.XI. Geneva, 1933.

————. *Minutes of the Eighteenth Session Held at Geneva, May 18–June 2, 1934.* C.317.M.142.1934.XI. Geneva, 1934.

————. *Minutes of the Twenty-first Session Held at Geneva, May 18–June 5, 1936.* C.290.M.176.1936.XI. Geneva, 1936.

————. *Minutes of the Twenty-second Session Held at Geneva, May 18–June 5, 1937.* C.315.M.211.1937.XI. Geneva, 1937.

————. *Minutes of the Twenty-third Session Held at Geneva, June 7–24, 1938.* C.249.M.147.1938.XI. Geneva, 1938.

————. *Minutes of the Twenty-fourth Session Held at Geneva, May 15–June 12, 1939.* C.209.M.136.1939.XI. Geneva, 1939.

Commission of Enquiry into the Control of Opium-Smoking in the Far East. *Report to the Council.* Vol. 1, *Report with Comparative Tables, Maps, and Illustrations.* C.635.M.254.1930.XI. Geneva, 1930.

First Geneva Opium Conference, November 3, 1924 to February 11, 1925: Minutes and Annexes. C.684.M.244.1924.XI. Geneva, 1925.

Records of the Second Geneva Opium Conference, November 17, 1924 to February 19, 1925. 2 vols. C.760.M.260.1924.XI. Geneva, 1925.

Traffic in Opium and Other Dangerous Drugs: Control of Opium Smoking in the Far East: Note by the Secretary General. A.40(a).1928.XI. Geneva, 1928.

United Nations

Commission on Narcotic Drugs. *Abolition of Opium Smoking in the Far East (26 April 1950)*. E/CN.7/193. Lake Success, N.Y, 1950.

―――. *Summary Record of the Third Session, 3–22 May 1948*. E/CN.7/155. Lake Success, N.Y., 1948.

―――. *Summary Record of the Fifth Session, One Hundred and Fourth Meeting, 4 December 1950*. E/CN.7/SR.104. Lake Success, N.Y., 1950.

Yearbook of the United Nations, 1953. New York: Columbia University Press in cooperation with the United Nations, 1954.

United States

Congressional Record. House of Representatives, 78 Cong., 2 sess., 1944.

The Pentagon Papers: The Defense Department History of United States Policymaking on Vietnam. The Senator Gravel Ed. Vols. 1–2. Boston: Beacon Press, 1971.

Philippine Commission. Opium Investigation Committee. *Use of Opium and Traffic Therein: Message from the President of the United States, Transmitting the Report of the Committee Appointed by the Philippine Commission to Investigate the Use of Opium and Traffic Therein. . . .* 59 Cong., 1 sess., S. Doc. 265. Washington, D.C.: Government Printing Office, 1906.

U.S. Congress. House. Committee on Foreign Affairs. *Hearing on Narcotics Review in Southeast/Southwest Asia, the Middle East, and Africa*. 100 Cong., 2 sess., 15 March 1988. Washington, D.C.: Government Printing Office, 1988.

―――. ―――. Select Committee on Narcotics Abuse and Control. *Report of a Study Mission to Korea, Thailand, Burma, Singapore, Malaysia, Indonesia, and Hawaii (14–25 January 1988)*. 100 Cong., 2 sess. Washington, D.C.: Government Printing Office, 1988.

―――. Senate. *Executive Sessions of the Senate Foreign Relations Committee (Historical Series)*. Vol. 6, 83 Cong., 2 sess., 1954. Washington, D.C.: Government Printing Office, 1977.

―――. ―――. Subcommittee of the Committee on Foreign Relations. *Hearing on International Opium Control*. 83 Cong., 2 sess., 17 July 1954. Washington, D.C.: Government Printing Office, 1954.

U.S. Department of State. *Papers Relating to the Foreign Relations of the United States, 1906*. Pt. 1. Washington, D.C.: Government Printing Office, 1909.

―――. *Papers Relating to the Foreign Relations of the United States, 1907*. Pt. 1. Washington, D.C.: Government Printing Office, 1910.

―――. *Papers Relating to the Foreign Relations of the United States, 1908*. Washington, D.C.: Government Printing Office, 1912.

―――. *Papers Relating to the Foreign Relations of the United States, 1909*. Washington, D.C.: Government Printing Office, 1914.

————. *Papers Relating to the Foreign Relations of the United States, 1913.* Washington, D.C.: Government Printing Office, 1920.

————. *Papers Relating to the Foreign Relations of the United States, 1915.* Washington, D.C.: Government Printing Office, 1924.

————. *Papers Relating to the Foreign Relations of the United States, 1917.* Washington, D.C.: Government Printing Office, 1926.

————. *Papers Relating to the Foreign Relations of the United States: The Paris Peace Conference, 1919.* Vol. 4. Washington, D.C.: Government Printing Office, 1943.

————. *Papers Relating to the Foreign Relations of the United States, 1926.* Vol. 1. Washington, D.C.: Government Printing Office, 1941.

————. *Papers Relating to the Foreign Relations of the United States, 1929.* Vol. 1. Washington, D.C.: Government Printing Office, 1943.

————. *Papers Relating to the Foreign Relations of the United States: Japan, 1931–1941.* 2 vols. Washington, D.C.: Government Printing Office, 1943.

————. *Papers Relating to the Foreign Relations of the United States, 1935.* Vol. 3, *The Far East.* Washington, D.C.: Government Printing Office, 1953.

————. *Papers Relating to the Foreign Relations of the United States, 1936.* Vol. 4, *The Far East.* Washington, D.C.: Government Printing Office, 1954.

————. *Papers Relating to the Foreign Relations of the United States, 1937.* Vol. 1, *General.* Washington, D.C.: Government Printing Office, 1954.

————. *Papers Relating to the Foreign Relations of the United States, 1938.* Vol. 4, *The Far East.* Washington, D.C.: Government Printing Office, 1955.

————. *Papers Relating to the Foreign Relations of the United States, 1939.* Vol. 4, *The Far East, the Near East, and Africa.* Washington, D.C.: Government Printing Office, 1955.

————. *Foreign Relations of the United States, 1940.* Vol. 4, *The Far East.* Washington, D.C.: Government Printing Office, 1955.

————. *Foreign Relations of the United States, 1941.* Vol. 5, *The Far East.* Washington, D.C.: Government Printing Office, 1956.

————. *Foreign Relations of the United States, 1944.* Vol. 6, *China.* Washington, D.C.: Government Printing Office, 1967.

————. *Foreign Relations of the United States, 1948.* Vol. 6, *The Far East and Australasia.* Washington, D.C.: Government Printing Office, 1974.

————. *Foreign Relations of the United States, 1949.* Vol. 7, *The Far East and Australasia,* pt. 1. Washington, D.C.: Government Printing Office, 1976.

————. *Foreign Relations of the United States, 1950.* Vol. 6, *East Asia and the Pacific.* Washington, D.C.: Government Printing Office, 1976.

————. *Foreign Relations of the United States, 1950.* Vol. 1, *National Security Affairs; Foreign Economic Policy.* Vol. 3, *Western Europe.* Washington, D.C.: Government Printing Office, 1977.

————. *Foreign Relations of the United States, 1951.* Vol. 6, pts. 1–2, *Asia and the Pacific.* Washington, D.C.: Government Printing Office, 1977.

————. *Foreign Relations of the United States, 1951.* Vol. 1, *National Security Affairs; Foreign Economic Policy.* Washington, D.C.: Government Printing Office, 1979.

————. *Foreign Relations of the United States, 1951.* Vol. 7, *Korea and China,* pt. 2. Washington, D.C.: Government Printing Office, 1983.

————. *Foreign Relations of the United States, 1952–1954.* Vol. 5, *Western European Security,* pt. 2. Washington, D.C.: Government Printing Office, 1983.

————. *Foreign Relations of the United States, 1952–1954.* Vol. 12, *East Asia and the Pacific,* pt. 2. Washington, D.C.: Government Printing Office, 1987.

————. *Foreign Relations of the United States, 1952–1954.* Vol. 13, *Indochina,* pt. 1. Washington, D.C.: Government Printing Office, 1982.

U.S. Department of the Treasury. Federal Bureau of Narcotics. *Traffic in Opium and Other Dangerous Drugs for the Year Ended December 31, 1933.* Washington, D.C.: Government Printing Office, 1934.

————. *Traffic in Opium and Other Dangerous Drugs for the Year Ended December 31, 1934.* Washington, D.C.: Government Printing Office, 1935.

————. *Traffic in Opium and Other Dangerous Drugs for the Year Ended December 31, 1936.* Washington, D.C.: Government Printing Office, 1937.

————. *Traffic in Opium and Other Dangerous Drugs for the Year Ended December 31, 1937.* Washington, D.C.: Government Printing Office, 1938.

C. Newspapers

Atlanta Constitution, 1945

Bangkok Post, 1950

Central China Post (Hankow), 1923, 1934

China Press Weekly, 1935

China Weekly Review, 1936–37

Christian Science Monitor, 1938

Honolulu Star-Bulletin, 1990

Japan Advertiser, 1937

Japan Chronicle, 1935

Le Monde (Paris), 1953

London Sunday Observer, 1952

Manchester Guardian, 1937

New York Herald Tribune, 1929

New York Times, 1937, 1942, 1951, 1953, 1988

North-China Daily News, 1915, 1918, 1930, 1935–38

North China Herald, 1918, 1928, 1930, 1933–34, 1936–37

Peiping Chronicle, 1934–37

Peiping News, 1937

Peking & Tientsin Times, 1922, 1931–33, 1935, 1937–38

Shanghai Evening Post and Mercury, 1931–32, 1934–38
South China Morning Post (Hong Kong), 1937, 1953
Washington Herald, 1934
Washington News, 1953
Washington Post, 1944, 1948, 1988
Washington Star, 1942

D. Books, Monographs, and Other Published Documents and Papers

Acheson, Dean. *Present at the Creation: My Years in the State Department.* New York: W. W. Norton & Company, 1969.

Adams, Frederick C. *Economic Diplomacy: The Export-Import Bank and American Foreign Policy, 1934–1939.* Columbia: University of Missouri Press, 1976.

Adams, Nina, and Alfred W. McCoy, eds. *Laos: War and Revolution.* New York: Harper & Row, 1970.

Allison, Graham T. *Essence of Decision: Explaining the Cuban Missile Crisis.* Boston: Little, Brown and Company, 1971.

Allison, John M. *Ambassador from the Prairie; or, Allison Wonderland.* Boston: Houghton Mifflin, 1973.

Anderson, Terry H. *The United States, Great Britain, and the Cold War, 1944–1947.* Columbia: University of Missouri Press, 1981.

Anslinger, Harry J., and Will Oursler. *The Murderers: The Shocking Story of the Narcotic Gangs.* New York: Farrar, Straus and Cudahy, 1961.

———, and William F. Tompkins. *The Traffic in Narcotics.* New York: Funk & Wagnalls Company, 1953.

L'Association culturelle pour le Salut du Viêt-Nam. *Témoignages et Documents français Rélatifs à la Colonisation française au Viêt-Nam.* [1945].

Attlee, C. R. *As It Happened.* New York: The Viking Press, 1954.

Bachrack, Stanley D. *The Committee of One Million: "China Lobby" Politics, 1953–1971.* New York: Columbia University Press, 1976.

Barnett, Correlli. *The Collapse of British Power.* London: Eyre Methuen, 1972.

Barnhart, Michael A. *Japan Prepares for Total War: The Search for Economic Security, 1919–1941.* Ithaca: Cornell University Press, 1987.

Bashford, James W. *China: An Interpretation.* 2d ed. New York and Cincinnati: The Abingdon Press, 1916.

Belden, Jack. *China Shakes the World.* New York: Monthly Review Press, 1970.

Berridge, Virginia, and Griffith Edwards. *Opium and the People: Opiate Use in Nineteenth-Century England.* London and New York: Allen Lane/St. Martin's Press, 1981.

Billingsley, Phil. *Bandits in Republican China.* Stanford: Stanford University Press, 1988.

Blaufarb, Douglas S. *The Counterinsurgency Era: U.S. Doctrine and Performance.* New York: The Free Press, 1977.

Blum, John M., ed. *The Price of Vision: The Diary of Henry A. Wallace, 1942–1946.* Boston: Houghton Mifflin, 1973.

Blum, Robert M. *Drawing the Line: The Origin of the American Commitment in East Asia.* New York: W. W. Norton & Company, 1982.

Board of Foreign Missions of the Methodist Episcopal Church. *Annual Report . . . for the Year 1907.* New York: Board of Foreign Missions, 1908.

———. *Annual Report . . . for the Year 1908.* New York: Board of Foreign Missions, 1909.

———. *Annual Report . . . for the Year 1917.* New York: Board of Foreign Missions, 1918.

———. *Annual Report . . . for the Year 1918.* New York: Board of Foreign Missions, 1919.

———. *Annual Report . . . for the Year 1920.* New York: Board of Foreign Missions, 1921.

———. *Annual Report . . . for the Year 1924.* New York: Board of Foreign Missions, 1925.

———. *Annual Report . . . for the Year 1925.* New York: Board of Foreign Missions, 1926.

Bohlen, Charles E., with the editorial assistance of Robert H. Phelps. *Witness to History, 1929–1969.* New York: W. W. Norton & Company, 1973.

Borden, William S. *The Pacific Alliance: United States Foreign Economic Policy and Japanese Trade Recovery, 1947–1955.* Madison: University of Wisconsin Press, 1984.

Borg, Dorothy. *American Policy and the Chinese Revolution, 1925–1928.* New York: Institute of Pacific Relations and The Macmillan Company, 1947.

———. *The United States and the Far Eastern Crisis of 1933–1938: From the Manchurian Incident through the Initial Stage of the Undeclared Sino-Japanese War.* Cambridge: Harvard University Press, 1964.

———, and Waldo Heinrichs. *Uncertain Years: Chinese-American Relations, 1947–1950.* New York: Columbia University Press, 1980.

———, and Shumpei Okamoto, with Dale A. K. Finlayson. *Pearl Harbor as History: Japanese-American Relations, 1931–1941.* New York: Columbia University Press, 1973.

Boyle, John Hunter. *China and Japan at War, 1937–1945: The Politics of Collaboration.* Stanford: Stanford University Press, 1972.

Brackman, Arnold C. *The Other Nuremberg: The Untold Story of the Tokyo War Crimes Trials.* New York: William Morrow and Company, 1987.

Bruner, Katherine F., John K. Fairbank, and Richard J. Smith, eds. *Entering China's Service: Robert Hart's Journals, 1854–1863.* Cambridge: Harvard University Press, 1986.

Bruun, Kettil, Lynn Pan, and Ingemar Rexed. *The Gentlemen's Club: International Control of Drugs and Alcohol.* Chicago: University of Chicago Press, 1975.

Buhite, Russell D. *Nelson T. Johnson and American Policy toward China, 1925–1941.* East Lansing: Michigan State University Press, 1968.

———. *Patrick J. Hurley and American Foreign Policy.* Ithaca: Cornell University Press, 1973.

———. *Soviet-American Relations in Asia, 1945–1954.* Norman: University of Oklahoma Press, 1981.

Bullock, Alan. *Ernest Bevin: Foreign Secretary.* New York: W. W. Norton & Company, 1983.

Bunge, Frederica M., ed. *Thailand: A Country Study.* 5th ed. Washington, D.C.: U.S. Department of the Army, Government Printing Office, 1981.

Bunker, Gerald E. *The Peace Conspiracy: Wang Ching-wei and the China War, 1937–1941.* Cambridge: Harvard University Press, 1972.

Burns, Richard Dean, and Edward M. Bennett, eds. *Diplomats in Crisis: United States–Chinese–Japanese Relations, 1919–1941.* Santa Barbara: ABC-Clio, 1974.

Burridge, Trevor. *Clement Attlee: A Political Biography.* London: Jonathan Cape, 1985.

Butow, Robert J. C. *Tojo and the Coming of War.* Stanford: Stanford University Press, 1961.

Cady, John F. *The History of Post-War Southeast Asia: Independence Problems.* Athens: Ohio University Press, 1974.

———. *The United States and Burma.* Cambridge: Harvard University Press, 1976.

Cameron, Meribeth E. *The Reform Movement in China, 1898–1912.* Stanford: Stanford University Press, 1931.

Chan, F. Gilbert, and Thomas H. Etzold, eds. *China in the 1920s: Nationalism and Revolution.* New York: New Viewpoints, 1976.

Chang Hsin-pao. *Commissioner Lin and the Opium War.* New York: W. W. Norton & Company, 1970.

Chang Kuo-t'ao. *The Autobiography of Chang Kuo-t'ao.* Vol. 2, *The Rise of the Chinese Communist Party, 1928–1938.* Translated by R. A. Berton. Lawrence: University Press of Kansas, 1972.

Ch'en, Jerome. *Yuan Shih-k'ai: Brutus Assumes the Purple.* London: Allen & Unwin, Ltd., 1961.

Chen, King C. *Vietnam and China, 1938–1954.* Princeton: Princeton University Press, 1969.

Ch'i Hsi-sheng. *Warlord Politics in China, 1916–1928.* Stanford: Stanford University Press, 1976.

China Centenary Missionary Conference Records: Report of the Great Conference Held at Shanghai, April 5th to May 8th, 1907. New York: American Tract Society, [1907].

The China White Paper, August 1949. Introduction by Lyman P. Van Slyke. 2 vols. Stanford: Stanford University Press, 1967.

Clifford, Nicholas R. *Retreat from China: British Policy in the Far East, 1937–1941.* Seattle: University of Washington Press, 1967.

Clubb, O. Edmund. *Twentieth-Century China.* New York: Columbia University Press, 1964.

———. *Communism in China as Reported from Hankow in 1932.* New York: Columbia University Press, 1968.

———. *China and Russia: The "Great Game."* New York: Columbia University Press, 1971.

———. *The Witness and I.* New York: Columbia University Press, 1974.

Clubb, Oliver E., Jr. *The Effect of Chinese Nationalist Military Activities in Burma on Burmese Foreign Policy.* Santa Monica: The Rand Corporation, P-1595-RC, 1959.

———. *The United States and the Sino-Soviet Bloc in Southeast Asia.* Washington, D.C.: The Brookings Institution, 1962.

Coble, Parks M., Jr. *The Shanghai Capitalists and the Nationalist Government, 1927–1937.* 2d ed. Cambridge: Harvard University Press, 1986.

Cochran, Sherman, and Andrew C. K. Hsieh, with Janis Cochran, eds. and trans. *One Day in China, May 21, 1936.* New Haven and London: Yale University Press, 1983.

Cohen, Warren I. *America's Response to China: An Interpretive History of Sino-American Relations.* New York: John Wiley & Sons, 1971.

———. *The Chinese Connection: Roger S. Greene, Thomas W. Lamont, George E. Sokolsky, and American–East Asian Relations.* New York: Columbia University Press, 1978.

———, ed. *New Frontiers in American–East Asian Relations: Essays Presented to Dorothy Borg.* New York: Columbia University Press, 1983.

Craigie, Robert. *Behind the Japanese Mask.* London: Hutchinson & Company, 1946.

Crowley, James B. *Japan's Quest for Autonomy: National Security and Foreign Policy, 1930–1938.* Princeton: Princeton University Press, 1966.

Dai, Bingham. *The Commission of Inquiry and Opium Monopoly: A Frank Discussion of the Problem of Opium-smoking in the Far Eastern Colonies of the Foreign Powers.* Shanghai: National Anti-Opium Association, 1928.

Dallek, Robert. *Franklin D. Roosevelt and American Foreign Policy, 1932–1945.* New York: Oxford University Press, 1979.

Davies, John Paton, Jr. *Dragon by the Tail: American, British, Japanese, and Russian Encounters with China and One Another.* New York: W. W. Norton & Company, 1972.

Decoux, Admiral Jean. *A la Barre de L'Indochine: Histoire de mon Gouvernement General (1940–1945).* Paris: Typographie Plon, 1949.

Denby, Charles. *China and Her People.* 2 vols. Boston: L. C. Page & Company, 1905.

Deverall, Richard L-G. *Red China's Dirty Drug War: The Story of the Opium, Heroin, Morphine, and Philopon Traffic.* Tokyo: [Toyoh Printing & Book-binding Co., Ltd.], 1954.

Dilks, David, ed. *The Diaries of Sir Alexander Cadogan, 1938–1945.* London: Cassell & Company, 1971.

Dingman, Roger. *Power in the Pacific: The Origins of Naval Arms Limitations, 1914–1922.* Chicago: University of Chicago Press, 1976.

Dommen, Arthur J. *Conflict in Laos: The Politics of Neutralization.* Rev. ed. New York: Praeger Publishers, 1971.

Dower, John W. *War without Mercy: Race and Power in the Pacific War.* New York: Pantheon Books, 1986.

Dunlop, Richard. *Behind Japanese Lines: With the OSS in Burma.* Chicago: Rand McNally & Company, 1979.

Eastman, Lloyd E. *The Abortive Revolution: China under Nationalist Rule, 1927–1937.* Cambridge: Harvard University Press, 1974.

———. *Seeds of Destruction: Nationalist China in War and Revolution, 1937–1949.* Stanford: Stanford University Press, 1984.

Eden, Anthony [Earl of Avon]. *The Memoirs of Anthony Eden: Full Circle.* Boston: Houghton Mifflin, 1960.

———. *The Memoirs of Anthony Eden: Facing the Dictators.* Boston: Houghton Mifflin, 1962.

———. *The Memoirs of Anthony Eden: The Reckoning.* Boston: Houghton Mifflin, 1965.

Egerton, George W. *Great Britain and the Creation of the League of Nations: Strategy, Politics, and International Organization, 1914–1945.* Chapel Hill: University of North Carolina Press, 1978.

Eisenlohr, L. E. S. *International Narcotics Control.* London: Allen & Unwin, Ltd., 1934.

Emerson, Rupert. *From Empire to Nation: The Rise to Self-assertion of Asian and African Peoples.* Cambridge: Harvard University Press, 1960.

Endicott, Stephen Lyon. *Diplomacy and Enterprise: British China Policy, 1933–1937.* Vancouver: University of British Columbia Press, 1975.

Esherick, Joseph W. *Reform and Revolution in China: The 1911 Revolution in Hunan and Hubei.* Berkeley and Los Angeles: University of California Press, 1976.

———. *The Origins of the Boxer Uprising.* Berkeley and Los Angeles: University of California Press, 1987.

———, ed. *Lost Chance in China: The World War II Dispatches of John S. Service.* New York: Random House, 1974.

Esterline, John H., and Mae H. Esterline. *"How the Dominoes Fell": Southeast Asia in Perspective.* Lanham, Md.: Hamilton Press, 1986.

Fairbank, John King. *Trade and Diplomacy on the China Coast: The Opening of the Treaty Ports, 1842–1854.* Stanford: Stanford University Press, 1969.

———. *The Great Chinese Revolution, 1800–1985.* New York: Harper & Row, 1986.

———, ed. *The Missionary Enterprise in China and America.* Cambridge: Harvard University Press, 1974.

———, ed. *The Cambridge History of China.* Vol. 10, *Late Ch'ing, 1800–1911,* pt. 1. Cambridge and New York: Cambridge University Press, 1978.

————, ed. *The Cambridge History of China*. Vol. 12, *Republican China, 1912–1949*, pt. 1. Cambridge and New York: Cambridge University Press, 1983.

————, Katherine Frost Bruner, and Elizabeth MacLeod Matheson, eds. *The I.G. in Peking: Letters of Robert Hart, Chinese Maritime Customs, 1868–1907*. 2 vols. Cambridge: The Belknap Press of Harvard University Press, 1975.

————, and Albert Feuerwerker, eds. *The Cambridge History of China*. Vol. 13, *Republican China, 1912–1949*, pt. 2. Cambridge and New York: Cambridge University Press, 1986.

————, and Kwang-ching Liu, eds. *The Cambridge History of China*. Vol. 11, *Late Ch'ing, 1800–1911*, pt. 2. Cambridge and New York: Cambridge University Press, 1980.

Fay, Peter Ward. *The Opium War, 1840–1842*. New York: W. W. Norton & Company, 1976.

Feis, Herbert. *The Road to Pearl Harbor*. Princeton: Princeton University Press, 1950.

————. *The China Tangle: The American Effort in China from Pearl Harbor to the Marshall Mission*. Princeton: Princeton University Press, 1953.

————. *Contest over Japan*. New York: W. W. Norton & Company, 1976.

Ferrell, Robert H. *American Diplomacy and the Great Depression: Hoover-Stimson Foreign Policy*. New Haven: Yale University Press, 1957.

————, ed. *Off the Record: The Private Papers of Harry S. Truman*. New York: Harper & Row, 1980.

Foot, Rosemary. *The Wrong War: American Policy and the Dimensions of the Korean Conflict, 1950–1953*. Ithaca: Cornell University Press, 1985.

Forman, Harrison. *Report from Red China*. New York: Henry Holt and Company, 1945.

Gaddis, John Lewis. *Strategies of Containment: A Critical Appraisal of Postwar American National Security Policy*. New York: Oxford University Press, 1982.

————. *The Long Peace: Inquiries into the History of the Cold War*. New York: Oxford University Press, 1987.

Gallicchio, Marc S. *The Cold War Begins in Asia: American East Asia Policy and the Fall of the Japanese Empire*. New York: Columbia University Press, 1988.

Gardner, Lloyd C. *Safe for Democracy: The Anglo-American Response to Revolution, 1913–1923*. New York: Oxford University Press, 1984.

————. *Approaching Vietnam: From World War II through Dienbienphu*. New York: W. W. Norton & Company, 1988.

George, Alexander. *Presidential Decisionmaking in Foreign Policy: The Effective Use of Information and Advice*. Boulder: Westview Press, 1980.

————, and Richard Smoke. *Deterrence in American Foreign Policy: Theory and Practice*. New York: Columbia University Press, 1974.

Gillin, Donald G. *Warlord: Yen Hsi-shan in Shansi Province, 1911–1949*. Princeton: Princeton University Press, 1967.

Girling, John L. S. *Thailand: Society and Politics*. Ithaca: Cornell University Press, 1981.

Greene, Robert W. *Calvary in China*. New York: G. P. Putnam's Sons, 1953.

Gregory, J. S. *Great Britain and the Taipings*. London: Routledge & Kegan Paul, 1969.

Grew, Joseph C. *Ten Years in Japan*. New York: Simon and Schuster, 1944.

————. *Turbulent Era: A Diplomatic Record of Forty Years, 1904–1945*. Edited by Walter Johnson, assisted by Nancy Harvison Hooker. 2 vols. Boston: Houghton Mifflin, 1952.

Grey, Sir Edward [Viscount Grey of Fallodon]. *Twenty-Five Years, 1892–1916*. 2 vols. New York: Frederick A. Stokes, 1925.

Gull, E. M. *British Economic Interests in the Far East*. New York: Institute of Pacific Relations, Oxford University Press, 1943.

Haggie, Paul. *Britannia at Bay: The Defence of the British Empire against Japan, 1931–1941*. New York: Oxford University Press, 1981.

Halifax, The Earl of. *Fulness of Days*. London: Collins, 1957.

Halperin, Morton H., with Priscilla Clapp and Arnold Kanter. *Bureaucratic Politics and Foreign Policy*. Washington, D.C.: The Brookings Institution, 1974.

Hamberger, Gerd. *The Peking Bomb: The Psychochemical War against America*. Translated by Sarah Banks Forman. Washington, D.C.: Robert B. Luce, Inc., 1975.

Hammer, Ellen J. *The Struggle for Indochina*. Stanford: Stanford University Press, 1954.

Harris, Kenneth. *Attlee*. New York: W. W. Norton & Company, 1982.

Harvey, John, ed. *The Diplomatic Diaries of Oliver Hardy, 1937–1940*. New York: St. Martin's Press, 1970.

Heinrichs, Waldo H., Jr. *American Ambassador: Joseph C. Grew and the Development of the United States Diplomatic Tradition*. New York: Oxford University Press, 1986.

Hess, Gary R. *The United States' Emergence as a Southeast Asian Power, 1940–1950*. New York: Columbia University Press, 1987.

[Ho Chi Mihn]. *Ho Chi Minh: Selected Works*. Vols. 2–3. Hanoi: Foreign Languages Publishing House, 1961.

Hughes, Richard. *Foreign Devil: Thirty Years of Reporting in the Far East*. Reprint ed. London: Century Publishing, 1984.

Hull, Cordell. *The Memoirs of Cordell Hull*. 2 vols. New York: The Macmillan Company, 1948.

Hunt, Michael H. *Frontier Defense and the Open Door: Manchuria in Chinese-American Relations, 1895–1911*. New Haven and London: Yale University Press, 1973.

————. *The Making of a Special Relationship: The United States and China to 1914*. New York: Columbia University Press, 1983.

Ienaga, Saburo. *The Pacific War: World War II and the Japanese, 1931–1945*. New York: Pantheon Books, 1978.

Ingram, James C. *Economic Change in Thailand, 1850–1970*. Stanford: Stanford University Press, 1971.

International Anti-Opium Association (Peking). *The War against Opium.* Tientsin: Tientsin Press, Ltd., 1922.

——. *Annual Report of the International Anti-Opium Association, Peking.* Vol. 4. May 1924.

——. *Morphia and Narcotic Drugs in China, Bulletin.* Vol. 5. February 1925.

Iriye, Akira. *After Imperialism: The Search for a New Order in the Far East, 1921–1931.* New York: Atheneum, 1969.

——. *Power and Culture: The Japanese-American War, 1941–1945.* Cambridge: Harvard University Press, 1981.

——, ed. *The Chinese and the Japanese: Essays in Political and Cultural Interactions.* Princeton: Princeton University Press, 1980.

Jackson, Karl D., and Wiwat Mungkandi, eds. *United States–Thailand Relations.* Research Papers and Policy Studies, no. 20. Berkeley: University of California Institute of East Asian Studies, 1986.

James, Robert Rhodes. *Anthony Eden: A Biography.* New York: McGraw-Hill, 1986.

Janis, Irving, and Leon Mann. *Decision Making: A Psychological Analysis of Conflict, Choice, and Commitment.* New York: The Free Press, 1977.

Jen Yu-wen. *The Taiping Revolutionary Movement.* New Haven and London: Yale University Press, 1973.

Jervis, Robert. *Perception and Misperception in International Politics.* Princeton: Princeton University Press, 1976.

——, Richard Ned Lebow, and Janice Gross Stein. *Psychology and Deterrence.* Baltimore: Johns Hopkins University Press, 1985.

Johnson, Chalmers. *Peasant Nationalism and Communist Power: The Emergence of Revolutionary China, 1937–1945.* Stanford: Stanford University Press, 1962.

Jones, F. C. *Shanghai and Tientsin.* San Francisco: American Council, Institute of Pacific Relations, 1940.

——, Hugh Borton, and B. R. Pearn. *The Far East, 1942–1946.* In *Survey of International Affairs, 1939–1946,* edited by Arnold Toynbee, vol. 7. London: Oxford University Press, 1955.

Kahin, George McT. *Intervention: How America Became Involved in Vietnam.* New York: Alfred A. Knopf, 1986.

Kahn, E. J., Jr. *The China Hands: America's Foreign Service Officers and What Befell Them.* New York: The Viking Press, 1975.

Kaku, Sagataro. *Opium Policy in Japan.* Geneva: Albert Kundig, 1924.

Kalicki, J. H. *The Pattern of Sino-American Crises: Political-Military Interactions in the 1950s.* New York: Cambridge University Press, 1975.

Kapp, Robert A. *Szechwan and the Chinese Republic: Provincial Militarism and Central Power, 1911–1938.* New Haven and London: Yale University Press, 1973.

Kennedy, Paul. *The Rise and Fall of the Great Powers: Economic Change and Military Conflict from 1500 to 2000.* New York: Random House, 1987.

Kimball, Warren F., ed. *Churchill and Roosevelt: The Complete Correspondence*. 3 vols., paper ed. Princeton: Princeton University Press, 1987.

Knatchbull-Hugessen, Sir Hughe. *Diplomat in Peace and War*. London: John Murray, 1949.

Koen, Ross Y. *The China Lobby in American Politics*. Edited with an introduction by Richard C. Kagan. New York: Harper & Row, 1974.

Kolko, Gabriel. *Anatomy of a War: Vietnam, the United States, and the Modern Historical Experience*. New York: Pantheon Books, 1985.

Kunstadter, Peter, ed. *Southeast Asian Tribes, Minorities, and Nations*. 2 vols. Princeton: Princeton University Press, 1967.

Kwitny, Jonathan. *The Crimes of Patriots: A True Tale of Dope, Dirty Money, and the CIA*. New York: W. W. Norton & Company, 1987.

LaMotte, Ellen. *Peking Dust*. New York: The Century Company, 1919.

Lansdale, Major General Edward Geary, USAF (Ret.). *In the Midst of Wars: An American's Mission to Southeast Asia*. New York: Harper & Row, 1972.

Larson, Deborah Welch. *Origins of Containment: A Psychological Explanation*. Princeton: Princeton University Press, 1985.

Lary, Diana. *Region and Nation: The Kwangsi Clique in Chinese Politics, 1925–1937*. Cambridge and New York: Cambridge University Press, 1974.

Leary, William M. *Perilous Missions: Civil Air Transport and CIA Covert Operations in Asia*. Tuscaloosa: University of Alabama Press, 1984.

Lebow, Richard Ned. *Between Peace and War: The Nature of International Crises*. Baltimore: Johns Hopkins University Press, 1981.

Lebra, Joyce C. *Japanese-trained Armies in Southeast Asia: Independence and Volunteer Forces in World War II*. New York: Columbia University Press, 1977.

Lee, Bradford A. *Britain and the Sino-Japanese War, 1937–1939: A Study in the Dilemmas of British Decline*. Stanford: Stanford University Press, 1973.

Leutze, James R. *Bargaining for Supremacy: Anglo-American Naval Collaboration, 1937–1941*. Chapel Hill: University of North Carolina Press, 1977.

Lindesmith, Alfred R. *The Addict and the Law*. Bloomington: Indiana University Press, 1965.

Link, Arthur S., et al., eds. *The Papers of Woodrow Wilson*. Vol. 32, *January 1–April 16, 1915*. Vol. 33, *April 17–July 21, 1915*. Princeton: Princeton University Press, 1980.

Lo, R. Y. *The Opium Problem in the Far East*. Shanghai: The Commercial Press, Ltd., 1933.

Louis, Wm. Roger. *British Strategy in the Far East, 1919–1939*. Oxford: Clarendon Press of Oxford University Press, 1971.

———. *Imperialism at Bay: The United States and the Decolonization of the British Empire, 1941–1945*. New York: Oxford University Press, 1978.

Lowe, Peter. *Great Britain and Japan, 1911–1915: A Study of British Far Eastern Policy*. New York: St. Martin's Press, 1969.

————. *Great Britain and the Origins of the Pacific War: A Study of British Policy in East Asia, 1937–1941*. Oxford: Clarendon Press of Oxford University Press, 1977.

McCammon, Dorothy Snapp. *We Tried to Stay*. Scottsdale, Pa.: Herald Press, 1953.

McCormack, Gavan. *Chang Tso-lin in Northeast China, 1911–1928: China, Japan, and the Manchurian Idea*. Stanford: Stanford University Press, 1977.

McCoy, Alfred W., with Cathleen B. Read and Leonard P. Adams II. *The Politics of Heroin in Southeast Asia*. New York: Harper & Row, 1973.

MacDonald, C. A. *The United States, Britain, and Appeasement, 1936–1939*. London: The Macmillan Press in association with St. Anthony's College, Oxford, 1981.

McGehee, Ralph W. *Deadly Deceits: My Twenty-Five Years in the CIA*. New York: Sheridan Square Publications, 1983.

MacKinnon, Stephen R. *Power and Politics in Late Imperial China: Yuan Shih-k'ai in Beijing and Tianjin, 1901–1908*. Berkeley and Los Angeles: University of California Press, 1980.

Mancall, Mark. *China at the Center*. New York: The Free Press, 1984.

[Mao Zedong]. *Selected Works of Mao Tse-tung*. Vols. 1–2. Peking: Foreign Language Press, 1965.

Marks, John. *The Search for the "Manchurian Candidate": The CIA and Mind Control*. New York: Times Books, 1979.

Martin, Edwin W. *Divided Counsel: The Anglo-American Response to Communist Victory in China*. Lexington: University Press of Kentucky, 1986.

Martinson, Harold H. *Under the Red Dragon*. Minneapolis: Augsburg Publishing House, 1961.

May, Ernest R. *The Truman Administration and China, 1945–1949*. Philadelphia: J. P. Lippincott Company, 1975.

————, ed. *Knowing One's Enemies: Intelligence Assessment before the Two World Wars*. Princeton: Princeton University Press, 1986.

————, and James C. Thomson, Jr., eds. *American–East Asian Relations: A Survey*. Cambridge: Harvard University Press, 1972.

May, Gary. *China Scapegoat: The Diplomatic Ordeal of John Carter Vincent*. Washington, D.C.: New Republic Books, 1979.

Mayers, David Allen. *Cracking the Monolith: U.S. Policy against the Sino-Soviet Alliance, 1949–1955*. Baton Rouge: Louisiana State University Press, 1986.

Meisner, Maurice. *Mao's China: A History of the People's Republic*. New York: The Free Press, 1977.

Melby, John F. *The Mandate of Heaven: Record of a Civil War: China, 1945–1949*. Toronto: University of Toronto Press, 1968.

Merrill, Frederick T. *Japan and the Opium Menace*. New York: Institute of Pacific Relations, Foreign Policy Association, 1942.

Miles, Vice Admiral Milton E., USN. *A Different Kind of War: The Little-known Story of the Combined Guerrilla Forces Created by the U.S. Navy and the Chinese during World*

War II. Prepared by Hawthorne Daniel from the original manuscript. Garden City: Doubleday & Company, 1967.

Minear, Richard. *Victors' Justice: The Tokyo War Crimes Trial*. Princeton: Princeton University Press, 1971.

Miners, Norman. *Hong Kong under Imperial Rule, 1912–1941*. New York: Oxford University Press, 1987.

Morley, James William, ed. *The Fateful Choice: Japan's Advance into Southeast Asia, 1939–1941*. New York: Columbia University Press, 1980.

———. ed. *The China Quagmire: Japan's Expansion on the Asian Continent, 1933–1941*. New York: Columbia University Press, 1983.

———, ed. *Japan Erupts: The London Naval Conference and the Manchurian Incident, 1928–1932*. New York: Columbia University Press, 1984.

Morley, John, Viscount. *Recollections*. 2 vols. New York: The Macmillan Company, 1917.

Morse, Hosea Ballou. *The International Relations of the Chinese Empire*. 3 vols. Vol. 1, *The Period of Conflict, 1834–1860*. Vol. 2, *The Period of Submission, 1861–1893*. Vol. 3, *The Period of Subjection, 1894–1911*. London: Longmans, Green and Co., 1918.

———. *The Trade and Administration of China*. 3d rev. ed., reprint. New York: Russell and Russell, 1967.

Moseley, George V. H., III. *The Consolidation of the South China Frontier*. Berkeley and Los Angeles: University of California Press, 1973.

Musto, David F., M.D. *The American Disease: Origins of Narcotic Control*. Expanded ed. New York: Oxford University Press, 1987.

Nagai, Yōnosuke, and Akira Iriye, eds. *The Origins of the Cold War in Asia*. New York: Columbia University Press, 1977.

Nathan, Andrew J. *Peking Politics, 1918–1923: Factionalism and the Failure of Constitutionalism*. Berkeley and Los Angeles: University of California Press, 1976.

Nee, Victor, and James Peck, eds. *China's Uninterrupted Revolution from 1840 to the Present*. New York: Pantheon Books, 1973, 1975.

Neu, Charles E. *The Troubled Encounter: The United States and Japan*. New York: John Wiley & Sons, 1975.

Nisbett, Richard, and Lee Ross. *Human Inference: Strategies and Shortcomings of Social Judgment*. Englewood Cliffs: Prentice Hall, 1980.

Nish, Ian H. *The Anglo-Japanese Alliance: The Diplomacy of Two Island Empires, 1894–1907*. London: The Athlone Press, University of London, 1966.

———. *Alliance in Decline: A Study in Anglo-Japanese Relations, 1908–1923*. London: The Athlone Press, University of London, 1972.

———, ed. *Anglo-Japanese Alienation, 1919–1952: Papers of the Anglo-Japanese Conference on the History of the Second World War*. Cambridge: Cambridge University Press, 1982.

Nixon, Edgar B., ed. *Franklin D. Roosevelt and Foreign Affairs*. 3 vols. Cambridge: Harvard University Press, 1969.

Oliphant, Laurence. *Elgin's Mission to China and Japan.* 2 vols. London: Oxford University Press, Oxford in Asia Historical Reprints, 1970.

Ovendale, Ritchie. *The English-speaking Alliance: Britain, the United States, the Dominions, and the Cold War, 1945–1951.* London: Allen & Unwin, Ltd., 1985.

———, ed. *The Foreign Policy of the British Labour Governments, 1945–1951.* Leicester: Leicester University Press, 1984.

Owen, David Edward. *British Opium Policy in China and India.* New Haven: Yale University Press, 1934.

Pal, Radha Binod. *International Military Tribunal for the Far East: Dissentient Judgment of Justice R. B. Pal, M.A., LL.D.* Calcutta: Sanyal & Company, 1953.

Parssinen, Terry M. *Secret Passions, Secret Remedies: Narcotic Drugs in British Society, 1820–1930.* Philadelphia: Institute for the Study of Human Issues, 1983.

Patti, Archimedes L. K. *Why Viet Nam? Prelude to America's Albatross.* Berkeley and Los Angeles: University of California Press, 1980.

Peers, William R., and Dean Brelis. *Behind the Burma Road.* London: Robert Hale Ltd., 1964.

Pelz, Stephen E. *Race to Pearl Harbor: The Failure of the Second London Naval Conference and the Onset of World War II.* Cambridge: Harvard University Press, 1974.

Pepper, Suzanne. *Civil War in China: The Political Struggle, 1945–1949.* Berkeley and Los Angeles: University of California Press, 1978.

Perry, Elizabeth J. *Rebels and Revolutionaries in North China, 1845–1945.* Stanford: Stanford University Press, 1980.

Pogue, Forrest C. *George C. Marshall: Statesman, 1945–1950.* New York: The Viking Press, 1987.

Popkin, Samuel L. *The Rational Peasant: The Political Economy of Rural Society in Vietnam.* Berkeley and Los Angeles: University of California Press, 1979.

Porter, Brian. *Britain and the Rise of Communist China: A Study of British Attitudes, 1945–1954.* London: Oxford University Press, 1967.

Prados, John. *Presidents' Secret Wars: CIA and Pentagon Covert Operations since World War II.* New York: William Morrow and Company, 1986.

Pugach, Noel H. *Paul S. Reinsch: Open Door-Diplomat in Action.* Millwood, N.Y.: KTO Press, 1979.

Randolph, A. Sean. *The United States and Thailand: Alliance Dynamics, 1950–1985.* Research Papers and Policy Studies, no. 12. Berkeley: University of California Institute of East Asian Studies, 1986.

Rankin, Karl Lott. *China Assignment.* Seattle: University of Washington Press, 1964.

Reardon-Anderson, James. *Yenan and the Great Powers: The Origins of Chinese Communist Foreign Policy, 1944–1946.* New York: Columbia University Press, 1980.

Records of the General Conference of the Protestant Missionaries of China Held at Shanghai, May 7–20, 1890. Shanghai: American Presbyterian Mission Press, 1890.

Renborg, Bertil A. *International Drug Control: A Study of International Administrations by and through the League of Nations.* Washington, D.C.: Carnegie Endowment for International Peace, 1947.

Reynolds, David. *The Creation of the Anglo-American Alliance, 1937–1941: A Study of Competitive Co-operation.* Chapel Hill: University of North Carolina Press, 1982.

Ridley, Jasper. *Lord Palmerston.* New York: E. P. Dutton & Company, 1971.

Rock, William R. *Chamberlain and Roosevelt: British Foreign Policy and the United States, 1937–1940.* Columbus: Ohio State University Press, 1988.

Romanus, Charles F., and Riley Sunderland. *Stilwell's Mission to China.* Washington, D.C.: U.S. Department of the Army, 1953.

———. *Stilwell's Command Problems.* Washington, D.C.: U.S. Department of the Army, 1956.

Rose, Lisle A. *Roots of Tragedy: The United States and the Struggle for Asia, 1945–1953.* Westport, Conn.: Greenwood Press, 1976.

Rosenberg, William G., and Marilyn B. Young. *Transforming Russia and China: Revolutionary Struggle in the Twentieth Century.* New York: Oxford University Press, 1982.

Rotter, Andrew J. *The Path to Vietnam: Origins of the American Commitment to Southeast Asia.* Ithaca: Cornell University Press, 1987.

Sainsbury, Keith. *The Turning Point: Roosevelt, Stalin, Churchill, and Chiang Kai-shek, 1943: The Moscow, Cairo, and Teheran Conferences.* New York: Oxford University Press, 1986.

Sainteny, Jean. *Histoire d'une Paix Manquée: Indochine, 1945–1947.* Paris: Librarie Fayard, 1967.

Salisbury, Harrison E. *The Long March: The Untold Story.* New York: Harper & Row, 1985.

Schaller, Michael. *The U.S. Crusade in China, 1938–1945.* New York: Columbia University Press, 1979.

———. *The American Occupation of Japan: The Origins of the Cold War in Asia.* New York: Oxford University Press, 1985.

Schoenbaum, Thomas J. *Waging Peace and War: Dean Rusk in the Truman, Kennedy, and Johnson Years.* New York: Simon and Schuster, 1988.

Schroeder, Paul W. *The Axis Alliance and Japanese-American Relations, 1941.* Ithaca: Cornell University Press, 1958.

Scott, James C. *The Moral Economy of the Peasant: Rebellion and Subsistence in Southeast Asia.* New Haven and London: Yale University Press, 1976.

———. *The Weapons of the Weak: Everyday Forms of Peasant Resistance.* New Haven and London: Yale University Press, 1985.

Seagrave, Sterling. *The Soong Dynasty.* New York: Harper & Row, 1985.

Selden, Mark. *The Yenan Way in Revolutionary China.* Cambridge: Harvard University Press, 1971.

Selle, Earl Albert. *Donald of China.* New York: Harper & Brothers, 1948.

Shai, Aron. *Britain and China, 1941–1947: Imperial Momentum.* New York: St. Martin's Press, 1984.

Sheridan, James E. *Chinese Warlord: The Career of Feng Yü-hsiang.* Stanford: Stanford University Press, 1966.

———. *China in Disintegration: The Republican Era in Chinese History, 1912–1949.* New York: The Free Press, 1975.

Shewmaker, Kenneth E. *America and the Chinese Communists, 1927–1945: A Persuading Encounter.* Ithaca: Cornell University Press, 1971.

Slade, John. *Narrative of the Late Proceedings and Events in China.* Canton: Canton Register Press, 1839.

Smedley, Agnes. *The Great Road.* New York: Monthly Review Press, 1972.

Smith, Arthur H. *The Uplift of China.* New York: Young People's Missionary Movement of the United States and Canada, 1907.

Smith, Bradley F. *The Shadow Warriors: O.S.S. and the Origins of the C.I.A.* New York: Basic Books, Inc., 1983.

Snow, Edgar. *Red Star over China.* New York: Grove Press, 1962.

Spector, Ronald H. *Advice and Support: The Early Years of the U.S. Army in Vietnam, 1941–1960.* New York: The Free Press, 1985.

———. *Eagle against the Sun: The American War with Japan.* New York: The Free Press, 1985.

Spence, Jonathan D. *The Gate of Heavenly Peace: The Chinese and Their Revolution, 1895–1980.* New York: The Viking Press, 1981.

Spencer, C. P., and V. Navaratnam. *Drug Abuse in East Asia.* Kuala Lumpur: Oxford University Press, 1981.

Spinelli, Lawrence. *Dry Diplomacy: The United States, Great Britain, and Prohibition.* Wilmington, Del.: Scholarly Resources, 1989.

Stein, Guenther. *The Challenge of Red China.* New York: McGraw-Hill, 1945.

Steinberg, David Joel, ed. *In Search of Southeast Asia: A Modern History.* Rev. ed. Honolulu: University of Hawaii Press, 1987.

Stuart, John Leighton. *Fifty Years in China: The Memoirs of John Leighton Stuart.* New York: Random House, 1954.

Stueck, William Whitney, Jr. *The Road to Confrontation: American Policy toward China and Korea, 1947–1950.* Chapel Hill: University of North Carolina Press, 1981.

Sues, Ilona Ralf. *Shark Fins and Millet.* Boston: Little, Brown and Company, 1944.

Taylor, Arnold H. *American Diplomacy and the Narcotics Traffic, 1900–1939: A Study in International Humanitarian Reform.* Durham: Duke University Press, 1969.

Taylor, Robert H. *Foreign and Domestic Consequences of the KMT Intervention in Burma.* Data Paper no. 93. Ithaca: Cornell University Southeast Asia Program, 1973.

Teng Ssu-yu. *The Taiping Rebellion and the Western Powers.* London: Oxford University Press, 1971.

———, and John K. Fairbank, eds. *China's Response to the West: A Documentary Survey, 1839–1923.* New York: Atheneum, 1965.

Thaxton, Ralph. *China Turned Rightside Up: Revolutionary Legitimacy in the Peasant World.* New Haven and London: Yale University Press, 1983.

Thomson, James C., Jr. *While China Faced West: American Reformers in Nationalist China, 1928–1937.* Cambridge: Harvard University Press, 1969.

———, Peter W. Stanley, and John Curtis Perry. *Sentimental Imperialists: The American Experience in Asia.* New York: Harper & Row, 1981.

Thorne, Christopher. *The Limits of Foreign Policy: The West, the League, and the Far Eastern Crisis of 1931–1933.* New York: G. P. Putnam's Sons, 1973.

———. *Allies of a Kind: The United States, Great Britain, and the War against Japan, 1941–1945.* New York: Oxford University Press, 1978.

———. *The Issue of War: States, Societies, and the Far Eastern Conflict of 1941–1945.* New York: Oxford University Press, 1985.

Tien Hung-mao. *Government and Politics in Kuomintang China, 1927–1937.* Stanford: Stanford University Press, 1972.

Tinker, Hugh. *The Union of Burma: A Study of the First Years of Independence.* London: Oxford University Press, 1961.

Trager, Frank N., Patricia Wohlgemuth, and Lu-yu Kiang. *Burma's Role in the United Nations, 1948–1955.* New York: Institute of Pacific Relations, 1956.

Trotter, Ann. *Britain and East Asia, 1933–1937.* London and New York: Cambridge University Press, 1975.

Truman, Harry S. *Memoirs.* Vol. 1, *Year of Decisions, 1945.* New York: Doubleday & Company, 1955.

Tsou, Tang. *America's Failure in China, 1941–1950.* Chicago: University of Chicago Press, 1963.

Tuchman, Barbara. *Stilwell and the American Experience in China, 1911–45.* New York: The Macmillan Company, 1970, 1971.

Tucker, Nancy Bernkopf. *Patterns in the Dust: Chinese-American Relations and the Recognition Controversy, 1949–1950.* New York: Columbia University Press, 1983.

Varg, Paul A. *Missionaries, Chinese, and Diplomats: The American Protestant Missionary Movement in China, 1890–1952.* Princeton: Princeton University Press, 1958.

Victoria, Sister Mary. *Nun in Red China.* New York: McGraw-Hill, 1953.

Vogel, Ezra. *Canton under Communism: Programs and Politics in a Provincial Capital, 1949–1968.* Cambridge: Harvard University Press, 1969.

Wakeman, Frederic, Jr. *Strangers at the Gate: Social Disorder in South China, 1839–1861.* Berkeley and Los Angeles: University of California Press, 1966.

———. *The Fall of Imperial China.* New York: The Free Press, 1975.

———, and Carolyn Grant, eds. *Conflict and Control in Late Imperial China.* Berkeley and Los Angeles: University of California Press, 1975.

Walker, William O., III. *Drug Control in the Americas.* Rev. ed. Albuquerque: University of New Mexico Press, 1989.

Warner, Denis. *The Last Confucian: Vietnam, Southeast Asia, and the West.* Baltimore: Penguin Books, 1964.

Wei, Betty Peh-t'i. *Shanghai: Crucible of Modern China.* New York: Oxford University Press, 1987.

Westermeyer, Joseph. *Poppies, Pipes, and People: Opium and Its Use in Laos*. Berkeley and Los Angeles: University of California Press, 1982.

Wheeler, Gerald E. *Prelude to Pearl Harbor: The United States Navy and the Far East, 1921–1931*. Columbia: University of Missouri Press, 1963.

White, Theodore H., ed. *The Stilwell Papers: General Joseph W. Stilwell's Iconoclastic Account of America's Adventures in China*. New York: Schocken Books, 1972.

————, and Analee Jacoby. *Thunder out of China*. New York: William Sloane Associates, Inc., 1946.

Wilbur, C. Martin. *Sun Yat-sen: Frustrated Patriot*. New York: Columbia University Press, 1976.

————. *The Nationalist Revolution in China, 1923–1928*. Cambridge and New York: Cambridge University Press, 1983.

Williams, Edward Thomas. *China Yesterday and Today*. New York: Thomas Y. Crowell Company, 1927.

Williams, Francis. *A Prime Minister Remembers*. London: Heinemann, 1961.

Williamson, The Reverend Alexander. *Journeys in North China, Manchuria, and Eastern Mongolia, with Some Account of Corea*. 2 vols. London: Smith, Elder & Company, 1870.

Williamson, H. R. *British Baptists in China, 1845–1952*. London: The Carey Kingsgate Press, Ltd., 1957.

Willmott, H. F. *Empires in the Balance: Japanese and Allied Pacific Strategies to April 1942*. Annapolis: Naval Institute Press, 1982.

Wilson, Joan Hoff. *American Business and Foreign Policy, 1920–1933*. Lexington: University Press of Kentucky, 1971.

Wise, David, and Thomas B. Ross. *The Invisible Government*. New York: Vintage Books, 1974.

Woodhead, H. G. W., ed. *The China Year Book, 1921–1922*. Tientsin: Tientsin Press, 1921.

————. *The China Year Book, 1923*. Tientsin: Tientsin Press, 1923.

————. *The China Year Book, 1928*. Tientsin: Tientsin Press, 1928.

Woodis, Jack, ed. *Ho Chi Minh: Selected Articles and Speeches, 1920–1967*. London: Lawrence and Wishart, Ltd., 1969.

Woodward, Sir Llewellyn. *British Foreign Policy in the Second World War*. Vol. 2. London: Her Majesty's Stationery Office, 1971.

————. *British Foreign Policy in the Second World War*. Vol. 4. London: Her Majesty's Stationery Office, 1975.

Wright, Mary Clabaugh, ed. *China in Revolution: The First Phase, 1900–1913*. New Haven and London: Yale University Press, 1968.

Wu Wen-tsao. *The Chinese Opium Question in British Opinion and Action*. New York: The Academy Press, 1928.

Young, Arthur N. *China's Nation-building Effort, 1927–1937: The Financial and Economic Record*. Stanford: Hoover Institution Press, 1971.

Young, Ernest P. *The Presidency of Yuan Shih-k'ai: Liberalism and Dictatorship in Early Republican China*. Ann Arbor: University of Michigan Press, 1977.

Zabriskie, Alexander C. *Bishop Brent: Crusader for Christian Unity*. Philadelphia: The Westminster Press, 1948.

Ziegler, Philip. *Mountbatten: The Official Biography*. London: Collins, 1985.

E. Articles and Dissertations

Adams, Nina S. "Patrons, Clients, and Revolutionaries: The Lao Search for Independence, 1945–1954." In *Laos: War and Revolution*, edited by Nina S. Adams and Alfred W. McCoy. New York: Harper & Row, 1970.

Allen, E. W. "Japanese Drug Trade Poisoning North China." *China Press Weekly*, 5 August 1933, 1010–11.

Anslinger, Harry J. "The Red Chinese Dope Traffic." *Military Police Journal* 10 (February–March 1961): 2–6.

Barney, G. Linwood. "The Meo of Xieng Khouang Province, Laos." In *Southeast Asian Tribes, Minorities, and Nations*, edited by Peter Kunstadter. 2 vols. Princeton: Princeton University Press, 1967.

Barnhart, Michael A. "Japanese Intelligence before the Second World War: 'Best Case' Analysis." In *Knowing One's Enemies. Intelligence Assessment before the Two World Wars*, edited by Ernest R. May. Princeton: Princeton University Press, 1986.

Bastid-Bruguiere, Marianne. "Currents of Social Change." In *The Cambridge History of China*. Vol. 11, *Late Ch'ing, 1800–1911*, pt. 2, edited by John K. Fairbank and Kwang-ching Liu. Cambridge and New York: Cambridge University Press, 1980.

Buhite, Russell D. " 'Major Interests': American Policy toward China, Taiwan, and Korea, 1945–1950." *Pacific Historical Review* 47 (August 1978): 425–51.

Burns, Richard Dean. "Stanley K. Hornbeck: The Diplomacy of the Open Door." In *Diplomats in Crisis: United States–Chinese–Japanese Relations, 1919–1941*, edited by Richard Dean Burns and Edward M. Bennett. Santa Barbara: ABC-Clio, 1974.

Chang, Hao. "Intellectual Change and the Reform Movement, 1890–1898." In *The Cambridge History of China*. Vol. 11, *Late Ch'ing, 1800–1911*, pt. 2, edited by John K. Fairbank and Kwang-ching Liu. Cambridge and New York: Cambridge University Press, 1980.

Ch'en, Jerome. "The Communist Movement, 1927–1937." In *The Cambridge History of China*. Vol. 13, *Republican China, 1912–1949*, pt. 2, edited by John K. Fairbank and Albert Feuerwerker. Cambridge and New York: Cambridge University Press, 1986.

Chern, Kenneth S. "The Politics of American China Policy, 1945: Roots of the Cold War." *Political Science Quarterly* 91 (Winter 1976–77): 631–47.

"A Chinese Charge against Japan." *Literary Digest* 61 (12 April 1919): 20.

Chutiyutse, M. "Japan and the Opium Scourge in China." *Opium: A World Problem* 1 (June 1928): 15–18.

Close, Upton. "Jehol: A Struggle Colored with Opium." *New York Times Magazine*, 15 January 1933, 4–5.

Cohen, Warren I. "Acheson, His Advisers, and China, 1949–1950." In *Uncertain Years: Chinese-American Relations, 1947–1950*, edited by Dorothy Borg and Waldo Heinrichs. New York: Columbia University Press, 1980.

———. "The United States and China since 1945." In *New Frontiers in American–East Asian Relations: Essays Presented to Dorothy Borg*, edited by Warren I. Cohen. New York: Columbia University Press, 1983.

"Control of Narcotic Drugs: U.N. to Assume Existing Functions." *UN Weekly Bulletin* 1 (30 September 1946): 10–13.

Crooker, Richard Allen. "Opium Production in North Thailand: A Geographical Perspective." Ph.D. dissertation, University of California, Riverside, 1986.

Eastman, Lloyd E. "Nationalist China during the Nanking Decade, 1927–1937." In *The Cambridge History of China*. Vol. 13, *Republican China, 1912–1949*, pt. 2, edited by John K. Fairbank and Albert Feuerwerker. Cambridge and New York: Cambridge University Press, 1986.

———. "Nationalist China during the Sino-Japanese War, 1937–1945." In *The Cambridge History of China*. Vol. 13, *Republican China, 1912–1949*, pt. 2, edited by John K. Fairbank and Albert Feuerwerker. Cambridge and New York: Cambridge University Press, 1986.

"Editorial: Mr. Attlee's Friends, the Chinese Commies, Are the World's Leading Dope Smugglers." *Saturday Evening Post*, 13 November 1954, 12.

"Editorial: On the Way to Absolute Prohibition." *Opium: A World Problem* 2 (January 1929): 1–2.

"Editorial: The Shaping of a Treaty." *Opium: A World Problem* 2 (July 1929): 2–3.

Etō, Shinkichi. "China's International Relations, 1911–1931." In *The Cambridge History of China*. Vol. 13, *Republican China, 1912–1949*, pt. 2, edited by John K. Fairbank and Albert Feuerwerker. Cambridge and New York: Cambridge University Press, 1986.

"Extraterritoriality and the Japanese Dope Trade in Manchuria." *China Weekly Review*, 18 April 1931, 224–25.

Feuerwerker, Albert. "Economic Trends, 1912–49." In *The Cambridge History of China*. Vol. 12, *Republican China, 1912–1949*, pt. 1, edited by John K. Fairbank. Cambridge and New York: Cambridge University Press, 1983.

Garver, John W. "Chiang Kai-shek's Quest for Soviet Entry into the Sino-Japanese War." *Political Science Quarterly* 102 (Summer 1987): 295–316.

Geddes, William R. "The Tribal Research Centre, Thailand: An Account of Plans and Activities." In *Southeast Asian Tribes, Minorities, and Nations*, edited by Peter Kunstadter. 2 vols. Princeton: Princeton University Press, 1967.

Gilbert, Rodney "Dope from Red China." *American Legion Magazine*, September 1954, 16–17, 52–54.

Goldstein, Steven M. "Chinese Communist Policy toward the United States: Opportunities and Constraints, 1944–1950." In *Uncertain Years: Chinese-American Relations, 1947–1950*, edited by Dorothy Borg and Waldo Heinrichs. New York: Columbia University Press, 1980.

"Great Britain, America, and the Chinese Opium Problem." *Millard's Review of the Far East* 12 (17 April 1920): 320–29.

Halpern, Joel, and Peter Kunstadter. "Laos: Introduction." In *Southeast Asian Tribes, Minorities, and Nations*, edited by Peter Kunstadter. 2 vols. Princeton: Princeton University Press, 1967.

Hao, Yen-p'ing, and Erh-min Wang. "Changing Chinese Views of Western Relations, 1840–1895." In *The Cambridge History of China*. Vol. 11, *Late Ch'ing, 1800–1911*, pt. 2, edited by John K. Fairbank and Kwang-ching Liu. Cambridge and New York: Cambridge University Press, 1980.

Hashikawa, Bunzō. "Japanese Perspectives on Asia: From Dissociation to Coprosperity." In *The Chinese and the Japanese: Essays in Political and Cultural Interactions*, edited by Akira Iriye. Princeton: Princeton University Press, 1980.

Hata, Ikuhiko. "The Army's Move into Northern Indochina." In *The Fateful Choice: Japan's Advance into Southeast Asia, 1939–1941*, edited by James William Morley. New York: Columbia University Press, 1980.

———. "The Marco Polo Bridge Incident, 1937." In *The China Quagmire: Japan's Expansion on the Asian Continent, 1933–1941*, edited by James William Morley. New York: Columbia University Press, 1983.

Hatano, Yoshihiro. "The New Armies." In *China in Revolution: The First Phase, 1900–1913*, edited by Mary Clabaugh Wright. New Haven and London: Yale University Press, 1968.

Herring, George C. "The Truman Administration and the Restoration of French Sovereignty in Indochina." *Diplomatic History* 1 (Spring 1977): 97–117.

Hess, Gary R. "Franklin Roosevelt and Indochina." *Journal of American History* 59 (September 1972): 353–68.

Hosoya, Chihiro. "Britain and the United States in Japan's View of the International System, 1919–1937." In *Anglo-Japanese Alienation, 1919–1952: Papers of the Anglo-Japanese Conference on the History of the Second World War*, edited by Ian H. Nish. Cambridge: Cambridge University Press, 1982.

Hsu, Immanuel C. Y. "Late Ch'ing Foreign Relations, 1866–1905." In *The Cambridge History of China*. Vol. 11, *Late Ch'ing, 1800–1911*, pt. 2, edited by John K. Fairbank and Kwang-ching Liu. Cambridge and New York: Cambridge University Press, 1980.

Ikei, Masaru. "Ugaki Kazushige's View of China and His China Policy, 1915–1930." In *The Chinese and the Japanese: Essays in Political and Cultural Interactions*, edited by Akira Iriye. Princeton: Princeton University Press, 1980.

Iriye, Akira. "The Role of the United States Embassy in Tokyo." In *Pearl Harbor as History: Japanese-American Relations, 1931–1941*, edited by Dorothy Borg and Shumpei Okamoto, with Dale A. K. Finlayson. New York: Columbia University Press, 1973.

———. "Japanese Aggression and China's International Position, 1931–1949." In *The Cambridge History of China*. Vol. 13, *Republican China, 1912–1949*, pt. 2, edited by John K. Fairbank and Albert Feuerwerker. Cambridge and New York: Cambridge University Press, 1986.

Jansen, Marius B. "Introduction: The Manchurian Incident, 1931." In *Japan Erupts: The London Naval Conference and the Manchurian Incident, 1928–1932*, edited by James William Morley. New York: Columbia University Press, 1984.

Jervis, Robert. "Deterrence Theory Revisited." *World Politics* 31 (January 1979): 289–324.

———. "Perceiving and Coping with Threat." In *Psychology and Deterrence*, by Robert Jervis, Richard Ned Lebow, and Janice Gross Stein. Baltimore: Johns Hopkins University Press, 1985.

Kinder, Douglas Clark. "Bureaucratic Cold Warrior: Harry J. Anslinger and Illicit Narcotics Traffic." *Pacific Historical Review* 50 (May 1981): 169–91.

———. "Foreign Fear and the Drug Specter: Harry J. Anslinger and the Illicit Narcotics Traffic." Ph.D. dissertation, Ohio University, 1991.

———, and William O. Walker III. "Stable Force in a Storm: Harry J. Anslinger and United States Foreign Policy, 1930–1962." *Journal of American History* 72 (March 1986): 908–27.

Kung Chung-wu. "Cultural Revolution in Modern Chinese History." In *China's Uninterrupted Revolution from 1840 to the Present*, edited by Victor Nee and James Peck. New York: Pantheon Books, 1973, 1975.

Kunstadter, Peter. "Burma: Introduction." In *Southeast Asian Tribes, Minorities, and Nations*, edited by Peter Kunstadter. 2 vols. Princeton: Princeton University Press, 1967.

———. Introduction to *Southeast Asian Tribes, Minorities, and Nations*, edited by Peter Kunstadter. 2 vols. Princeton: Princeton University Press, 1967.

LaFeber, Walter. "Roosevelt, Churchill, and Indochina, 1942–1945." *American Historical Review* 80 (December 1975): 1277–95.

LaMotte, Ellen. "'Limiting' Drug Manufacture." *The Nation* 134 (13 April 1932): 418–19.

La Raw, Maran. "Toward a Basis for Understanding the Minorities in Burma: The Kachin Example." In *Southeast Asian Tribes, Minorities, and Nations*, edited by Peter Kunstadter. 2 vols. Princeton: Princeton University Press, 1967.

Lee, P. H. "Opium and Extraterritoriality." *Opium: A World Problem* 2 (April 1929): 34–39.

Leffler, Melvyn P. "The United States and the Strategic Dimensions of the Marshall Plan." *Diplomatic History* 12 (Summer 1988): 277–306.

Lifschultz, Lawrence. "Bush, Drugs, and Pakistan: Inside the Kingdom of Heroin." *The Nation* 247 (14 November 1988): 477, 492–96.

Lo, Dr. R. Y. "A Review of the People's Anti-Opium Movement in China." *Opium: A World Problem* 2 (January 1929): 20–27.

Lowe, Peter. "Britain and the Opening of the War in Asia, 1937–1941." In *Anglo-Japanese Alienation, 1919–1952: Papers of the Anglo-Japanese Conference on the History of the Second World War*, edited by Ian H. Nish. Cambridge and New York: Cambridge University Press, 1982.

———. "Great Britain's Assessment of Japan before the Outbreak of the Pacific War." In *Knowing One's Enemies: Intelligence Assessment before the Two World Wars*, edited by Ernest R. May. Princeton: Princeton University Press, 1986.

McAlister, J. T., Jr. "Mountain Minorities and the Viet Minh: A Key to the Indochina War." In *Southeast Asian Tribes, Minorities, and Nations*, edited by Peter Kunstadter. 2 vols. Princeton: Princeton University Press, 1967.

Marshall, Jonathan. "Opium and the Politics of Gangsterism in Nationalist China, 1927–1945." *Bulletin of Concerned Asian Scholars* 8 (July–September 1976): 19–48.

May, Herbert L. "The Tasks of the Permanent Central Opium Board." *UN Weekly Bulletin* 4 (15 April 1948): 336–38.

———. "Narcotic Drug Control." *International Conciliation*, no. 485 (November 1952): 489–536.

Merrill, Frederick T. "The Opium Menace in the Far East." *Foreign Policy Reports* 12 (1 March 1937): 293–304.

Moorehead, Helen H. "International Narcotics Control, 1939–1946." *Foreign Policy Reports* 22 (1 July 1946): 94–103.

Morlock, George A. "Recent Developments in the International Control of Narcotics." *Department of State Bulletin* 31 (13 September 1954): 366–71.

Mote, F. W. "The Rural 'Haw' (Yunnannese Chinese) of Northern Thailand." In *Southeast Asian Tribes, Minorities, and Nations*, edited by Peter Kunstadter. 2 vols. Princeton: Princeton University Press, 1967.

Mungkandi, Wiwat. "Thai-American Relations in Historical Perspective." In *United States–Thailand Relations*, edited by Karl D. Jackson and Wiwat Mungkandi. Research Papers and Policy Studies, no. 20. Berkeley: University of California Institute of East Asian Studies, 1986.

Nagaoka, Shinjirō. "The Drive into Southern Indochina and Thailand." In *The Fateful Choice: Japan's Advance into Southeast Asia, 1939–1941*, edited by James William Morley. New York: Columbia University Press, 1980.

Nakamura, Takafusa. "Japan's Economic Thrust into North China, 1933–1938: Formation of the North China Development Corporation." In *The Chinese and the Japanese: Essays in Political and Cultural Interactions*, edited by Akira Iriye. Princeton: Princeton University Press, 1980.

Nish, Ian H. "Japan in Britain's View of the International System, 1919–1937." In *Anglo-Japanese Alienation, 1919–1952: Papers of the Anglo-Japanese Conference on the History of the Second World War*, edited by Ian H. Nish. Cambridge and New York: Cambridge University Press, 1982.

"Old and New Narcotic Perils: World Drug Control in Operation." *UN Weekly Bulletin* 3 (16 September 1947): 364.

Ovendale, Ritchie. "Britain, the United States, and the Cold War in South-East Asia, 1949–1950." *International Affairs* 58 (Summer 1982): 447–64.

———. "Britain and the Cold War in Asia." In *The Foreign Policy of the British Labour Governments, 1945–1951*, edited by Ritchie Ovendale. Leicester: Leicester University Press, 1984.

Peck, Jim. "America and the Chinese Revolution, 1942–1946." In *American–East Asian Relations: A Survey*, edited by Ernest R. May and James C. Thomson, Jr. Cambridge: Harvard University Press, 1972.

Pepper, Suzanne. "The KMT-CCP Conflict, 1945–1949." In *The Cambridge History of China*. Vol. 13, *Republican China, 1912–1949*, pt. 2, edited by John K. Fairbank and Albert Feuerwerker. Cambridge and New York: Cambridge University Press, 1986.

"Poisoning the Chinese." *Literary Digest* 68 (26 February 1921): 30.

Reins, Thomas David. "China and the International Politics of Opium, 1900–1937: The Impact of Reform, Revenue, and the Unequal Treaties." Ph.D. dissertation, Claremont Graduate School, 1981.

Rinehart, Robert. "Historical Setting." In *Thailand: A Country Study*, edited by Frederica M. Bunge. 5th ed. Washington, D.C.: U.S. Department of the Army, Government Printing Office, 1981.

Sbrega, John J. "The Anticolonial Policies of Franklin D. Roosevelt: A Reappraisal." *Political Science Quarterly* 101 (Issue no. 1, 1986): 65–84.

Schaller, Michael. "Securing the Great Crescent: Occupied Japan and the Origins of Containment in Southeast Asia." *Journal of American History* 69 (September 1982): 392–414.

Schlesinger, Arthur M., Jr. "The Missionary Enterprise and Theories of Imperialism." In *The Missionary Enterprise in China and America*, edited by John K. Fairbank. Cambridge: Harvard University Press, 1974.

Sheridan, James E. "The Warlord Era: Politics and Militarism under the Peking Government, 1916–1928." In *The Cambridge History of China*. Vol. 12, *Republican China, 1912–1949*, pt. 1, edited by John K. Fairbank. Cambridge and New York: Cambridge University Press, 1983.

Shimada, Toshihiko. "Designs on North China, 1933–1937." In *The China Quagmire: Japan's Expansion on the Asian Continent, 1933–1941*, edited by James William Morley. New York: Columbia University Press, 1983.

Soonthornojana, Andulyasak. "The Rise of United States–Thai Relations, 1945–1975." Ph.D. dissertation, University of Akron, 1986.

Spall, Richard Francis, Jr. "Reform Ideas and the Anti-Corn–Law Leaguers." Ph.D. dissertation, University of Illinois, 1985.

Spence, Jonathan. "Opium Smoking in Ch'ing China." In *Conflict and Control in Late Imperial China*, edited by Frederic Wakeman, Jr., and Carolyn Grant. Berkeley and Los Angeles: University of California Press, 1975.

Stein, Janice Gross. "Building Politics into Psychology: The Misperception of Threat." *Political Psychology* 9 (June 1988): 245–71.

Thomson, James C., Jr. "The Role of the Department of State." In *Pearl Harbor as History: Japanese-American Relations, 1931–1941*, edited by Dorothy Borg and Shumpei Okamoto, with Dale A. K. Finlayson. New York: Columbia University Press, 1973.

Thorne, Christopher. "Indochina and Anglo-American Relations, 1942–1945." *Pacific Historical Review* 45 (February 1976): 73–96.

Usui, Katsumi. "The Politics of War, 1937–1941." In *The China Quagmire: Japan's Expansion on the Asian Continent, 1933–1941*, edited by James William Morley. New York: Columbia University Press, 1983.

Van Slyke, Lyman. "The Chinese Communist Movement during the Sino-Japanese War, 1937–1945." In *The Cambridge History of China*. Vol. 13, *Republican China, 1928–1949*, pt. 2, edited by John K. Fairbank and Albert Feuerwerker. Cambridge and New York: Cambridge University Press, 1986.

Wakeman, Frederic, Jr. "The Canton Trade and the Opium War." In *The Cambridge History of China*. Vol. 10, *Late Ch'ing, 1800–1911*, pt. 1, edited by John K. Fairbank. Cambridge and New York: Cambridge University Press, 1978.

Walker, William O., III. "Drug Control and the Issue of Culture in American Foreign Relations." *Diplomatic History* 12 (Fall 1988): 365–82.

Wang, Y. C. "Tu Yueh-sheng (1888–1951): A Tentative Political Biography." *Journal of Asian Studies* 26 (May 1967): 433–55.

Watt, D. C. "Britain and the Cold War in the Far East, 1945–1958." In *The Origins of the Cold War In Asia*, edited by Yōnosuke Nagai and Akira Iriye. New York: Columbia University Press, 1977.

White, Peter T. "The Poppy—For Good and Evil." *National Geographic*, February 1985, 143–89.

———. "Laos Today." *National Geographic*, June 1987, 772–95.

Wilkins, Mira. "The Role of U.S. Business." In *Pearl Harbor as History: Japanese-American Relations, 1931–1941*, edited by Dorothy Borg and Shumpei Okamoto, with Dale A. K. Finlayson. New York: Columbia University Press, 1973.

Wright, Mary Clabaugh. "Introduction: The Rising Tide of Change." In *China in Revolution: The First Phase, 1900–1913*, edited by Mary Clabaugh Wright. New Haven and London: Yale University Press, 1968.

Wu Lien-teh, Dr. "Opium Problem Reaches Acute Stage." *The Chinese Nation*, 28 January 1931, 818–19, 836.

Wu Tien-wei. "Chiang Kai-shek's April Twelfth Coup of 1927." In *China in the 1920s: Nationalism and Revolution*, edited by F. Gilbert Chan and Thomas H. Etzold. New York: New Viewpoints, 1976.

Young, Ernest P. "Yuan Shih-k'ai's Rise to the Presidency." In *China in Revolution: The First Phase, 1900–1913*, edited by Mary Clabaugh Wright. New Haven and London: Yale University Press, 1968.